Sport Management in the Ibero-American World

This book explores innovation in technology, products, and services in sport management in the Ibero-American region, one of the most rapidly developing regions in world sport. This timely volume captures a sense of the potential impact and opportunities presented in the region for international sport businesses and sporting organizations.

The book presents cutting-edge research into topics as diverse as digitization in the Chilean sport industry; responses to COVID-19 by sports clubs in the region; consumer behavior in the Portuguese fitness industry; multiplatform content distribution in Brazilian basketball; and the strategy behind the growth and development of the Valencia marathon in Spain. It is full of insight, data, and examples of best practice in innovation.

This is fascinating reading for any student, researcher, or practitioner working in sport management, sport business, sport governance, international business and management, or Ibero-American studies.

Gabriel Cepeda Carrión is Professor in the management and marketing department at the Universidad de Sevilla, Spain. His main research topics include knowledge management, absorptive capacity, dynamic capabilities, and organizational learning and unlearning. He is currently working on several research projects on leadership and soft skills in sports funded by the European Commission and the Spanish Government.

Jerónimo García-Fernández is Associate Professor in sports science in the department of physical education and sport at the University of Seville, Spain. His research focuses on the management of fitness centers, customer loyalty, consumer perception, digital transformation, customer satisfaction, and analysis of professional profiles linked to the sport and fitness sector. In 2016, he was the President of the Ibero-American Congress on Sports Economics that took place in Spain, and in 2020 and 2021, he was President of the International Conference on Technology in Physical Activity and Sport. He also belongs to the board of the Spanish Society of Sports Economy (SEED) and the Andalusian Association of Sports Managers (AGESPORT).

James J. Zhang is Professor of sport management at the University of Georgia, USA. His primary research interests are applied measurement and/or applied studies examining sport consumer behavior. He has previously been Editor of the *International Journal of Sport Marketing and Sponsorship*, Sport Management Section Editor of the *Measurement in Physical Education and Exercise Science* journal, and President of North American Society for Sport Management (NASSM).

World Association for Sport Management Series

Series Editors:
Brenda G. Pitts, Georgia State University, USA
James J. Zhang, University of Georgia, USA

The World Association for Sport Management (WASM) was founded to facilitate sport management research, teaching and learning excellence, and professional practice, across every continent. The WASM book series is designed to support those aims by presenting current research and scholarship, from well-established and emerging scholars and practitioners, on sport management theory, policy, and practice. Books in the series will explore contemporary issues and key challenges in sport management and identify important new directions for research and professional practice. Above all, the series aims to encourage and highlight the development of international perspectives, international partnerships, and international best practice in sport management, recognizing the globalized nature of the contemporary sport industry.

Available in this series:

Sport Governance and Operations
Global Perspectives
Edited by James J. Zhang and Euisoo Kim

Sport Marketing in a Global Environment
Strategic Perspectives
Edited by Ruth M. Crabtree and James J. Zhang

Marketing Analysis in Sport Business
Global Perspectives
Edited by Kevin K. Byon, Brian H. Yim, and James J. Zhang

Sport Management in the Ibero-American World
Product and Service Innovations
Edited by Gabriel Cepeda Carrión, Jerónimo García-Fernández and James J. Zhang

For more information about this series, please visit: https://www.routledge.com/World-Association-for-Sport-Management-Series/book-series/WASM

Sport Management in the Ibero-American World

Product and Service Innovations

Edited by Gabriel Cepeda Carrión, Jerónimo García-Fernández and James J. Zhang

LONDON AND NEW YORK

First published 2023
by Routledge
4 Park Square, Milton Park, Abingdon, Oxon OX14 4RN

and by Routledge
605 Third Avenue, New York, NY 10158

Routledge is an imprint of the Taylor & Francis Group, an informa business

© 2023 selection and editorial matter, World Association of Sport Management (WASM); individual chapters, the contributors

The right of World Association of Sport Management (WASM) to be identified as the author of this work has been asserted by them in accordance with sections 77 and 78 of the Copyright, Designs and Patents Act 1988.

All rights reserved. No part of this book may be reprinted or reproduced or utilised in any form or by any electronic, mechanical, or other means, now known or hereafter invented, including photocopying and recording, or in any information storage or retrieval system, without permission in writing from the publishers.

Trademark notice: Product or corporate names may be trademarks or registered trademarks, and are used only for identification and explanation without intent to infringe.

British Library Cataloguing-in-Publication Data
A catalogue record for this book is available from the British Library

Library of Congress Cataloging-in-Publication Data
Names: Cepeda Carrión, Gabriel, editor. | García-Fernández, Jerónimo, editor. | Zhang, James J., editor.
Title: Sport management in the Ibero-American world : product and service innovations / edited by Gabriel Cepeda Carrión, Jerónimo García-Fernández and James J. Zhang.
Description: Abingdon, Oxon ; New York City : Routledge, 2023. | Series: World association for sport management series | Includes bibliographical references and index. |
Identifiers: LCCN 2023001019 | ISBN 9781032482385 (hardback) | ISBN 9781032482408 (paperback) | ISBN 9781003388050 (ebook)
Subjects: LCSH: Sports administration--Latin America. | Sports administration--Spain. | Sports administration--Portugal.
Classification: LCC GV713 .S67755 2023 | DDC 796.06/9--dc23/eng/20230207
LC record available at https://lccn.loc.gov/2023001019

ISBN: 978-1-032-48238-5 (hbk)
ISBN: 978-1-032-48240-8 (pbk)
ISBN: 978-1-003-38805-0 (ebk)

DOI: 10.4324/9781003388050

Typeset in Goudy
by KnowledgeWorks Global Ltd.

Contents

List of contributors   viii

1 Ibero-American Sport Management: Challenges and Opportunities   1
GABRIEL CEPEDA-CARRIÓN, JERÓNIMO GARCÍA-FERNÁNDEZ,
ROSA LÓPEZ D'AMICO AND JAMES J. ZHANG

PART I
Innovations in Technologies   13

2 Digitization in Services of the Emerging Chilean Sport
Industry: The Case of BoxMagic Inc.   15
DANIEL DUCLOS-BASTÍAS, KYLE HEPP, DANIEL ÁVILA ARIAS,
FRANO GIAKONI-RAMÍREZ AND PABLO LARENAS CALDERON

3 Managing Employee's Health While They Are Teleworking: A
Corporate Well-Being Model in Times of COVID-19   25
JOSÉ M. NÚÑEZ-SÁNCHEZ, CARMINA JAMBRINO-MALDONADO,
JERÓNIMO GARCÍA-FERNÁNDEZ AND RAMÓN GÓMEZ-CHACÓN

4 Innovation and Sport Policy in Brazilian Sports: The Sport
Intelligence Research Institute   42
FERNANDO MARINHO MEZZADRI, GONZALO A. BRAVO,
NATASHA SANTOS-LISE AND GUSTAVO BAVARESCO

5 Crisis Management during COVID-19: Sport Clubs'
Initiatives and Innovations   58
PALOMA ESCAMILLA-FAJARDO, JUAN M. NÚÑEZ-POMAR AND
FERRAN CALABUIG-MORENO

vi Contents

PART II
Innovations in Fitness Industry   71

6 Innovation in Training Service for the Sport Management
   Sector in Ecuador   73
   ROSA LÓPEZ DE D'AMICO, LUISA VELEZ, MARÍA DOLORES GONZÁLEZ-
   RIVERA AND SUMMAR GÓMEZ

7 Healthy Universities: The Case of Nebrija University and Its
   Program of Physical Activity and Sport   86
   DAVID DE LA FUENTE FRANCO, JERÓNIMO GARCÍA-FERNÁNDEZ AND
   RAMÓN GÓMEZ-CHACON

8 Satisfaction with Services of a Public
   Sport Organization in Mexico   106
   MARINA REYES ROBLES, ROSA ELENA MEDINA RODRÍGUEZ,
   MARÍA GRETHEL RAMÍREZ SIQUEIROS AND
   OSWALDO CEBALLOS GURROLA

9 Impact of Products and Services Innovations on Consumer
   Behavior: The Portuguese Fitness Industry   123
   VERA PEDRAGOSA, JAIRO LEÓN-QUISMONDO AND THIAGO SANTOS

10 Educational Quality in Physical Education during
    Covid-19 Pandemic   138
    RAQUEL MORQUECHO SÁNCHEZ, MARÍA FERNANDA LEÓN
    ALCERRECA, LINA GUADALUPE SIERRA GARCÍA, ERIKA ALEXANDRA
    GADEA CAVAZOS AND ALMA ROSA LYDIA LOZANO GONZÁLEZ

11 Innovation in Sport Centres: Accessibility and
    Adapted Sports Programmes   148
    ZACARÍAS ADAME GARCÍA, ALBERTO NUVIALA NUVIALA,
    JERÓNIMO GARCÍA-FERNÁNDEZ AND NICOLÁS FERNÁNDEZ MARTÍNEZ

PART III
Innovations in Sports Events   165

12 Innovative Management Model and Multiplatform
    Distribution Content: The Liga Nacional de Basquete and
    Novo Basquete Brasil   167
    ARY JOSÉ ROCCO JÚNIOR AND GUILHERME BUSO

Contents vii

13 Innovative Promotions to Attract Non-Resident Spectators: A
Case Study in Portugal 186
MARIA JOSÉ CARVALHO, MARISA SOUSA AND CELINA GONÇALVES

14 Success Factors in Sporting Events through IPA Approach:
The Case of an International Horse Show Jumping 204
JAIRO LEÓN-QUISMONDO, PABLO BURILLO, THIAGO SANTOS AND
ÁLVARO FERNÁNDEZ-LUNA

15 Key Strategic and Innovative Decisions That Explain the
Success of the Valencia Marathon 224
RAMÓN LLOPIS-GOIG AND JUAN L. PARAMIO-SALCINES

16 Ecuador as a Destination for International Events:
A Case Study of Oceanman in Manta 246
E. SU JARA-PAZMINO AND SIMON M. PACK

17 Sport Events as a Catalyst for Economic, Sociocultural,
Tourism and Environmental Sustainability in Portugal 258
MÁRIO COELHO TEIXEIRA, AGAMENON CARVALHO JÚNIOR AND
ANDRÉ DIONÍSIO SESINANDO

18 Beach Volleyball Management in Brazil:
Reflections on the Modality's Autonomy 274
FERNANDO MARQUES D'OLIVEIRA, SILVIO COSTA TELLES, LUIZ
CARLOS NERY AND MÁRIO COELHO TEIXEIRA

Index 295

Contributors

Zacarías Adame García is Associate Professor in sports science at the Centro de Estudios Universitarios Cardenal Spínola CEU, Spain. His studies are focused on the situation in the practice of sport for people with disabilities in sports centers, in addition to the management policies of the managers of these centers. In terms of teaching, her profile is focused on Adapted and Paralympic Sport and Physical Education in schools.

Daniel Ávila Arias is CTO and Co-Founder of Boxmagic, Computer Engineer, and Postgraduate in Computer Management.

Gustavo Bavaresco is a doctoral student in the Department of Physical Education at Federal University of Parana in Brazil. His research examines policy and governance of sport in national sports organizations.

Gonzalo A. Bravo is Professor of Sport Management in the School of Sport Sciences in the College of Applied Human Sciences at West Virginia University, USA. His research examines issues in policy and governance of sport and organizational behavior in sport.

Pablo Burillo is Director of the Executive MBA in Sports Management at Real Madrid Graduate School, Spain, as well as a specialist in sport management (mostly about football management). His research topics are about sports planning models, economic impact in sport events, and sport equipment and facilities.

Guilherme Buso is the Business Development Manager of Genius Sports in Latin America. He is a Sports Marketing Executive who has worked with important sport organizations in Brazil, such as NBB and Federação Paulista de Futebol.

Ferran Calabuig-Moreno is Associate Professor at the University of Valencia, Spain, where he is also Director of the Sport Management and Innovation research group (SMIrg). His research interests are sport consumer behavior, sport entrepreneurship, and the social and economic impact of sporting events.

Agamenon Carvalho Júnior completed his studies by getting his master's degree in sport management at the University of Évora, Portugal. He is interested in the study of sports development and major sport events.

Contributors   ix

Maria José Carvalho is Assistant Professor in Sport Management in the Faculty of Sport at the University of Porto, Portugal. Her research interests include sport law, gender and sport, sport policies, and professional sport. She is also disciplinary judge (Disciplinary Board) of the Portuguese Football Federation and a member of the Centre of Research, Education, Innovation and Intervention in Sport (CIFI2D).

Oswaldo Ceballos Gurrola is Associate Professor and Coordinator of the PhD Program in Physical Activity and Sport Sciences at the Facultad de Organización Deportiva of the Universidad Autónoma de Nuevo León, Mexico. He is also Founder President of the Latin American Association of Sport Sciences, Physical Education and Dance (ALCIDED), and ICSPES North America Regional Representative. His research focuses on physical education, physical activity, and health.

Mário Coelho Teixeira is Professor in Sport Management at the University of Évora, Portugal, Coordinator of the Sport Management PhD and International Postdoctoral Supervisor. Mário participates in International Research Centers and Scientific Committees of events and journals and is a Researcher of the FIFA World Cup 2030 bid studies.

Silvio Costa Telles is Associate Professor at the Federal University of Rio de Janeiro and at the State University of Rio de Janeiro, Brazil. He has a PhD in Physical Education and Culture from the Gama Filho University, Brazil, and Post-Doctorate degree from the Institute for Advanced Research and Training at the University of Évora, Portugal.

Rosa López D'Amico is Emeritus Professor at the Universidad Pedagógica Experimental Libertador, Venezuela, and Coordinator of the Research Center EDUFISADRED. She is also Invited Professor at Universidad Nacional Experimental del Magisterio (UNEM), President of the ISCPES, Treasurer of WASM, and Founder President of the Latin America Sport Management Association (ALGEDE).

David de la Fuente Franco is Lecturer in the area of sports management and event organization in the Faculty of Physical Activity and Sport Sciences and Director of the Sports Service at Nebrija University, Spain. He is also a member and technical advisor of the Madrid Committee for University Sport (COMADU), Spain.

Daniel Duclos-Bastías is Assistant Professor and Researcher in sport management at the Pontificia Universidad Católica de Valparaíso, Chile, Coordinator of the iGEO – Sport Management and Olympic Studies Research Group, and Head of Sports at the Pontificia Universidad Católica de Valparaíso.

Paloma Escamilla-Fajardo collaborates with the University of Valencia, Spain. Her research interests are related to entrepreneurial orientation and its impact on the performance of sports clubs.

x Contributors

Nicoías Fernández is Associate Professor in sports science at the Centro de Estudios Universitarios Cardenal Spínola CEU, Spain. His research focuses on sports management geared toward racket sports.

Álvaro Fernández-Luna is Professor of Sport Management at Universidad Europea de Madrid, Spain, where he is also the Director of the Sport Management European Research Group. His research interest is in sports marketing and the economic and social impact of sports events.

Erika Gadea is Associate Professor A at the Autonomous University of Nuevo León, Mexico. Among her titles is that of teacher, researcher, and soccer coach, as well as the specialty in sports management, she has a doctorate in cultural sciences physics and is currently a level 1 researcher at the SNI.

Frano Giakoni-Ramírez is Director of the Sports Science career at Universidad Andrés Bello, Chile, Researcher with WoS and SCOPUS publications, in Sport Management, Physical Education, Esports, technology and Sport, Director of the scientific journal *Latin American Journal of Sport Management*, and an Active member of research groups in Chile and Spain, and in the Latin American Association of Sport Management (ALGEDE).

Summar Gómez is a teacher-researcher at the Metropolitan University of Ecuador. His line of research focuses on management culture in sports organizations in Latin America and the Caribbean. He is the Academic Director of the Center for Research and Sports Studies-CIED, an organization dedicated to the formulation and execution of research projects at the highest academic level in the field of management and administration in sports organizations.

Ramón Gómez-Chacón is Lecturer in the Department of Physical Activity and Sports at the Centro Estudios Universitario Cardenal Spínola CEU and Lecturer at the International University of Valencia, Spain. Ramón has professional experience and is a researcher in "Healthy Organisations" and "Healthy Universities", Spain.

Celina Gonçalves is Professor in Sport Management at the University of Maia, Portugal. Her research interests include consumer behavior in sport and its relationship with sports organizations and services, most cited research on retention of members in fitness centers, consumer perception, and customer satisfaction. She is also a member of Research Center in Sports Sciences, Health Sciences and Human Development (CIDESD).

María Dolores González-Rivera is Assistant Professor in the Faculty of Medicine and Health Science at University of Alcalá, Spain. She serves on the Executive Board of the International Association of Physical Education and Sport for Girls and Women (IAPESGW). Her teaching focus is Physical Education teaching and sport management.

Kyle Hepp is CEO of BoxMagic and has a bachelor's degree in Sports Management.

Contributors   xi

Carmina Jambrino-Maldonado is Associate Professor at the University of Málaga, Spain. She teaches in economics bachelor and master's degree.

E. Su Jara Pazmino is Assistant Professor in the Sport Management program at the University of West Georgia, USA, and collaborates with Universidad San Francisco de Quito in Ecuador. Her research interests include organizational behavior, collegiate athletics in the United States, international student-athletes, athlete brand building, and Latin American Sport.

Pablo Larenas Calderon is CFO and Co-Founder of Boxmagic and Civil Industrial Engineer.

María Fernanda León Alcerreca recently completed a doctorate in Physical Cultural Sciences, has a Master's in Physical Activity and Sports Orientated to Sports Management. She is a teacher at the Autonomous University of Nuevo León, Mexico. Her research interests are management and marketing, personal and professional sports brand.

Jairo León-Quismondo is Associate Professor of Sport Management at Universidad Europea de Madrid, Spain. His research interests include organizational management and quality service, specifically in fitness centers, sporting events, and other sport organizations. In 2019, he was awarded the Young Researcher Award by the Spanish Society for Sports Economics.

Ramon Llopis-Goig is Professor in Sociology at the University of Valencia, Spain.

Alma Rosa Lydia Lozano González is Associate professor A at the Facultad de Organización Deportiva of the Universidad Autónoma de Nuevo León, Mexico, and General Manager of social and cultural sports promotion of the Centro Bancario de Monterrey. She is also Head of the Extension Department of the Instituto Tecnológico y de Estudios Superiores de Monterrey (ITESM).

Fernando Marques d'Oliveira is a member of the Sports Development Department of the Brazilian Olympic Committee. He has a Master in Sports Science and Physical Education from the State University of Rio de Janeiro, Brazil, and Postgraduate degree in Sports Management and is also certified in Management of Olympic Sports Organizations by the International Olympic Committee.

Fernando Marinho Mezzadri is Professor of Sport Public Policies in the Department of Physical Education at Federal University of Parana in Brazil. His research examines issues in policy and governance of sport and sport sociology.

Rosa Elena Medina Rodríguez is Associate Professor and Research Coordinator in the Faculty of Sports Organization, member of the National System of Researchers Level 1, and belongs to the Latin American Association of Sports Sciences, Physical Education and Dance (ALCIDED, 2021), the Latin American Association of Sports Management (ALGEDE, 2009); and World Association for Sport Management (WASM 2012).

xii Contributors

Raquel Morquecho Sánchez completed her PhD in Sports Sciences (Sports Management) in 2012, from the Faculdade de Motricidade Humana at the Universidade de Lisboa, Portugal. She has been a manager in fitness centers (owning her own gym and opening others gyms) and she was member of Portugal Activo (Association of Gyms and Fitness Centers of Portugal) in the social bodies.

Juan M. Núñez-Pomar is Professor at the University of Valencia, Spain. He is also professional sports manager and his research interests are sport management, sport entrepreneurship, and service quality.

José M. Núñez-Sánchez is Associate Professor in the Business and Management Department at the University of Málaga, Spain, in degrees such as Business Administration, Industrial Engineering or Marketing. With more than 20 years of career in the Wellness private sector, he also works as the Corporate Wellness Business Unit manager in O2 Centro Wellness, where he also works as the Chief Marketing Officer. His main research topics are corporate wellness and well-being programs, healthy employees and healthy organizations, happiness at work, internal and external marketing, and the fitness industry. He is also founding trustee of World Happiness Foundation.

Alberto Nuviala is Associate Professor in sports science at the Universidad Pablo de Olavide, Spain. His research focuses on the consumer perception, customer satisfaction, and customer loyalty in the sport services.

Simon M. Pack is Associate Professor in the Division of Sport Management at St. John's University in New York, USA. His research interests include student-athletes, organizational behavior, and using sport as a tool for development.

Juan L. Paramio-Salcines is Senior Lecturer at Loughborough University, UK.

Vera Pedragosa is Associate Professor and Scientific Coordinator of the degree in Sports Management at the Autonomous University of Lisbon, Portugal. She is currently responsible for the subjects of Sports Marketing and Internships. She is also an integral member of the Research Centre in Economic and Business Sciences (CICEE) and collaborates with the Research Centre in Psychology (CIP).

Luiz Carlos Pessoa Nery is Doctor of Knowledge Management in Sport, Coordinator of the Research Center on Knowledge Management in Sport and Sport Management, Member of the Brazilian Society of Knowledge Management, Member of the Asociación Latinoamericana Gestor Deportiva, and Member of the Center for Studies in Politics and Management of Sport and Leisure.

Maria Grethel Ramirez Siqueiros is Research Professor 1 in Sports Training, and General Academic Secretary at the State University of Sonora, Mexico.

Marina Reyes Robles is Professor 1 at Sonora State University, Mexico. Her research is related to the quality and satisfaction of sports services.

Contributors xiii

Ary José Rocco Júnior is Associate Professor in sports management in the School of Physical Education and Sport at the University of São Paulo (EEFE/USP). His research focuses on sports marketing, customer behavior, and sports organizations. He is member of the São Paulo State Sports Council and was President of the Brazilian Association of Sport Management (Abragesp).

Thiago Santos is Assistant Professor of Sport Management at Universidade Europeia, Portugal. His research interest is in consumer behavior, service quality, and social responsibility in sports. In 2014, he received an award from the Portuguese Olympic Committee for the most relevant scientific research in the field of sport management.

Natasha Santos-Lise is Professor of Sociology in the Department of Physical Education at the State University of Ponta Grossa in Brazil. Her research examines issues on policy and governance of sport, also sport sociology and history.

André Dionísio Sesinando is Researcher, Author, and PhD Student in sport management (public spending in sport). He holds a master's degree in sport management and a bachelor's degree in sport sciences. His research focuses on sport management at the local authorities, sport policies, and leadership in sport management.

Lina Guadalupe Sierra García coordinates and participates in research projects, scientific congresses, fundraising for research projects, and organizes scientific events and conferences. Her research interests are consumer behavior in the fitness industry.

Marisa Sousa is a PhD Student in Sport Sciences in the Faculty of Sports at the University of Porto, Portugal, where she is also Aquatic Activities Manager in the Sports. She is also Professor of sports management at the University of Maia, Portugal.

Luisa Velez teaches in the Department of Exercise Science at the Universidad Sagrado Corazon in San Juan, Puerto Rico.

Chapter 1

Ibero-American Sport Management
Challenges and Opportunities

Gabriel Cepeda-Carrión
Universidad de Sevilla, Seville, Spain

Jerónimo García-Fernández
Universidad de Sevilla, Seville, Spain

Rosa López D'Amico
Universidad Pedagógica Experimental Libertador, Venezuela

James J. Zhang
University of Georgia, USA

Chapter Contents

Introduction	1
The Ibero-American Market and Sports Management	3
Sport Practice and Governance	3
Academic Development of Sport Management	4
Innovations in Sport Management in Ibero-America	5
About This Book	10
References	11

Introduction

Ibero-America is a term formed from the words Iberia and America to designate the group of territories in the Americas where Ibero-Romance languages are spoken. Ibero-America is one of the largest and most culturally cohesive linguistic regions in the world. The Pan-Hispanic Dictionary of Doubts defines Ibero-America as the region made up of the American nations that belonged as viceroyalties and provinces to the former Spanish and Portuguese Iberian empires. According to this definition, Ibero-America would refer only to an American region. However, this definition also includes what refers to Spain and Portugal. Likewise, the dictionary of the Real Academia Española de la Lengua includes one of the definitions of this "gentilicio": "that which belongs to or relates to Ibero-America,

DOI: 10.4324/9781003388050-1

Spain and Portugal". Sometimes, the same term also includes Andorra. Therefore, Ibero-America is composed for the following 22 countries: Andorra, Argentina, Bolivia, Brazil, Chile, Colombia, Costa Rica, Cuba, Dominican Republic, Ecuador, El Salvador,Guatemala, Honduras, Mexico, Nicaragua, Panama, Paraguay, Peru, Portugal, Spain, Uruguay, and Venezuela.

The First Ibero-American Summit of Heads of State and Government held in 1991 enshrined in its Final Declaration the recognition of a common Ibero-American space for political coordination and cooperation, which has been given more depth and content from year to year. "We have decided to establish the Ibero-American Summit of Heads of State and Government with the participation of the Spanish and Portuguese-speaking sovereign States of America and Europe" (International Organization serving Ibero-America, 1991, p. 7). The Ibero-American Conference has its central axis the biennial celebration of the Ibero-American Summit, a meeting of the highest political level among the listed countries, which was annually until 2014. This meeting is coordinated by the Pro Tempore Secretary that is constituted by the host country of the Summit, working together with the Ibero-American General Secretariat. The Meeting of Ministers of Foreign Affairs is the second most important decision-making entity after the Summit. The meeting continues to be held annually to follow up on the mandates issued by the Heads of State and Government during the immediately preceding Summit.

In addition to the aforementioned, the meetings of National Coordinators and Cooperation Officers are the usual management and discussion bodies and are convened several times a year. The Ministerial Meetings are held every 2 years and bring together Ibero-American ministers and senior officials from different areas to discuss sectoral issues. In turn, there are various forums and meetings in various levels of governance, parliamentarians, business sectors, academic disciplines, civil society, and different types of organizations that also hold technical meetings. All of these meetings, forums, and gatherings serve to enable Ibero-American leaders to discuss and prioritize the issues to be addressed during the Summit. The meetings are a privileged forum for dealing with multilateral issues. They create a climate of trust among governments, organizations, and individuals that allow them to exchange ideas and experiences, establish shared diagnoses, and agree on common positions in the face of the challenges facing the Ibero-American community and beyond.

The Ibero-American Summit includes Associate Observers (States) and Consultative Observers (international organizations). Their presence promotes closer ties with other members of the international community and thus opens Ibero-America to linguistically and culturally similar countries and areas. One of the tools for Ibero-American countries is the Ibero-American counsel of sport. Among central tasks is the definition of objectives and central strategies for sport. With the aim of being a roadmap to expand the impact of sport on the 2030 Agenda, the main alternatives proposed include the following:

1 Sport to support some or all of the Sustainable Development Goals (SDGs), looking at "active" (participants) and passive (fans) participation in sport.

2 Arguments around a systematic approach to support the design, management and evaluation of Sport for Development programs and initiatives, considering how most effectively to educate, guide, and empower sport fans.
3 Multi-sectoral partnerships, public policy opportunities, and around the Well-Being Index.

The Ibero-American Market and Sports Management

In order to explain the evolution of sport management in Ibero-America, this section is divided in two parts. The first one looks at the sport practice and its governance, i.e., events, practice, and structures. The second one looks at the academic development of sport management as a scientific discipline and training area.

Sport Practice and Governance

In the Ibero-American region, sport places an important role in society; its increasing value is visible in various projects, activities, and active participation in the private and public sphere (e.g., Consejo Iberoamericano de Deporte & Secretaría General Iberoamérica 2019a, 2019b). In all countries, there are national bodies from government and private sectors that organize sport and they are all connected with the international umbrella organizations that govern sport. The national and regional political divisions do incorporate sport in its structure, and budget is assigned to it either to sport for all or elite sport (Martínez, 2013), being the latest the most benefit one in most countries (Schausteck, 2010). The countries of the region participate in all major events internationally, such us: Olympic and Paralympic Games, Winter and Paralympics Games, Junior Olympic Games, University Sport Games, Military Sport Games, Pan American Games, Central American and the Caribbean Games, Central American Games, South American Games, and Bolivarian Games. Besides, some countries participate in other major events that might not be celebrated in the region, e.g., Andorra in the Games of the Small States of Europe. The organization of the events in the region represents a major economic investment, besides the educational and cultural impact that a major event represents. On the other hand, there is a long series of world championships of all sport disciplines that have been celebrated in the region. Besides, many of the countries celebrate internal national games or their national Olympics, and again it represents important business. The school sport games are another major event that is celebrated in the countries at national level as well as internationally.

The development of professional sport is a visible component in the region. There are many leagues and sports that contribute significantly with players to other regions of the world. Football by far is the most popular sport in the region (Consejo Iberoamericano de Deporte & Secretaría General Iberoamérica, 2019b), but there are other professional sports that also have important number of followers, such as baseball, tennis, volleyball to mention but a few. Professional sport implies the celebration of important events and again important economic impacts (e.g., Bravo et al., 2016; Da Costa et al., 2008). Besides, the relevance of the touristic activities connected with events is a major component in the socio-economic dynamic that occurs in the region with the celebration of any of the events mentioned before, other highlights are activities such as Rally Dakar, extreme sport events, Caribbean Series, among others. In terms of sport for leisure and recreation, the activities are many with particular experiences in many places (Chin & Edginton, 2014; Consejo Iberoamericano de Deporte & Secretaría General Iberoamérica, 2019a). The industry of fitness has grown impressively, and the input from this sector has increased the training demands for professionals and definitely in the economic sector as well (e.g., García-Fernández et al., 2018). The development of sport, physical activity, and recreation is a demanding sector in the region and is at the same level of the global demands.

It will be naïve to believe that the innovation and market chances are developed at the same level in the region. Spain by far has an important visibility with professional events in football (e.g., Cubeiro & Gallardo, 2010) or tennis; Argentina, Brazil, and Portugal have a strength in football as well. The socio-cultural and political situation of some countries and its foreign relations affect the attraction of major sport events; however, each one has an attractive sport interest or celebrates any international event. There are other destinations that might be attractive because of training camps, such as baseball in Dominican Republic or Venezuela, for example. The good opportunities for sport management are many. Let's first address the training of the staff that is needed to respond to the high demands that sport management requires in practice. As an academic field, it could be said that it is an area that is in the process to grow in the region, this is understood by the social recognition it has in terms of its professionalization, employability, profile, and academic programs to train professionals. Spain and Portugal do have more stability as there are academic and non-academic organizations for sport management or its sub-disciplines (e.g., García & Pradas, 2017). In Latin America, particularly in Brazil, Colombia, Mexico, Chile, and Costa Rica, there are national organizations for sport managers; Brazil has the eldest national academic organization in sport management, just since 2009 (López de D'Amico et al., 2017).

Academic Development of Sport Management

The academic programs to train professionals are an important indicator. In the region there are some in few countries. In Latin America, in particular, there is still the tradition to have undergraduate programs either in Physical Education or Sport Science, so there is limited reference about bachelor programs in Sport Management, just one in Venezuela and Brazil (Ibid). So, graduate programs mean the place to specialize in the field and in that respect again, Spain and Portugal are the countries in which more academic programs can be found, for example, at master level (Gallardo, 2017). In Latin America in the last 10 years, there has been an increase in the programs, being Cuba, Venezuela, Brazil, and Mexico the ones that have some masters in place since late 1990s and early 2000, more recent there are in Colombia, Chile, Argentina, and Ecuador (Bastos et al., 2021). In Latin America still, there are no doctoral programs in sport management, just Sport Science, Physical Education, or Education with perhaps a research cluster in sport management. In the other side of the ocean there are ones (Portugal and Spain), but they are not too many ones. This is important as it is a source of continuous research and enrichment in the field.

The region, particularly Latin America, has been influenced by academics from diverse regions of the world. The academic tradition comes from those who went to study abroad and came back with terminologies and literature either from North America, Europe, Former Soviet Union, and Australia, that is why we do not have a unify term to refer to "sport management" in Spanish and there is a history of translations and adaptations (López de D'Amico, 2022). Academic organizations do play an important role to support the presence of academic programs in the region. In the Iberian Peninsula, the European Sport Management Association has supported the growth of the field since it was initiated in the 1990s. The Latin American Association of Sport Management (ALGEDE, acronym in Spanish) is more recent. Since 2009, however, it has been crucial to start making an important network in the whole region and promote publications. Bastos (2019) highlights the good connection Brazil has with Portugal in terms of academic programs in the field and interestingly, the publications and activity with the Intercontinental Alliance for Sport Management since 2011. The COVID-19 pandemic made all of us change and the educations systems in consequence. Despite the negative effects of the pandemic, it must be said that in education, it has pushed major changes to adapt. ALGEDE has done a series of webinars that have managed to incorporate more interested people in the field, academic and practitioners from both sides of the ocean have participated in many virtual experiences as never before; the importance to speak the same language and to make efforts to understand ourselves between Spanish and Portuguese has been a major input. So, in general, Ibero-America is an important market for sport management and its academic field is growing.

Innovations in Sport Management in Ibero-America

Increasingly, studies and experiences related to innovative products and services in Ibero-America are better known. In fact, these experiences help to work and improve the sports system in Latin America and, therefore, help to professionalize the sports sector. For this reason, the objective of this book is to show experiences and studies related to the sports system in Ibero-America where innovation and research have been the differentiating element to achieve this goal. The content provides knowledge about the current situation and what are the challenges of the future. In turn, a great strength of this book is the great diversity of authors and countries that have participated, providing great value from their points of view and professional and academic experiences.

In particular, this book is organized into three sections. The first section shows studies and experiences related to innovation in technologies. Specific, Daniel Duclos-Bastías, Kyle Hepp, Daniel Ávila Arias, Frano Giakoni-Ramírez, and Pablo Larenas Calderon show the sports industry, innovation in Chile and its digital transformation. The chapter gives an overview of the country's economy and governance, as well as the country's evolution and current state of sport, as well as how it has evolved into an emergent sector. In addition, the company BoxMagic's expertise is shared. In terms of digitalization of the fitness market in Chile and Latin America, BoxMagic is a success story. The steps taken to become more inventive are described in depth. It is a cutting-edge company that assists gym owners in managing less, generating more revenue, and maximizing their time. Regarding the chapter of José M. Núñez-Sánchez, Ramón Gómez-Chacón, Carmina Jambrino-Maldonado, and Jerónimo García-Fernández study the improvement of health of employees through sports as a strategic element in business management. As a result, corporations concerned about their employees' well-being have developed corporate wellness programs in the workplace. The current COVID-19 pandemic, as well as the rise in teleworking, has created a slew of health concerns for workers, and businesses must adapt their workplace wellness programs to reflect this new reality. On the basis of the successful case study of Mahou San Miguel, qualitative research was conducted. The goal of this chapter is to develop a management model that can be used by firms of various sizes and types to adapt corporate wellness programs in the workplace, especially when that workplace is the employees' home. The chapter of Fernando Marinho Mezzadri, Gonzalo A. Bravo, Natasha Santos-Lise, and Gustavo Bavaresco shows the Sport Intelligence Research Institute of Brazil. The Sport Intelligence Research Institute was founded in 2013 as a result of a collaboration between the Federal University of Parana and the Brazilian National High-Performance Sport Secretariat. The purpose of this collaborative initiative was to gather, organize, and disseminate information regarding high-performance sport in order to offer crucial data for evidence-based decision-making in sport policies at the federal, state, and local levels. The Sport Intelligence Research Institute is a managerial and organizational type of innovation in the field of sport management and policy in Brazil, with the goal of producing germane information that can be used not only to evaluate existing programs but also to foster informed conversations among key stakeholders for the evaluation, change, or creation of new policies in sport. The first section ends with the chapter of Paloma Escamilla-Fajardo, Juan M. Núñez-Pomar, and Ferran Calabuig-Moreno that analyzed 148 Spanish sports clubs in April and May 2020. The crisis that resulted from COVID-19 has had a significant impact on sports teams and their operations. As a result, they've been obliged to react to the situation in order to maintain their relationship with users and members, as well as ensure the organization's long-term viability. According to the findings, sports clubs believe that it was vital to reinvent themselves in the light of the lockdown situation. As a result, the vast majority of participants have implemented projects or innovations that were not contemplated before to COVID-19. The results were compared between sports clubs with a high-felt COVID-19 impact on their economic-financial status and those with a low-perceived COVID-19 impact on their economic situation. On the basis of the findings, practical consequences and managerial solutions have been offered.

The second section brings innovations from fitness industry. Rosa López de D'Amico, Luisa Velez, María Dolores Gonzalez, and Summar Gómez show a case of success in adapting to market needs. In 2020, Ecuador's Center for Research and Studies of Sport (Centro de Investigación y Estudios del Deporte-CIED) launched on an innovative road with a series of webinars on Sport Management. It was a slow-starting movement, but by the end of the year, they had organized and hosted multiple events, forming a network of practitioners and academics in the Ibero-American sport management sector. A document review procedure and participant experience observation were utilized as part of the qualitative technique used to address this case. The Ibero-American Forum of Sport Management 2020 (Foro Iberoamericano de Gerencia Deportiva, 2020) is analyzed for a series of five events and the publication of proceedings. This ground-breaking procedure shifted the Latin American landscape and allowed for the formation of new networks. It also sparked other intriguing consequences in the region, which has already begun to create more goods and services. In relation to the chapter written by David de la Fuente Franco, Ramón Gómez-Chacon, and Jerónimo García-Fernández shows the sport case of Nebrija University and its Program of Physical Activity and Sport in the workplace. This is a program aimed at improving the overall health of employees, with the primary goal of having a positive influence on both employees and the organization. It focuses on the Nebrija University teachers, researchers, and employees (Madrid, Spain). Also, it offers a model of sports management applied to the healthy area in the university environment, with the correct and adequate coordination of the various departments, the optimization of the company's existing resources for its implementation and follow-up, as well as the entity's support and institutional backing.

On the other hand, Marina Reyes Robles, Rosa Elena Medina Rodríguez, María Grethel Ramírez Siqueiros, and Oswaldo Ceballos Gurrola analyzed the sports context in Mexico and the services offered by a public sports organization. A total of 453 users/athletes took part, with males accounting for 58.9% and women for 41.1%. With 11 factors and 40 items, a viable and valid tool was employed to measure satisfaction in sports services. Trainer performance and training tasks were the most highly regarded elements, whereas cafeteria services and sports facilities were the least highly rated. Gender and age had no bearing on the results. Public policies in the country encourage sports participation, but quality of life development requires human resources, financial resources, and suitable facilities. In relation to the chapter of Vera Pedragosa, Jairo León-Quismondo, and Thiago Santos explains the fitness industry in Portugal like an innovation region in the world. One of the reference services for boosting societal adherence to physical activity is the fitness sector. The necessity to adapt to new circumstances has arisen as a result of increased demand, professionalization of the sector, and the pandemic breakout. As a result, in the contemporary fitness sector climate, innovation is critical. Portugal is one of the most promising sports markets in Ibero-America. Fitness service providers must seek innovative tactics to effectively impact consumer behaviors, with over 1,100 fitness clubs servicing 688,210 members (a fall of 30% after COVID-19). In Portugal, three primary areas of innovation are driving change: new business models, new pricing classes, and high technology. All of these factors could have a favorable impact on customer behavior. The case of GoFit is presented in order to demonstrate the good practices followed by this fitness operator, which is a shining example in the Ibero-American fitness market. On the other hand, Raquel Morquecho Sánchez, María Fernanda de León Alcerreca, Lina Guadalupe Sierra García, Erika Alexandra Gadea Cavazos, and Alma Rosa Lydia Lozano González analyzed the online education in Mexico. Due to the health crisis caused by COVID-19, online education has taken on a new significance that will usher in a new era in pedagogical practices and educational institutions around the world. Faced with this paradigm shift, Mexican educational institutions are concentrating on developing guidelines to aid in the adaptation of the learning methodology framework and the use of evaluation instruments. In recent months, the challenge for education systems has been to sustain the vibrancy of education while encouraging the growth of meaningful learning. It has two major supporters in this: its professors and virtuality (use of ICT). The SERVQUAL Model is an effective evaluation mechanism for demonstrating service quality in a variety of corporate, institutional, educational, social, and health-related settings. The diversity of ideas based on the paradigm of the suitable way to measuring quality management in educational services appears to be obvious. As a result, implementing this paradigm in physical education, whether face-to-face or online, as well as building continuous improvement methods in the quality of Mexican educational services, is critical. The second block ends with the chapter of Zacarías Adame, Alberto Nuviala, Jerónimo García-Fernández, and Nicolás Fernández that analyzes the problems encountered by sports facilities in a Spanish city in relation to the accessibility of fitness centers. Thus, the aim of the chapter is to describe sports facilities in a total of 87 sports centers, in order to determine which are the accessibility elements in sports centers that influence the practice of physical-sports activities by people with disabilities. The main conclusions show that there are still improvements in accessibility elements that can be directed to new business initiatives, taking as an opportunity for an integral innovation of the centers the inclusion policies expressed by the managers of the sports centers.

To end with the three sections that structure the book, studies and innovative experiences are presented as specific sports events. Thus, Ary José Rocco Júnior, and Guilherme Buso present the case of Liga Nacional de Basquete (LNB), the Brazilian National Basketball League, founded in 2008 by the union of the most important men's basketball clubs in Brazil, in order to revitalize the sport in the country. LNB was born out of an amateur and semi-professional environment but was inspired by a series of mega events held in Brazil over the last decade to adopt an innovative management model that involves the clubs administering the organization through an electoral college, professional, and business vision. LNB's organizational approach is unique in Brazil, and it has produced outstanding benefits for its stakeholders. LNB's broad and original strategy stands out for its technological and communicational advancements, as well as the unique content distribution through the multiplatform concept, which has led to a higher level of engagement and a better branding experience for its followers. Concerning to the chapter of Maria José Carvalho, Marisa Sousa, and Celina Gonçalves, they analyzed the profile and consumption patterns of non-resident spectators of Liga NOS. In five games played at Futebol Clube Paços de Ferreira's stadium, 343 randomly selected fans were given study questionnaires. The SPSS software was used to conduct the analysis, which included descriptive statistics, nonparametric testing, and linear regression. Non-resident Liga NOS fans are predominantly men, with an average age of 36.12 years, a secondary education, and a monthly salary of less than 1,000€. In the city of Paços de Ferreira, fans spent an average of 25€. This study provided insight into the demographics and consumption patterns of non-resident spectators that attend Liga NOS football matches in Paços de Ferreira. As a result, stronger marketing methods can be used to attract more spectators and boost their expenditure at sporting events.

The chapter of Jairo León-Quismondo, Pablo Burillo, Thiago Santos, and Álvaro Fernández-Luna offers an innovative approach to determine success factors in an international horse show jumping event. The chosen event takes place in Madrid, Spain, as part of a broader international championship with economic significance. It discusses Importance-Performance Analysis (IPA), a novel way for assessing strengths and weaknesses in the sports sector. It's a simple yet powerful tool for event planners who want to enhance their processes and increase their chances of success. This chapter is based on a case study that takes a practical approach to event evaluation. The studied data yields a number of priorities, most of which are connected to food and beverage service, organizational aspects, comfort, and the event setting. Despite the fact that this is an event-focused chapter, it has significant ramifications for other sports marketplaces. As a result, practitioners, educators, university students, and researchers will benefit greatly from this publication. With regard to the chapter of Ramón Llopis-Goig, and Juan L. Paramio-Salcines, they identify and analyze the main decisions that have been key in the evolution of the Valencia Marathon over the last 40 years, from its inception on 29 March 1981, organized by a local athletic club, Sociedad Deportiva Correcaminos (SDC), as a popular race marathon (known at this time as Marathon Popular de Valencia) with only 800 runners to its current name, Marathon Valencia Trinidad Alfonso as is renamed today, and status as one of the leading marathons worldwide. Evans Chebet, from Etyopia, reached the height of growth on 6 December 2020, when he crossed the finish line at the 2020 Marathon Valencia Trinidad Alfonso in an incredible time of 2 hours 3 minutes.

Unlike previous academic works that have focused on the event's economic, tourist, social, and sporting impact, as well as participant satisfaction with the event's organization, this chapter has focused on the analysis of the organizers' strategic decisions and innovation proposals made during this time period that could explain the benchmark race's long-term success (1981–2020). The chapter of E. Su Jara-Pazmino and Simon Pack shows Ecuador as a destination for International Events. In particular, on Ecuador's Pacific Coast, Manta is one of the most important cities for commerce and tourism. Ecuador has lately held international events such as the 2014 Adventure Race World Championship, the Huairasinchi Adventure Race since 2003, the 2016 Galapagos CAMTRI Sprint Triathlon American Cup, Ironman 70.3 Ecuador from 2015 to 2019, and the Oceanman Manta 2021 open water swimming. The inaugural edition of the Oceanman Manta 2021 is the subject of this case study. The case study's main research question is: what factors influenced Sara Palacios, the event manager's decision-making process when designing and executing the Oceanman for the first time in Manta, Ecuador? Sara Palacios, the event organizer, and the Oceanman franchise gave a fantastic chance to expand the Open Water Competitions and encourage high-quality event execution. The chapter of Mário Teixeira, Agamenon Júnior, and André Sesinando investigated an urban running sport event in the capital of Portugal, with the aim of analyzing and evaluating its potential economic, socio-cultural, and environmental sustainability impacts. Methodologically, 2,771 questionnaire surveys were distributed to event attendees, yielding 590 validated responses. The significant findings show that the main reason for traveling was to participate in the event, that environmental preservation efforts were acknowledged, and that the majority of people plan to attend future editions. They observed that most participants' brief trips to Lisbon (less than 20 kilometers) had no substantial economic consequences on various expenses, restricting the promotion and growth of the local economy and tourism. Finally, this section closes by the chapter of Fernando Costa Marques d'Oliveira, Silvio de Cassio Costa Telles, Luiz Carlos Nery, and Mário Coelho Teixeira. By studying the operational dynamics in these regions, the chapter intends to map beach volleyball practice locations in the main regions of its development in Brazil and explore the autonomy with which they interact with the various actors in the field in which this sport finds itself. In terms of methodology, they used a field diary to analyze the data collected in the Metropolitan Regions of Rio de Janeiro, Joo Pessoa, Fortaleza, and Vitória to map the conditions under which this technique is incorporated in Brazilian territory. They came to the conclusion that the geographical territories where high-performance volleyball is practiced have a high level of reliance on the Brazilian Volleyball Confederation and its sponsors. The sites recognized for informal practice, on the other hand, have a degree of autonomy in relation to these actors.

About This Book

This book is purported to provide knowledge of the reality and current affairs of innovation in Ibero-America and identify what are the experiences and studies that can help professionalize and innovate in the Ibero-American sports system.

The co-editors of this book have selected research papers relevant to the topical issues. In addition to this introduction chapter, this book contains a total of 17 chapters. The chapters are contributed by a total of 53 scholars representing eight Ibero-American countries or territories, including Chile, Spain, Venezuela, Puerto Rico, Ecuador, Brazil, Portugal, and Mexico. Co-editors Gabriel Cepeda-Carrión, Jerónimo García-Fernández, and James J. Zhang would like to take this opportunity to thank these eminent scholars for their remarkable contributions to the completion of this book project. This book is commissioned by the WASM Executive Board, representing this organization's leadership and commitment to develop, summarize, synthesize, and analyze knowledge that helps enhance global sport industry. It covers a range of key research and practical issues of sport management in diverse contexts and settings of Ibero-American regions and countries. The book combines scholarly output derived from diverse inquiry protocols, such as review of literature, documentary analysis, qualitative research, and quantitative investigations.

References

Bastos, F. (2019). Sport management scientific development in Brazil. In J. J. Zhang, & B. Pitts (Eds.), *Globalized sport management in diverse cultural contexts* (pp. 136–153). Routledge.

Bastos, F., D'Amico, L., Rocco, R., & Furegato, A., I. (2021). Gerencia Deportiva en América Latina. Brasil

Bravo, G., de D'Amico, L., & Parrish, R. (2016). *Sport in Latin America policy, organization, management*. Routledge.

Centro de Investigación y Estudios del Deporte (2020). Memorias foro iberoamericano de gerencia del deporte. Quito, Ecuador: Cámara Ecuatoriana del Libro.

Chin, M. K., & Edginton, C. R. (2014). *Physical education and health. Global perspectives and Best practices*. Sagamore.

Consejo Iberoamericano del Deporte & Secretaría General Iberoamérica. (2019a). *Iberoamérica y la Agenda 2030. El deporte como herramienta para el desarrollo sostenible: perspectivas, avances y oportunidades – Parte 1*. Montevideo: Author.

Consejo Iberoamericano del Deporte & Secretaría General Iberoamérica. (2019b). *Iberoamérica y la Agenda 2030. El deporte como herramienta para el desarrollo sostenible: perspectivas, avances y oportunidades – Parte 2*. Montevideo: Author.

Cubeiro, J., & Gallardo, L. (2010). *El Mundial De La Roja*. Alienta.

Da Costa, L., Corrêa, D., Rizzuti, E., Villano, B., & Miragaya, A. (2008). *Legados de megaeventos esportivos*. Ministério do Esporte.

Gallardo, A. (2017). La formación de postgrados de gestión deportiva, clave para los gestores deportivos. In M. García Tascón, & M. Pradas García (Eds.), *El Gestor Deportivo En La Organización Del Deporte En La Sociedad Actual* (pp. 172–175). Wanceulen.

García-Fernández, J., Galvez-Ruiz, P., Pitt, B., Vélez-Colón, L., & Bernal-García, A. (2018). Consumer behaviour and sport services: An examination of fitness centre loyalty. *International Journal of Sport Management and Marketing, 18*(1/2), 8–23.

García, M., & Pradas, M. (Coord.). (2017). *El Gestor Deportivo En La Organización Del Deporte En La Sociedad Actual* (2a ed.). Wanceulen.

International Organization serving Ibero-America (1991). *Declaration of Guadalajara. Mexico. July 19, 1991*. Retrieved from https://www.segib.org/wp-content/uploads/Primera-Cumbre-Iberoamericana-de-Jefes-de-Estado-y-de-Gobierno.pdf

López de D'Amico (2022). *El libro de la gerencia deportiva*. Editorial Kinesis.

López de D'Amico, R., da Cunha Bastos, F., & Hojas, J. (2017). Gerencia deportiva en latinoamérica: Formación del talento humano. In A. Silva, & V. Molina (Eds.), *Educación Física En América Latina: Currículos Y Horizontes Formativos* (pp. 22–36). Paco.

Martínez, D. (2013). *La Gestión Deportiva Municipal En Iberoamérica: Historia, Teoría Y Práctica*. Editorial ESM.

Schausteck, B. (2010). O finaciamento do comitê olímpico brasileiro e suas relações com a política no Brasil. In W. Marchi Junior (Ed.), *Ensaios Em Sociologia Do Esporte* (pp. 141–160). Factash.

Part I

Innovations in Technologies

Chapter 2

Digitization in Services of the Emerging Chilean Sport Industry

The Case of BoxMagic Inc.

Daniel Duclos-Bastías
Pontificia Universidad Católica de Valparaíso, Chile

Kyle Hepp
BoxMagic Inc., Chile

Daniel Ávila Arias
Sports Tech Chile, Chile

Frano Giakoni-Ramírez
Universidad Andrés Bello, Chile

Pablo Larenas Calderon
BoxMagic Inc., Chile

Chapter Contents

Introduction	15
BoxMagic as a Success Case in Chile	18
Conclusion	22
References	23

Introduction

Chile is a country located in South America that is made up of a territorial strip with 16 regions, the most populated of which is the Metropolitan Region. The regions, in turn, are divided into a total of 54 provinces which are organized into 346 municipalities. The estimated Chilean population in 2020 is 19.5 million (48.9% men and 51.1% women), with a life expectancy of 80.8 years and 1.5 million foreign residents. According to age group, the population is distributed as: 0–14 years (21.1%), 15–64 years (68.5%), and 65 years or older (11.4%) according to data from the Instituto Nacional de Estadísticas (2018). In the political-administrative sphere, its executive capital is the city of Santiago, while its legislative capital is

DOI: 10.4324/9781003388050-3

the city of Valparaíso. The Political Constitution (since 1980) defines Chile as a centrally driven unitary state. Its political organization is based on a presidential regime in which the executive power is vested, while the legislative power is organized into the Senate and Chamber of Deputies and finally the judiciary is organized through autonomous and independent courts established by law.

In the economic sphere, Chile has a per capita income estimated at U$15,000 of medium-high level (World Bank, 2020) and is similar to other countries in the region such as Panama or Uruguay. However, this disaggregated reality has shown high levels of inequality in the distribution of income, which affects the population's access to goods and services. Despite this, in recent decades, the country has had an economic performance highlighted by international organizations for having a "solid" economic framework and sustained growth, which has allowed for a significant reduction in poverty, but gaps still persist in terms of social security. This reveals a significant difference between macroeconomic indicators and those related to human capital, so that income distribution, health and education are far from being satisfactorily completed (Riveros & Báez, 2014). However, in the international framework, the Human Development Index Development places Chile at the highest level in Latin America (0.847) according to a report from the United Nations Development Program ([UNDP], 2019). Specifically, in relation to the education sphere, over the last three decades, governments have focused educational public policies on expanding the coverage of the education system, which has resulted in an increase in the educational level of the population.

Although the Chilean sports system can be defined as mixed, in the last two decades it has been led by public institutions which, after the civil-military dictatorship, created the Instituto Nacional de Deportes (IND) in 2001 and the Ministerio del Deporte (MINDEP) in 2013. The implementation of sports began at the municipal level as a result of a reform to the Organic Constitutional Law of Municipalities (Ministerio del Interior, 2006). The above has led to an increase in public spending on sports (Figure 2.1), which has had an impact on the increase in the availability of fitness and sports activities aimed at the population through programs such as: Social Participation, Comprehensive Sports Schools, National System of Sports Competitions, Strengthening of Conventional and Paralympic Performance Sports and Assistance to Sports Career executed by the IND in addition to the supply of municipal sports services. Both MINDEP and IND have decentralized bodies in all regions of the country and regional capitals throughout the country. Together these have as their main functions, the execution of fitness and physical activity programs in the municipalities, complementing the municipal offer.

Municipal sports are one of the most beneficial tools that municipalities have to improve the quality of life of their citizens (Gallardo & Jiménez, 2004). The Organic Constitutional Law of Municipalities establishes that municipalities have among their attributions the development of functions related to sports and recreation (Ministerio del Interior, 2006) using different organizational forms of municipal sports such as: directorate, department, coordination, units or sports office;

Digitization in the Emerging Chilean Sport Industry 17

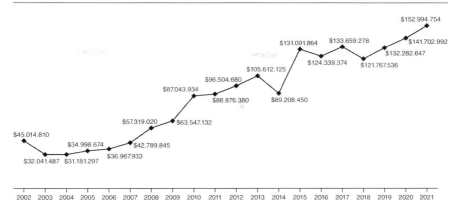

Figure 2.1 Fiscal Spending on Sports and Physical Activity 2002–2021 in Billions CLP$.

and in some cases, external figures to the municipal structure such as corporations or local sports councils (non-profit organizations). However, some studies have shown an evidence of a high number of entities in charge, which would affect their management capabilities (Cornejo Améstica et al., 2017). This accounts for shortcomings at the level of human resources for a better approach to their tasks and responsibilities, and that adds to funding problems (Feller et al., 2013). In many cases, these entities depend on external financing through competitive funds with the purpose of maintaining an offer of municipal sports services that complement what is executed directly from the IND, the latter in many cases poorly articulated alongside its municipal counterpart.

Along with public entities, there is the Institution of Federated Sports, which currently groups 57 National Sports Federations under the umbrella of the Chilean Olympic Committee. The Chilean Paralympic Committee oversees 15 Paralympic Federations. The official data of the National Registry of Organizations show that there are more than 25,000 sports organizations. In terms of federated sports development, and considering the international sports performance in the last Pan American Games, the Chilean delegation obtained its best performance with 50 medals (13 golds, 19 silvers, and 18 bronzes), while in the Parapan American Games, the national Paralympic delegation also achieved its best results with 32 medals (10 golds, 12 silvers, and 10 bronzes). The development of federated sport in Chile, according to Bravo and Silva (2014), shows a clear orientation toward the development of high performance sport, which could be confirmed in the distribution of the budget of sports programs that are precisely oriented to performance and high performance sport, which concentrate 62.3% of spending on IND programs (Ministerio del Deporte, 2020). On the other hand, sports successes are not consistent with the levels of physical activity and sports in the general population, since official figures, evidence high levels of physical inactivity in the adult population with 80.4% (Instituto Nacional de Deportes, 2018) while in the child and adolescent population 83.5%, when taken into account the recommendations of international organizations.

It is important to point out that in Chile, sport is not recognized as an economic activity, so there is no data available to determine its impact on the national economy through the gross domestic product. However, the economic activity around physical activity and sport has had an exponential development in the last two decades mainly due to the so-called fitness industry, developed by gym chains, franchises, and ventures that at the end of 2015 invoiced, according to industry data, about US$150 million and that as of March 2018, its revenues increased by 17% to US$176 million. This has positioned Chile in fifth place at the Latin American level (Global Fitness Industry Association [International Health, Racquet and Sports Club Association], 2019). The fitness market has undoubtedly experienced significant growth in Chile due to the increase in physical activity mainly in segments of the population with purchasing power and people's interest in leading a healthier lifestyle. It has reached a figure of 490 thousand customers (International Health, Racquet and Sports Club Association, 2019) generating higher than expected revenues for the sector. However, the COVID-19 pandemic has strongly impacted this sector as most gyms have remained closed in the last year, destroying close to 10 thousand jobs. This can be evidenced by the sales deficit of the sector grouped in "Artistic, Entertainment and Recreational Activities" which contracted by 81.3% from the period of January 2019 to June 2020 (Instituto Nacional de Estadísticas, 2018). The current scenario is challenging, since the supply of this type of service must adapt to the needs of users (in lockdown), and will be decisive for the survival of this industry until the economy is activated in the medium term, allowing it to reach the projected levels of previous years (Duclos-Bastías & Giakoni-Ramírez, 2021). In this sense, the innovation of the sports industry is fundamental.

BoxMagic as a Success Case in Chile

BoxMagic is a success case in Chile and the Latin American fit-tech marketplace. BoxMagic, a gym management platform for gyms in Latin America, was founded in 2017 as the brainchild of Kyle Hepp and Daniel Ávila. Hepp is a former CrossFit gym owner and Ávila is a Chief Technology Officer (CTO) of various Latin American startups. When Hepp first opened her CrossFit gym, she was shocked that she couldn't find a decent gym management software in Spanish. CrossFit Headquarters had been very vocal that Latin America and Asia were their two fastest growing markets, so she couldn't understand why there were not more options available in terms of technology for managing reservations and payments.

Outside of Latin America, Mindbody is the oldest most storied company that has delved into the gym management arena. As of 2015, Mindbody was grossing $32 million USD per year and eventually sold to a private equity firm for almost $2 billion USD. The company operates not only in the fitness sector, but also offers their product to spas, hair salons, massage parlors, and other such wellness

Digitization in the Emerging Chilean Sport Industry   19

entities in their target market. As Mindbody has grown, they've acquired other smaller startups, adding to their portfolio of subsidiaries. These subsidiaries include but are not limited to – FitMetrix (a heart rate tracking and progress tracking app), BowTie Labs (AI for customer service messaging), and ZeeZor (measuring staff engagement and benchmarking). These buyouts have essentially made Mindbody into an industry giant but they've chosen to continue expanding their product offerings into the English-speaking market, rather than making a heavy focus on Latin America a priority.

Taking note of Mindbody's success, other US and European-based startups have begun popping up. Among many others, we see Triib, ZenPlanner, Wodify, GloFox, Mariana Tek, and Pike13 all attacking niches within the same market as Mindbody, some focusing more heavily on CrossFit, while others branding themselves as general "wellness" management software. While GloFox and a few others have run ads in Latin America from time to time, they have not translated their ads into Spanish or Portuguese and have not taken any significant portion of market share. While all these startups were growing outside of Latin America, within Latin America, countries were not only very quickly expanding internet and cell phone access, but fitness on the whole was on the rise. Globe News Wire (Markets, 2021) projects that the Latin American health and fitness club market will grow at a Compound Annual Growth Rate (CAGR) of 6.49%, even coming out of the pandemic. Of these markets, Brazil is by far the largest, while Argentina has the highest penetration rate. All of the above goes to show that the Latin American market, while an exceptionally difficult market to break into, is ripe for the picking, should a startup fully understand the cultural differences and technology barriers that make it so unique.

According to BoxMagic's data, the majority of their clients have never used a management software prior to onboarding with BoxMagic. This has meant that the technological barrier is much higher. In 2017, according to a survey by the company, less than 15% of boutique fitness studios in Chile (yoga, Pilates, kickboxing, CrossFit, etc.) were using a gym management platform to manage their payments and reservations. While developing BoxMagic, their team had to take into account several important factors that make the Latin American market different from the European and US markets.

There is still no overarching payment solution in Latin America. There is no Stripe that would allow payments in the different currencies used in the 33 countries making up the continent. Many gym owners in Latin America do not own a computer and expect to do all gym operations from their cell phone. Android is the primary phone of choice, averaging between 60% and 80% of the market share over iPhone, depending on the country. Most boutique/small gyms and fitness studios have never used a fitness management software before. BoxMagic would not be competing with other software, but working to educate the potential market on why using their technology was superior to using a pen and a pencil, or excel to run their operations and keep track of payments. The end user (gym member, the client of our client) is less accustomed to using an app or even a web app to reserve classes. The end user (gym member, the client of our client) is less accustomed to making payments online (Halcrow, 2021), in Latin America, prior to the pandemic, approximately 85% of all payments on the continent were made in cash. In Latin America, 55% of all people are underbanked, according to the *International Monetary Fund* (IMF) (Halcrow, 2021). Receipt requirements are generally stricter in Latin America, in governmental efforts to avoid tax fraud.

When Hepp opened a gym in Santiago, Chile, and tried to use the foreign software options on the market, she quickly found that none of popular choices outside of Latin America connected to payment options in Chile. She was obliged to enter payments into the system she was using at the time (Wodify) manually. For a gym management system to work the way it is intended to, it normally connects to a payment aggregator (in the US, these would be systems like Stripe or BrainTree). When the client makes their payment via one of those aggregators connected to a gym management system, the payment is automatically uploaded to the gym management system and the client's monthly plan is activated. The plan would then be frozen the next month if the client does not make their payment on time or automatically renewed if they do make their payment on time. This automates the gym owner's task of receiving and recording payments, keeping track of individual monthly plans and charging their members manually every month. Alas, as Wodify does not connect to payment aggregators working in Chile, the functionality of Wodify's features was lost to Hepp's gym.

Hepp's next option was to attempt to connect WebPay, a service available to businesses in Chile, allowing them to receive online payments. To connect to WebPay is a slow and bureaucratic process involving contracts that must be notarized and a significant amount of documentation. Communication with WebPay is generally inefficient, as the company has a monopoly on Chile's digital payment services and thus it is not incentivized to improve their services. It took Hepp almost a full year of going back and forth with WebPay to get set up to be able to receive credit cards and debit cards in person and be able to receive online payments. This translated into a year of waiting to be able to receive credit and debit cards in person and to be able to receive online payments. In addition to this, Hepp was required by Chilean tax laws to give each person who paid her gym, what's called a "boleta" or legal sales receipt. This legal process required first printing out massive books of the legal sales receipts, then going to the Chilean *Internal Revenue Service* (IRS) (the SII or Servicio de Impuestos Internos) location, waiting in long lines and getting these sales receipts officially stamped by the government. Without the stamps, they were not official and the business could be fined by the government.

The SII did offer a way to connect to their system online but Hepp still would've had to manually input the payment information in their website in order to send her clients the required legal sales receipt. This is where BoxMagic came into play. Ávila began developing a gym management system that would both connect to online payments, first in Chile and then beyond in Latin America, as well as connect to the SII's online receipt system. Now, when a client paid Hepp's gym, their payment would be uploaded into BoxMagic, their monthly membership would be renewed automatically and they would receive their legal sales receipt online automatically, all without Hepp having to lift a finger. The time savings that came

Digitization in the Emerging Chilean Sport Industry 21

from having all of these processes automated were immense – according to a survey conducted by BoxMagic, using BoxMagic gave gym owners approximately 70% more time to spend outside of gym management.

Because so many people in Latin America are underbanked, being able to receive online payments would be nearly impossible if they were to have to sign up for WebPay on their own. But Daniel developed BoxMagic in a way so that each gym can use BoxMagic as the payment aggregator. All the gym owners have to do is connect their information and BoxMagic can begin to receive payments on their behalf. They can be connected to online payments within 24 hours of signing up, as opposed to months' worth of bureaucracy that Hepp went through when she signed up for WebPay. BoxMagic has walked a fine line in making their platform simple enough for clients who have never used a gym management software, yet sophisticated enough that larger gyms and studios would also be satisfied. Currently about 4% of BoxMagic clients are traditional gyms (larger than 500 members, operating on a free-entry model, rather than a class-based model), franchises (2+ locations), or government entity gyms (universities or municipal gyms). BoxMagic has also developed an exceptionally simple payment experience for the gym goer, taking into account that they may never have made an online purchase before. BoxMagic tries to make things as easy as possible for the gym members, because when gym members have a good user experience, BoxMagic gyms make more money and therefore BoxMagic also thrives! The pandemic has accelerated the digital transformation in Latin America and online payments are on the rise. Mercado Pago (Latin America's answer to China's Ali Baba) saw online transactions rise by 111% in Q2 of 2020 (Garrison, 2021). BoxMagic itself has also seen tremendous success with payment processing.

Prior to the pandemic of 2020, BoxMagic saw payments online growing at a slow but steady rate. By September 2020, the amount of payments they were processing online was growing by 40–55% per month, reaching $44 million CLP processed in March. The growth has not been 100% regular as the country of Chile itself goes in and out of lockdown, but when the economy opens up, BoxMagic has seen that online payments boom. Blue in Figure 2.2 represents BoxMagic's online payment processing in 2019, green represents 2020, and pink is 2021. April has seen a sharp decline as gyms are forced to close because of government restrictions again. It is safe to say that the pandemic has altered the way the average Latin American consumer interacts with online payments, as well as the expectations they have for a small business. It is becoming normalized and expected that the places they frequent will accept debit and credit cards via an online system or will receive payment in person via credit cards or debit cards.

In addition to online payments, the pandemic has seen the use of software for business management becomes essential. For purposes of this chapter, we will talk specifically about the gym industry. Pre-pandemic, traditional and/or large gyms had no need to control the amount of members coming and going. They did not limit capacity and if clients had to wait for machines because they were full, that was part of the business model. In boutique gyms such as CrossFit or yoga studios,

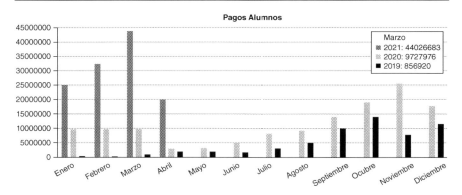

Figure 2.2 BoxMagic Online Payment Processing Volume 2019 to 2021.

these gyms traditionally did have class limits, but would often surpass those limits during peak hours as a way to bring in maximum revenue, and coaches would adapt to more people in a limited space. Now for safety reason during the COVID-19 pandemic, as well as government restrictions as to tracking outbreaks, all gyms, large and small, are required to limit the amount of clients they can let in, as well as keep a registry of who attended and at what time, in order to do contact tracing. This has meant that the use of a software to manage attendance is obligatory.

Prior to 2020, BoxMagic had a steady growth rate and reached close to 400 clients before the pandemic hit. Post March 2020, BoxMagic lost almost 200 clients, however the company changed strategy, revamped their platform to a high-end look, with more sophisticated reporting and the addition of new paid add-on features. BoxMagic's business model is that of a SaaS company in which the gyms pay a monthly subscription fee for the platform's services. They started out using a pay-per active member model but in September 2020, BoxMagic raised their prices to a fixed monthly fee, enabling them the ability to offer a 3-month, 6-month, or yearly plans with a discount. This option has been popular with gyms and every month approximately 40% of their sales have come from the sale of these long-term plans. Although BoxMagic lost a significant amount of clients during the pandemic, they are currently making significantly more monthly recurring revenue with less clients, than what their target monthly recurring revenue (MRR) was, with more clients, prior to the pandemic.

Conclusion

The gym industry globally has historically been a laggard industry. Gym owners have been slow to adapt and this trend was seen even more so in Latin America prior to the pandemic. But the ongoing crisis of 2020/2021, while hurting the sector tremendously financially, has accelerated the digital transformation of the industry in ways not previously imaginable. BoxMagic is an example of the potential for massive success in Latin America, when a company takes the time to truly understand their target market. The same things that work in the US and European markets do not work in Latin America. Nor is it possible to look at Latin America as a monolith – the continent is made up of different countries, each with not only their own currency, but also their own distinct culture and consumer behavior and to try to generalize to facilitate business is a grave mistake. By adapting to the specific needs of the Latin American consumer, BoxMagic has seen growth, even during these unprecedented times, and is poised for tremendous success coming out of the pandemic.

References

Bravo, G., & Silva, J. (2014). Sport policy in Chile. *International Journal of Sport Policy and Politics*, 6(1), 129–142.

Cornejo Améstica, M., Matus Castillo, C. A., & Tello Silva, D. (2017). El deporte extraescolar chileno y su funcionamiento. Una mirada a la región del Biobío.

Duclos-Bastías, D., & Giakoni-Ramírez, F. (2021). The fitness industry in Chile. In J. García-Fernández, & P. Gálvez- Ruiz (Eds.). *The global private health & fitness business: A marketing perspective (1)* (pp. 85–91). Emerald.

Feller, C., Alvarado, P., Bossay, C., & García, I. (2013). In D. Martínez (Ed.). *La Gestión Deportiva Municipal En Iberoamérica: Historia, Teoría Y Práctica.* (pp. 133–157) Librerías Deportivas Esteban Sanz.

Gallardo, L., & Jiménez, A. (2004). *La Gestión De Los Servicios Deportivos Municipales. Vías Para La Excelencia.* Editorial INDE.

Garrison, C. (2021). *Latin American payment giant rises amid pandemic, with an eye on China's Ant. Reuters.* Retrieved from https://www.reuters.com/article/us-latam-mercadolibre-payments-focus-idUKKBN2751FB

Halcrow, A. (2021). *Mobile & digital payments rise in Latin America | Amex US.* Retrieved from https://www.americanexpress.com/us/foreign-exchange/articles/digital-payments-in-latin-america-rise/

Instituto Nacional de Deportes. (2018). *Encuesta nacional de hábitos de actividad física y deporte en población mayor de 18 años.* Retrieved from https://www.mindep.cl/encuesta-actividad-fisica-y-deporte-2018/

Instituto Nacional de Estadísticas. (2018). Memoria Censo 2017. Retrieved from https://www.ine.es/ine/planine/informe_anual_2017.pdf

International Health, Racquet and Sports Club Association (2019). *The 2019 IHRSA global report.* IHRSA.

Markets, R. (2021). *South American Health and Fitness Club Market Growth, Trends and Forecasts to 2025. GlobeNewswire News Room.* Retrieved from https://www.globenewswire.com/news-release/2021/01/04/2152307/28124/en/South-American-Health-and-Fitness-Club-Market-Growth-Trends-and-Forecasts-to-2025.html

Ministerio del Deporte. (2020). *Cuenta Pública 2020.* Retrieved from https://cdn.digital.gob.cl/public_files/Campa%C3%B1as/Cuenta-P%C3%BAblica-2020/CP-sectoriales/23-2020-SECTORIAL-MINISTERIO-DEL-DEPORTE.pdf

Ministerio del Interior. (2006). Ley N° 18.695, Orgánica Constitucional de Municipalidades. Retrieved from http://www.leychile.cl/Navegar?idNorma=251693

Riveros, L., & Báez, G. (2014). Chile y la OCDE. La dicotomía entre lo macroeconómico y el desarrollo humano. *Estudios Internacionales, 46*(179), 9–34.

United Nations Development Program Desarrollo (2019). *Human Development Report 2019, Beyond income, beyond averages, beyond today: Inequalities in human development in the 21ˢᵗ century.* Retrieved from https://hdr.undp.org/system/files/documents/hdr2019pdf.pdf

World Bank (2020). Global Economic Prospects, June 2020. Washington, DC: World Bank.

Chapter 3

Managing Employee's Health While They Are Teleworking

A Corporate Well-Being Model in Times of COVID-19

José M. Núñez-Sánchez
University of Malaga, Spain

Carmina Jambrino-Maldonado
University of Economics – Málaga, Spain

Jerónimo García-Fernández
Universidad of Seville, Spain

Ramón Gómez-Chacón
Cardenal Spínola CEU, Spain

Chapter Contents

Introduction	25
Method	30
Results	31
Discussion	35
References	38

Introduction

This chapter arises from the recommendations gathered in research on the corporate well-being programme in times of COVID, through the case study of Mahou San Miguel (MSM) conducted by Núñez-Sánchez et al. (2021). The history of this company officially began in 1890, being today the first Spanish company in the brewing sector in Spain and with a presence in more than 70 countries, a family of more than 4,250 employees. This company was selected because it is considered a benchmark in Spain in the field of corporate wellness and health care programmes for its employees, which have won several national awards, encouraging them to continue to constantly improve its programmes. The company was the first company in the sector to be certified as a Healthy Company in 2012.

DOI: 10.4324/9781003388050-4

In 2010, a milestone for the company took place, as the Sports and Health Area of the Higher Sports Council of the Ministry of Education, Culture and Sport, in collaboration with the National Institute of Social Security and Hygiene at Work, initiated an investigation in MSM, aware of the need to promote corporate physical activity programmes, and of the innovative development in the application of these programmes. This study was pioneering in Spain as it demonstrated that investment in corporate wellness has a positive ROI (return on investment) for the company (CSD, 2013). Moreover, MSM has been named "the best brewery to work for" for several years by international Corporate Reputation Observatories, such as the Merco Business Monitor. In 2020, due to the situation caused by COVID-19, the company had to adapt its successful corporate workplace wellness programme to a hybrid format, meeting and even exceeding the World Health Organisation (WHO) recommendations (World Health Organisation, 2020) as can be seen in Figure 3.1. The authors have not found similar case studies in scientific literature. Therefore, this case study is considered to be unique in corporate well-being programmes in COVID-19 times.

The COVID-19 pandemic, and the increase of working-from-home, have drastically changed many aspects of work life, causing very negative effects on employees' physical and psycho-social well-being (Núñez-Sánchez et al., 2022), increasing stress and depression (Lai et al., 2020; Xiang et al., 2020), among others, creating a challenging environment for human resources management (HRM) – with managers having to quickly venture into the "unknown unknowns" as they strive to help their workforce adapt to and cope with radical changes occurring in the work environment (Carnevale & Hatak, 2020). The COVID-19 pandemic can be related to many stressors that may drain employees' mental health, not only during, but after this pandemic (Hamouche, 2020). The negative consequences of the confinement caused by COVID-19 were reflected in a multi-country research highlighting the impact on mental, emotional and even behavioural health related to an increase in sedentary lifestyles and a decrease in physical activity (Ammar et al., 2020).

Chen et al. (2020) indicate that maintaining regular physical activity and routinely exercising in a safe home environment is an important strategy for healthy living during the coronavirus crisis and there is a link between improved immune system function and exercise (Nieman & Wentz 2019). In addition, physical activity reduces the severity of respiratory infections (Grande et al., 2020), reduces symptoms of depression (Cooney et al., 2013), anxiety (Aylett et al., 2018), stress and improves sleep quality (Altena et al., 2020), has anti-inflammatory properties and reduces the risk of disease (Nieman & Wentz 2019), reduces cardiovascular and brain-vascular risks (Hupin et al., 2019), and reduces significantly body weight (Mulchandani et al., 2019), which is what is of particular importance, as obesity is a risk factor in patients with COVID-19 (Simonnet et al 2020). Regular physical activity is positively related to muscle tone and general fitness (Bezner et al., 2020), enthusiasm and psychological well-being (Boix Vilella et al., 2018), as well as to reduced stress levels, improved job satisfaction and more positive work emotions (Gil-Beltrán et al., 2020).

Managing Employee's Health 27

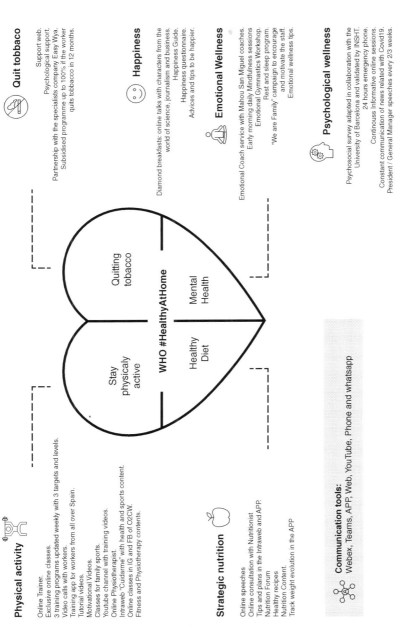

Figure 3.1 Mahou San Miguel Corporate Well-being Programme Adapted to the COVID- (Cuidarme) in Comparison with the Recommendations of the WHO.

Salgado-Aranda et al. (2021) conclusively found that people who exercise regularly are up to eight times more likely to survive to COVID-19, than sedentary people, with the group that maintained a constant, light, or moderate physical activity having a mortality risk of 1.8% compared to 13.8% in the group with a sedentary lifestyle. On the other hand, one of the consequences of the pandemic has been the substantial increase in teleworking, having several governments recommending companies to facilitate working from home (Belzunegui-Eraso & Erro-Garcés, 2020). The COVID-19 pandemic has increased the negative effects that teleworking can have on workers' health, as can be seen in Table 3.1. Maintaining a physical activity routine at home is a necessary strategy to combat citizens' long days at home, which are impacting on depression, physical inactivity and anxiety, leading to a sedentary lifestyle (World Health Organisation, 2020), generating numerous recommendations from the WHO in 2020, concerned about the devastating effects that confinement can have on people's health. According to Roschel et al. (2020), the aggravation of physical inactivity emerges as a relevant adverse effect of the social isolation measures taken to combat the spread of COVID-19.

Following Wright et al. (2017) well-being is a broad and multidimensional concept that not only includes the absence of ill-being (e.g., strain and emotional exhaustion) but also involves positive states (e.g., happiness and work engagement). Companies that successfully implement corporate wellness programmes

Table 3.1 Risks Associated with Telework

Family of risk	Effect of telework	Amplification or reduction in the context of COVID-19-related containment	Key prevention measures for employers
Risks associated with home working environment			
	Increased risks associated with workstation (musculoskeletal pain)	Ambiguous (potentially amplified due to the lack of anticipation, poorly suited home working environment and reduced physical activity, but short duration of exposure)	Diffusion of simple, pragmatic messages on ergonomics; financial contribution to adapted equipment; **promotion of physical activity**
Psychosocial risks			
	Increased risks of social isolation in the professional sphere	Reduced (universalisation of telework)	Adoption of virtual collective working periods (teleconferences)
Behavioural risks (diet, sleep, addiction)			
	Ambiguous	Amplified (confinement, COVID-linked anxiety)	Allow and promote teleconsultations with occupational practitioners

achieve very positive results as there is a positive relationship between physical activity and increased work productivity (Whitsel et al., 2019) and job satisfaction (Laroche et al., 2020). In other words, investing in employee health will reduce health care costs, decreasing absenteeism, increasing productivity and high employee satisfaction (Sparling, 2010), leading to a successful and healthy business (Grawitch & Ballard, 2016). According to Kent et al. (2016), employers recognise that it is in their interest to keep workers healthy, engaged and productive. In addition, healthy employees are identified with certain personal strengths such as self-efficacy, hope, optimism and resilience (Luthans & Youssef, 2004) and work engagement, as well as teamwork performance (Salanova & Schaufeli, 2009). These strengths of the healthy employee are of particular importance in these times of pandemic and teleworking.

Employees are aware of the positive benefits of exercise and in a recent survey conducted by Gympass (Gympass, 2021) with over 9,000 employees in nine countries, almost 70% consider that a wellness routine is a very important factor that positively affects their performance, while 77% say it is important or very important that their companies care about their health and offer corporate wellness plans. Despite these figures, half of the respondents say that their companies have not contributed to their well-being since the pandemic began. The research concludes that there is still a long way to go towards cultural change in companies, highlighting that stress, lack of motivation and absenteeism are still factors that are present and need to be tackled in some way. From the employees' point of view, they want leaders who value their well-being, as health-oriented leadership goes beyond the management task itself and, unlike other leadership styles, puts employee well-being first (Kaluza et al., 2021). This health-oriented leadership improves employees' health and well-being through employees' own self-care (Franke et al., 2014), being more important than ever, as the employee is at home and not at the workplace.

Throughout this introduction, it has been shown that the physical and psychological well-being of employees is being severely affected by the pandemic. Therefore, health-oriented leadership, adapted to the current circumstances, can reduce these negative effects. According to Núñez-Sánchez et al. (2021), the pandemic has challenged organisations around the world, so they must work on adapting their wellness programmes to offer their employees a programme through which they can continue to take care of their health also remotely. These authors concluded, based on the successful results of MSM, with an overall satisfaction ratio of nine out of ten and 87.6% of its employees stating that they felt well or very well guided by the company during this period, that it would be advisable to design a model adoptable by small, medium, or large companies. It was not possible to find this kind of research in scientific literature.

Taking all these factors into account, this research seeks to offer organisations the management of a practical corporate wellness programme framework, which could be adopted by any type of company. This research contributes by providing a corporate wellness management proposal, based on a successful case, to update corporate wellness in pandemic and telework times. This model should be flexible and modular so that it can be adopted by companies of different characteristics and locations. It responds to the recommendations of Carnevale and Hatak (2020), to coordinate research efforts into actionable insights to help organisations tackle one of the greatest challenges in modern history.

Method

This research is a continuation of the one carried out by Núñez-Sánchez et al. (2021) in which the case of MSM was analysed in depth, showing how they successfully adapted their traditional corporate welfare programme to the circumstances caused by the pandemic. The authors have employed a qualitative case study approach to analyse the key features of this corporate well-being programme during the most difficult periods of the COVID-19 crisis. This research tool is adequate when the objective is exploratory and when it focuses more on understanding rather than on verification. Case studies allow contemporary phenomena to be described and examined and provide insights into the interaction between the various parts involved in a system (Merriam, 1988; Yin, 2013). According to Bartunek et al. (2006), when theory is built from case studies, these are often reflected as one of the most interesting research methods. A case study is appropriate for understanding a phenomenon (Bryman et al., 2011), on the other hand, this method has been widely used in management research and as a source of knowledge and as a source of experience (Mariotto et al., 2014). Finally, extracting lessons learned by employers who have built a culture of health and excellent communications strategies and apply them more broadly in workplace settings is a necessary endeavour (Kent et al., 2016).

Once the observation phase and the documentary analysis necessary to design the interviews had been carried out, the next step was to interview the Wellbeing Manager of the company MSM. This person is Manuel Palencia, who together with other people has led the Cuidarme en Casa (Take care of me at home) programme, having also been the initiator of the employee wellness care programmes at MSM with the "A tu Salud" (At your Health) programme in 2000 and a benchmark professional in corporate wellness in Spain, having received the National Healthy Leader Award 2016. The instrument chosen was in-depth semi-structured interviews. It was considered to be the most appropriate means to support, contrast and expand on various aspects of the analysis conducted previously and to guide the objective of exploring corporate welfare programmes during the COVID-19 pandemic, with the interviews being transcribed on the spot and subsequently discussed by the authors. The phases of the research can be seen in Figure 3.2.

The qualitative phase was subdivided into four sub-phases to facilitate the final objective of the research. Four semi-structured interviews were conducted on 9, 11, 16 and 23 March 2021, lasting 2 hours each, and carried out via video call due to the limitations caused by the pandemic. Following this phase, results were discussed, a graphical model was designed showing how it works, concluding the

Managing Employee's Health

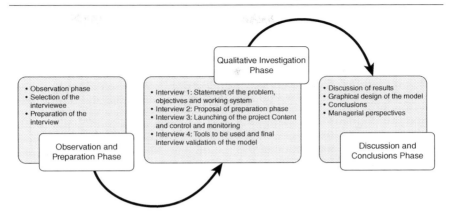

Figure 3.2 The Three Sequential Phases of the Investigation.

research with managerial perspectives. In the initial interview, the problem to be solved and the objectives of the interviews were set out, as well as the specific phases of the interview and the objective of designing an operating model based on the successful experience of MSM's Cuidarme en Casa (Take care of me at home), which could help other organisations to adapt their traditionally physical corporate well-being programmes to the new remote environment caused by the pandemic. In this phase, the interviewee is asked to describe the MSM model of success, which will later serve as a basis and example for the model proposal. This model had to be adoptable by different type of companies in Spain, and in other parts of the world, as it had to be flexible enough to be able to work even if some aspects of it were applied according to the company's characteristics and budgets.

Results

Based on MSM's experience, an initial phase prior to the launch of the programme, called the Preparation Phase, was recommended and discussed in the second interview, once the objectives of the programme were clear. This interview indicated that the whole process should begin with an analysis of the situation and the resources available to carry out the project: human, material, financial and technological, so that later, based on these resources and the initial diagnosis, the responsible team can design a welfare plan adapted to the company's external and internal circumstances. All of these steps had the clear objective of continuing to take care for the welfare of workers while they were teleworking. At this point, indicators to measure the success of the project were discussed and general recommendations were made:

1. Satisfaction level measured through periodic surveys, to be decided by the company. The proposed measurement system is a self-administered, anonymous

survey sent to employees by email. It is important not to saturate employees with excessive surveys.

2 Number of views of the different group exercise classes, seminars and sessions: measured through the statistics of the website, the fitness application (APP) or the streaming platform used, e.g., YouTube or Vimeo.

3 Number of participants in online activities. The measurement is done by measuring the statistics of the system used in broadcasting.

4 Global physical activity data (activity, km and kcal): measured through statistics provided by the training APP. If the training APP is not available, this physical activity data must be measured by means of a self-reported survey.

5 Evolution of physical and psychosocial well-being: survey using a validated tool or the one normally used in the company and with the agreed periodicity.

Once these five objectives have been defined, as no more than five KPIs (key performance indicators) are recommended, all that remains is the approval of the plan, the organisational and economic resources and the objectives to be achieved by the management team or direct superior, depending on how the company is organised. The importance of having the involvement of the management team was highlighted to be successful. In addition, a person responsible for the implementation of the plan, monitoring and compliance with the KPIS is necessary. It is recommended that this person is the one responsible for employee well-being in the company and that, as the person ultimately responsible for the success of the project, he or she defines the team, whether internal or outsourced, to achieve these objectives. The selection would range from fitness trainer/s, personal trainer/s, physiotherapist/s, nutritionist, professional in charge of the psychosocial programme, somebody responsible for the technological support team (support for video calls, app …) and last but not least, coordinated with the head of the Marketing Department, define the marketing and communication person who would oversee designing the tools and executing the communication plan with employees. Manuel Palencia assured that "it is essential to have a good communication plan to be successful". Once the plan is perfectly defined, the first phase of the preparation plan is completed and the next phase could be developed, which would be carried out in the following interview.

In the third interview, the objective was to ensure the correct launching of the programme, to describe the main sections that should be included in the programme, and to propose a monitoring and follow-up system to ensure the success of the programme. The communication strategy in this moment is fundamental for the success of the project. For this reason, he recommended calling all the employees to a video call in which the CEO would inform them of the importance of taking care of their health at this time, thus conveying to the employees that their health is a priority for the company. Finally, the person responsible of the wellness programme would provide more detailed information on what this programme consists of. Subsequently, an informative email would be sent to all employees, expanding the information and explaining the functioning of the programme in more detail. In this way, the employees perceive that their health is important to the company, as well as ensuring that all employees know and understand the programme. Once the plan has been designed and approved, and excellent communication to the teams has taken place, we would be able to implement the programme with the multidisciplinary team selected and coordinated by the project manager.

Next, the services that workers should be able to receive in each section were discussed in more detail. Firstly, the training section was highlighted and it was recommended to offer an online personal trainer, who would establish training plans for the workers. He/she would communicate with them by phone, WhatsApp, emails or individual/group video calls. Online activities should also be offered, recorded and made available to the employees, as well as video recordings with proposed routines for the employees. The video support will be YouTube, Vimeo, or the Company's Wellbeing website. Its main function will be to encourage, motivate and contact all employees with the periodicity agreed by the company, ensuring their well-being all the time.

Secondly, it is important to offer an online nutrition service, which would be carried out by means of individual video calls, recording and sharing nutritional advice and healthy recipes, complemented by a weekly online seminar, with a theme chosen by the manager or according to the demand of the workers, which would be recorded later. Thirdly, the work of the physiotherapist is important, who could work either in person or at the worker's home, depending on the worker's needs, the indications of the company manager and current health regulations. Mr. Palencia points out that it is also important for him to carry out individual video calls to accompany and update existing rehabilitation programmes and, in a similar way to the nutritionist, to offer a weekly online seminar, which would also be recorded. He/she should contact, accompany and encourage his/her patients with the frequency agreed by the company and ensure their recovery and/or successful treatment. Fourthly, there would be the care of psychosocial well-being, so important in these times of pandemic times, advising to offer mindfulness sessions practically every day, of no more than 15 minutes, which would also be recorded. As before, it is important to monitor workers individually, especially those who may need it most, through individual or group video calls, by department, offering individual support on demand, encouraging the sharing of videos with success stories of colleagues or recommended routines, family activities, sharing the healthy recommendation of the week (sleep, motivation, etc.), recommendations of series, films, books, music, etc., by workers.

Last, the wellness manager recommended offering medical consultation services on demand, with the option of online consultation, publication of advice and recommendations on how to take care of oneself and information on existing preventive measures. This service, according to Manuel, would offer workers peace of mind and security, as well as a quick and reliable response within the company. The idea is not to offer a medical treatment service, but above all to offer information, consultation and support to workers. Once everything is running, it was discussed how to follow up to ensure the smooth running of the programme and to ensure compliance with the KPIs. It was recommended that the monitoring of the KPIs should be done on a weekly basis, except for the satisfaction survey and the psychosocial well-being survey, as it would not make sense to do this on a weekly basis and it would also saturate the workers. A coordination meeting should be held monthly (weekly during the first month) by video call involving all team members, analysing data on attendance, physical activity, visualisations and suggestions, and updating the plan if necessary. It is advisable to prepare positive communications to workers, either about the fulfilment of objectives, success stories, or simply positive and motivating messages.

Finally, once the first phase of the programme has been completed, it is recommended to evaluate its success by measuring the KPIs established in the first phase. Once the data has been analysed, return to the first phase to update the programme according to the data, the suggestions of the employees, the team implementing the programme and the level of employee satisfaction, communicating the conclusions to the teams and holding a meeting with General Management to report on the results of the programme if important changes to the initial project are necessary.

In the fourth and final interview, the aim was to find out what tools are needed to successfully meet the programme's objectives. Manuel Palencia has no doubts in this regard, it is essential to have sufficient and quality technological tools, otherwise it is very difficult to guarantee success and traceability. Among the basic tools, he recommends a training and/or nutritional APP, if the training APP does not have this functionality. In addition to the above, companies could use a YouTube account or similar for online and recorded classes (possibility of including Instagram), WhatsApp and email, as well as a Teams-type video call system or similar, as well as a health and wellness web section for workers. One of the objectives of this last interview was to review the previous interviews and the data collected in order to, if necessary, modify or correct errors. In this sense, to take advantage of MSM's experience, Mr. Palencia was requested to share the mistakes to avoid in order to guarantee the success of the programme:

1 Failure to communicate the programme well to employees.
2 Not having the involvement and support of the top management.
3 Introduce totally unknown and unused services in pre-pandemic times.
4 Failure to listen to suggestions from workers and the implementation team.
5 Do not saturate or overwhelm workers.
6 Avoid incorporating 100% unknown personnel: in case there is a need, make a good selection process and presentation to the workers. They must be very communicative and empathetic people.

At the end of the fourth and last interview, it was discussed why he believed that this model could be applicable in any company and anywhere, depending on the objective of the research. Manuel pointed out that when MSM started working on the Employee Wellbeing project (as it was conceived 20 years ago), the aim was to strive to ensure that the people who make up the Company were a corporate force that had the necessary tools to carry out their professional work with the minimum physical and emotional impact. Any corporate wellness programme that a company, regardless of its size, sets out to implement will be a success and he assured that with very reasonable investment, providing that the top management and leaders of the company are convinced of the project and support it. For Manuel, the ideal is a wellness programme that includes face-to-face activities and social spaces, taking advantage of the digital tools that we have at our disposal today and that allow us to reach anyone, anywhere. The important thing is to diagnose the needs of the company, detect what people need and what has a significant influence on their life and profession and adapt the programme to each company according to their needs, regardless of size or sector. His final recommendations for the project to be a success are, first of all, to sincerely believe in the project and to look internally for suitable, empathetic, trained and enthusiastic people to lead and drive the project forward. In addition to valuing the project as an investment and not an expense. Along these lines, he recommends that the costs of the services offered in the programme be borne by the company, and that the activities and webinars that are organised be held, as far as possible, during working hours. With these valuable recommendations, the four interviews conclude, and the last phase of the research begins, in which the researchers will design, based on this research, a model of corporate well-being management adapted to the times of pandemic.

Discussion

Once the transcribed interviews have been analysed, the researchers propose, based on the interview, the following flexible and modular management model, as the content of the programme will be finally decided by each company according to its human, technological and financial resources (Figure 3.3). Companies wishing to take care of their workers in these challenging times must adapt their corporate wellness programmes to the new situation brought about by COVID-19. In this sense, Bouziri et al. (2020) stated that maximising health benefits of teleworking in times of containment while minimising its negative impacts constitutes a continuity in their duty to preserve the health of their employees.

The proposed model is divided into three phases: the preparation phase, the operation phase and the evaluation phase. This model is based on previous research and, above all, on the interview with the MSM expert, and is flexible enough to be adapted by different companies, from different sectors, as long as they had previously had a traditional employee well-being programme. On the other hand, it is a modular proposal, so that, depending on the services that the company can or wishes to offer, it can eliminate some of them and/or expand some others, based on its experience and available resources, although the ideal is to offer them all to a greater or lesser extent, depending on the resources available in each company, with the services of physical well-being, nutrition and psychosocial activities being

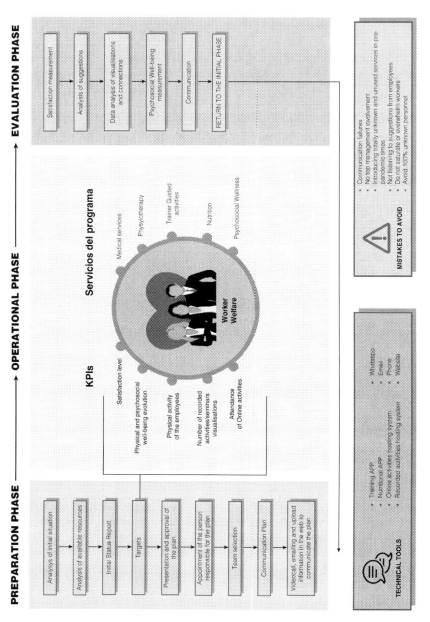

Figure 3.3 Framework for Adapting Corporate Wellbeing Programs to Pandemic and Telework Times.

essential. These priorities are in line with research by Ammar et al. (2020) which concluded that COVID-19 home confinement had a negative effect on all physical activity intensity levels (vigorous, moderate, walking and overall), additionally, daily sitting time increased from 5 to 8 hours per day and food consumption and meal patterns were unhealthier during confinement. Chen et al. (2020) agree that physical activity is the best natural medicine to prevent the consequences of confinement and teleworking and stress the urgency of sharing good practices to help in the fight against this global pandemic. On the psychological side, Trougakos et al. (2020) stated that organisations should help employees mitigate anxiety broadly by offering training in effective emotional coping methods as well as strategies to ensure they fulfil their psychological needs offering webinars in the time of COVID-19 on topics such as resilience, stress management and work-life balance may be particularly beneficial.

For the model to be successful, it should have the support of the managers and a responsible person to lead the project. This recommendation is in line with Franke et al. (2014) as health-oriented leadership improves the health and well-being of employees. According to Salanova et al. (2021), groups and people entail having a management team that is committed to both comprehensive health and the development and promotion of health at work. Communication is also pivotal according to Kent et al. (2016) who investigated best practices in different companies, and these include establishing a culture of health and using strategic communications, designed to educate, motivate and build trust, with optimum timing, frequency, multichannel and bidirectional. It is also recommended that the company adopting this model should have corporate well-being as part of its philosophy and strategy as in MSM where it is one of their strategic lines of company's corporate social responsibility (CSR), included in its strategic sustainability framework. This is in line with Singh & Misra (2021), indicating that CSR towards employees is related to employee well-being and business ethics, which enables management to better guide and serve employees.

Finally, for the model to work properly, it must be supported by technological tools, which is in line with Iglesias-Sánchez et al. (2020), who indicated that the only way to adapt to the new environment of confinements and teleworking is through social media and digital ecosystems. Social media and the use of technologies have a positive influence on customer retention in gyms (Barbosa et al., 2021) from which we can infer that it also has a positive influence on employees in their follow up of corporate physical activity programmes. On the other hand, it was proposed that the programme should be open to all employees, at no cost, which is in line with Sparling (2010). Furthermore, Heise et al. (2021) indicate that by subsidising the cost of services, employees value health status more because they do not have to worry about costs. The authors consider that the proposed model, based on a successful case study, meets the initial objective, although it has the limitation of not having been tested in companies of different sizes, sectors and locations. Anyhow it responds to the urgent need worldwide to share best practices to help in the fight against this global pandemic (Chen et al., 2020), sharing a model based on a success story. For this reason, they propose as a future line of research for practitioners and scholars to test the results of the proposed management model in different types of companies. The grand challenge we currently face is not a singular, anomalous event, but rather constitutes a "new reality" that offers new opportunities to which organisational scholars and practitioners alike will need and want to remain attentive (Carnevale & Hatak, 2020).

The traditional, physical workplace has moved to the home due to teleworking, but this does not mean, on the contrary, that work and the obligation to take care of the health of employees can be abandoned. This proposed well-being management model fulfils the initially stated objective and offers companies that wish to adopt it a proven, modular and flexible model so that the size of the company, location or sector is not a constraint. Numerous studies indicate that telework will continue to grow in the coming years, so the model will continue to be useful even when the pandemic is over. Moreover, it will allow companies to be better prepared to deal with an extraordinary situation such as COVID-19, thus preventing problems in the well-being of their workers that would affect the company's bottom line. Increased efforts are needed to disseminate lessons learned from employers who have built cultures of health and excellent communications strategies and apply these insights more broadly in workplace settings (Kent et al., 2016). Similar proposals have not been found in the scientific literature, so the present research can shed light on an issue of growing interest for companies, and for their leaders as they will need to develop skills to manage their employees working remotely and provide physical and mental support (De Klerk et al., 2021).

References

Altena, E., Baglioni, C., Espie, C. A., Ellis, J., Gavriloff, D., Holzinger, B., Schlarb, A., Frase, L., Jernelöv, S., & Riemann, D. (2020). Dealing with sleep problems during home confinement due to the COVID-19 outbreak: Practical recommendations from a task force of the European CBT-i academy. *Journal of Sleep Research*, 29(4), e13052.

Ammar, A., Brach, M., Trabelsi, K., Chtourou, H., Boukhris, O., Masmoudi, L., & Hoekelmann, A. (2020). Effects of COVID-19 home confinement on eating behaviour and physical activity: Results of the ECLB-COVID-19 international online survey. *Nutrients*, 12(6), 1583.

Aylett, E., Small, N., & Bower, P. (2018). Exercise in the treatment of clinical anxiety in general practice-a systematic review and meta-analysis. *BMC Health Services Research*, 18(1), 1–18.

Barbosa, H. F., García-Fernández, J., & Carrión, G. C. (2021). Influéncia das tecnologias na retencao de socios em ginásios. Revisao Sistemática. *Movimento*, 26, 26070.

Bartunek, J. M., Rynes, S. L., & Irland, R. D. (2006). What makes management research interesting, and why does it matter? *The Academy of Management Journal*, 49(1), 9–15.

Belzunegui-Eraso, A., & Erro-Garcés, A. (2020). Teleworking in the context of the covid-19 crisis. *Sustainability*, 12(9), 3662.

Bezner, J. R., Franklin, K. A., Lloyd, L. K., & Crixell, S. H. (2020). Effect of group health behaviour change coaching on psychosocial constructs associated with physical activity among university employees. *International Journal of Sport and Exercise Psychology, 18*(1), 93–107.

Boix Vilella, S., León Zarceño, E., & Serrano Rosa, M. (2018). Levels of psychological and occupational health in pilates adherents. *Revista Costarricense De Psicología, 37*(2), 145–162.

Bouziri, H., Smith, D. R., Descatha, A., Dab, W., & Jean, K. (2020). Working from home in the time of covid-19: How to best preserve occupational health? *Occupational and Environmental Medicine, 77*(7), 509–510.

Bryman, A., Bell, E., & Harley, B. (2011). *Business research methods.* Oxford University Press.

Carnevale, J. B., & Hatak, I. (2020). Employee adjustment and well-being in the era of COVID-19: Implications for human resource management. *Journal of Business Research, 116*(4), 183–187.

Chen, P., Mao, L., Nassis, G. P., Harmer, P., Ainsworth, B. E., & Li, F. (2020). Coronavirus disease (COVID-19): The need to maintain regular physical activity while taking precautions. *Journal of Sport and Health Science, 9*(2), 103–104.

Cooney, G. M., Dwan, K., Greig, C. A., Lawlor, D. A., Rimer, J., Waugh, F. R., McMurdo, M., & Mead, G. E. (2013). Exercise for depression. *Cochrane Database of Systematic Reviews, 12*(9), CD004366.

CSD (Consejo Superior de Deportes). (2013). *Socio-economic assessment of a Physical Activity Programme for the employees of a company.* Available online: https://www.researchgate.net/publication/322605407_Socio-economic_determinants_of_physical_activity_across_the_life_course_A_DEterminants_of_DIet_and_Physical_ACtivity_DEDIPAC_umbrella_literature_review

De Klerk, J. J., Joubert, M., & Mosca, H. F. (2021). Is working from home the new workplace panacea? Lessons from the COVID-19 pandemic for the future world of work. *SA Journal of Industrial Psychology/SA Tydskrif Vir Bedryfsielkunde, 47*, a1883.

Franke, F., Felfe, J., & Pundt, A. (2014). The impact of health-oriented leadership on follower health: Development and test of a new instrument measuring health-promoting leadership. *German Journal of Human Resource Management: Zeitschrift Für Personalforschung, 28*(1/2), 139–161.

Gil-Beltrán, E., Llorens, S., & Salanova, M. (2020). Workers' physical exercise, resources, engagement and performance: A cross-sectional study with the HERO model. *Revista De Psicología Del Trabajo y De Las Organizaciones, 36*(1), 39–47.

Grande, A. J., Keogh, J., Silva, V., & Scott, A. M. (2020). Exercise versus no exercise for the occurrence, severity, and duration of acute respiratory infections. *Cochrane Database Cochrane Database of Systematic Reviews, 16*(6), CD010596.

Grawitch, M. J., & Ballard, D. W. (2016). *The psychologically healthy workplace: Building a win-win environment for organizations and employees.* American Psychological Association.

Gympass (2021). Impact of Covid-19 on the Fitness and Wellness universe. Available online: https://hs.gympass.com/es/ebook-impacto-covid-19-en-el-universo-del-fitness (accessed on 10 May 2021)

Hamouche, S. (2020). COVID-19 and employees' mental health: Stressors, moderators and agenda for organizational actions. *Emerald Open Research, 20*(2), 15.

Heise, T. L., Frense, J., Christianson, L., & Seuring, T. (2021). Using financial incentives to increase physical activity among employees as a strategy of workplace health promotion: Protocol for a systematic review. *BMJ Open, 11*(3), e042888.

Hupin, D., Raffin, J., Barth, N., Berger, M., Garet, M., Stampone, K., Celle, S., Pichot, V., Bongue, B., Barthelemy, J.-C., & Roche, F. (2019). Even a previous light-active physical activity at work still reduces late myocardial infarction and stroke in retired adults aged> 65 years by 32%: The PROOF cohort study. *Frontiers in Public Health, 7*, 51.

Iglesias-Sánchez, P. P., Vaccaro Witt, G. F., Cabrera, F. E., & Jambrino-Maldonado, C. (2020). The contagion of sentiments during the COVID-19 pandemic crisis: The case of isolation in Spain. *International Journal of Environmental Research and Public Health, 17*(16), 5918.

Kaluza, A. J., Weber, F., van Dick, R., & Junker, N. M. (2021). When and how health-oriented leadership relates to employee well-being—the role of expectations, self-care, and LMX. *Journal of Applied Social Psychology, 51*(4), 404–424.

Kent, K., Goetzel, R. Z., Roemer, E. C., Prasad, A., & Freundlich, N. (2016). Promoting healthy workplaces by building cultures of health and applying strategic communications. *Journal of Occupational and Environmental Medicine, 58*(2), 114–122.

Lai, J., Ma, S., Wang, Y., Cai, Z., Hu, J., Wei, N., Wu, J., Du, H., Chen, T., Li, R., Tan, H., Kang, L., Yao, L., Huang, M., Wang, H., Wang, G., Liu, Z., & Hu, S. (2020). Factors associated with mental health outcomes among health care workers exposed to coronavirus disease 2019. *JAMA Network Open, 3*(3), e203976.

Laroche, E., L'Espérance, S., & Mosconi, E. (2020). Use of social media platforms for promoting healthy employee lifestyles and occupational health and safety prevention: A systematic review. *Safety Science, 131*, 104931.

Luthans, F., & Youssef, C. M. (2004). Human, Social, and Now Positive Psychological Capital Management: Investing in People for Competitive Advantage. *Organizational Dynamics, 33*(2), 143–160.

Mariotto, F. L., Zanni, P. P., & Moraes, G. H. S. (2014). What is the use of a single-case study in management research? *Revista De Administração De Empresas, 54*(4), 358–369.

Merriam, S. B. (1988). *Case study research in education: A qualitative approach.* Jossey-Bass.

Mulchandani, R., Chandrasekaran, A. M., Shivashankar, R., Kondal, D., Agrawal, A., Panniyammakal, J., Tandon, N., Prabhakaran, D., Sharma, M., & Goenka, S. (2019). Effect of workplace physical activity interventions on the cardio-metabolic health of working adults: Systematic review and meta-analysis. *International Journal of Behavioral Nutrition and Physical Activity, 16*(1), 1–16.

Nieman, D. C., & Wentz, L. M. (2019). The compelling link between physical activity and the body's defense system. *Journal of Sport and Health Science, 8*(3), 201–217.

Núñez-Sánchez, J. M., Gómez-Chacón, R., Jambrino-Maldonado, C., & García-Fernández, J. (2021). Corporate well-being programme in COVID-19 times. The Mahou San Miguel case study. *Sustainability, 13*(11), 6189.

Núñez-Sánchez, J. M., Gómez-Chacón, R., Jambrino-Maldonado, C., & García-Fernández, J. (2022). Can a corporate well-being programme maintain the strengths of the healthy employee in times of COVID-19 and extensive remote working? An empirical case study. *European Journal of Government and Economics, 11*(1), 51–72.

Roschel, H., Artioli, G. G., & Gualano, B. (2020). Risk of increased physical inactivity during COVID-19 outbreak in older people: A call for actions. *Journal of American Geriatrics Society, 68*(6), 1126–1128.

Salanova, M., Acosta-Antognoni, H., Llorens, S., & Le Blanc, P. (2021). We trust you! A multilevel-multireferent model based on organizational trust to explain performance. *International Journal of Environmental Research and Public Health, 18*(8), 4241.

Salanova, M., & Schaufeli, W. (2009). *Engagement at work: When work becomes passion.* Alianza Editorial.

Salgado-Aranda, R., Pérez-Castellano, N., Núñez-Gil, I., Orozco, A. J., Torres-Esquivel, N., Flores-Soler, J., Chamaisse-Akari, A., McInerney, A., Vergara-Uzcategui, C., Wang, L., González-Ferrer, J. J., Filgueiras-Rama, D., Cañadas-Godoy, V., Macaya-Miguel, C., & Pérez-Villacastín, J. (2021). *Infectious Diseases and Therapy, 10*(2), 801–814.

Simonnet, A., Chetboun, M., Poissy, J., Raverdy, V., Noulette, J., Duhamel, A., & Verkindt, H. (2020). High prevalence of obesity in severe acute respiratory syndrome coronavirus-2 (SARS CoV-2) requiring invasive mechanical ventilation. *Obesity, 28*(7), 1195–1199.

Singh, K., & Misra, M. (2021). Linking corporate social responsibility (CSR) and organizational performance: The moderating effect of corporate reputation. *European Research on Management and Business Economics, 27*(1), 100139.

Sparling, P. B. (2010). Worksite health promotion: Principles, resources, and challenges. *Preventing Chronic Disease, 7*(1), A25.

Trougakos, J. P., Chawla, N., & McCarthy, J. M. (2020). Working in a pandemic: Exploring the impact of COVID-19 health anxiety on work, family, and health outcomes. *Journal of Applied Psychology, 105*(11), 1234–1245.

Whitsel, L. P., Arena, R., Kaminsky, L. A., Berrigan, D., Katzmarzyk, P. T., Calitz, C., Grossmeier, J., Pshock, J., Lobelo, F., & Pronk, N. P. (2019). Assessing physical activity, sedentary behavior, and cardiorespiratory fitness in worksite health promotion. *American Journal of Health Promotion, 33*(2), 318–326.

World Health Organisation (WHO). (2020). Connecting the World to Combat Coronavirus. Available online: https://www.who.int/campaigns/connecting-the-world-to-combat-coronavirus/healthyathome? (accessed on 30 March 2021).

Wright, T. A., Emich, K. J., & Klotz, D. (2017). The many 'faces' of well-being. In *Research handbook on work and well-being*. Edward Elgar. https://doi.org/10.4337/9781785363269.00008

Xiang, Y. T., Yang, Y., Li, W., Zhang, L., Zhang, Q., Cheung, T., & Ng, C. H. (2020). Timely mental health care for the 2019 novel coronavirus outbreak is urgently needed. *The Lancet Psychiatry, 7*(3), 228–229.

Yin, R. K. (2013). Validity and generalization in future case study evaluations. *Evaluation, 19*(3), 321–332.

Chapter 4

Innovation and Sport Policy in Brazilian Sports

The Sport Intelligence Research Institute

Fernando Marinho Mezzadri

Universidade Federal do Paraná, Brazil

Gonzalo A. Bravo

West Virginia University, USA

Natasha Santos-Lise

Universidade Estadual do Ponta Grossa, Brazil

Gustavo Bavaresco

Universidade Federal do Paraná, Brazil

Chapter Contents

Introduction	42
Innovation and Public Policies in Brazil	45
The Sport Intelligence Research Institute	46
The Subprojects and Programs	50
Bolsa Atleta	50
National Training Network	50
Brazilian School Games	51
Governance of National Sport Entities	52
Management of Sport within the State and Municipalities	53
Conclusion	54
References	56

Introduction

Brazilian athletes have historically occupied a privileged place not only in Latin American sport but also in the global sporting scene. Since the late 1950s, the men's national football team has reached the world stage by winning five FIFA World Cup, making it the most successful national football team in the world.

DOI: 10.4324/9781003388050-5

Brazilian athletes have also reached world and Olympic success in many other sports including men's and women's volleyball, sailing, swimming, Formula One, tennis, track and field, judo, and mixed martial arts (Bravo, 2013). Moreover, since the 2000s, the Brazilian sport industry has shown significant growth reaching the fifth largest market in the world (DeMelo Neto & Feitosa, 2006). The success and growth of sport in Brazil have not occurred spontaneously. Instead, it reflects that the direct involvement of the federal government has exerted since the 1940s, particularly through the enactment of laws that have allowed not only the promotion and funding of sport but also by giving sport a special status within the Brazilian Constitution (Rocha, 2016). Undoubtedly, all these actions and steps have contributed to strengthening, even more, the cultural appeal most Brazilians feel toward sport.

The organizational architecture of the governance of sport in Brazil has its origins in the Decree-Law 3199 of 1941, which gave the State a central role. This Law centralized in the hands of the State all of the actions of governmental and non-governmental entities related to sport. In Brazil, the higher national governing body in each sport is called Sport Confederation and at the state level is called Sport Federation. Other entities that fall below the sport federations are sport leagues and sport clubs. Knowing the geopolitical organization of Brazil becomes critical for an understanding of how sport is organized in this country. Brazil is a federative republic, made of 26 federative states and 5,570 municipalities. There is also the Federal District of Brasilia, which is the only federative unit that does not have municipalities but houses the country's capital (IBGE, 2010).

Brazilian sport, which involves governmental and non-governmental entities, has presence in all three levels (Godoy, 2013; Starepravo, 2011). Among the governmental organizations, the highest authority lies in the federal government through the Special Secretariat for Sport (SEE). Among non-governmental organizations, the highest authorities are the Brazilian Olympic Committee (COB) and the Brazilian Paralympic Committee (CPB), although these two entities also depend on public funding for their operation. In Brazil, most sport organizations are funded via public resources that come from the SEE and are channeled to the state and municipal levels and also to those sport entities that are part of the COB and CPB. From 2002 to 2019, the federal government allocated 20.15 billion *Reais*, or approximately 4 billion dollars, to sport projects. During the same period, state funding for sport was 20.77 billion *Reais* or 4 billion dollars, and municipalities invested 50.25 billion *Reais*, equivalent to 6 billion dollars in sport projects. Funding was significantly increased during the years 2006–2017 as a result of the hosting of several sport mega-events such as the Rio de Janeiro 2007 Pan American Games, the World Military Games in 2011, the 2013 FIFA Confederation Cup, the 2014 FIFA World Cup, and the 2016 Rio Olympic and Paralympic Games (IPIE, n.d.). Part of the federal funding that goes to the COB and CPB is distributed to the Brazilian Club Committee (CBC) and also to the sport confederations and sport federations that are under the umbrella of the COB and CPB (Meira et al., 2012).

When examining the institutional relationships among sport entities in Brazil, two things are important to keep in mind. First, the link between governmental and non-governmental entities occurs at all three levels, federal, state, and municipal, and the link is almost exclusively through financing. While there exist other financial resources that also support the operations of clubs, federations, and confederations, public funding through governmental agencies assumes a large share of that responsibility. One explanation for this is that a large portion of the sport participation in Brazil is associated with the most popular sports, such as men's football and volleyball on a small scale. Without government support, many other sports would not survive because of the lack of funding. Second, and still, from a relational point of view, there is no fiscal accountability from the sport organizations that receive public funding. Decisions about where to invest public resources are not based on data, cost-effective analysis, demand and supply, or return of investment, but more on windows of opportunity (Kingdon, 2003; Zahariadis, 2007), including political will, special circumstances, or by the explicit demand of key stakeholders such as athletes, coaches, or sport participants. Thus, in Brazil, there is minimal program evaluation based on data regarding the effectiveness for the funding of sport programs; goals to be achieved; or how a decision to invest can or could impact the broader sport development in the country. In other words, Brazilian sport relies heavily on the subsidization provided by governmental organizations to private sport entities that operate with a great deal of autonomy.

Based on the above scenario, in 2013, the then Ministry of Sport, today SEE, established a joint venture with a group of researchers from the Federal University of Paraná (UFPR) to conduct a four-year project (2013–2016) of national scope to collect, organize, and analyze data on sport programs. The goal of this initiative was to collect data that will serve to establish metrics and indicators of performance which will help to assess the effectiveness of such programs and to guide conversations for the evaluation of existing and future public policies. The initial partnership between UFPR and the Ministry of Sport was formalized in the creation of the Sport Intelligence Project or *Projeto Inteligência Esportiva* which in 2019 expanded and became the Sport Intelligence Research Institute or *Instituto de Pesquisa Inteligência Esportiva* (IPIE).

This chapter seeks to discuss the role of the Sport Intelligence Research Institute as an innovative action in the management of sport in Brazil. Innovative action, because it enabled a close dialogue between the political entities (the Ministry) and the academic community (the university) to influence the actions of the sporting community, was represented by both public and private sport organizations. The chapter is organized into four sections. The first section discusses the role of innovation as a tool to influence public policies in Brazil; the second section explains the evolution and the role of the IPIE; the third section discusses the subprojects and programs conducted by the IPIE; finally, the fourth section offered a few concluding remarks on the innovation role play by the Sport Intelligence Research Institute and how it facilitates evidence-based decision-making in policymaking.

Innovation and Public Policies in Brazil

Innovation in Brazil has played a critical role within most government agendas, particularly after 1985 when the country returned to democracy (Hochstetler & Montero, 2013). Compared to many other countries, innovation in Brazil has been historically state-driven where more than 50% of the research and development (R&D) is supported through public funding (Limoeiro & Schneider, 2019). The big jump to innovate started in the early 2000s with the enactment of two laws, the Innovation Act of 2004 and the Good Law of 2005. These two legislations provided important incentives to increase R&D initiatives and establish partnerships and joint ventures between the government, the business sector, and universities (Arbix, 2019). Although most innovation strategies in Brazil have been technological innovation on sectors with industrial policies that have a direct impact on the country's economic growth (Schneider & Reynolds, 2019), managerial and organizational innovations also occur but have received less attention from the agencies that track the state of innovation in Brazil (Lopes & Barbosa, 2014). Because managerial and organizational innovations involve the development of new ways of managing a business, creation of new policies, processes, and organizational structures (Lopes & Barbosa, 2014) to make a product or services more cost-efficient and competitive, the Sport Intelligence Research Institute represents an example of managerial and organizational innovation as it produces relevant information which can be used to evaluate existing programs and help to re-design policies in sport.

Although through the years, policymaking in Brazil has shifted from a centralized approach where the federal government was responsible to develop policies at all three levels, today there exists a decentralized approach where states and municipalities create and adopt policies that best suit their needs. As a result, policy analysis today in many sectors has become highly professionalized through the work done by research institutes that are part of universities, think tanks, and other non-governmental agencies acting at the federal, state, and municipal level (Vaitsman et al., 2013). In this regard, innovation and policy analysis has become intrinsically related as both require the creation and analysis of knowledge to advance their goals. Considering that in Brazil, most sport organizations receive funding from the state, then there is a legitimate reason for the government (federal, state, or municipal) to evaluate the effectiveness of both programs and policies. Without data, it is not possible to know if those programs should continue to be funded. The need for program and policy evaluation in sport has been addressed by many studies (i.e., Brouwers et al., 2015; Cavill et al., 2006; Chen, 2018; Coalter, 2017; Lindsey & Bacon, 2016) to be an essential part within the policymaking cycle (Dye, 1972; Frey, 2000). These evaluations allow policymakers to have a perspective on the impact of a given action. Thus, the emergence of evidence-based policies, which allow policymakers to build interventions relevant to a specific target audience, has become the way policies should be built upon. Because of the relevance of the evaluation and monitoring process, the question is how sport policies are evaluated in Brazil.

As previously noted, the governance structure of sport in Brazil includes governmental (municipal, state, and federal secretariats) and non-governmental entities (confederations, federations, and clubs). Despite the existence of these two branches, the federal government still exerts great centralization, specifically with the regulation of sport through laws and also with the funding of both public and private sport organizations (Godoy, 2013). Because of this, there is a need to evaluate existing policies, programs, and allocation of resources not only of public sport entities but also private organizations, particularly the sport confederations.

The Sport Intelligence Research Institute

The Sport Intelligence project was born as a partnership established between the UFPR and the National High-Performance Sport Secretariat (SNEAR), which, in 2012, was part of the Ministry of Sport and today is the SEE. The project started in 2013 to collect, organize, and disseminate information about high-performance sport in Brazil to provide critical information for the review of existing sport policies as well as to foster discussions for new sport policies at the federal, state, and municipal levels. Initially, the Sport Intelligence project was conceived as a four-year project (2013–2016), ending with the Rio 2016 Olympic and Paralympic Games. However, after a positive evaluation from the Ministry of Sport, the SNEAR decided to continue Sport Intelligence until 2021. In 2019, the Sport Intelligence Research Institute (IPIE) was launched, an autonomous non-profit entity affiliated with UFPR. Since 2019, the IPIE has kept similar goals as those established in 2013 and has continued working with both governmental and non-governmental sport entities. Since 2021, the IPIE has received funding through public and private sources. Figure 4.1 shows the projects and phases of the Sport Intelligence project and the Sport Intelligence Research Institute. Figure 4.2 shows the entire *eco-system* of Sport Intelligence, which refers to all of the organizations that have been directly and indirectly served or consulted by the IPIE.

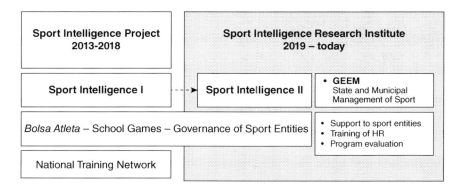

Figure 4.1 Evolution of the Sport Intelligence Research Institute.

Innovation and Sport Policy 47

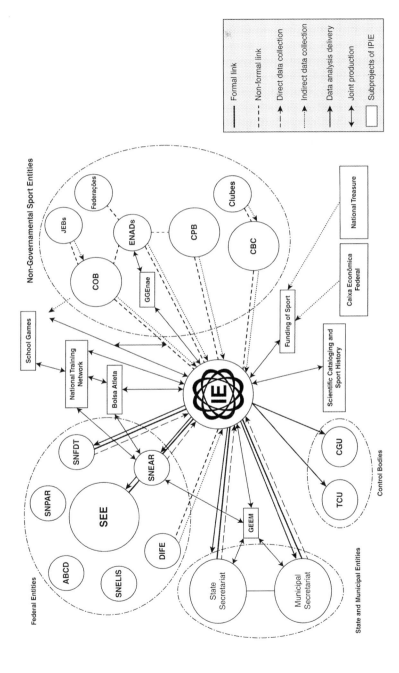

Figure 4.2 Sport Intelligence Eco-System.

The Sport Intelligence project aimed at four goals. First, build a data bank collected from a wide range of activities, programs, and processes related to the development of high-performance Olympic and Paralympic sports in Brazil. Some of the data included tracking the sources of funding for athletes, places of training, types of venues, coaching staff, ranking of athletes, etc. Second, interact with critical stakeholders in the Brazilian sport system, including Brazilian researchers, universities, sport confederations, policymakers, and other non-governmental sport organizations through seminars, scientific symposiums, and policy round tables to discuss challenges and issues affecting the development of high-performance sport in Brazil. Third, establish an international network with academic centers and institutes, coaching associations, sport scientists, and policy experts, to better understand how other more advanced nations organize and plan the development of high-performance athletes. Finally, the fourth goal was to organize, analyze, and index the scientific production related to Olympic and Paralympic sports in Brazil. This goal was aimed to support not only the traditional academic community but also making this information available to critical stakeholders such as coaches, athletes, referees, sport officials, and policymakers.

The methodological approach in this project focused on gathering critical information on three key stakeholders: athletes, sport entities, and sport modalities. Thus, it was deemed important to collect evidence of the issues and challenges that affect and intervene during the process of high-performance sport from the angle and experience of these three stakeholders. To achieve this purpose, the project was organized into two parts that were developed simultaneously. One part was geared exclusively toward the interests of athletes, coaches, officials, and other stakeholders that are part of the Brazilian sport system. Therefore, all sorts of data were collected and analyzed to assist decision-makers to evaluate the process of high-performance sport, including analysis of existing sport programs and policies developed by either the sport confederations, the COB, or the SNEAR. The other part of the project was more geared toward the interests of sport scientists and academicians. Here, thousands of scientific material produced in Brazil since the early 20th century were organized and cataloged. That type of information and getting access to it, through one platform, was almost unknown to most practitioners that work directly with high-performance athletes, coaches, officials, and sport administrators in Brazil.

During the first six years of the Sport Intelligence project, three of the most important programs that were under the umbrella of the SNEAR were thoroughly analyzed. This included the *Bolsa Atleta* and *Bolsa Atleta Podium*, the National Training Network, and the Brazilian School Games. The analysis of these programs included collecting and organizing information from 26,700 athletes and 73,786 grants from the *Bolsa Atleta* and *Bolsa Atleta Podium* programs. Regarding the National Training Network, more than 55,000 pieces of relevant data were collected; and for the Brazilian School Games, more than 7,000 student-athletes of school age, who ranked among the top three in Brazil, were analyzed. Finally, the analysis of sport entities included data on 7,200 of these organizations at the national, state, and municipal level.

At the end of 2018, Sport Intelligence 1 ended and Sport Intelligence 2 began. During this time, a few of the initial subprojects ended, others continued, and new subprojects were added, particularly the Governance of National Sport Entities, or *Gestão e Governança em Entidades Nacionais de Administração do Esporte* (GGEnae), and the Management of Sport within the States and Municipalities, also known as *Gestão do Esporte nos Estados e Municípios* (GEEM). It is through these two subprojects that Sport Intelligence has started to work more directly with decision-makers, assisting in their decision-making. Therefore, the process of innovation and influence on sport policies is not linear (Figure 4.3). The impact of data on policy takes several steps, including a political discussion before any change can be implemented. The role of the Sport Intelligence project and now Institute has been primarily focused on providing and analyzing data. The final word on how data will impact policy always depends on decision-makers who have been charged to lead the sport in Brazil as well as political players who weigh how new decisions or policies might affect the interests of the constituencies they represent (Filgueiras & Rocha, 2013).

After the Sport Intelligence Research Institute was born, one of its objectives was to foster an informed discussion on the benefits and worthiness of a National Sport System for Brazil. To start such a conversation, one of the first tasks was to assess how sport was developed at the municipal level. To do that, a questionnaire was developed and piloted in the state of Parana, given that is where the IPIE is located. In 2021, the municipal assessment has been expanded to several states and municipalities across Brazil. One of the distinguishing aspects of the Sport Intelligence Research Institute with the initial Sport Intelligence project is that it not only addressed high-performance sport but also expanded to include sport participation at the grassroots and local level. At the time this chapter is written, some of the original sub-projects that were part of Sport Intelligence I such as *Bolsa Atleta* and the Brazilian School Games are still part of the Institute's agenda. However, more recently, the emphasis has slowly shifted to address the needs of sport organizations at the municipal and state levels. Currently, the Sport Intelligence Research Institute is centered on three strands: support sport entities (public and private), the training of managers, and program evaluation of these sport entities. The next section describes the main subprojects and programs that have been developed since the beginning of the Sport Intelligence project.

Figure 4.3 From Data to Decision-making.

The Subprojects and Programs

Bolsa Atleta

This is a federal program that provides grants to support the career of elite athletes, particularly those prospects of succeeding internationally. Athletes who qualify for these grants receive a 12-month stipend that can be renewed based on the attainment of performance goals. Currently, the program includes six categories that provide a monthly stipend between 370 *Reais* to up to 15,000 *Reais*, equivalent to 100–3,750 US dollars (Camargo, 2020). Since the beginning of *Bolsa Atleta* in 2005, more than 24,000 athletes have benefited from receiving more than 63,000 grants for a total of 884 million *Reais*, equivalent to 221 million US dollars (Instituto de Pesquisa Inteligência Esportiva, 2019). This program not only has dramatically increased the amount of money elite athletes had received until that time but also changed the way financial support for athletes had been administered. In *Bolsa Atleta,* grants are directly channeled to the athletes without going through the sport governing body. Because of that, *Bolsa Atleta* has become extremely popular among athletes. Although *Bolsa Atleta* is one of the main public sport policies in Brazil and the largest program for elite sport, the National High-Performance Secretariat (SNEAR) lacked a database that included critical information to evaluate the effectiveness of the program. Without relevant information, SNEAR cannot know, for example, how many Olympic medals an athlete had won that had received funding from this program; or how much money has been invested by categories of athletes (i.e., beginners, advanced, Olympic, etc.).

In this subproject, the main task of Sport Intelligence has been to collect and organize all sorts of data that relates directly to the athletes who have received these grants. By crosschecking and combining data, it is possible to know the amount of money received by sport, by categories of athletes, know regions of the country with the highest concentration of athletes who have benefited from the program, know the clubs from where these athletes trained, etc. Overall, this information has helped not only to better understand who has benefited but also allows an athlete's career and performance to be followed.

National Training Network

This program was created in 2011 by Federal Law 12395 (Brasil, 2011) and aimed to serve the development of high-performance sport through the creation of a network of training centers across Brazil. In these training venues, elite athletes from all over the country could train under one roof and interact with coaches and sport scientists. The idea of a network evolves from the notion that a high-performance center acts as a node that interacts with other sport entities, including local sport clubs, state federations, and confederations, creating a synergy in the process of developing high-performance athletes. The National Training Network (RNT) was also conceived as a part of the legacy of the Rio 2016 Olympic and Paralympic

Games. The plan intended that all these venues were going to be in full operation before the Rio Olympics, serving as the headquarters for athletes from the same sport who were prospects to compete in this event. Considering that most venues were completed after Rio 2016, it was unclear if the actual network was operating as it was originally planned. Therefore, one of tasks of this subproject was to assess the extent whether this network existed.

Therefore, in this subproject, the data collected focused not only on identifying the different entities that participate as a part of the broader sport system in Brazil, such as clubs, federations, and confederations, but also confirm if these entities were operating in the logic of a network. In this subproject, data was collected from the website of each confederation that was part of the Olympic program. In those websites, it was possible to identify the history and results of the top elite Olympic athletes which also allowed tracking and identifying the sites and places where these athletes were training. After the information was collected and entered into a database, it was possible to understand the strengths of the links among the different stakeholders that were part of the network. All this helped to advance a serious discussion on the challenges that exist when developing a National Training Network, particularly in a large country like Brazil.

Brazilian School Games

This event is the largest sport festival for children and adolescents from public and private schools in Brazil. Participants come from all over the country and compete in 17 different sports every year. The Brazilian School Games (BSG) have been organized since 1969 under the patronage of different government agencies. Since 2005, the COB has taken the responsibility to organize this event, which is also supported by the Ministry of Sport, and the *Globo* Organization which is the largest media organization in Latin America. Many stakeholders believe that the BSG is a platform that helps identify talent and future champions (Arantes et al., 2019). Because of the relevance and tradition of this event, Sport Intelligence examined and analyzed data about athletes who competed in the BSG to shed light on how this event has evolved since 2005. Data collected in this subproject included all participating student-athletes since 2005, the type of schools (private or public) they attended, and the number of medals achieved by school, state, and region in each category.

Data regarding the operation and development of the BSG such as goals, objectives, and regulation, and financial, human, and physical resources used in this event were also collected. One of the findings of this subproject showed that private schools excel in sports that require greater infrastructure, such as swimming. Conversely, public schools excel in sports that require less equipment, such as running in athletics or basketball. These findings suggest that the socio-economic status of athletes correlates with success in certain sports. In other words, athletes with a more privileged background most likely will attend a private school that will provide better training conditions (i.e., infrastructure, equipment, coaches, etc.)

when compared to athletes from a less privileged socio-economic background. One question for future policy analysis that surfaces after these findings: what can critical stakeholders (i.e., confederations, COB, etc.) do? Especially those that have a vested interest in high-performance sport to level the playing field for students who attend public schools.

Governance of National Sport Entities

The governance of Olympic sport in Brazil is no different from other countries that are part of the Olympic movement. This structure involves several non-governmental organizations that relate in a pyramidal hierarchy way (Skinner et al., 2019). At the bottom of this pyramid are the sport clubs and at the top are the sport confederations. Above all these organizations is the National Olympic Committee or NOC, which is a non-governmental organization affiliated with the International Olympic Committee (IOC). NOCs represent, promote, and protect the interests of the Olympic Movement and the IOC in each country. In Brazil, the Brazilian Olympic Committee, or COB, is one of the main organizations responsible to promote the development of high-performance sport (COB, 2021a). Currently, 54 organizations are part of the COB. Of those, 34 are sport confederations part of the summer and winter Olympic programs (COB, 2021b). As previously noted, sport confederations, which govern sport at the national level, also relate and interact with the state federations, sport associations, clubs, and finally the athletes (Ribeiro, 2012).

Over the past decade, several high-profile cases of corruption have tainted Brazilian sport, including the arrest of the former President of COB Carlos Nuzman, who was charged with paying cash for votes in favor of Rio de Janeiro's candidature in 2009. Other cases of corruption involved the sport confederations of judo, volleyball, and handball with the mismanagement of public money that was channeled through the COB. These and other cases of mismanagement and governance failures not only affect the reputation and image of these confederations but also their financial sustainability. Recent modifications to the Sport Law 9615 of 1998 have stressed the need for compliance and good governance practices. Because the main source of funding of the COB as well as the sport confederations are the resources they received from the Federal Lottery, compliance with these norms becomes a must for these organizations. In response to these issues, in 2015, the IPIE start surveying the state of governance of sport confederations in Brazil. This survey, conducted in collaboration with the non-profit, non-governmental organization *Sou do Esporte* ('I am from Sport') advocates for good governance practices in sport. The survey included five dimensions of governance: transparency, equity, accountability, institutional integrity, and modernization. This framework is based on the instrument developed by the Sport Governance Observer project run by the Danish organization Play the Game (Geeraert, 2015). Furthermore, in 2018, and in partnership with the Ministry of Sport, the *Governance Booklet on Sport Entities* was launched to assist sport entities to adopt good governance practices in their management (Mezzadri et al., 2018).

Sport confederations in Brazil have recently gone through important changes in their management. These changes have been driven both by external factors (i.e., modification in the sport legislation, social pressure for greater transparency, difficulties in raising financial resources), as well as internal ones (i.e., organizational restructuring, institutional planning, budget distribution, among other factors). Interestingly, these changes have resulted that many sport confederations have raised their scores in the governance dimensions. These changes and the pressure to comply with the standards of good governance have contributed to developing more fair, transparent, and accountable sport organizations in Brazil.

Management of Sport within the State and Municipalities

In Brazil, most cities do not have enough qualified human resources for the administration of sport, and when they do, many municipal secretariats do not have enough personnel to address the complexity of running a public sport program. This reality prevents not only that administrators cannot effectively attend to their day-to-day programming but also prevents them from evaluating the needs of their communities. For this reason, the IPIE, seeking to facilitate the dialogue between local sport organizations and their constituencies, launched in 2019 the Management of Sport within the State and Municipalities program (GEEM). This program aims to support sport organizations at the state and municipal levels by assisting their planning, training personnel, and conducting program evaluations to assess the effectiveness of their policies. To reach that goal, in 2019, the IPIE developed a questionnaire that provides a comprehensive view of the state-of-the-art sport reaches in each municipality. The idea to develop and apply the GEEM questionnaire is intended to facilitate evidence-based decision-making. As previously noted in this chapter, information represents a critical part and an efficient tool that assists decision-making, particularly in policy building (Batista, 2013). Results from data allow managers to assess the investment made, the strategies implemented, and the outcomes that resulted from their actions.

The GEEM questionnaire was adapted from an existing instrument (developed by researchers at the IPIE) that assessed how resources allocated to sport confederations were used to support the development of sport in these confederations. Likewise, the questionnaire adapted several dimensions and indicators from an instrument developed by the Working Group of the National Sport System in the Ministry of Sport. The GEEM questionnaire asked administrators to provide information in six areas: (a) institutional; (b) governance, including data regarding transparency, accountability, equity and democracy; (c) human resources, asking how many people work in the organization and the level and type of training and expertise they have; (d) sport policies, including financing of programs and type of programs offered; (e) facilities, collecting data on the sport infrastructure that is managed by the entity; and finally, information about (f) the sport culture of the community, including data on the types of sport offered and sport preferences of the population.

In addition to the data collected through the GEEM questionnaire, IPIE collects demographic information on the municipalities such as total population, population density, and human development index among others. All this information is retrieved from the website of the Brazilian Institute of Geography and Statistics (IBGE) and the data is analyzed with other information collected from the GEEM questionnaire. These results help administrators to have an inside look at possible weaknesses or strengths in the sport offers, for example, if the overall supply of programs, activities, and facilities meet the demand of the population. IPIE seeks partnerships with state public sport entities. These institutions facilitate contact with their respective cities. IPIE trains municipal managers on how to administer the GEEM questionnaire and how to interpret the data that is collected. Every month the IPIE delivers a report to the states that shows the results. In May 2021, there were 930 municipalities from 16 states that have completed the GEEM questionnaire. This represents 16.7% of the total number of municipalities in Brazil.

Conclusion

The Sport Intelligence Research Institute started in 2013 as a partnership between the UFPR and the National High-Performance Sport Secretariat (SNEAR) of Brazil. The purpose of this collaboration was the gathering of information related to the process of high-performance sport to influence evidence-based decision-making in future sport policymaking. In the beginning, the project focused exclusively on matters related to high-performance sport. As the project progressed, the overall discussion began to expand to include other dimensions of sport such as participatory sport, particularly at the grassroots level. The rationale and justification to expand the scope of the project were simple as it was found that many sport policies in Brazil had been built with minimal or total lack of evidence. Therefore, researchers involved in the project concluded that it was not possible to make a complete contribution to the development of sport in Brazil if other dimensions of sport, such as educational and participatory, were not included in the overall analysis. As a result, in 2019, the Sport Intelligence project turned into the Sport Intelligence Research Institute. Nonetheless, and although the scope of the project was now much larger, the purpose remained unaltered, which is the collection and organization of sport information to influence future sport policymaking in Brazil.

Another point of inspiration to transform the Sport Intelligence project into the Sport Intelligence Research Institute was the existence of other well-established institutions that had the mission to organize data on sport, making it available for public debate or just to advance the body of knowledge in sport sciences. Some of these organizations are the Sport Information Resource Center, SIRC, in Canada; the Danish Institute for Sport Studies IDAN, and the European Institute of Sport Development and Leisure Studies linked to the German Sport University in Cologne, Germany. However, in Brazil, before the creation of the Sport Intelligence Research Institute, there were no other similar organizations that sought to develop sport and contribute to the debate on public policies. The closest initiative to the Sport Intelligence Research Institute was the National Institute of Educational Studies and Research Anísio Teixeira – INEP, a federal agency that works with the Ministry of Education, whose mission is to subsidize the formulation of educational policies to contribute to the economic and social development of the country. In this regard, the Sport Intelligence Research Institute is not an initiative that emerges totally out of the blue, but instead, it was inspired by existing models that aim at similar goals but in other social and cultural contexts and different fields.

The Sport Intelligence Research Institute represents a managerial and organizational innovation within the field of sport management and sport policy as it produces germane information that can be used to evaluate existing programs and help to re-design or create new policies in sport. Such initiatives are particularly important in a country like Brazil, where despite the relevant place sport has in society, the country still has a long list of social and economic challenges that perhaps require more urgent attention. This does not suggest that sport should not be given attention, but instead, it urges policymakers and decision-makers to base future policy on evidence, meaning that for every Brazilian Real invested in sport, there should always be a clear idea of what the return on investment might be.

Arguably, among emerging economies, Brazil is a country with one of the largest public budgets allocated to sport behind China and Russia. Data collected from the Sport Intelligence Project has shown that despite the large investment the government has allocated to sport, many initiatives had been developed without evaluation plans or even were pursued with diffused goals. In this regard, it is necessary to bring a more scientific approach to the debate of both planning and future policymaking in sport. This does not mean ignoring the harsh reality of the policymaking process, which involves many other 'non-factual factors' in addition to the 'scientific facts', but as noted by Batista (2013), data and facts still constitute a reliable and effective way to influence policy: 'academic studies are unlikely to provide the whole basis for political decisions... [but] academic research results [still] constitute an important source of information [as] they contribute to discussion and debate and thus influence action taken by decision-makers, thus impacting public policies, even if indirectly or partly' (p. 256).

The historical context provided by the hosting of several sport mega-events in Brazil left important legacies for the country as well as created a momentum that could elevate Brazil as a world-class sport nation. This new context could significantly benefit athletes, coaches, and sport scientists to reach the new boundaries of excellence in sport. However, that could only be possible if sport bureaucrats, politicians, and sport researchers listen, debate, and put attention to what each other has to say, and particularly understand the weight and relevancy of facts when deciding what, where, and why to invest, develop, or pursue programs, projects, or policies related to sport in Brazil.

References

Arantes, A., Silva, F. M., Lopes, J. P. S. R., Bravo, G., & Melo, G. F. (2019). A percepção dos gestores de esporte sobre jogos escolares brasileiros [the perception of sport managers about the Brazilian school games]. *Pensar a Prática, 22*(55738), 1–13.

Arbix, G. (2019). Innovation policy in Brazil since 2003. Advances, incoherencies, and discontinuities. In E. B. Reynolds, B. R. Schneider, & E. Zylberberg (Eds.), *Innovation in Brazil. Advancing development in the 21st century* (pp. 73–89). Routledge.

Batista, C. (2013). Policy analysis by academic institutions in. In J. Vaitsman, & J. M. Ribeiro (Eds.), *Policy analysis in Brazil* (pp. 249–260). Policy Press at the University of Bristol.

Brasil (2011). Lei n° 12.395, de 16 de março de 2011. Altera as Leis n°s 9.615, de 24 de março de 1998, que institui normas gerais sobre desporto, e 10.891, de 9 de julho de 2004, que institui a Bolsa-Atleta; cria os Programas Atleta Pódio e Cidade Esportiva; revoga a Lei n° 4.354, de 2 de setembro de 1976; e dá outras providências. Retrieved from: http://www.planalto.gov.br/ccivil_03/_ato2011-2014/2011/lei/l12395.htm

Bravo, G. (2013). Brazil. In I. O'Boyle, & T. Bradbury (Eds.), *Sport governance: International case studies* (pp. 142–155). Routledge.

Brouwers, J., Sotiriadou, P., & De Bosscher, V. (2015). Sport-specific policies and factors that influence international success: The case of tennis. *Sport Management Review, 18*(3), 343–358.

Camargo, P. R. D. (2020). *O programa bolsa-atleta: Desenvolvimento da performance esportiva e política de welfare state.* [The scholarship-athlete program: development of sport performance and welfare state policy]. Doctoral Dissertation. Universidade Federal do Paraná, Curitiba, Paraná, Brazil.

Cavill, N., Foster, C., Oja, P., & Martin, B. W. (2006). An evidence-based approach to physical activity promotion and policy development in Europe: Contrasting case studies. *Promotion & Education, 13*(2), 104–111.

Chen, S. (2018). Sport policy evaluation: What do we know and how might we move forward? *International Journal of Sport Policy and Politics, 10*(6), 1–19.

Coalter, F. (2017). Sport and social inclusion: Evidence-based policy and practice. *Social Inclusion, 5*(2), 141–149.

COB. (2021a). Sobre o COB. *Comitê Olímpico do Brasil.* Retrieved from: https://www.cob.org.br/pt/cob/home/sobre-o-cob

COB. (2021b). Confederações. *Comitê Olímpico do Brasil.* Retrieved from: https://www.cob.org.br/pt/cob/confederacoes

DeMelo Neto, F. P., & Feitosa, M. (2006). Marketing esportivo. In L. DaCosta (Ed.), *Atlas do esporte no Brasil.* CONFEF.

Dye, T. D. (1972). *Understanding public policy.* Prentice-Hall.

Filgueiras, C. A. C., & Rocha, C. A. V. (2013). Production of policy-related information and knowledge in Brazil: The state government agencies. In J. Vaitsman, & J. M. Ribeiro (Eds.), *Policy analysis in Brazil* (pp. 95–106). Policy Press at the University of Bristol.

Frey, K. (2000). Políticas públicas: Um debate conceitual e reflexões referentes à prática da análise de políticas públicas no Brasil. *Planejamento e Políticas Públicas, 21,* 211–259.

Geeraert, A. (2015). *Sports governance observer 2015: The legitimacy crisis in international sports governance.* Play the Game.

Godoy, L. (2013). *O sistema nacional de esporte no Brasil: Revelações e possíveis delineamentos.* [The National Sport System in Brazil: revelations and possible designs]. Doctoral Dissertation. Universidade Federal do Paraná, Curitiba, Paraná, Brasil.

Hochstetler, K., & Montero, A. P. (2013). The renewed developmental state: The national development bank and the Brazil model. *Journal of Development Studies*, 49(11), 1484–1499.

IBGE, 2010. Panorama. *Instituto Brasileiro de Geografia e Estatística*. Retrieved from: https://cidades.ibge.gov.br/brasil/panorama.

Instituto de Pesquisa Inteligência Esportiva. (2019). *Banco de dados*. IE-UFPR/Secretaria Nacional de Esportes de Alto Rendimento, Curitiba, Parana, Brasil.

IPIE (n.d.). Nossos relatórios de BI. [Our business intelligence reports]. *Instituto de Pesquisa Inteligência Esportiva*. Retrieved from: http://www.inteligenciaesportiva.ufpr.br/site/index.php/nossos-relatorios-de-bi/

Kingdon, J. W. (2003). *Agendas, alternatives, and public policies* (2nd ed). University of Michigan.

Limoeiro, D., & Schneider, B. R. (2019). Institutions, politics, and state-led innovation. In E. B. Reynolds, B. R. Schneider, & E. Zylberberg (Eds.), *Innovation in Brazil, Advancing development in the 21st century* (pp. 23–44). Routledge.

Lindsey, I., & Bacon, D. (2016). In pursuit of evidence-based policy and practice: A realist synthesis-inspired examination of youth sport and physical activity initiatives in England (2002–2010). *International Journal of Sport Policy and Politics*, 8(1), 67–90.

Lopes, D. P. T., & Barbosa, A. C. Q. (2014). Management and organizational innovation in Brazil: Evidence from technology innovation surveys. *Production*, 24(4), 872–886.

Meira, T. B., Bastos, F. C., & Böhme, M. T. S. (2012). Análise da estrutura organizacional do esporte de rendimento no Brasil: Um estudo preliminar. *Revista Brasileira De Educação Física e Esporte*, 26(2), 251–262.

Mezzadri, F. M., Haas, L. G. N., Neto, R. C. S., & Santos, T. O. (2018). *Cartilha de governança em entidades esportivas lei 9.615/98* (2nd ed). Ministério do Esporte.

Ribeiro, M. A. D. S. (2012). *Modelos de governança e organizações esportivas: uma análise das federações e confederações esportivas brasileiras* [Governance models and sport sport organizations: An analysis of Brazilian sport federations and confederations]. Doctoral Dissertation. Fundação Getúlio Vargas. Rio de Janeiro. Brazil.

Rocha, C. (2016). Public sector and sport development in Brazil. In G. Bravo, R. López de D'Amico, & C. Parrish (Eds.), *Sport in Latin America. Policy, organization & management* (pp. 101–112). Routledge.

Schneider, B. R., & Reynolds, E. B. (2019). Introduction: Innovation in Brazil: Advancing development in the 21st century. In E. B. Reynolds, B. R. Schneider, & E. Zylberberg (Eds.), *Innovation in Brazil. Advancing development in the 21st century* (pp. 1–20). Routledge.

Skinner, J., Mueller, J., & Swanson, S. (2019). Professional sport leagues and tours. In E. MacIntosh, G. Bravo, & M. Li (Eds.), *International sport management* (2nd ed., pp. 211–225). Human Kinetics.

Starepravo, F. A. (2011). *Políticas públicas de esporte e lazer no Brasil: aproximações, intersecções, rupturas e distanciamentos entre os subcampos político/burocrático e científico/acadêmico.* [Public policies on sport and leisure in Brazil: Proximities, intersections, ruptures and distances between the political/bureaucratic and scientific/academic subfields]. Doctoral Dissertation. Universidade Federal do Paraná.

Vaitsman, J., Lobato, L., & Andrade, G. (2013). Professionalization of policy analysis in Brazil. In J. Vaitsman, & J. M. Ribeiro (Eds.), *Policy analysis in Brazil* (pp. 13–26). Policy Press at the University of Bristol.

Zahariadis, N. (2007). The multiple streams framework: Structure, limitations, prospects. In P. A. Sabatier (Ed.), *Theories of the policy process* (pp. 65–92). Westview.

Chapter 5

Crisis Management during COVID-19

Sport Clubs' Initiatives and Innovations

Paloma Escamilla-Fajardo
University of Valencia, Spain

Juan M. Núñez-Pomar
University of Valencia, Spain

Ferran Calabuig-Moreno
University of Valencia, Spain

Chapter Contents

Introduction	58
Dealing with the COVID-19 Crisis	60
Conclusions and Managerial Perspectives	66
References	67

Introduction

The practice of sports and sport in its different aspects occupy a large part of the lives of people in Spain. This growing interest and repercussion has led to a high degree of standardization and professionalization of sports organizations in recent years. Since the 1980s, sport has been considered a social phenomenon (Lefèvre et al., 2020) with a great capacity to mobilize and attract people. Nowadays, it is difficult to find anyone who does not practice or has not practiced physical activity, or who is not a follower or fan of an athlete or team. Therefore, it is understandable that the sports sector has gone from being a scarcely regulated practice to representing 3.3% of the Gross Domestic Product (GDP) in Spain in 2018 (PwC España, 2020p. 21).

Sport is a sector of the first magnitude, in which a liquidated public expenditure has been invested that has been increasing in recent years. Its highest value in the last decade has been reached in 2018, with a total of €2,340 million. This amount encompasses spending, among other destinations, on sports promotion and dissemination, aid to sports or sports entities, as well as the creation, conservation,

DOI: 10.4324/9781003388050-6

and operation of sports facilities. This expenditure is understandable since Spain has a large number of sports facilities and spaces. Specifically, according to the last National Census of Sports Facilities published in 2005, in our country, there are a total of 255,260 sports facilities and spaces that are used by sports organizations of different character or nature. In Spain, there are different types of sports organizations involved in the promotion and encouragement of physical activity (Escamilla-Fajardo et al., 2018). Among them, we can highlight public sports organizations and private sports organizations.

Within private sports organizations, we can differentiate (1) sports organizations of a mercantile nature and (2) sports organizations of an associative nature, among which sports clubs could be highlighted. The number of all of them has increased significantly in recent years, gaining importance and representation with respect to the rest of the activity sectors. According to the latest data collected, in 2019, the number of organizations of a mercantile nature linked to sports was 36,793, with 83.5% being companies engaged in sports activities. This number has grown since 2018, when 34,529 companies were counted. However, it should be noted that these data were taken at a time when COVID-19 was not contemplated, therefore, it is still unknown how much change will be experienced in 2020 compared to the previous year.

On the other hand, attending to federated sport and private organizations of an associative nature (registered sports clubs), according to the annual report presented by the Spanish government, in 2019, there were 3,945,510 federative licenses, the highest number in recent years. With these objective data, there is evidence of the important rate of practice and the growing impact that sport has in our country. However, federated people are a group of practicing population, but it is far from being the total population that practices sport in our society. According to the same report, in 2019, there were a total of 75,455 clubs. These clubs are attached to national sports federations that receive public aid and subsidies, however, they operate in a competitive sector in which they must adopt attitudes and behaviors typical of for-profit organizations despite their non-profit nature. The above data were collected and evaluated prior to the emergence of COVID-19 in Spanish society.

In recent months, we have encountered restrictions derived from COVID-19 that have directly affected the global economy (Kraus et al., 2020), and the sports sector has not been oblivious to this. Social and mobility constraints have changed the lives of millions of people (World Health Organization, 2020b), affecting in a high percentage the sport practice performed (Stanton et al., 2020). Among these restrictions are the cancellation of sporting events and competitions, or the limitation of practice in sports facilities, even in open public spaces. Depending on the country and the period in which we were, the restrictions have been more or less strict. However, in addition to changing people's lives dramatically, they have also had a considerable impact on sports organizations, regardless of their commercial or associative nature. Sports organizations have been forced to make changes to their sports offer (Parnell et al., 2020), through initiatives and innovations adapted to the situation and the needs of members, users, and athletes.

Within the different types of sports organizations, in general, sports clubs have been highly impacted by the crisis resulting from COVID-19. Their non-profit nature, the impossibility of counting on profits from previous seasons, or the cancellation of sports leagues and competitions have placed these kind of entities in a complicated situation. Therefore, sports clubs have been forced to evaluate and develop initiatives that could maintain the quality of their services and satisfy, as far as possible, the sports and social needs of their members and users.

The role of sports clubs in developed societies can be approached from an economic, social, or health perspective. From the economic perspective, their impact on GDP has been discussed previously. On the other hand, from a social perspective, sport clubs have an undeniable role (Escamilla-Fajardo et al., 2020). As important social objectives of sports clubs, we find the promotion of sports practice through an offer that covers as many people as possible. This can be achieved through a wide range of sports services that meet the needs of users. However, from a social perspective, this is not the only objective of this type of entity. Associative sport also has the objective of involving groups at risk of exclusion, adapting the sports offer to their personal characteristics and leaving aside the economic return that this can mean for the organization. All this can have as a consequence the improvement of the well-being of the people who practice it and the increase of their social relationships. Finally, from the health field, the positive role of sport in people's health is an important aspect. Therefore, during this pandemic, the physical and mental health of people has been affected by the impossibility of performing physical activity in sports or outdoor spaces, and the reduction of general sports practice during this period (Maugeri et al., 2020; Slater et al., 2020). With the purpose of changing this trend, a large part of sport organizations have carried out innovative strategies and proactive initiatives to continue with the sport offer and maintain the relationship with their partners and users.

In this hostile and changing context derived from COVID-19, sports clubs have had the social responsibility to adapt their offer to the situation and offer the possibility to their members and users to continue practicing sports. In times of crisis, entities with an entrepreneurial attitude are more likely to maintain, even thrive (Devece et al., 2016). However, despite knowing the positive impact that innovation can have on the final performance of the organization in times of crisis, developing an entrepreneurial attitude and behavior has not been easy, nor has it been supported by all clubs. Therefore, it is necessary to analyze it in order to obtain more information on how these types of organizations have responded to a situation they had never faced before.

Dealing with the COVID-19 Crisis

In this study, 148 Spanish sports clubs were analyzed. Information was obtained from them on their response to a period of restrictions and limitations in the development of the sports offer. The questionnaire was filled in between the months of April and May 2020. At that time Spain was living a complicated situation.

Physical activity in sports centers was limited, sports events had been cancelled, and there were social and mobility restrictions. Sports organizations were facing a hostile situation they had never experienced before. However, despite the undeniable impact of COVID-19 on all organizations, the crisis resulting from this virus may not have affected all sports organizations equally. Consequently, their actions may have been different. To find this out, the sample studied has been divided between sports clubs that perceive a high impact of COVID on their economic-financial situation and those that perceive a low impact. This has been evaluated through the result obtained to the question "To what extent has your club been affected economically or financially by the crisis derived from Covid-19?". This question has been previously asked in previous studies with the same purpose (Saebi et al., 2017). This question has been considered relative to the economic-financial aspect as the sporting impact was determined by the restrictions and the social impact was also subject to the social and mobility constraints that existed during the lockdown.

According to the results obtained, two ranges have been established: low perceived impact (LPI) (≤ 3.49; n = 33) and high-perceived impact (HPI) (≥ 3.50; n = 115). The data obtained regarding this question were to be expected, since the virus has impacted the sports sector in a way that had not been seen before (Ratten, 2020). As can be seen in Table 5.1, nine questions were asked related to the novel initiatives developed, the level of risk of these proposals, the previous analysis carried out of the competition, or the collaboration of institutions such as national or autonomic federations during this period. The degree of agreement with the statement was answered with a Likert-type response scale with 1 being "strongly disagree" and 7 "strongly agree".

According to the results obtained, the sports clubs that perceived a high impact of COVID-19 on their economic-financial situation (HPI) are the ones that present higher values in all the items, compared to the clubs that perceived a low impact of COVID-19 on their situation (LPI). These differences are significant in four of the nine items analyzed. First, according to the results of the first item, clubs with LPI (mean (M) = 5.00; standard deviation (SD) = 2.24) and clubs with HPI (M = 5.41; SD = 1.87) considered it highly necessary to reinvent themselves in light of the lockdown situation we were in. Clubs should be open to exploring new alternatives to adapt to changes instead of relying on the actions they have developed before (Doherty et al., 2020). To do this, it is important to know in advance the needs of members and users and the constraints at any given time. In this way, it is possible to adapt the sports offer and the most appropriate communication channel to carry out the initiatives with maximum efficiency.

However, the response to this changing and hostile situation resulting from a crisis can be approached differently depending on how the situation is perceived (Kraus et al., 2020). If the sports club's management team interprets the crisis as a threat, they are likely to see a danger in it and react more conservatively. On the contrary, if the management team perceives the crisis positively, as an opportunity, it will have a more open and proactive attitude toward change. Considering

Table 5.1 General Descriptions of the Analyzed Items

Items	Low perceived impact		High perceived impact		
	M	SD	M	SD	p
1 Due to the situation of lockdown, it has been necessary to reinvent ourselves.	5.00	2.24	5.41	1.87	
2 We have carried out some initiatives to approach or contact users (online training, activity monitoring, etc.).	5.12	1.98	5.34	1.89	
3 This situation has led to innovative initiatives that would not have been considered in a normal situation.	4.61	1.98	5.15	1.83	
4 The initiatives we have taken may put the sustainability of my organization at risk.	1.85	1.50	2.08	1.61	
5 The innovative initiatives taken may improve our positioning compared to our competitors.	3.64	1.99	4.52	1.66	*
6 These initiatives will continue to be developed after the current lockdown situation has passed.	3.33	1.88	4.10	1.73	*
7 Some of the initiatives taken in this situation have been implemented before other competing organizations.	3.85	1.89	4.65	1.88	*
8 The sport sector was analyzed before the initiatives developed were implemented.	3.12	1.99	4.45	1.99	**
9 Institutions or federations have assisted in the elaboration and development of innovative initiatives during this lockdown situation.	2.48	1.98	2.89	1.95	

Note: A = Average; SD = Standard Deviation; * = $p < .05$; ** = $p < .01$; *** = $p < .001$.

the results of the second item, the sports clubs analyzed carried out some outreach initiative or contact with users, since both in clubs with LPI (M = 5.12; SD = 1.98) and in clubs with HPI (M = 5.34; SD = 1.89), the results are high. Social and mobility restrictions were very strict in Spain during the months of March and April. As a result, a large number of sports clubs were forced to change the channel of communication with their members and users. Communication went from being face-to-face before the outbreak of the virus in society to being completely online during the period of tighter restrictions. Some sports organizations already had open online contact with their members, users, and followers, however, others were forced to establish these communication channels (Instagram, Facebook, Twitter, TikTok, etc.) in a new way for their entity, and on many occasions, to significantly vary the use that was made of them. This fits with what was presented by Santos et al. (2017), who state that in times of crisis, it is necessary to seek alternative paths that can meet the needs of users and alleviate the loss that limitations can cause.

Crisis Management during COVID-19   63

In this time of lockdown, online communication has experienced unprecedented growth (Donthu & Gustafsson, 2020). This growth has taken place in different fields and sport has not been oblivious to this. The offer of online sports training, the opening of new social networks to maintain and strengthen contact with members and users, or the online monitoring of the activity of their athletes are some of the initiatives that Spanish sports clubs have carried out. However, according to the results of the third item, these innovative initiatives have been proposed due to the situation, since both clubs with LPI (M = 4.61; SD = 1.98) and clubs with HPI (M = 5.15; SD = 1.83) in a normal situation would not have proposed them. This fits with Faulkner (2001), who associates crises with negative effects, but highlights the positive effect they can have on innovation and the search for new markets. "Necessity is the mother of invention" fits the situation of Spanish sports clubs. These types of entities have been forced to reinvent their products and services in order to make them more attractive and accessible to members and users. In this sense, technological innovation can provide the tools to adapt services to a dynamic and changing environment (Miao & Popp, 2014).

In this context, the great majority of clubs have considered it important to explore new technologies and market opportunities from an entrepreneurial approach. The use of social networks to offer physical activity, online platforms to track training sessions, or a greater effort in analyzing the environment are some of the actions that have been carried out in an uncertain scenario, but full of opportunities. The use of online platforms and communication tools such as social networks or communication and messaging APPS have gone from being communication channels for news related to the club to being the means through which training and preparation sessions were developed, individualized training programs were prepared, sent, and supervised, and a minimum level of activity was maintained in the athletes so that, when the time came, they could return to normality in the best possible conditions. Up to this point, for most of these organizations, many of these utilities were not even remotely part of their plans.

Other adaptations that sports clubs have been forced to address during the hardest times of total lockdown, and even in times when practice has been allowed with significant limitations, have been that of an important organizational and technical adaptation: once sports practice was allowed to resume in the facilities, it was resumed in a progressive and limited way. Initially, the size of the training groups was very small and there have been important limitations in terms of interaction between athletes, with prohibitions on contact and the obligation to maintain a safe social distance. In these circumstances, the organizations have also faced important challenges at a technical sports level, as they have had to adapt their activity to these circumstantial limitations, which in many cases have meant a technical challenge that they have had to solve with initiative and innovation. For example, for a few months, training activities in Spain could only be carried out individually, with social distance, in small groups and without sharing any material, which meant a considerable effort to adapt any team or contact activity to the new circumstances. The appearance of strict prevention protocols has also meant a considerable adaptation effort, given that not only have restrictions been imposed on access to the facilities, but there are also strict obligations regarding registration of attendees, hand hygiene, temperature controls, differentiated entry and exit circulations in the facilities, avoiding crossings and agglomerations, etc.

Last but not least, the restrictions and even prohibition of the public to attend sporting events have meant an important change in the conditions for the development of the activity, not only from a purely social and support point of view, but also in some cases at an economic level, due to the loss of often scarce, but not negligible, income. This absence of the public has also had consequences in terms of difficulties in obtaining sponsorships linked to the social impact of the activity. These latter limitations have been solved in some cases with initiatives such as streaming retransmissions that are totally amateurish, but effective in terms of fulfilling the function of disseminating the club's activity. According to the results of the fourth item, the clubs analyzed stated that the initiatives developed did not jeopardize the sustainability of the organization. Both clubs perceiving a low impact of COVID-19 (M = 1.85; SD = 1.50) and those perceiving a high impact (M = 2.08; SD = 1.61) planned and carried out actions that did not greatly compromise the resources and sustainability of the organization. This traditional and conservative stance can be understood as sports clubs were facing an unpredictable and totally unknown situation. When you carry out an action that commits the organization's resources and there is a possibility of failure, it has been necessary to evaluate the risk–benefit ratio beforehand.

Actions that have a high probability of failure or that imply the commitment of high organizational resources are not wise if the benefit that could be returned is not considerably higher than what it would be if that risk had not been assumed. Therefore, in hostile and highly changing times, it is necessary to analyze the risk–benefit balance in detail. However, the response to the crisis and the speed of this response are vital in times of recession (Kuckertz et al., 2020). In this case, there was not much time to assess the potential impact of the actions as they had to be carried out quickly. This may be one reason for the results obtained. In the fifth item analyzed, which shows whether the innovative initiatives adopted can improve positioning in relation to competitors, significant differences were found (t(148) = 2.09, p < .05, d = .48, r = .23), with sports clubs with HPI obtaining significantly higher values (M = 4.52; SD = 1.66) than clubs with LPI (M = 3.64; SD = 1.99). Previous literature exposes that sports entrepreneurship has ceased to be an option to become a necessity if the organization's goal is to be highly competitive and maintain the sustainability of its organization (Legg & Gough, 2012). It does not seem unreasonable to think that a good number of the initiatives undertaken as a result of the pandemic could remain incorporated into the club's offerings as alternatives or complements to traditional services. However, in an activity such as sports, with an unquestionable requirement for attendance, it does not seem that we will see a substitution of some for others, but rather the incorporation of the new ones as a complementary offer.

In line with the above, and considering the sixth item, which analyzes whether the initiatives will continue to develop after the current situation of lockdown, there are significant differences (t(148) = 2.33, p < .05, d = .43, r = .21), with sports clubs with HPI showing significantly higher results (M = 4.10; SD = 1.73), with respect to clubs with LPI (M = 3.33; SD = 1.88). If entrepreneurial initiatives have the necessary characteristics, they can lead to superior performance in times of crisis (Hammerschmidt et al., 2021). Therefore, sports clubs should see this period as an opportunity to explore and exploit new opportunities and to sustain them over time. Many of the changes that have resulted from COVID-19 have revolutionized the work, social, family, and sports environments. But are they here to stay? New technologies have helped in this time of crisis to increase teleworking and improve family reconciliation (Ayuso et al., 2020). To this has also been added the increase in the consumption of online sports offerings, so that it has been possible to adapt the type of physical activity and the time of day at which it is performed. This has been increased by the situation arising from COVID-19. However, it may be an opportunity to offer it to users and partners in a complementary way to the sports offer provided before the irruption of the virus in society.

According to the seventh item analyzed "Some of the initiatives adopted in this situation have been implemented before other competing organizations", there are significant differences (t(148) = 2.16, p < .05, d = .42, r = .21). Similarly, clubs with HPI (M = 4.65; SD = 1.88) show significantly higher results than sports clubs with LPI (M = 3.85; SD = 1.89). These differences according to the perceived impact of COVID-19 may be due to Reynolds et al. (2001), who state that necessity-driven entrepreneurship is widely developed in times of crisis. In this sense, sports clubs with HPI are more likely to perceive a need and, consequently, to carry out initiatives quickly and ahead of the competition. However, according to previous studies in professional sports, necessity-driven entrepreneurship has a low effectiveness compared to innovation based on opportunity recognition in times of crisis (Hammerschmidt et al., 2021). Organizations during times of crisis carry out proactive responses and, in turn, also develop a reactive attitude, which is just the opposite of proactivity. According to Petzold et al. (2019), proactive initiatives have a positive impact on the final performance of the entity, however, reactive responses do as well. Therefore, finding a balance and knowing how to identify when it is right to be proactive and when it is better to adopt a more entrepreneurial stance is a factor that will mark an added value in the sports club.

On the other hand, there are significant differences in the eighth item analyzed (t(148) = 3.39, p < .01, d = .69, r = .32), which alludes to whether the sports sector was analyzed before carrying out the initiatives developed. Sports clubs with HPI (M = 4.45; SD = 1.99) present significantly higher results than sports clubs with LPI (M = 3.12; SD = 1.99). This fits with the previous item, since before carrying out an action, the context in which it will be developed should be analyzed. However, within similar possibilities, a characteristic that can differentiate one entrepreneur from another is the ability to interpret the situation based on their experiences (Ratten, 2017). In this context, an analysis of the competition, of the organization itself, of the needs of the users, and of the situation in which such an initiative will be developed is of vital importance. If the sports club has extensive knowledge of the above factors in normal times, it may have a better chance of elaborating and developing an effective initiative ahead of the competition in hostile and changing times because it has valuable information.

Finally, all the analyzed sport clubs present low values in the ninth item "Institutions or federations have helped in the elaboration and development of innovative initiatives during this lockdown situation". Both sports clubs with HPI (M = 2.89; SD =1.95) and clubs with LPI (M = 2.48; SD = 1.98) expose the low collaboration of institutions or federations in the development of innovative initiatives. On 14 April 2020, general considerations for sport federations were published in which sport limitations and restrictions were exposed (World Health Organization, 2020a). Hence, the knowledge of all federations or public institutions about the difficult situation sports clubs face is essential.. However, the results obtained in the present study expose that the sports clubs consider that the federations did not collaborate with them to a great extent to respond to this difficult situation.

On the one hand, it seems normal and understandable that a sports club would look to its federation as the superior organization responsible for its activity in such complicated and uncertain circumstances for guidance and support, although in order to make a rigorous judgment of this last circumstance, different factors should be taken into account. Sports federations in Spain constitute a group of sports governing organizations as diverse and heterogeneous as their clubs themselves. Their size, budget, and, consequently, organizational capacity differ significantly from one to another. As a result, the capacity to respond to this unprecedented crisis has also been limited and diverse. It is enough to glance at the number of federated licenses that exist in different disciplines to get an idea of the great differences that exist between their respective federations (Llopis-Goig, 2017).

On the other hand, traditionally the federations exercise an organizing and regulating function of their sport that is embodied in multiple actions, but which have always revolved around a central one, which is the organization of the competition in their discipline. Although other functions are developed, such as the training of coaches, specialization, etc., the existing restrictions seem to have left the federations orphaned of their raison d'être and somewhat misplaced and perhaps missing an excellent opportunity to position themselves as a support and a reference for their sports clubs. In any case, it would be unfair to say all this without recognizing that the exceptionality and singularity of the situation derived from this pandemic has surprised and dislocated not only sports federations, but society as a whole, with all the systems that compose it.

Conclusions and Managerial Perspectives

According to the results obtained, valuable conclusions have been drawn for the sports and organizational sphere. In the first place, sports clubs consider that in the face of this situation of lockdown, it has been necessary to reinvent themselves.

This need has led many of the sports clubs to elaborate and develop initiatives and innovations to gain a competitive advantage over the rest of the competition. In addition, in order to cover part of the most important social and sporting functions of this type of entity, the vast majority of sports clubs have carried out some initiative to approach or contact users (online training, monitoring of the athlete's activity, etc.). However, they generally agree that it has been this hostile situation that has led them to develop initiatives or innovations that in a normal situation would not have been considered.

Virtually all of the sports clubs have carried out initiatives that did not jeopardize the sustainability of the organization. Not compromising the club's resources or reducing the chances of failure were important requirements to be met in the initiatives developed. The sports clubs that perceived a high impact of COVID-19 think that the initiatives carried out could improve their positioning in relation to competitors. This may be because they needed the improvement to a much greater extent than sports clubs that did not perceive such a high impact of COVID-19 on their economic-financial situation. Similarly, sports clubs that perceived a high impact were more likely than clubs that perceived a low impact to continue to develop these initiatives beyond the current lockdown situation. As in the previous questions, sports clubs that perceived a high impact of COVID-19 on their situation have been significantly more proactive in carrying out initiatives earlier than other competing organizations. Prior to undertaking these initiatives, sports clubs that perceived a high impact have conducted an industry analysis more significantly than clubs that did not perceive such an impact. Finally, all sports clubs generally felt that they received little assistance or collaboration in the design and development of innovative initiatives during this lockdown situation from institutions or federations.

The present study has several limitations that should be considered. First, the sample is not very representative, since only 148 sports clubs were analyzed. Similarly, the questions asked have not been previously validated; however, in a practical and experiential way, they can provide new information in a period when it is difficult to access such information. Finally, the quantitative methodology could have been complemented with quantitative methodology through semi-structured interviews that could provide more focused information. As future lines of research, it would be interesting to know the impact of the results obtained on the final performance of the sports clubs. In this case, social performance, sporting performance, and economic performance could be assessed. In addition, an analysis could be carried out in a situation of new normality in which there were no such strict restrictions and limitations. This would allow a comparison of averages that would provide relevant information.

References

Ayuso, L., Requena, F., Jiménez-Rodriguez, O., & Khamis, N. (2020). The effects of COVID-19 confinement on the Spanish family: Adaptation or change? *Journal of Comparative Family Studies, 51*(3–4), 274–287.

Devece, C., Peris-Ortiz, M., & Rueda-Armengot, C. (2016). Entrepreneurship during economic crisis: Success factors and paths to failure. *Journal of Business Research*, 69(11), 5366–5370.

Doherty, A., Millar, P., & Misener, K. (2020). Return to community sport: Leaning on evidence in turbulent times. *Managing Sport and Leisure*, 27(1–2), 7–13.

Donthu, N., & Gustafsson, A. (2020). Effects of COVID-19 on business and research. *Journal of Business Research*, 117(3), 284–289.

Escamilla-Fajardo, P., Alguacil, M., & del Carmen Giménez-Espert, M. (2018). Tipos de organizaciones deportivas en españa. *Kairós. Revista De Ciencias Económicas, Jurídicas y Administrativas*, 1(1), 32–39.

Escamilla-Fajardo, P., Núñez-Pomar, J. M., & Gómez-Tafalla, A. M. (2020). Exploring environmental and entrepreneurial antecedents of social performance in Spanish sports clubs: A symmetric and asymmetric approach. *Sustainability*, 12(10), 4234–4252.

Faulkner, B. (2001). Towards a framework for tourism disaster management. *Tourism Management*, 22(2), 135–147.

Hammerschmidt, J., Durst, S., Kraus, S., & Puumalainen, K. (2021). Professional football clubs and empirical evidence from the COVID-19 crisis: Time for sport entrepreneurship? *Technological Forecasting and Social Change*, 165, 120–136.

Kraus, S., Clauss, T., Breier, M., Gast, J., Zardini, A., & Tiberius, V. (2020). The economics of COVID-19: Initial empirical evidence on how family firms in five European countries cope with the corona crisis. *International Journal of Entrepreneurial Behavior & Research*, 26(5), 1067–1092.

Kuckertz, A., Brändle, L., Gaudig, A., Hinderer, S., Reyes, C. A. M., Prochotta, A., Steinbrink, K., & Berger, E. S. (2020). Startups in times of crisis–A rapid response to the COVID-19 pandemic. *Journal of Business Venturing Insights*, 13(1), 169–183.

Lefèvre, B., Routier, G., & Llopis-Goig, R. (2020). Sports participation in France and Spain: An international comparison of voraciousness for sport. *Poetics*, 81, 101429.

Legg, D., & Gough, V. (2012). Calgary flames: A case study in an entrepreneurial sport franchise. *International Journal of Entrepreneurial Venturing*, 4(1), 32–41.

Llopis-Goig, R. (2017). Spain: Putting the pieces of the sport system in place—the role of the sport federations. In Scheerder, J., Willem, A. and Claes, E. (Eds.), *Sport policy systems and sport federations* (pp. 243–262). Springer.

Maugeri, G., Castrogiovanni, P., Battaglia, G., Pippi, R., D'Agata, V., Palma, A., Di Rosa, M., & Musumeci, G. (2020). The impact of physical activity on psychological health during covid-19 pandemic in Italy. *Heliyon*, 6(6), e04315.

Miao, Q., & Popp, D. (2014). Necessity as the mother of invention: Innovative responses to natural disasters. *Journal of Environmental Economics and Management*, 68(2), 280–295.

Parnell, D., Widdop, P., Bond, A., & Wilson, R. (2020). COVID-19, networks and sport. *Managing Sport and Leisure*, 27(1–2), 1–7.

Petzold, S., Barbat, V., Pons, F., & Zins, M. (2019). Impact of responsive and proactive market orientation on SME performance: The moderating role of economic crisis perception. *Canadian Journal of Administrative Sciences/Revue Canadienne Des Sciences De l'Administration*, 36(4), 459–472.

PricewaterhouseCoopers España (PwC) (2020). Termómetro del ecosistema del deporte en España. Termómetro del ecosistema del deporte en España. https://www.pwc.es/es/entretenimiento-medios/assets/informe-termometro-ecosistema-deporte-espana.pdf

Ratten, V. (2017). Entrepreneurial sport policy. *International Journal of Sport Policy and Politics*, 9(4), 641–648.

Ratten, V. (2020). Coronavirus disease (COVID-19) and sport entrepreneurship. *International Journal of Entrepreneurial Behavior & Research, 26*(6), 1379–1388.

Reynolds, P. D., Bygrave, W., Autio, E., Cox, L. W., & Hay, M. (2001). Global Entrepreneurship Monitor (GEM) 2001 Executive Report. *Kaufman Center for Entrepreneurial Leadership.*

Saebi, T., Lien, L., & Foss, N. J. (2017). What drives business model adaptation? The impact of opportunities, threats and strategic orientation. *Long Range Planning, 50*(5), 567–581.

Santos, S. C., Caetano, A., Spagnoli, P., Costa, S. F., & Neumeyer, X. (2017). Predictors of entrepreneurial activity before and during the European economic crisis. *International Entrepreneurship and Management Journal, 13*(4), 1263–1288.

Slater, S. J., Christiana, R. W., & Gustat, J. (2020). Peer Reviewed: Recommendations for keeping parks and green space accessible for mental and physical health during COVID-19 and other pandemics. *Preventing Chronic Disease, 17*(59), 1–5.

Stanton, R., To, Q. G., Khalesi, S., Williams, S. L., Alley, S. J., Thwaite, T. L., Fenning, A. S., & Vandelanotte, C. (2020). Depression, anxiety and stress during COVID-19: Associations with changes in physical activity, sleep, tobacco and alcohol use in Australian adults. *International Journal of Environmental Research and Public Health, 17*(11), 4065.

World Health Organization (2020a). *Considerations for sports federations/sports event organizers when planning mass gatherings in the context of COVID-19: Interim guidance, 14 April 2020.* World Health Organization.

World Health Organization (2020b). *Mental health and psychosocial considerations during the COVID-19 outbreak, 18 March 2020.* World Health Organization.

Part II

Innovations in Fitness Industry

Chapter 6

Innovation in Training Service for the Sport Management Sector in Ecuador

Rosa López de D'Amico
Universidad Pedagógica Experimental Libertador – Maracay, Venezuela

Luisa Velez
Universidad Sagrado Corazón, Puerto Rico

María Dolores González-Rivera
Universidad de Alcalá – Madrid, Spain

Summar Gómez
Centro de Investigación y Estudios del Deporte – Ecuador

Chapter Contents

Introduction	73
Review of Literature	76
Method	78
Results	79
Trends and Prospects of the Conferences	80
Manifestos from the Statements of the Speakers	82
Conclusion	82
References	83

Introduction

The Republic of Ecuador has an extension of 256,370 km and it is located in the equatorial line in South America, its capital is Quito. It borders with Colombia on the north, Peru on the east and south, and the Pacific Ocean on the west. It is divided in four regions: Coast, Mountain, East, and Galapagos; it is geographically divided in 24 provinces. Due to its geographical location, it is considered as one of the countries with more biodiversity (Programa de Naciones Unidas para el Desarrollo (PNUD), 2019). The globalized impact of sport on the economic, social, and political spheres of many countries is irrefutable. The Olympic charter indicates that sport is a human right (Comité Olímpico Internacional, 2004) and that

DOI: 10.4324/9781003388050-8

everybody should practice it without discrimination. Sport provides a platform for social relations and cultural exchange among nations, besides its important role in the cultivation of values, physical, and mental wellbeing (Carta Europea del Deporte, 1992). This is also a reality that is accepted in Ecuador.

According to UNESCO Statistic Institute (UNESCO, 2020), Ecuador joined this organization in 1947. It is a presidential republic in which the president is elected by simple majority of the popular vote, two rounds if necessary; the president can be re-elected just for one period. The United Nations Development Programme (Programa de Naciones Unidas para el Desarrollo 2019) indicates that Ecuador has a population of 17.1 million and the human development index was 0.758 in 2019, besides life expectancy is 76.6 years old. The public expenditure for education represents 5% of the GDP, school years expected 14.9, internet users 57.3%, and enrolment in secondary education 85.34%. Ecuador has a rich heritage with around 180,000 goods and cultural manifestation, besides ten world heritage sites recognized by UNESCO.

The National Sport Structure is based on the Law of Sport, Physical Education and Recreation (Ley del Deporte, Educación Física y Recreación, 2010) and the General Regulation of the Sport Law, Physical Education and Recreation (Reglamento General a la Ley del Deporte, Educación Física y Recreación, 2011). Both documents are the highest statements for the organization of sport, Physical Education, and recreation at national level. Sport is classified as educational professional, high performance, and adapted/paralympic. Each one of them has its organizational bodies and norms to which they are affiliated (Uyaguari, 2016). The Ministry of Sport was established in 2007 but it was eliminated just 11 years later, in 2018. Since then the highest sport body is the Ecuador Sport Secretary that is under the umbrella of the Ministry of Education. However, there is high expectation that in 2021, the Ministry of Sport will be a reality once again (El Telégrafo, 2021)

The Ecuador National Institute of Statistics and Census (Instituto Nacional de Estadística y Censos Ecuador, 2015) indicates that 37.3% of the population practice some sort of physical activity or sport – in a population older than 15 years old – which represents 39.5% from the urban area and 32.5% of the rural area. In general terms, there is a high level of inactivity and the main illness is provoked by smoking and alcohol consumption. More recently, the Direction for Research and Cooperation in Physical Culture (Dirección de Investigación y Cooperación en Cultura Física, 2018), a dependency from the Ecuador Sport Secretary, indicated that from the population older than 12 years old, a sample (1,257,554 people) that represents 10.1% of the total population (13,466,326) indicated that they do exercise or practice sport in their free time for more than 3.5 hours weekly.

The Ecuador Olympic Committee was created in 1948 and recognized by the International Olympic Committee (IOC) in 1959. The first participation of Ecuador at the Olympic Games was in Paris in 1924, then it was interrupted until 1968; in total, it has participated in 14 Olympic Games and has obtained one gold and one silver medals, both by Jefferson Pérez (men's 20 km walk). Ecuador has just had one participation at the Winter Olympic Games, Pyeongchang 2018. Football is by far the most popular sport and the male team has participated at the FIFA World Cup on three occasions; the women's team has had one participation in the FIFA World Cup. Due to sponsorship rights, Ecuador also enjoys a professional basket league called Direct TV Cup. All sports in Ecuador are practiced and organized by their individual sport bodies. Ecuador participates in all continental Games, such as Bolivarian, South American, and Pan American among others.

Academic studies in the field of Physical Education, Physical Activity and Sport are not widely spread in the country. There are no graduate studies related to Sport Management; only one private university offers an undergraduate program in Sport Management (Universidad de Las Américas, 2020). Ecuador has a need for trained professionals, particularly in the area of human resources in sport management and administration in order to support the effectiveness of the organizations, public, and privates. It is evident at the grass-roots level and high performance that many offices and organizations are run by people who do not have the technical, professional, and humanitarian competences. Sport management specific preparation consists of weak academic training in the managerial aspects (Gómez, 2019). Sport within the university also presents weaknesses and inconsistencies as there is lack of continuous training and limited support and abilities; this affects the expected results in the management of sport (Gómez, 2018).

The Center for Research and Studies of Sport (Centro de Investigación y Estudios del Deporte (CIED), 2021) is a profit organization (a company) founded in Quito on February 2017. Its purpose is to be a recognized sport management organization in Latin America, particularly connected with the administrative, management sciences and public policies related with human resources that provide quality process with social pertinence. The mission of CIED is to offer advisory and consultancy services as well as research and management training in order to promote institutional competence and increase the economic value of the sport enterprise in Latin America. CIED services are offered by professionals with practical experience in sport management, adapt and transform possible scenarios for the benefit of all involved, and understand the changing global context. The CIED mission and vision is supported by its values: (1) strategic sense, (2) responsibility and discipline, (3) entrepreneurship connection, (4) excellence centered, (5) anticipatory projection, and (6) developer Instinct. These values guide the fulfilment of the objectives, strategies, and guidelines that contribute to the development of physical activity and sport in Ecuador in all sectors. CIED is committed to the innovation of products and services particularly in the complex and wide business of sport. The projection the CIED has had in the last 2 years has been visible in various countries in the region and this is precisely what made of it an interesting case to be studied.

The pandemic situation with COVID-19 has brought terrible consequences to the world and together it has widened the existent gaps in all sectors, particularly those related to the economy Jensen (2020) and education (Hallgarten et al., 2020). In the training sectors, many initiatives were pushed to emerge in order to

Review of Literature

Innovation is often used interchangeably with the word *change* (Wright et al., 2006). Innovation has been defined, explained, and studied by several scholars. Kahn (2018) explains innovation as three different things: an outcome, emphasizes what output is sought, including product innovation, process innovation, marketing innovation, business model innovation, supply chain innovation, and organizational innovation; a process, attends to the way in which innovation should be organized so that outcomes can come to fruition including innovation and development; and a mindset, addresses the internalization of innovation by individual members of the organization where innovation is instilled and ingrained along with the creation of a supportive organizational culture that allows innovation to flourish. Tjønndal (2017) proposes five types of innovations: social innovation, technological innovation, commercial innovation, community-based innovation, and organizational innovation. While Rogers (1995) argued that innovation by diffusion has four elements: invention of the innovation, diffusion (or communication) through the social system, an adoption period, and consequences (Rogers & Shoemaker, 1971). Furthermore, and specific to the sport sector, the concept of innovation is at the forefront of every social, management, and educational sector of physical activity and sport, and even more strongly during uncertain times. Efficiency and effectiveness in processes cannot be separated from innovation. Specific to the sport industry, innovation and entrepreneurship are necessary to deal with uncertainties but also integrate new societal advancements (Andersen & Ronglan, 2015).

Physical education has gone through an innovation by diffusion process. Preservice teachers' beliefs about teaching and learning is strongly influenced by their lived experiences of teachers and schools and more influential than the eventual practice of physical educators (Brennan, 2006; Oslin et al., 2001). Pill et al. (2012) sought to provide a site of pedagogical innovation by presenting 'the possible' for sport teaching in secondary physical education, a curriculum and pedagogical model that contrasted traditional Physical Education Teacher Education (PETE). *Sport literacy* has been the term used when referring to pedagogical innovation for sport teaching (Drummond & Pill, 2011; Pill, 2010). Researchers describe literate sport participants as those who understand the culture, ritual, traditions, and participations of a sport, and research sport literacy as the functional use of sport knowledge for active and engaged citizenship (Siedentop, 1994; Siedentop et al., 2011). Innovation in educational practice enhanced Physical Education by shifting from a traditional teaching approach to dialectic where teachers facilitate (Mitchell et al., 2006) and lead students to the discovery of knowledge (Griffin et al., 1997; Oliver et al., 2015).

Innovations in the sport industry cannot be discussed without delving into innovations in Sport Management education (Funk et al., 2016). Common practice in user innovation systems is the involvement of specific lead users into the innovation process frequently described as openness to the realized and unrealized needs of potential and existing customers (Sattler, 2011). Innovation in Sport Management has revolutionized the sport industry. There is a growing interest from innovation management researchers due to the developments in the sports industry and its influence on other industries of the economy (Sivrikaya et al., 2018). Types of innovation in sport include social innovations which can be appreciated through initiatives creating awareness for women and girls in sport, education, and building relationships between communities, among others. Furthermore, the popularization of social media revolutionized consumption, access, information, communication, and just about every major aspect of the industry (Ciletti, 2012; Tjønndal, 2017). Sivrikaya et al. (2018) argue that the most essential mechanism for technology integration in the sports industry is technology innovation mechanisms which maintain motivation for technological and innovative progress. Nevertheless, Hyysalo (2009) comments that innovativeness in the industry development is not limited to technology and technique, but also requires the contribution of user practice, market, environmental, and organizational dimensions, including ecological factors, regulations, and cultural values.

Much the same as in Physical Education, curricular innovations are innovative teaching strategies within sport management education. Questioning is the foundation of a life-long learning mindset. Furthermore, open-ended, thought-provoking, and intellectually engaging questions will empower students to develop higher cognitive-thinking skills. Effective questioning strategies changes the traditional teaching-learning dynamic, changes student perspective, and enhances the capacity to explain, interpret, apply, and transfer their learning in new situations (Lumpkin, n.d.) but also requires the contribution of user practice, market, environmental, and organizational dimensions, including ecological factors, regulations, and cultural values (Hyysalo, 2009). Due to the global nature of sport, scholars understand the need for sport managers to have competencies in international business. This and the competitive factor of the educational environment have brought curricular innovation to the forefront of Sport Management Education. Such is the case of Ohio University, United States and University of Bayreuth, Germany; two long standing sport management programs that innovated their program to enhance international education global internship and job-placement opportunities (Ströbel et al., 2020).

The ongoing COVID-19 pandemic has made sport entities change their current market strategies in order to cope with the new normal. The sport industry has been affected by unprecedented changes in terms of social distancing requiring the use of new broadcast technologies and games played with fans. Thus, innovation and entrepreneurship provide a way to deal with change and allow the sport industry to continue (Radaelli et al., 2018). This is important particularly in the current COVID-19 times in which sport provides a much needed source of entertainment.

The COVID-19 pandemic has forced sport markets to innovate to survive. Sport entities have found no other way but to innovate and change their business strategies and operate within the new normal. Innovation and entrepreneurship provide a way to deal with change, make the necessary adjustments, and continue operating during the current COVID-19 times where business as usual is increasingly challenging yet the consumers need a much-needed source of entertainment (Radaelli et al., 2018). There is a certain element of uncertainty that comes with innovation, due to insufficient information to predict the future. However, this uncertainty must be looked at as an opportunity for new sport products or services to enter the marketplace (McSweeney, 2020). Sport innovation requires a system approach due to the need to get input from multiple stakeholders. Increasingly sport innovation requires the feedback from different entities in order to gain acceptance in the marketplace. Innovation in sport requires the input from multiple stakeholders and feedback from different entities (Ratten, 2021). Furthermore, Ratten and Babiak (2010) assert that sport innovations are shaped by the sharing and dissemination of knowledge from multiple sources. Innovations are generated through the collective sharing of knowledge and practices.

Method

This case study emerged from a series of conferences that took place at the Ibero-American Forum of Sport Management (IFSM) (*Foro Iberoamericano de Gerencia Deportiva*) held in Quito, Ecuador. The purpose of this study is to analyze the innovative academic initiative consisting of a series of five events that took place in 2020 during pandemic times from an emerging organization in a region of the world where initiatives for sport management training are a few. The aim of this section is to analyze the process followed in a series consisting of five events, and understand the outcome and the mindset that resulted from the innovative initiative. The analytical process sought to identify the current trends, perspectives, and challenges of sports management in Latin America in an extraordinary context of a global pandemic, where sport management has plenty to say, transforming and innovating in order to constitute an extensive and efficient tool for sustainable development while integrating political agendas at global, regional, and local levels as well as multilateral organizations and a comprehensive treatment not only from the sport but also from of all areas of intervention. Besides, the identification of speakers in those conferences from various countries of the region, the methodology used to study this case is qualitative in nature with a document review process. The five events were published in five books of proceedings, which were reviewed for the purpose of this study: four books of the *Proceedings of the Ibero-American Forum of Sport Management 2020* (Gómez, 2020a; 2020b; 2020c; 2020d) and the book of the *Proceedings of the Encounter of Students- Latin American Forum of Sport Management* (Gómez, 2021).

The IFSM were four in total and were identified as chapters, so each one represents a chapter. A total of 71 keynote conferences were analyzed (corresponding to all the proceedings published in the five events), among which: 15 conferences correspond to the Book of Proceedings that make up Chapter I of the Forum held from 16 to 18 July 2020 (Gómez, 2020a); 16 conferences of the Proceedings – chapter II (Gómez, 2020b) of the Forum that took place from 20 to 22 August 2020; 14 conferences from chapter III (Gómez, 2020c) celebrated from 25 to 26 September 2020; nine conferences of chapter IV (Gómez, 2020d) held on 30 October 2020; and 17 conferences from the Students Encounter Forum conducted on 10 April 2021 (Gómez, 2021). In addition, the manifestos derived from the statements of the speakers (Manifesto of the Forum of Sport Management) and the manifestos derived from the encounter with students (Student Manifesto of the Latin American Forum of Sport Management) were analyzed. These manifestos were also published in each of the five books. All the conferences were held online, before each forum multiple activities pre-event were conducted, the most successful ones were the 'Instagram live' sessions that were open to anyone following the CIED Instagram.

Results

The total number of speakers who participated in the five events was 72 (54 in the first four forums, and 17 in the Student Forum, with one speaker in each conference except one where there were two speakers). Regarding gender of the speakers, there was a greater number of men than women, with a total of 16 women (22.2%) and 56 men (77.8%). It should be noted that in the fifth Forum where the students participated, the number of women speakers rose considerably with six women compared to 12 men, while in the first four events, there were three women in each, except in the third Forum, where there was only one woman. This confirms the tendency of the underrepresentation of women in sports management that is mentioned in numerous studies. For example, in Spain, the study by Campos-Izquierdo et al. (2016) found a low representation of women in this labor market with a clear dominance of men in sports management (79% men and 21% women), in Latin America, it is also a reality (López de D'Amico et al., 2016) as well as in the global village (Lough & Geurin, 2019).

The speakers came from a wide geographic variety of Ibero-American countries, with a total of 13 countries. In the first four forums, the countries with greater representation of speakers were Argentina and Brazil (with nine speakers from each), followed by Colombia and Venezuela (six speakers from each), Ecuador, Spain, and Mexico (five speakers from each), Chile (four speakers), and from Costa Rica, Guatemala, Portugal, Puerto Rico, and Uruguay, one speaker. Regarding the Encounter of Students Forum, the majority were from Colombia (12), Guatemala had two speakers, and one speaker from Ecuador, Mexico, and Venezuela, respectively. This great variety of nationalities of the speakers promoted the exchange of knowledge, good practices, and innovations from different contexts and realities to achieve a common objective: to create a space for dialog and training to learn about the advances of sports management in Latin America from a theoretical perspective and good practices, to share experiences of the implementation processes, improvements, and new challenges (Gómez, 2020a, 2020b, 2020c, 2020d, 2021), and the final, to know about the tendencies in research from the younger generation.

Likewise, the academic profile of the speakers was varied. In the first four forums, there were 16 Doctors, 12 Masters, seven CEO, and 13 Bachelors. In the case of the Student Encounter Forum, the speakers came from different university and study levels, such as Bachelor of Physical Education (1), Bachelor of Sports (1), Sports Management Program (1), Social Communication (1), Sciences Economics and business (1), Sports Administration Professional Program (1), Members of Research Groups (5), Center for Studies in Sports and Leisure Management policy (2), and Business Administration (2). This allowed a space for dialog and debate of ideas, from different perspectives according to their training, collaborative learning in the area of sports management, and other fields directly related. It is important to note that one of the student speakers was studying with a scholarship abroad, specifically in a program at Seoul National University, Korea.

Job profile of these speakers was diverse, which also contributed to knowledge building from different universities, research centers, companies, institutions, and organizations, allowing both the transmission of theoretical contributions and good practices for the establishment of synergies from public and private entities at all levels. The purpose – to debate toward a more extensive and efficient sport management in the region – was achieved. The speakers were members of universities (15), consultancies and company managers and directors (11), research centers, technological institutes and research foundations (8), business organizations as CEOs (5), programs of specialized studies (3), international and national federations (3), associations (2), sports secretariats (2), sports clubs (2), municipal entities (1) and sports clubs as coaches (1), and sports centers (1).

Trends and Prospects of the Conferences

Due to the great diversity of speaker profiles, nine main lines of research have been identified in the analysis. In the case of the four forums, the predominant research line was Management (31.5%), followed by Governance (13%), Leadership and Communication (11.1%), Sports Events (9.3%), and Education/Training (9.3%). Other lines of research identified were Technology and Innovation (7.4%), Gender Equity (7.4%), Marketing (5.6%), and Research (5.5%). The Management research line has been approached from a broad perspective, with trends such as post-COVID-19 sport management as an opportunity for sports organizations to reinvent themselves, sports management for the development of sustainable sports facilities and social responsibility, sports management and its influence on health and economic growth, the management of sports clubs and teams as an example of good practices, models and new paradigms of sports management for the transformation and improvement of organizations, and challenges of managers and sports directors. Likewise, a comprehensive perspective has been obtained in the

Governance research line, where the speakers did analysis from various perspectives: governance in sports federations, sports legislation, corporate governance and social responsibility in sports, public policies in sports, governance for agile and sustainable systems, and sports alliances between multiple public, private, and civil sectors and their transformation in government agendas.

The Leadership and Communication topic was approached in terms for innovation, such as the leadership of the managerial role for innovation and change, neuro-management as a tool for the sport manager to effectively manage and transmit an assertive communication for building relationships, communicational neurolinguistics, and communicative competence of coaches. The Sports Events topic was focused on sustainability, entrepreneurship, and innovation, such as Gamification in the management of sporting events, sports events based on sustainable management, planning to undertake in the management of sporting events, Olympism, and sustainable development and social innovation.

Regarding the Education/Training topic, it was focused on quality education from different viewpoints, such as the necessary connection between pedagogy and sports management, the significant and sustainable development for sports training and the training of sustainable working relationships. In the case of the Student Forum, the main topics were Management (47%), followed by Marketing (17.6%), Gender Equity (11.8%), Education/Training (11.8%), Governance (5.9%), and Research (5.9%). Concerning the Management Research topic, the most widely addressed with respect to the rest, some of the studies were focused on the perspective of responsibility and sustainability, as well as job performance, sponsorship programs, supply and demand, and emotional salary. These topics were also grouped to be analyzed by the keywords present in each of the abstracts, since there is a great variety. From among 226 words in the four forums, the most repeated (considering from four repeated words) are: Management (36); followed by Sport (22); Organization (7), Sustainability (5), Marketing (4), Leadership (4); and Public Policies (4). Among the 76 keywords of the Forum with the students, the most repeated (considering from four repeated words) were Management (6) and Sport (4).

Likewise, the research topic was in accordance with the Sustainable Development Goals (SDGs) promoted by the United Nations, due to the five events were framed in the SDGs. Some of the conferences were related to different SDGs because of the transversal scope of physical activity and sport; nevertheless, this analysis has been carried out by identifying a main SDG at each conference. The objective that has been most addressed is Decent work and economic growth (n = 31), followed by Quality education (n = 6), Partnerships for the goals (n = 5), Gender equality (n = 4), Sustainable cities and communities (n = 4), Industry, innovation, and infrastructure (n = 2), Good health and well-being (n = 1), and Reduced inequalities (n = 1). Regarding the Student Forum, the SGD most approached has also been Decent work and economic growth (n = 10), followed by Quality education (n = 2), Gender equality (n = 2), Peace, justice, and strong institutions (n = 2), and Sustainable cities and communities (n = 1).

Manifestos from the Statements of the Speakers

In relation to the manifestos of the speakers derived from the statements of the speakers (Manifesto of the Forum of Sport Management), the speakers placed a greater emphasis on promoting the SDGs of the 2030 Agenda from sports management. In this way, they focused on proposals in sports management of social responsibility for economic development, social inclusion, and environmental protection. Another one of the emphasized statements was the necessary support and creation of training programs for updating skills and competences in order to adapt to changes in society. Proposals have also been found regarding the formation of alliances, cooperation, and interdisciplinary work. Other statements that were also emphasized, although with less impact on the manifestos, were those related to the need to create spaces for the exchange of knowledge, experiences, and good practices. Research was also declared as an aspect that should be addressed through the development of more research projects, the promotion of lines of research, and the publication of scientific articles in this field. Likewise, the speakers also expressed the importance of technology and innovation for an improvement in management at all levels. Regarding the manifestos derived from the encounter with students (Student Manifesto of the Latin American Forum of Sport Management), the most emphasized proposals were those related to the need for greater academic training to adapt to the new demands of society. Likewise, the need for research and the strengthening of scientific networks and institutions for the training of sports managers in Latin America was stressed.

Conclusion

Today's increasingly changing competitive environment, social challenges, and growing opportunities force organizations to seek valuable external sources. As in the case of the study presented, much can be achieved through social and formal networks which provide benefits such as efficient use of internal resources and increased competitiveness by exploiting the valuable opportunities obtained from external resources. The data from the case study was examined through a content analysis as the methodological process, and the outcome and mindset revealed intelligences developed from customer/participant input. The innovation process is characterized by various organizational elements and inputs. The major factors of products development process include available knowledge in workforce, external networks, explicit knowledge management, cross-functional coordination, competitor intelligence, reduced cycle time, proficiency in product development process and customer input, and the process and emergence of innovative initiatives. As for Latin America, this research center provided a platform to exchange knowledge and connect people working in the sport management field, not just from academia, but many practitioners, people from diverse generations, and new students in the field. It started to create a network that has even benefited the existent Latin American Sport Management organization (ALGEDE by its acronym in Spanish) that exists in the region. In general, the CIED has provided a benefit

Innovation in Training Service **83**

to the sport management field as it embraced all those who wanted to contribute, in a historical moment of society.

References

Andersen, S., & Ronglan, L. (2015). Historical paths and policy change: Institutional entrepreneurship in Nordic elite sport systems. *International Journal of Sport Policy and Politics, 7*(2), 197–216.

Brennan, P. (2006). From rhetoric to reality: A case study of partnerships for improvement. *The Bulletin of Physical Education, 42*(1), 16–33.

Campos-Izquierdo, A., González-Rivera, M., & Taks, M. (2016). Multifunctionality and occupations of sport and physical activity professionals in Spain. *European Sport Management Quarterly, 16*(1), 106–126

Carta Europea del Deporte. (1992). Declaración política sobre la nueva carta europea del deporte. http://femp.femp.es/files/566-69-archivo/CARTA%20EUROPEA%20DEL%20 DEPORTE.pdf

Centro de Investigación y Estudios del Deporte – CIED. (2021). Filosofía Organizacional.

Ciletti, D. (2012). Sports entrepreneurship: A theoretical approach. In D. Ciletti, & S. Chadwick (Eds.), *Sports entrepreneurship: Theory and practice* (pp. 1–10). WV Fitness Information Technology.

Comité Olímpico Internacional. (2004). Carta olímpica. https://www.um.es/documents/ 933331/0/CartaOlimpica.pdf/8c3b36b2-11a2-4a77-876a-41ae33c4a02b

Dirección de Investigación y Cooperación en Cultura Física. (2018). INEC-ENEMDU, diciembre de los años 2007, 2009, 2013-2017. INEC-MULTIPROPÓSITO. https:// servicios.deporte.gob.ec/incentivoTributarioMinisterio/documentosAnexos/ESTRATE-GIAS%20PARA%20ALINEAR%20PROGRAMAS%20Y%20PROYECTOS.pdf

Drummond, M., & Pill, S. (2011). The role of physical education in promoting sport participation in school and beyond. In S. Georgakis, & K. Russell (Eds.), *Youth sport in Australia: History and culture* (pp. 165–178). Sydney University Press.

El Telégrafo. (2021, May 13). Secretaría del Deporte volverá a ser ministerio en el gobierno de Guillermo Lasso. https://www.eltelegrafo.com.ec/noticias/actualidad/44/ secretaria-del-deporte-volvera-a-ser-ministerio-en-el-gobierno-de-guillermo-lasso

Funk, D., Lock, D., Karg, A., & Pritchard, M. (2016). Sport consumer behavior research: Improving our game. *Journal of Sport Management, 30*(30), 113–116.

Gómez, S. (2018). Cultura gerencial del deporte en Ecuador: Una mirada desde los actores sociales. *Podium, 34*(34), 24–38.

Gómez, S. (2019). Deporte universitario y cultura gerencial en Ecuador. *EmásF, 10*(57), 35–56.

Gómez, S. (2020a). *Memorias foro iberoamericano de gerencia del deporte.* Centro de Investigación y Estudios del Deporte-CIED.

Gómez, S. (2020b). *Memorias foro iberoamericano de gerencia del deporte. Capítulo IV.* Centro de Investigación y Estudios del Deporte-CIED.

Gómez, S. (2020c). *Memorias foro iberoamericano de gerencia del deporte. Capítulo III.* Centro de Investigación y Estudios del Deporte-CIED.

Gómez, S. (2020d). *Memorias foro iberoamericano de gerencia del deporte. Capítulo II.* Centro de Investigación y Estudios del Deporte-CIED.

Gómez, S. (2021). *Memorias encuentro de estudiantes-foro latinoamericano de gerencia del deporte.* Centro de Investigación y Estudios del Deporte-CIED.

Griffin, L., Mitchell, S., & Oslin, J. (1997). *Teaching sport concepts and skills: A tactical games approach*. Human Kinetics.

Hallgarten, J., Gorgen, K., & Sims, K. (2020, May). *Report Overview of emerging country-level response to providing educational continuity under COVID-19*. https://edtechhub.org/wp-content/uploads/2020/05/supporting-education-conflict.pdf

Hyysalo, S. (2009). User innovation and everyday practices: Micro-innovation in sports industry development. *R&D Management, 39*(3), 247–258.

Instituto Nacional de Estadística y Censos Ecuador. (2015). Compendio de resultados encuesta condiciones de vida ECV sexta ronda. https://www.ecuadorencifras.gob.ec//documentos/web-inec/ECV/ECV_2015/

Jensen , L. (Ed.). (2020). *Informe de los objetivos de desarrollo sostenible 2020*. Naciones Unidas.

Kahn, K. (2018). Understanding innovation. *Business Horizons, 61*(3), 453–460.

Ley del Deporte, Educación Física y Recreación. (2010). Registro Oficial Suplemento 255 de 11-ago-2010. https://www.deporte.gob.ec/wp-content/uploads/downloads/2015/03/Ley-del-Deporte.pdf

López de D'Amico, R., Benn, T., & Pfister, G. (2016). *Women and sport in Latin America*. Routledge.

Lough, N., & Geurin, A. (Eds.) (2019). *The Routledge handbook of the business of women's sport*. Routledge.

Lumpkin, A. (n.d). Effective questioning strategies for the sport management classroom, sport management classroom. *Sport Management Education Journal, 13*(1), 23–25. http://journals.humankinetics.com/view/journals/smej/13/1/article-p23.xml

McSweeney, M. J. (2020). Returning the 'social' to social entrepreneurship: Future possibilities of critically exploring sport for development and peace and social entrepreneurship. International *Review for the Sociology of Sport, 55*(1), 3–21.

Mitchell, S., Griffin, L., & Oslin, J. (2006). *Teaching sport concepts and skills: A tactical games approach*. Human Kinetics.

Oliver, K. L., Oesterreich, H. A., Aranda, R., Archeleta, J., Blazer, C., de la Cruz, K., Martinez, D., McConnell, J., Osta, M., Parks, L., & Robinson, R. (2015). The sweetness of struggle': Innovation in physical education teacher education through *student-centered inquiry as curriculum* in a physical education method course. *Physical Education and Sport Pedagogy, 20*(1), 97–115. doi: 10.1080/17408989.2013.803527.

Oslin, J., Collier, C., & Mitchell, S. (2001). Living the curriculum. *Journal of Physical Education, Recreation and Dance, 72*(5), 47–51.

Pill, S. (2010). Sport literacy - It's not just about learning to play sport via 'textbook techniques'. *Journal of Student Wellbeing, 4*(2), 32–42.

Pill, S., Penney, D., & Swabey, K. (2012). Rethinking sport teaching in physical education: A case study of research based innovation in teacher education. *Australian Journal of Teacher Education, 37*(8), 117–138.

Programa de Naciones Unidas para el Desarrollo. (2019). Más información-Ecuador, datos y cifras. https://en.unesco.org/system/files/countries/ecu_facts_figures.pdf

Radaelli, G., Dell'Era, C., Frattini, F., & Petruzzelli, A. (2018). Entrepreneurship and human capital in professional sport: A longitudinal analysis of the Italian soccer league. *Entrepreneurship Theory and Practice, 42*(1), 70–93.

Ratten, V. (2021). Introduction: Innovation and entrepreneurship in sport management. In V. Ratten (Ed.). *Innovation and entrepreneurship in sport management* (pp. 1–8). doi: 10.4337/9781783473960.00008.

Ratten, V., & Babiak, K. (2010). The role of social responsibility, philanthropy and entrepreneurship in the sport industry. *Journal of Management and Organization, 16*(4), 482–487.

Reglamento General a la Ley del Deporte, Educación Física y Recreación. (2011). Registro Oficial Suplemento 418 de 01-abr.-2011. https://www.gob.ec/sites/default/files/regulations/2018-10/Reglamento%20a%20la%20Ley%20del%20Deporte.pdf

Rogers, E. (1995). *Diffusion of innovations*. Free Press.

Rogers, E., & Shoemaker, F. (1971). *Communication of innovations*. Macmillan.

Sattler, M. (2011). *Excellence in innovation management*. Gabler Verlag.

Siedentop, D. (1994). *Sport education: Quality PE through positive sport experiences*. Human Kinetics.

Siedentop, D., Hastie, P., & van der Mars, H. (2011). *Complete guide to sport education*, (2nd ed). Human Kinetics.

Sivrikaya, K., Demir, A., & Fisek, T. (2018). Innovation in sports management and the role of users, open innovation and sport-based entrepreneurship. *Journal of Research in Business and Management, 6*(17), 9–14.

Ströbel, T., Ridpath, B. D., Woratschek, H., O'Reilly, N., Buser, M., & Pfahl, M. (2020). Co-branding through an international double degree program: A single case study in sport management education. *Sport Management Education Journal, 14*(2), 119–128.

Tjønndal, A. (2017). Sport innovation: Developing a typology. *European Journal for Sport and Society, 14*(4), 291–310. doi: 10.1080/16138171.2017.1421504.

UNESCO. (2020). Más información- Ecuador, datos y cifras. https://unesdoc.unesco.org/search/db3536ec-1b07-441d-9c82-48a98cd7f81d

Universidad de Las Américas. (2020). Gestión deportiva. https://www.udla.edu.ec/carreras/programas-academicos/pregrados/facultad-de-ciencias-economicas-y-administrativas/ingenieria-de-negocios-y-marketing-deportivo/

Uyaguari, K. (2016). La estructura del sistema deportivo nacional. *Revista Ecuatoriana De Investigación En Deporte y Actividad Física - REINDAF, 1*(1), 9–14. http://biblioteca.unae.edu.ec/cgi-bin/koha/opac-detail.pl?biblionumber=59967

Wright, S., McNeill, M., Fry, J., Tan, W., Tan, K., & Schempp, P. (2006). Implications of student teachers' implementation of a curricular innovation. *Journal of Teaching in Physical Education, 25*(3), 310–328.

Chapter 7

Healthy Universities

The Case of Nebrija University and Its Program of Physical Activity and Sport

David de la Fuente Franco
Universidad Antonio de Nebrija, Spain

Jerónimo García-Fernández
University of Seville, Spain

Ramón Gómez-Chacon
CEU Cardenal Spínola CEU, Spain

Chapter Contents

Introduction	86
Program Analysis	88
Practical Implications	100
References	102
Appendix I	103

Introduction

The work environment takes on special relevance in our society as it is the playing field where individuals develop on a personal level and as part of the collective in which they live, establishing conditions that directly affect their overall health: physical, emotional, and social (Gómez-Chacón and Fernández-Martínez, 2020). Thus, healthy organizations emerge in this line of action and creation of initiatives that seek to improve or maintain the health of workers in the workplace (Salanova et al., 2012; Salanova et al., 2019). On the other hand, the practice of physical activity and sports in the work environment is understood as that practice through which the employer directly or indirectly favors and facilitates employees being able to carry it out in their workplace (Consejo Superior de Deportes, 2009).

The implementation of physical activity and sport programs focused on improving and caring for the health of workers is considered positive and favorable to the work environment. This causes companies and organizations to change the concept of the workplace for that of a space that favors the promotion and

DOI: 10.4324/9781003388050-9

encouragement of physical activity and sport focused on improving its employees' health and productivity based on the physical and psychological benefits that this practice brings (Gil-Beltrán et al., 2020; Gómez-Chacón and Fernández-Martínez, 2020; Madden et al., 2020). This promotion and encouragement of physical activity in the work environment is aligned with the new guidelines of the World Health Organization (WHO) on physical activity and sedentary habits (World Health Organization [WHO], 2020) which, for the age group associated with working life (18–64 years), recommends accumulating a minimum of 150–300 minutes of moderate-intensity aerobic physical activity, or a minimum of 75–150 minutes of vigorous-intensity aerobic physical activity, or an equivalent combination of moderate- and vigorous-intensity activities over the course of the week, in order to achieve significant health benefits (WHO, 2020).

Networking is essential in this globalized world in which we live. The Bangkok Charter for Health Promotion (World Health Organization [WHO], 2005) sets out the major challenges, actions, and commitments needed to address the determinants of health and calls for the involvement of the many actors and stakeholders that are critical to achieving health for all. In addition, the WHO (2013) presented a healthy business model where it stressed that the health, safety, and welfare of workers are a fundamental part of the business system, for the workers themselves and their families, and also for the productivity, competitiveness, and sustainability of companies and, therefore, for the economies of countries and the world. In order to face these challenges, the help of the university is essential and, even more so, if it acquires the commitment to promote the principles, values, and proposals for health promotion in and by the university that are set out in the Edmonton Charter (WHO, 2005).

The Spanish Network of Healthy Universities (REUS) (2017) emphasizes that in this context of a new social and business model and of priorities regarding workers' health, universities have taken a step forward to be active agents of it from their strategic position in society, having a clear role in the training and education of citizens. Universities make up one of the environments of the social context where people develop daily activities and where environmental, organizational, and personal factors that affect the health and well-being of those who live, work, and learn in it interact (REUS, 2017). These are brought together, on the one hand, by being a workplace, on the other hand, by being an educational center, as well as being an institution that researches and guarantees the advancement of our society through education (REUS, 2017). In this sense, the implementation of healthy programs of physical activity and sport in the work environment (the University is also a work center) should be based on a correct and contrasted previous contextualization and, inevitably, adapted to the reality of each company or organization so that its viability can be maintained over time, an indispensable condition to measure its impact on the university community.

Nebrija University (Madrid, Spain) has launched this program – the Healthy Program for Physical Activity and Sport in the Work Environment – aimed exclusively at its workers. It also belongs to REMUS (Madrid Network of Healthy

Universities), created by the Ministry of Health and all the universities in the Community of Madrid in 2009, and whose main objective is to generate healthy university environments, including the physical and working environment. This program is led by the University Sports Service, in collaboration with other departments that should be part of the project for its proper and useful implementation and aims to offer a Healthy Plan for Physical Activity and Sport to all the institution's TRS (Teaching and Research Staff) and SAS (Services and Administration Staff). In addition, the value that Nebrija University wants to project with this new program is that of a healthy alternative from which they will benefit: the workers themselves, who will be able to do physical activity and sport in the work environment, and the organization itself, which seeks with the implementation of this program to see reflected an increase in productivity rates, a reduction in sick leave due to musculoskeletal and psychological disorders associated with a sedentary life and/or stress, as well as an improvement in the work climate.

Program Analysis

After the previous analysis of the different aspects of the environment of Nebrija University and its study through diagnosis with dynamic Strengths, Weaknesses, Opportunities and Threats (SWOT) methodology, Figure 7.1 describes the main issues associated with the implementation of the program, as well as for the achievement of the objectives set by the institution, its economic viability, and development logistics. The implementation aims to make Nebrija University a

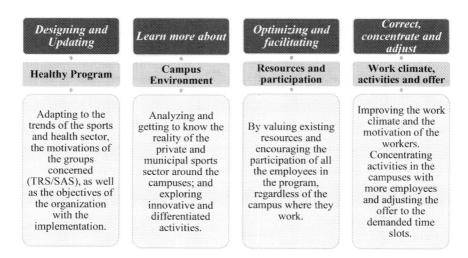

Figure 7.1 Main Aspects of Program Monitoring Based on the Institution's Analysis. Note: Main Conclusions of the Institution's Diagnosis by Using the Dynamic SWOT methodology.

healthy university committed to the development of its workers and, to this end, it establishes the following main objectives:

1 To facilitate and increase the practice of regular physical activity among workers in the university environment.
2 To improve the welfare and quality of life of these workers.
3 Likewise, in the short term, the following specific objectives are defined:
   a To improve the work climate.
   b To reduce the amount of sick leave.
   c To reduce absenteeism.

With the implementation of this Healthy Program of Physical Activity and Sport in the working environment for TRS/SAS, the image that is intended to project from the University Management is that of a company committed to and responsible for the health of its employees and therefore with our society. Therefore, the main beneficiaries of the program will be the workers, who will improve their working conditions and environment as well as their quality of life with an improvement in their health. The company, which will see reflected with the implementation of this program an increase in productivity rates, a reduction in sick leave due to musculoskeletal and psychological disorders associated with a sedentary life, and an improvement in the working environment, as well as the image it projects to society of being a responsible company. The families of the workers, who will also benefit from the improved conditions in which they work. The society and the environment in which the University develops its activity (Figure 7.2).

For the implementation of the program, an initial marketing plan is designed in order to articulate a promotional strategy to inform, persuade, and convince that a healthy program of physical activity and sport will be implemented in the work environment of the Nebrija University aimed at the workers of the organization. The slogan and claim used will make the job much easier. It is the first message that potential users receive and it is important for it to be easy to retain and to associate with the organization's values, mission, and vision. In this case, directly related to these three elements will be sought for the following:

- **UNIVERSITY.** Bearing in mind that the values of excellence and responsibility to society and the formation of the citizens of a country or state are directly related to educational institutions, and more so at the level of Higher Education, such as a University.
- **HEALTHY**. Associated concept, to a new way of understanding life from an approach of contrasted knowledge of what is beneficial or not for the individual, the society in which he/she lives and his/her environment.
- **ACTIVE LIFE**. Associated with health. Through physical activity and sport. A concept of *active life* that tries to arouse the interest of the University's teaching staff and administration and services personnel.

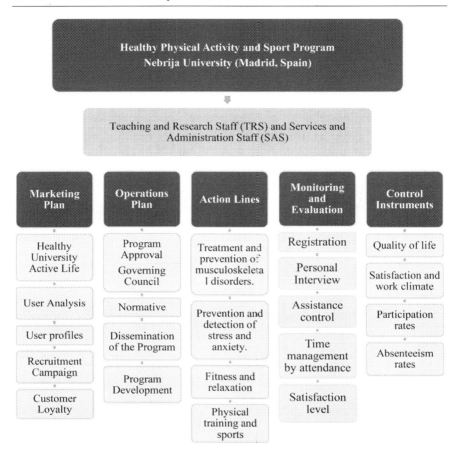

Figure 7.2 Healthy Physical Activity and Sports Program at Nebrija University.

Relating these three elements (University, Healthy, and Active Life), the proposals for the slogan and the claim of the campaign can be found in Figures 7.3 and 7.4.

In the phase of the identification of the user (TRS/SAS of the Nebrija University), understanding and analyzing their profiles, as well as the interactions between the organization and their interests, a previous participation questionnaire is handed out to the employees, in collaboration with the Human Resources (HR) Department. With this, relevant data can be extracted about the profile of the typical user (majority), as well as being able to establish a correct segmentation of the different profiles and adapt the program to the results of this questionnaire. According to Kotler (1991), it is very useful for the management of sports centers and services to be able to group their users into a limited number of types or characteristic groups in order to respond correctly to a growing competitive market,

Figure 7.3 Slogan Proposal for Marketing Campaign Healthy Program.

and also with the direct intention of adapting supply to demand (Nuviala et al., 2014). User segmentation consists of identifying similar behaviors among people in a given market, trying to form a group or groups with similar characteristics and needs, as well as their behavior (Elasri-Ejjaberi et al. 2021), with the main objective of dividing consumers into homogeneous groups using different criteria or variables. The result of this process is the possibility of applying a differentiated commercial strategy to each group in order to satisfy their needs more effectively and to achieve the proposed objectives of the company or sports organization in a more direct and efficient way (Santesmases, 2001). In order to establish this user segmentation for the Nebrija University, with the previous participation questionnaire will define the standard profile that the organization has, as well as the different most representative segments, providing an image with this information:

- Knowledge of TRS/SAS about healthy programs.
- Sports practice habits.
- Interest in participating in such a program.
- Campus where they work.
- Gender and age group.
- Time slot in which they would like to participate in this program.
- Type of activities they are interested in.
- Objectives they have when joining the Program.
- Interest in Physiotherapy Service.
- Suggestions or comments.

#FitwithNebrija, ¡Take care of yourself and get going!
Healthy Physical Activity Program in the workplace for TRS/SAS

Figure 7.4 The Claim's Proposal for a Marketing Campaign for the Healthy Program.

After linking the information gathered, both from the Department of HR (Volume of employees by gender and category – TRS/SAS – as well as by age ranges) and the result of the questionnaire on the intention to participate in the Healthy Activity and Sport Program, it is concluded that there are three large groups (profiles) of users at the Nebrija University in relation to the practice of sport in the work environment (Table 7.1).

With all this data, the final design of the Healthy Physical Activity and Sport Program is adapted to the interests, peculiarities, and characteristics of the potential users. In view of the clear segmentation into three well-defined and differentiated groups, and in order to respond to those interests of the employees and in line with the objectives of the company, as well as the available resources, four lines of action with specific objectives are established:

- Treatment and prevention of musculoskeletal disorders.
- Prevention/detection of stress/anxiety, meditation.
- Fitness, relaxation.
- Competition/physical conditioning.

After identifying the potential users in the previous phase of analysis, we move on to the phase of attracting users. This phase should begin with the presentation and approval of the healthy program by the University's Governing and Management Council, in order to provide it with value at the institutional level and with the necessary support in the eyes of the organization's workers and middle management to promote the TRS/SAS's participation in it. Once approved, the promotion and recruitment campaign begins by using the techniques and tools detailed below, also involving the Area Directors and Deans, as well as establishing a flexible and open registration and trial period (Table 7.2).

Table 7.1 Profiles of Possible Users of the Nebrija University Healthy Program

Segment	Majority profile (Group I)	Second profile (Group II)	Third profile (Group III)
Sex	Woman	Man	Woman
Age	31–40 years	31–40 years	31–40 years
TRS/SAS	TRS	TRS	SAS
Sports habits	Fitness	Competition	Health
Campus (workplace)	Madrid – princess	Madrid – princess	La berzosa
Time zone (sports activity)	2 PM – 4PM	2PM – 4PM	2PM – 4PM
Type of activity	Pilates, yoga, and back	Paddle, running, soccer, basketball ...	Yoga, relaxation, and physiotherapy
Objective	Exercise	Sporting	Improve health
Other interests	Conciliation	Eliminate stress	Eliminate stress

Healthy Universities 93

Table 7.2 Promotion and Recruitment Campaign for the Healthy Program

Action	Techniques
Human Resources Welcome Manual	Within the Welcome Manual that is given to the workers who join the University, a section explaining the Program
University Intranet	A space with the details of the program, including schedules, objectives, benefits, etc.,
Web Sports Service	A section for "Healthy Program in the Workplace" will be included in the Sports Service's web space
Flyers and traditional signs in the cafeterias and dining rooms	Distribution and installation of static advertising by means of flyers and posters of the program
Promotional actions in transit areas	Actions to make visible and promote/inform about the program through "Healthy Breaks" in transit areas
Promotional activities among the University's Faculties	Offering the *Healthy Pause Service* if someone plans to organize a seminar, conference, congress, long meeting, etc.,
Training Courses	About healthy physical activity, postural habits, and risk prevention in relation to bad habits

In order to gain customer loyalty, the customer must first be a user and have gone through a customer acquisition process. Thus, we can differentiate between the loyalty of those who are already customers and, on the other hand, the constant search for new subscribers to attract them and subsequently turn them into loyal users (García-Fernández et al., 2017) through determining elements such as the perceived value of the service and customer satisfaction (Baena-Arroyo et al., 2016). In this third phase of loyalty and retention of users (TRS/SAS) of the healthy program, a database will be generated in which all interactions, queries, suggestions, cancellations, and so forth, that reach the promotion and dissemination points of the program will be recorded, either in person, online, or in specific actions that have been implemented. These records must be analyzed by segments to extract patterns or relationships that allow us to identify new user profiles to anticipate the users' interest. Likewise, once the users are registered in the program, a satisfaction questionnaire will be passed periodically to facilitate correct decisions in the process of the program's correction or continuity. So, the final objective of this phase is to make the user feel part of the program and want to continue in it, apart from other alternatives outside the University, as well as having high and positive future intentions to recommend the service and use it again when he/she has the chance to do so (Elasri-Ejjaberi et al., 2021). In this sense, and to monitor and control the level of satisfaction of users, and their intention to recommend to other potential users, an EPOD2 validated sports services assessment questionnaire (Nuviala et al., 2013) of 25 questions and adapting the statements of the sports services sector to the university environment of the healthy program implemented will be handed out. For example, in the statements of block 1 or block 5, the term "sports center" or "facility" is replaced by "Healthy Program".

This Evaluation and Satisfaction Questionnaire of the Healthy Program of Physical Activity and Sport in the Work Environment (Nebrija University) – EPOD2 – will consist of eight blocks of questions (Appendix I) and will generate a data report with all the answers that will allow extracting the level of satisfaction and evaluation of the users and, above all, their intention of recommendation to other possible users, facilitating the correct decision-making in the process of correction or continuity of the healthy program. The dimensions to be measured will be: the activity itself (five items), the sports equipment (three items), the materials (three items), the staff (four items), the communication (two items), the general satisfaction (one item), and the relationship between the organization and the activity itself (four items). Using a Likert scale from 1 to 5, where 1 – Strongly disagree, 2 – Disagree, 3 – Agree, 4 – Quite agree, and 5 – Strongly agree.

In order to implement the program, different actions, techniques, and tools will be implemented for each of the phases of dissemination, development, and monitoring of the program. Prior to the start of the dissemination and development of the program, the necessary steps must be taken to provide it with institutional support, security for the employee, and in line with the organization's conciliation policies, in addition to making it attractive for the worker to join the program.

- Approval of the program by the Governing Council of the University. To provide the project with greater value at the institutional level and the necessary support for the organization's workers to promote the TRS/SAS's participation.
- Program participation regulations. To encourage the TRS/SAS's participation in the program, the University, through the Department of HR, will establish the procedure and regulations that will govern this participation.

For the actions, techniques, and tools to disseminate the program, this section describes the elements used for the implementation of the program at the level of its dissemination and communication, as well as for the recruitment of users (Table 7.3). This section differentiates the general actions that will be carried out for the program's development (Table 7.4) and the specific actions that will be implemented in each of the program's four lines of work.

For specific actions for the development of the program, this section details the specific actions to be implemented in each of the four lines or blocks of work that make up the program (Figure 7.5).

- Block 1: treatment and prevention of musculoskeletal disorders.
  - Healthy Pauses
    - Objectives: to improve body mobility, self-care, use of free time, personal relationships, work environment, mood, stress, occupational diseases, and musculoskeletal disorders.
    - Description: 15 minutes of active rest, 2 days a week.

Healthy Universities 95

Table 7.3 Actions, Techniques, and Tools for Dissemination of the Program

Action	Technique	Tool(s)
Dissemination of the program to the newly incorporated TRS/SAS	HR Welcome Manual. Including a section explaining the healthy program for TRS/SAS and its regulations	Digital support (PDF) on the University's intranet and sent by email to workers who join the organization
Diffusion of the program among all the TRS/SAS	Official communiqué signed by the Rector promoting the program and a link to information about it	Sending of institutional emails with the Communiqué to all workers
Dissemination and practical information of the program to the entire TRS/SAS	Create a space with all the details of the program and its regulations, in the section "Benefits to employees" of the Intranet	Specific space in the University Intranet: "Healthy Program in the Work Environment"
Diffusion of the program at an external level, to transmit the image of a responsible company to its workers	Create a section for "Healthy Program in the Workplace" within the Sports Service website	Nebrija University website
Dissemination of the program throughout the University Campus	Flyers and traditional posters with program information	Distribution and installation of static advertising
Dissemination and promotion of the program among the Faculties of the University	Offering the Healthy Pause Service	Healthy breaks in the rest time for the participants
Dissemination and promotion of the Program among all University workers	Training courses on healthy physical activity, postural habits, risk prevention in relation to bad habits associated with sedentarism and smoking	Workshops about the importance and benefits of practicing physical activity in a healthy way
Dissemination and promotion of the program on social networks	Publications in the official profiles of the University in the main networks: Twitter, Facebook, Instagram ...	Share promotional videos and motivational images, as well as practical information

Table 7.4 Actions, Techniques, and General Tools for the Development of the Program

Action	Technique	Tool(s)
Updated Program information for registered users	Program-specific application for mobile devices (iOS and ANDROID) – "Nebrija Saludable"	Development of a mobile application that can only be accessed by workers enrolled in the program
Updated Program information for registered users	Specific section for the Healthy Program on the Sports Service website	Create a section in that web space with the basics in relation to schedules and facilities
Updated program information for registered users	Specific section for the University's Healthy INTRANET Program	Specific section for the University's Healthy INTRANET Program
Training courses on healthy habits for users of the program	Classroom courses and courses through streaming platforms	Schedule one course per month on healthy habits
To make visible on the screens outside the classrooms, the specific activity of the Healthy Program that is taught in each one of them	Inclusion in the digital calendar of classroom schedules of the University	Add the activities of the Healthy Program
Promotion of "engagement" among program users	With the sportswear brand, KAPPA, garments of this brand will be used for the users of the Healthy Program	All the users of the Program will have a technical T-shirt

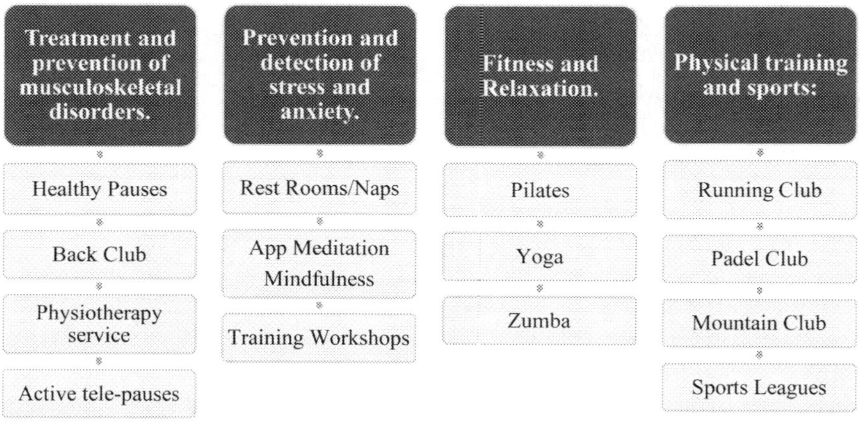

Figure 7.5 Lines of Action of the Healthy Program.

Healthy Universities 97

- Back Club
  - Objectives: to correct bad habits and acquire good ones in terms of postural control of the back's skeletal muscle group.
  - Description: postural education classes, 2 days a week.
- Physiotherapy service.
  - Express sessions (30') of physiotherapy.
- Active Tele-Pauses - Intranet videos.
  - Tutorial videos with activation, stretching, and relaxation exercises.
- Block 2: Prevention and detection of stress and anxiety.
  - Rest Rooms/Naps.
    - Objectives: generation of spaces of rest and disconnection to facilitate the relaxation of the mind and the body.
    - Description: rooms with *ad hoc* resources for rest. Music and relaxing light, resources to be able to lie down or to be comfortable.
  - App Meditation/Mindfulness
    - Offer to all users of the Healthy Nebrija Program the subscription to the "Feel" App (Creating Health, 2020).
    - Goal: improve well-being by learning to accept life situations, be flexible in the face of change, share the pain of others, be confident, improve relationships, find purpose, gain accuracy, and be kind.
  - Training Workshops.
    - Objective: focused on the detection and prevention of stress.
    - Description: classroom and tele-presence courses to raise awareness about the importance of practicing healthy physical activity.
- Block 3: Fitness and relaxation
  - Pilates, Zumba and Yoga classes
    - Objective: to respond to the demand of Group I, majority profile of users, who want to practice fitness and relaxation activities.
    - Description: classes led by a qualified professional, 2 days a week.
- Block 4: Physical training and sports competition.
  - Running, paddle, and mountain clubs and sports leagues
    - Objective: to respond to the demand of Groups I, II, and III of the majority user profiles, in terms of interest in exercising, competing, and improving health.

98 D. de la Fuente Franco, J. García-Fernández and R. Gómez-Chacon

- Description: guided training for runners, competitions between paddle, soccer, and basketball workers, and excursions to the mountains for guided group tours.

For techniques, actions, and tools for monitoring and evaluation, in this section, we detail, in a differentiated way, on the one hand, the actions for the follow-up and control with respect to the compliance by the workers of the participation rules of the healthy program in the work environment and, on the other hand, the correct follow-up and control of the activities and actions that comprise the plan (Tables 7.5. and 7.6). In order to follow up the participation for the subsequent hourly compensation, as well as for the analysis of the development itself and possible adjustment of the program according to this data, a rigorous control of attendance in the different activities of the four blocks that make up the program will be carried out.

For actions associated with the level of satisfaction, in order for the program to be alive, get feedback from users, and for correct decisions to be made in the process of correcting, adapting, and continuing the program, it is essential to measure the overall level of satisfaction of the TRS/SAS participating in it. For this purpose, two well-differentiated actions will be carried out (Table 7.7). All the actions detailed in this section, whether on compliance and monitoring of the rules of participation in the program, or on the level of user satisfaction, must be aimed at a constant review and adaptation of the program according to the data that

Table 7.5 Actions, Techniques, and Tools for the Registration and Monitoring of the Program

Action	Technique	Tool(s)
PROGRAM REGISTRATION	Registration of workers	Telematic platform to access the program for the TRS/SAS through the University intranet
PERSONAL INTERVIEW	Interview with the worker	Personal interviews with a technician from the occupational risk prevention area and a technician from the sports service
SPORTS SERVICE ASSISTANCE CONTROL	Fortnightly attendance record of participants in each activity	Attendance sheets with name, signature, and ID of the workers. Every 15 days
HUMAN RESOURCES ATTENDANCE CONTROL	Monthly attendance record of participants in each activity	Monthly participation report

Healthy Universities 99

Table 7.6 Actions, Techniques, and Tools for Hourly Compensation

Action	Technique	Tool(s)
HOURLY COMPENSATION – SUITABLE	Communication to the worker of the achievement of the objective of participation in the program	Once the four-month period is over, HR will communicate by email the achievement of the objective to the people who have achieved it, based on the participation reports
HOURLY COMPENSATION TRS/SAS	Extension of 1 day (8 hours) in the "Paid Permits" bag to the TRS/SAS who has been eligible in the achievement of the program participation objective	On the University's TRS/SAS platform, which can be accessed through the intranet with a username and password, HR will add 1 day to the pool of days off available to the worker

Note: the follow-up will be done by four-month periods: from September to January and from February to June, following the start and end dates of the four-month periods of the sports activities people are registered for.

these actions will generate. The evaluation, adaptation, and possible correction of the program should be done periodically after the end of each quarter of activity (January and June).

For evaluation/monitoring instruments for the Program's objectives, an initial implementation of the program is proposed for a period of three academic years, although it is essential and necessary to establish a control and make an annual evaluation in relation to the program's main and specific objectives. For this purpose,

Table 7.7 Actions, Techniques, and Tools for Measuring Satisfaction of the TRS/SAS

Action	Technique	Tool(s)
GENERAL SATISFACTION QUESTIONNAIRE	Compilation of user satisfaction levels on the main aspects of the program	EPOD2 validated sports services assessment questionnaire (Nuviala et al., 2013) Sending the link by email to each user at the end of each quarter
NPS SATISFACTION LEVEL (Reichheld, 2006)	Single question: From zero to ten, what is your level of satisfaction with the Healthy Program?	Through the App "Nebrija Saludable". Monthly notification on the employee's mobile device to be completed with a single value (0 to 10)

in coordination with the HR Department, the following instruments will be used for the following:

1 Quality of Life. The SF36 Health Questionnaire, developed by the Health Institute, New England Medical Center, Boston, Massachusetts, adapted to the Spanish environment, will be used (Alonso et al., 1998).
2 Job satisfaction. Through the Work Satisfaction Questionnaire S10/12, developed by Meliá and Peiró (1989), composed of 12 items.
3 Intention of abandonment and work environment. Using the scale developed by Alcover et al. (2007), composed of five items.
4 Calculation of percentage of TRS/SAS participating in the Healthy Program between course 1 and course 2 of implementation. And so on every year.
5 HR report with data on sick leave and absenteeism from previous years and from years with the implemented Healthy Program.

In addition, as a future line of research and in parallel to the use of these instruments to monitor the program's main objectives, a more comprehensive model of a healthy university can be carried out that includes students, using new tools to measure their psychosocial health (Gómez-Chacón et al., 2021).

Practical Implications

The implementation of physical activity and sports programs in the work environment can be a transforming and transversal element for any university institution; an instrument that permeates the entire educational community and is appreciated in a positive way both internally and in the image that the institution projects to society: a healthy university. These programs will generate a double improvement impact: on the employees themselves, improving their well-being and quality of life, and on the organization itself, generating different benefits that can be measured in the medium and long term. Other concepts to take into account, directly related to the implementation of this type of programs in the field of healthy universities, are those of transversality and integral transformation that can be developed in the institution; highlighting several aspects that will provide value and content to this transversal and integrating vision of the program. On the one hand, as well as the HR associated with their implementation, the necessary collaborative and interdepartmental strategy to materialize each and every one of the lines of work raised is highlighted, promoting work between different departments of the University and conveying to workers a common project message and shared goals.

The shared leadership in the direction of the program, between the Sports Service of the university and the area of Human Resources and Prevention of Occupational Risks, acquires an essential relevance to provide the program with institutional position in the eyes of the employee and projection outside of the organization. This outward projection that a healthy program of physical activity and sport in the work environment generates must also be framed and aligned with the Sustainable Development Goals (SDGs) and Agenda 2030 of the United Nations Organization (2015). In this line of commitment to society, Nebrija University may be a reference of good practice in the field of healthy organizations in the university environment. This circumstance shows itself as a reference for other organizations in the field of corporate health, which can be extended to the business world, without forgetting the possible attraction of external talent that may be drawn by this type of compensation and benefits policies for employees with this kind of program and its multiple ramifications or associated lines of work (Figure 7.6).

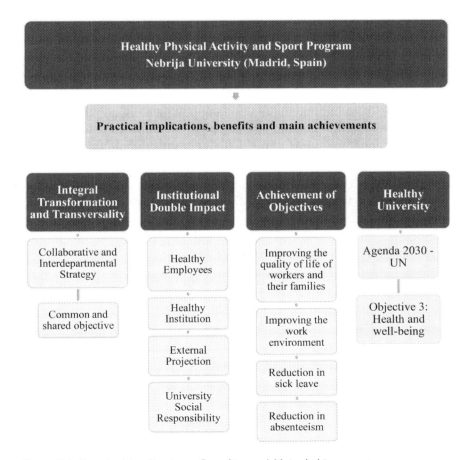

Figure 7.6 Practical Implications, Benefits, and Main Achievements.

References

Alcover, C. M., Martínez, D., & Zambrano, Z. (2007). Effects of the opportunities of incorporation to the labor market on the development of the psychological contract and attitudes towards work: The case of workers with disabilities in the call/contact center sector. *Psychology, 21*(1), 151–176.

Alonso, J., Alderman, E., Barrio, G., Prieto, L., Rodríguez, C., & de la Fuente, L. (1998). Reference population values of the Spanish version of the SF-36 health questionnaire. *Clinical Medicine, 111*(11), 410–416.

Baena-Arroyo, M. J., García-Fernández, J., Bernal-García, A., Lara-Bocanegra, A., & Gálvez-Ruiz, P. (2016). Perceived value and customer satisfaction in virtual directed activities and with a technician in fitness centers. *Journal of Sports Psychology, 25*(2), 219–227.

Consejo Superior de Deportes. (2009). *Integral plan for physical activity and sport.* https://www.csd.gob.es/es

Creating Health (2020). *Feel.* Retrieved January 24, 2020. https://crearsalud.org/siente/

Elasri-Ejjaberi, A., Triadó-Ivern, X., & Aparicio Chueca, P. (2021). Users of public sports centers: A segmentation approach to sports habits and satisfaction. *Journal of Sports Psychology, 25*(1), 15–18.

García-Fernández, J., Sánchez-Oliver, A., Grimaldi-Puyana, M., Fernández-Gavira, J., & Gálvez-Ruíz, P. (2017). Quality and customer loyalty: A segmentation analysis in low-cost fitness centers. *Journal of Sports Psychology, 26*(3), 17–22.

Gil-Beltrán, E., Llorens, S., & Salanova (2020). Employees' physical exercise, resources, engagement, and performance: A cross-sectional study from HERO model. *Journal of Work and Organizational Psychology, 36*(1), 39–47.

Gómez Chacón, R., & Fernández Martínez, N. (2020). Relationship between the practice of physical activity and healthy employees. *Sports Psychology Notebooks, 20*(3), 64–73.

Gómez-Chacón, R., Fernández Martinez, N., & Gálvez Ruiz, P. (2021). Healthy students: Adaptation and validation of the instrument from the workplace to the educational field. *Sustainability, 13*(3), 1134.

Kotler, P. (1991). *Marketing management: Analysis, planning, implementation and control.* Prentice Halls.

Madden, S., Cordon, E., Bailey, C., Skouteris, H., Ahuja, K., Hills, A. P., & Hill, B. (2020). The effect of workplace lifestyle programs on diet, physical activity and weight-related outcomes for working women: A systematic review. *Obesity Reviews, 21*(10), e13027.

Meliá, J. L., & Peiró, J. M. (1989). The satisfaction questionnaire S10/12: Factorial structure, reliability and validity. *Journal of Work and Organizational Psychology, 4*(11), 179–187.

Nuviala, A., Grao-Cruces, A., Tamayo, J. A., Nuviala, R., Álvarez, J., & Fernández-Martínez, A. (2013). Design and analysis of the sports services assessment questionnaire (EPOD2). *International Journal of Medicine and Sciences of Physical Activity and Sport, 13*(51), 419–436.

Nuviala, R., Teva-Villén, R. M., Pérez-Ordás, R., Grao-Cruces, A., Tamayo, A., & Nuviala, A. (2014). Segmentation of users of sports services. *New Trends in Physical Education, Sports and Recreation, 25,* 90–94. http://redalyc.org/pdf/3457/345732291019.pdf

Pan American Health Organization. (2005, October). *Letter from Edmonton to Health Promoting Universities and Institutions of Higher Education.* Second International Conference of Health Promoting Universities, Edmonton, Canada. https://www.paho.org/es

Reichheld, F. (2006). *The ultimate question: Driving good profits and true growth.* Harvard Business School Press.

Salanova, M., Llorens, S., Cifre, E., & Martínez, I. M. (2012). We need a hero! Towards a validation of the healthy and resilient organization (hero) model. *Group and Organization Management, 37*(6), 785–822.

Salanova, M., Llorens, S., & Martínez, M. I. (2019). *Healthy organizations. A view from positive psychology* (1st ed.). Aranzadi. http://www.want.uji.es/wp-content/uploads/2019/02/2019_Salanova-Llorens-y-Martinez_Organizaciones-Saludables.pdf

Santesmases, M. (2001). *Marketing: Concepts and strategies.* Pirámide.

Spanish Network of Healthy Universities. (2017). *Statutes of the Spanish Network of Healthy Universities.* https://www.unisaludables.es/es/

United Nations Organization. (2015, September 25). *Sustainable Development Goals.* https://www.un.org/sustainabledevelopment/es/

World Health Organization (WHO). (2005, August). *Bangkok Charter for Health Promotion in a Globalized World.* Sixth International Conference on Health Promotion, Bangkok, Thailand. https://www.who.int/teams/health-promotion/enhanced-well-being/sixth-global-conference/the-bangkok-charter

World Health Organization (WHO). (2013). *Healthy Workplaces: A Model for Action.* https://apps.who.int/iris/bitstream/handle/10665/44317/9789243599311_spa.pdf;jsessionid=509B672EFD444362582F3EC292E481CE?sequence=1

World Health Organization (WHO). (2020, November 25). *WHO Guidelines on Physical Activity and Sedentary Habits.* https://www.who.int/es/publications/i/item/9789240014886

Appendix I

Evaluation/Satisfaction Questionnaire of the Program of Healthy Physical Activity in the Work Environment (Nebrija University)—EPOD2. (Scale of 1 to 5, 1 being—Strongly Disagree and 5—Strongly Agree)

Q. 1. How would you evaluate the following aspects, in relation to the **monitor/coach** you have in your activity of the Healthy Program

	Strongly Disagree	Disagree	Agree	Quite agree	Strongly agree
I am happy with the treatment received by the monitor/coach.	1	2	3	4	5
I believe that the instructor pays adequate attention to users' problems from day one.	1	2	3	4	5
I believe that the instructor adapts the classes/trainings to the interests/needs.	1	2	3	4	5
I think the monitor/coach is encouraging the group enough.	1	2	3	4	5

Q. 2. In relation to the **facilities**, what is your opinion about the following elements.

	Strongly Disagree	Disagree	Agree	Quite agree	Strongly agree
The changing rooms are clean enough.	1	2	3	4	5
The changing rooms are spacious enough.	1	2	3	4	5
The facilities are sufficiently clean.	1	2	3	4	5

Q.3. In relation to **sports equipment**, what is your opinion about the following elements.

	Strongly Disagree	Disagree	Agree	Quite agree	Strongly agree
Sufficient material is available for training.	1	2	3	4	5
The material is in optimal condition for use.	1	2	3	4	5
The material is modern.	1	2	3	4	5

Q.4. To what extent do the **activities** you perform conform to the following statements?

	Strongly Disagree	Disagree	Agree	Quite agree	Strongly agree
The activity is enjoyable.	1	2	3	4	5
The tasks that the instructor develops in the trainings/sessions are sufficiently varied.	1	2	3	4	5
The activities end in the time indicated.	1	2	3	4	5
With this activity I get the results I expected.	1	2	3	4	5
It has been easy for me to join the activity I am participating in.	1	2	3	4	5

Q.5. As a user of the Healthy Program, what is your perception of the following aspects of **communication**?

	Strongly Disagree	Disagree	Agree	Quite agree	Strongly agree
Some means of transmitting suggestions are available (suggestion box, bulletin board, etc).	1	2	3	4	5
The information on the activities that are developed is adequate.	1	2	3	4	5
The range of activities is constantly being updated.	1	2	3	4	5

Q.6. The **staff of the Program organization** is a key element, what is your perception of the following aspects?

	Strongly Disagree	Disagree	Agree	Quite agree	Strongly agree
The staff of the Healthy Program is friendly.	1	2	3	4	5
There is a good relationship among the staff of the Healthy Program.	1	2	3	4	5

Q.7. We would like to know your satisfaction in relation to the organization and the activity carried out.

	Strongly Disagree	Disagree	Agree	Quite agree	Strongly agree
Choosing the Healthy Program was a good choice.	1	2	3	4	5
I am happy to have enrolled in the Healthy Program.	1	2	3	4	5
It was a good decision to do sports activities in the Healthy Program.	1	2	3	4	5
I am pleased to have enrolled in the Healthy Program.	1	2	3	4	5

Q.8. State the extent to which you agree with this statement

	Strongly Disagree	Disagree	Agree	Quite agree	Strongly agree
I am satisfied with the Healthy Program.	1	2	3	4	5

Chapter 8

Satisfaction with Services of a Public Sport Organization in Mexico

Marina Reyes Robles
Universidad Estatal de Sonora, Mexico

Rosa Elena Medina Rodríguez
Universidad Autónoma de Nuevo León, Mexico

María Grethel Ramírez Siqueiros
Universidad Estatal de Sonora, Mexico

Oswaldo Ceballos Gurrola
Universidad Estatal de Sonora, Mexico

Chapter Contents

Introduction	106
Public Sport Organization in Mexico	109
Method	110
Results	111
Discussion	114
Conclusion	116
References	119

Introduction

The history of sports in Mexico has a pre-Hispanic origin with the practice of the ball game (purépecha or tlachtli) and traditional games, some that are still practiced as a form of recreation, religious practice, or to preserve culture. Through the years, Mexico has been a venue for international events such as the Olympic Games, world championships, the Pan-American Games, and the Central American and Caribbean Games. These events have promoted and encouraged competitive sports, resulting in talented athletes representing the country with excellent sports achievements. The structure of the physical culture and sport system in Mexico is characterized by the highest legislative authority, Congress (the Chamber of Senators and the Chamber of Representatives), which establishes how sports

DOI: 10.4324/9781003388050-10

systems will work. At the federal level, the National Physical Culture and Sports Commission coordinates with civil associations from the academic sector, sports associations, the Paralympic Committee, and the Mexican Olympic Committee. At the state (provincial) level, the state organizations of physical culture and sports (State Sports Institutes) as government agencies connect with other sports civil associations. At the municipal level, the government organisms (Municipal Sports Committees) connect with multiple sports leagues and civil associations.

The regulation related to these constitutional entities is the General Law of Physical Culture and Sports, published in the Official Journal of the Federation (DOF 2022). This law designates the National Commission of Physical Culture and Sports (CONADE, in Spanish) as the maximum authority for the application and interpretation of the law and the planning of diverse sports programs. There is a National System of Physical Culture and Sports (SINADE, in Spanish) that promotes, encourages, and stimulates physical culture and sport in all its manifestations. It is a collegiate body that comprises agencies, public and private organizations and institutions, societies, national associations, and national sports councils. Its objective is to provide advice regarding creating a National Program and coordinating, following-up, and evaluating programs that carry out public policy. The CONADE promotes, coordinates, and encourages, together with the Public Education Secretariat, teaching, research, the promotion of technological development, the application of scientific knowledge concerning physical activity, physical culture, sports, and the construction of teaching and training centers related to these activities.

Education is considered the principal tool to transform vulnerable social environments into safe and harmonious spaces. For this, strategies have been established in which one of the main axes of action is sports (Lara Rodríguez & Juárez Lozano, 2020). In countries like Mexico, sports have been considered the primary protector to keep society away from violence, insecurity, and inequality. Considered as rights, physical activity and sports are part of the essential privileges that make people's well-being possible. Numerous benefits in favor of individual and collective quality of life emerge from their practice, impacting important matters such as healthcare and the creation of healthy habits, social integration, intellectual development, and the strengthening of community life (Martínez León, 2020). Worldwide, around 20% of adults do not have healthy physical activity habits, with this being worse in regions such as Latin America, where it is 39% (Mondaca et al., 2020). Recent numbers reported by the National Institute of Statistics and Geography (Instituto Nacional de Estadística y Geografía, 2022) show the status of sports in the Mexican context and identify related problems and trends. Among the population over 18 years of age, less than half of Mexican men and women (42.1%) are physically active. Of this percentage, 49.5% are men and 35.6% are women. There is also a substantial gender gap, with a higher percentage of women than men physically inactive (8% worldwide and 9% in Latin America) (Mondaca et al., 2020).

The educational level reflects different settings and conditions for the practice of physical activity. Among those who have not finished primary education, only

26.4% spend time in physical activities; in people who have finished primary education or have some level of middle education, it is 41.1%, and in those that have a higher education, 54.8% practice some activity; in other words, this reflects a trend to increase the practice of physical activity or sports when the individual has a higher educational level. Regarding the spaces for practicing a physical activity or sport, 65.7% who are physically active exercise in installations or public areas, of which only 51.9% reach a level sufficient to obtain health benefits. Private installations or places are used for exercise or sport by 21.6%; of these, only 66.4% achieve health benefits (Instituto Nacional de Estadística y Geografía, 2022). The socioeconomic level is another variable involved in the possibility of practicing or not a physical activity. In this situation, it is necessary to refer to the unequal access to sports installations and programs, the practical and theoretical knowledge needed to practice physical activity, and the time available to practice it. Specifically, in Mexico, physical activity is practiced mainly in public spaces related to men (soccer and baseball) and in private places related to women (fitness centers). The segmentation of productive activities demands that women dedicate more time to tasks such as homemaking or caretaking, which reduces their free time to practice sports activities; there is also a binary division by gender with sports being considered a male practice that serves to display masculinity and women are excluded (Leyra, 2019).

Sports are also a setting to establish and spread fair play and a gender perspective. The importance of the gender perspective lies in the fact that it is a crucial element to prevent or counteract the different types of violence that are indirectly formed, considering that gender is one facet of sport, especially if it is not forgotten that this ludic, competitive, recreational, educational, commercial, and political endeavor integrates sociocultural scenarios, behaviors, and traditions. When a sports discipline is practiced as a spectator, promoter, trainer, or disseminator of sports in different areas, one continues to be a social entity (Lara Rodríguez, 2020). Thus, the importance of increasing usual levels of practice, where the issue of barriers perceived by the population to carry out physical activity, has enormous importance. The literature has identified aspects such as social physique anxiety linked to body image, fatigue or laziness, lack of time due to obligations or the environment, and the lack of facilities as the main reasons for physical inactivity at different ages (Ceballos-Gurrola et al., 2020; Hernández-Cortés et al., 2019; Niñerola et al., 2006). The professional sports environment in Mexico, another feature of sports, has become a large recreation and business industry, a product that has grown and is consumed by thousands of fans. This industry produces an average of 211 million pesos a year, considering investments, economic benefits, publicity, and sales of souvenirs and tickets, according to the Economists and Associates Group (Pérez, 2020). There are 92 teams in the four main sports (soccer, baseball, basketball, and football), divided into seven leagues in 42 cities in 27 different states (Vernet, 2020). Another aspect to point out is the increase in the last decade of fitness gyms in the whole country (INFOBAE, 2020). A total of 12,500 fitness clubs and gyms are registered in Mexico; these generate 759 direct and indirect jobs and represent more than four million users (Villafranco, 2016).

Satisfaction with Services   109

The states that aim to improve their administration system must effectively and efficiently respond to the needs, motivations, and interests of the different social actors that intervene in the process. The evaluation of worker satisfaction in these states regarding their activities presents as a social interaction related to the service offered (Reyes-Robles et al., 2018). The evaluation of services by users in sports organizations allows continuous improvement by considering their predilections and needs (Morquecho-Sánchez et al., 2016). This study shows the evaluation of services provided by a public sports organization in Mexico to identify the aspects that are best valued and those that require improvement to meet the expectations of users (athletes). With this information, it is intended that public sector entities achieve continuous improvement but above all escalate toward a condition of self-sustainability, making adjustments in specific areas demanded by society and becoming safe scenarios for the development and growth of Mexican sports talent.

Public Sport Organization in Mexico

Sports practice is currently the ideal means to obtain multiple health benefits and the social well-being of individuals (Macarro et al., 2012). For this reason, in the last two decades, there has been a greater citizen demand for sports services from public and private sports organizations (Ruíz-Alejos, 2015). Among these, at the state level, the Sonora State Sports Commission (CODESON, in Spanish) is an institution in charge of promoting and regulating physical culture and sports in the state of Sonora. Its mission is to develop, create, and implement policies and actions that stimulate massive integration of the population into the practice of physical, recreational, and sports activities, thus strengthening their human and social development, improving their levels of well-being, promoting equal opportunities, and achieving participation and excellence in sport. The user/athlete has become demanding since they know the characteristics that a service must have and that they expect to receive, as in other settings (Rial et al., 2010). It is necessary to offer quality service to guarantee continuity and processes; therefore, administrators must consider establishing strategies to improve service, generating a benefit for clients, administrators, employees, and the organization (Calabuig et al., 2010). Based on the above, all those responsible in the sports organization must understand client service satisfaction to make a general diagnosis of the aspects that greatly influence satisfaction (Nuviala et al., 2010; Vegara et al., 2011).

It is essential to improve public sports services administration, especially those offered by municipalities and local entities. These services are a constant concern, which is why the process of evolution must be accompanied by improvement in public services (Dorado & Gallardo, 2005). Continuous improvement processes in sports administration are more frequent, and they become necessary tools to help improve the quality of current sports services (Ruíz-Alejos, 2015). Research in sports administration has gained much interest as a consequence of the growth in physical culture sports; this has caused an increase in sports practice consumption (Martínez & Martínez, 2007; Nuviala et al., 2012). In this way, studies related to customer satisfaction regarding the quality of sports services comprise an area that has produced a large amount of literature in recent years, in different fields, and from different perspectives (Calabuig et al., 2012; García et al., 2016; Granero et al., 2008; Larson & Steinman, 2009).

Management of a sports entity finds in research a means to determine the appropriate formula to achieve effectiveness and efficiency, directing toward quality the management of services and elements that intervene, since the quality of service not only refers to the internal experience of each individual but also to the evaluation of attributes external to the service (Sánchez-Hernández et al., 2009). Specifically, the administration of public sports services by government administrations in Mexico offers different physical activities-sports programs using sports facilities that are usually shared with municipalities and rural areas. This study aims to analyze user/athlete satisfaction regarding the sports service administered by a state sport institute in Mexico and establish differences in the function of user characteristics.

Method

A descriptive, comparative, correlational, nonexperimental, cross-sectional, cohort design study with a quantitative focus was conducted to answer the objective of this research (Hernández et al., 2014). The sample consisted of 453 users/athletes from the Sonora State Sports Institute (Mexico); 58.9% were men and 41.1% were women. According to the age range group, the most significant percentage was 13–15 years (39.3%), followed by the group from 16 to 18 years (38.2%). Regarding the use of installations and sports programs, 59.2% attended more than 5 days a week with a duration between 60 and 120 minutes a day (54.3%). According to the type of sport, 57.4% practiced individual sports, 15.2% sport team sports, 21.9% combat sports, and 5.5% aquatic activities.

A satisfaction survey of users/athletes adapted to the Mexican context by Reyes-Robles (2018) was used. The instrument consisted of 40 items grouped into 11 factors: Attention (six items), Facilities (five items), Training tasks (three items), Trainer performance (six items), Activities offered (three items), Cost (two items), Complaints and suggestions (three items), Medical service (three items), Parking (three items), Cafeteria/store/snack (four items), and Service attitude (two items), with a Likert-type response scale with options from 1 to 4, where 1 = Not at all satisfied and 4 = Very satisfied. Reliability and validity were performed independently by dividing the sample, performing an exploratory factor analysis (EFA) with sample 1 ($N = 231$). Reliability (α) using Cronbach's alpha for the different factors ranges between .73 and .88. The method used was main axes extraction and orthogonal rotation (Promax, kappa = 4). The KMO index had a value of .87. The Bartlett test was statistically significant with an $\chi^2 = 4660.85$, df = 780; $p < .001$); the resulting factor structure consisted of the 11 factors that together explain 69.04% of the total variance. The goodness of fit indices of the resulting model from the confirmatory factor analysis (CFA) with sample 2 ($N = 222$)

Satisfaction with Services   111

achieved adequate values (χ^2/df = 1.30, TLI = .98, CFI = .99 and RMSEA = .03). The compound reliability indices varied from .82 to .91, and the average variance extracted indices were above the recommended value of .50.

After obtaining authorization for the instrument's application from the sports entity's administration, a group of interviewers trained in this type of data collection went to the different sports spaces. They introduced themselves to the users/athletes, requested consent for their participation, commented on the objective of the study, and described the survey and its completion. To complement the previously mentioned and facilitate understanding of the procedure, the interviewers explained that the information collected would be used with responsibility, ensuring the anonymity and confidentiality of the information. It is important to mention that the questionnaire was self-administered, which means that it was provided directly to the participants who answered it. The statistical software program SPSS v.24 was used to evaluate the data using different analysis techniques. In the first step, data were cleaned and quality was established. Descriptive statistics were performed using standard parameters (mean ± standard deviation) to determine the general value of each factor. After descriptive statistics, as a third step due to the number of participants in the study, an inferential analysis was performed to statistically verify the existence of differences in the means using parametric tests, Student's t for independent samples, and a one-way ANOVA. Finally, correlations between factors were established using Pearson's r.

Results

The global evaluation of user/athlete satisfaction had high scores in most factors, especially trainer performance (M = 3.48, SD = .50) and training tasks (M = 3.44, SD = .50), while lower values were found in cafeteria services (M = 2.97, SD = .76) and sports facilities (M = 3.02, SD = .59) (see Figure 8.1). No significant differences were found (p > .05) in the analysis comparing satisfaction with the different services based on gender. However, in the results, it was found that women gave slightly higher scores in facilities, training tasks, activities offered, cost, medical services, cafeteria, and attitude. Men focused their attention on the organization, the trainer, and complaints and suggestions (see Table 8.1). After grouping the different ages of the users/athletes into six groups (see Table 8.2), no statistically significant differences were found (p > .05). Nevertheless, it was found that the user/athlete group 22–24 years of age provided slightly higher scores in most of the factors, while individuals over 28 years of age provided the lowest scores.

Regarding satisfaction based on weekly frequency with which users/athletes attend the service to practice sports, significant differences were found with higher scores in those that attend 3–5 days a week (see Table 8.3), facilities (t = 2.53; p < .05), complaints and suggestions (t = 1.91; p < .05), and medical service (t = 2.52; p < .05). When analyzing satisfaction with regard to time that the user/athlete dedicates to practice during the day, significant differences were found in

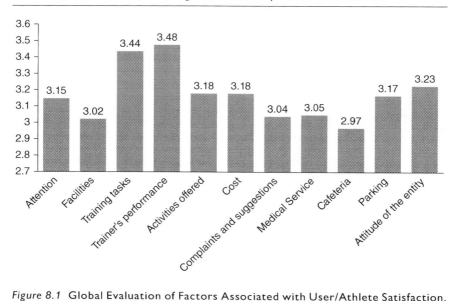

Figure 8.1 Global Evaluation of Factors Associated with User/Athlete Satisfaction.

training tasks ($F = 2.65$; $p < .05$), cost ($F = 3.45$; $p < .05$), and medical service ($F = 1.58$; $p < .05$); no group predominates (see Table 8.4). Regarding the comparison of satisfaction in relation to sports modality, significant differences were found in facilities ($F = 3.36$, $p < .05$), training tasks ($F = 3.58$, $p < .05$), and medical service ($F = 11.61$, $p < .05$); no sports modality predominated (see Table 8.5). Table 8.6 shows the positive and significant correlations of the 11 factors studied.

Table 8.1 User/Athlete Satisfaction Based on Gender

Factors	Men		Women			
	Mean	SD	Mean	SD	T	Sig
Attention	3.16	.51	3.13	.58	.516	.606
Infrastructure	3.01	.59	3.02	.59	−.096	.923
Training tasks	3.40	.56	3.49	.53	−1.62	.105
Trainer performance	3.48	.49	3.46	.51	.332	.740
Activity offered	3.14	.61	3.22	.61	−1.20	.230
Cost	3.13	.71	3.24	.66	−1.71	.087
Complaints and suggestions	3.05	.69	3.02	.72	.506	.613
Medical service	3.00	.74	3.11	.70	−1.46	.143
Cafeteria	2.92	.77	3.03	.72	−1.35	.177
Parking	3.16	.66	3.17	.73	.047	.962
Service Attitude	3.20	.64	3.28	.59	−1.22	.223

Table 8.2 Users/Athletes Satisfaction Based on Age (Years)

Factors	13–15	16–18	19–21	22–24	25–27	>28	F	Sig
Attention	3.10 ± .52	3.18 ± .57	3.17 ± .58	3.23 ± .32	3.22 ± .68	3.20 ± .62	.619	685
Facilities	3.98 ± .57	2.99 ± .60	3.14 ± .59	3.26 ± .55	3.02 ± .73	2.76 ± .57	1.66	.141
Training tasks	3.40 ± .59	3.47 ± .55	3.48 ± .48	3.40 ± .56	3.47 ± .52	3.33 ± .66	.497	.779
Trainer performance	3.48 ± .49	3.49 ± .54	3.44 ± .50	3.49 ± .41	3.46 ± .62	3.30 ± .67	.207	.959
Activities offer	3.16 ± .60	3.16 ± .64	3.25 ± .61	3.28 ± .49	3.28 ± .63	2.80 ± .73	.784	.561
Cost	3.20 ± .69	3.12 ± .74	3.30 ± .59	3.26 ± .48	3.12 ± .85	2.60 ± 1.19	1.45	.205
Complaints and suggestions	2.95 ± .73	3.08 ± .68	3.14 ± .66	3.20 ± .46	2.97 ± 1.03	2.93 ± .64	1.16	.327
Medical service	3.00 ± .78	3.04 ± .71	3.16 ± .68	3.10 ± .58	3.41 ± .55	2.66 ± .40	1.38	.228
Cafeteria	2.93 ± .80	2.98 ± .74	3.3 ± .77	3.00 ± .40	3.06 ± .75	2.80 ± .76	.296	.915
Parking	3.13 ± .71	3.18 ± .71	3.24 ± .64	3.30 ± .54	3.11 ± .78	2.80 ± .77	.721	.608
Service attitude	3.19 ± .63	3.25 ± .63	3.27 ± .58	3.50 ± .52	3.08 ± .70	2.90 ± .82	1.34	.244

Note: Data are expressed as mean ± standard deviation ($M \pm SD$) unless stated otherwise.

Table 8.3 Users/Athletes Satisfaction Based on Frequency

Factors	3–5 days		More than 5 days			
	Mean	SD	Mean	SD	t	Sig
Attention	3.14	.53	3.15	.55	−.172	.863
Facilities	3.10	.60	2.95	.57	2.53	.011
Training tasks	3.42	.52	3.45	.57	−.651	.513
Trainer performance	3.47	.53	3.47	.48	−.025	.980
Activities offer	3.14	.64	3.19	.60	−.965	.335
Cost	3.21	.69	3.15	.70	.806	.421
Complaints and suggestions	3.11	.67	2.99	.72	1.91	.049
Medical service	3.15	.66	2.98	.76	2.52	.012
Cafeteria	3.01	.74	2.93	.76	1.18	.235
Parking	3.21	.66	3.14	.71	1.05	.291
Service attitude	3.25	.62	3.22	.62	.527	.598

Discussion

The aim of this work was to analyze user/athlete satisfaction regarding the sports service managed by a state sports institute in Mexico and establish differences based on user characteristics. The results showed that the highest scores were for trainer performance and training/exercise tasks, results that coincide with other studies that positively value training tasks (Camino & García-Fernández, 2014; Ruíz-Alejos, 2015) and trainer performance (Camino & García-Fernández, 2014; Elasri et al., 2015; García et al., 2016; Nuviala et al., 2008; Ruíz-Alejos, 2015). On the other hand, the lowest scores were for the cafeteria, considering aspects such as the service provided, cleanliness, and adequate physical space, as a minimum.

Table 8.4 Users/Athletes Satisfaction Concerning the Time of Practice

Factors	Between 60 and 120 minutes	Between 121 and 180 minutes	>180 minutes	F	Sig
	$M \pm SD$	$M \pm SD$	$M \pm SD$		
Attention	3.16 ± .54	3.12 ± .55	3.17 ± .49	.241	.786
Facilities	3.01 ± .57	3.03 ± .62	2.92 ± .61	.540	.583
Training tasks	3.39 ± .54	3.49 ± .57	3.56 ± .53	2.65	.029
Trainer performance	3.44 ± .50	3.51 ± .48	3.50 ± 54	1.20	.299
Activities offer	3.15 ± .62	3.23 ± .60	3.20 ± .62	.265	.768
Cost	3.15 ± .68	3.26 ± .67	2.95 ± .84	3.45	.033
Complaints and suggestions	3.08 ± .66	2.99 ± .73	2.92 ± .77	1.29	.276
Medical service	3.10 ± .66	2.99 ± .79	2.95 ± .76	1.58	.027
Cafeteria	3.02 ± 71	3.10 ± .79	3.03 ± .78	2.84	.059
Parking	3.14 ± .67	3.23 ± .65	2.99 ± .92	2.11	.122
Service attitude	3.23 ± .58	3.25 ± .66	3.09 ± .69	.965	.382

Satisfaction with Services 115

Table 8.5 Users/Athletes Satisfaction Concerning Time Sports Modality

Factors	Individual sports	Team sports	Combat sports	Aquatic sports		
	M ± SD	M ± SD	M ± SD	M ± SD	F	Sig
Attention	3.13 ± .59	3.16 ± .46	3.18 ± .48	3.17 ± .50	.188	.905
Facilities	2.99 ± .61	3.16 ± 48	2.89 ± .56	3.01 ± .68	3.36	.019
Training tasks	3.49 ± .53	3.46 ± .48	3.26 ± .59	3.33 ± .77	3.58	.014
Trainer performance	3.52 ± .51	3.40 ± .45	3.41 ± 48	3.41 ± 54	1.85	.137
Activities offer	3.17 ± .65	3.19 ± .52	3.17 ± .59	3.12 ± .60	.082	.970
Cost	3.15 ± 73	3.30 ± .58	3.16 ± .68	3.02 ± .72	1.61	.186
Complaints and suggestions	3.00 ± .72	3.13 ± .62	3.06 ± .70	2.98 ± .70	1.00	.390
Medical service	3.01 ± .73	3.23 ± .64	2.89 ± .74	3.10 ± .77	3.63	.013
Cafeteria	2.90 ± 78	3.11 ± .64	2.96 ± .70	3.02 ± .90	1.91	.126
Parking	3.15 ± .68	3.25 ± .65	3.03 ± .75	3.33 ± .70	1.80	.145
Service attitude	3.20 ± .64	3.31 ± .50	3.21 ± .66	3.26 ± .70	.824	.481

These findings coincide with the study by Medina-Rodríguez (2010) regarding other services that the municipal sports entity provides, such as the snack bar, which operates under minimal hygiene conditions, does not offer nutritious food and does not have adequate physical space and staff service. In another study by Liu et al. (2009), good scores were obtained with the rest of the evaluated attributes, except for the availability and quality-price related to food/beverages services, which had low scores.

When comparing satisfaction with the different services based on gender, no significant differences were found. Other studies show that women are more satisfied with the facilities and programs offered (Aznar, 2015; Calabuig et al., 2010;

Table 8.6 Correlation between User/Athlete Satisfaction Factors

Factors	1	2	3	4	5	6	7	8	9	10	11
1	-										
2	.506**	-									
3	.390**	.390**	-								
4	.304**	.283**	.563**	-							
5	.418**	.458**	.450**	.422**	-						
6	.359**	.346**	.392**	.374**	.477**	-					
7	.470**	.459**	.323**	.350**	.507**	.431**	-				
8	.457**	.493**	.334**	.225**	.419**	.366**	.461**	-			
9	.397**	.488**	.293**	.217**	.415**	.335**	.419**	.469**	-		
10	.344**	.450**	.345**	.302**	.462**	.474**	.430**	.553**	.413**	-	
11	.480**	.416**	.340**	.329**	.495**	.437**	.452**	.405**	.399**	.481**	-

Note: N = 231, 1 = Attention, 2 = Infrastructure, 3 = Training tasks, 4 = Trainer performance, 5 = Activities offered (disciplines), 6 = Cost, 7 = Complaints and suggestions, 8 = Medical service, 9 = Cafeteria, 10 = Parking, 11 = Service Attitude; **P <.01

Nuviala et al., 2012; Sánchez et al., 2017; Vila et al., 2009). No significant difference was recorded regarding age, a result that coincides with Elasri et al. (2013) and Sánchez et al. (2017). On the other hand, Medina-Rodríguez (2010) found significant differences in clients 13–21 years of age who gave higher scores than people >40 years, who gave the lowest scores. Concerning the latter, Boceta (2012) and Nuviala (2013) report that the group >65 years gave the best scores. Thus, the satisfaction of sports services offered varies depending on the age of the user/athlete, which is determined by their experience with the service. When analyzing satisfaction based on weekly frequency, significant differences were recorded for this work; data similar to the study by Boceta (2012). Notably, users/athletes who practice three times a week gave higher positive scores, while in the study by Ruíz-Alejos (2015), it was individuals who practice four times a week.

Our study results show that individuals who practice between 121 and 180 minutes give slightly higher scores, as in the study by Ruíz-Alejos (2015). In contrast, in the studies by Bernal (2013) and Boceta (2012), the athletes who practice less than 60 minutes are those who give better evaluations. On the other hand, sports modality was compared considering individual, team, combat, and aquatic sports, registering a better evaluation in team sports. These results differ from Aznar (2015) since individual sports and combat sports gave a better evaluation of the service, while collective sports had the worst evaluations. In contrast, Nuviala (2013) reported that combat, fitness, and swimming were better evaluated. Aspects related to human, physical/tangible resources, and the service itself are decisive in forming user/athlete satisfaction (Bernal, 2013; Calabuig et al., 2008; Medina-Rodríguez, 2010). Adequate importance and continuous reflection must be given to the method used to evaluate the quality of service (García-Fernández et al., 2012; Larson & Steinman, 2009).

Conclusion

Human resources are essential in activities in which they intervene directly with the users/athletes during the service provision, confirming that trainer performance and training tasks are decisive for assessing satisfaction. Next, a model that integrates the factors associated with a sports organization's service quality from the perspective of the user/athlete is proposed. When they are integrated, service quality, sports performance, and quality of life of the people who use them in rural areas, municipalities, and cities improve (see Figure 8.2). The perceived quality and loyalty of users/athletes are related to the attention they receive, the interpersonal skills and technical capabilities of the sports entity (García et al., 2016), its proximity, accessible costs, the variety of activities, and schedules (Vila et al., 2009). In Mexico, a mentality of distrust prevails regarding the access and use of sports facilities and programs of public organizations; although there are entities with extensive experience concerning human capital and successful programs, these are affected by the changes in government administration that occur every 3 years at the municipal level, and every 6 at the state and national level.

Satisfaction with Services 117

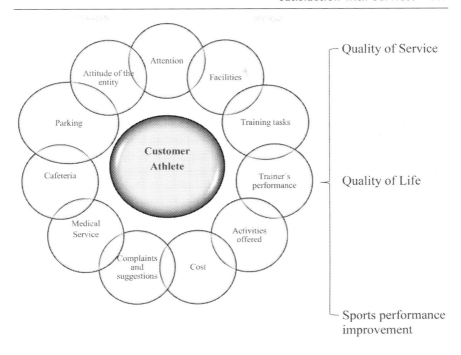

Figure 8.2 Factors Associated with the Service Quality of a Sport Organization from the Customers/Athlete's Perspective.

Sports facilities require adequate equipment with official measures, universal accessibility, user rules, and permanent maintenance for recreational or competitive users. Some factors that affect use are maintenance and the risk of suffering a lesion, little or no sports programs, vandalism, and a lack of security, administrative, and coaching personnel (Flores Allende et al., 2019). The content and characteristics of the tasks related to training must be appropriate to the interests and needs of the athlete, who seek well-being and health. Simultaneously, these tasks must be presented in a recreational, practical, and varied manner, seeking an approach that favors interaction. Instructors/coaches must communicate strategies to the athlete and design them to have a controlled and progressive intensity that favors self-evaluation (Imbroda, 2014; Vila et al., 2009).

The coach must have a series of skills and extensive knowledge to transmit positive attitudes and provide individualized attention to athletes (Vila et al., 2009). Therefore, it is essential to have technically qualified trainers to develop physical activities or practices within an entity, company, or sports organization (Imbroda, 2014; Mestre, 2013). The activities offered related to the strengthening of health and well-being that a sports services organization offers have changed, adapting to unexpected situations such as the COVID-19 pandemic and the trends of private fitness companies (Gambau i Pinasa, 2020; Moscoso-Sánchez, 2020). Thus, these organizations have focused on diversifying programs and services, impacting other population sectors (García et al., 2016). These changes in conception have led to a modification of the physical activity programs offered, the adaptation and/or modification of existing sports facilities and spaces to achieve maximum functionality, and the optimization of the interaction between customers and the organization (Morales Sánchez & Gálvez-Ruiz, 2011).

Cost is a factor that directly influences satisfaction, so it must be taken into account when the objective is to improve (Elasri et al., 2013). This factor is decisive in decision-making since clients tend to evaluate the price value of the sports activity or discipline (Medina et al., 2015). Public sports organizations in Mexico need to adapt the strategies of private sports entities (fitness centers) or companies in the search for self-sustainability, which allows them to improve their facilities and services (Román Miranda et al., 2020). The complaints and suggestions box is a very useful tool for organizations since valuable information is collected from customers and workers. These complaints or suggestions can manifest dissatisfaction or a proposal for improvement, but if the client does not communicate the reasons for his or her complaint, disappointment, or displeasure, he or she practically leaves no opportunity for the organization to become aware of this dissatisfaction. In contrast, clients who complain continue talking to the organization, allowing them to return to a state of satisfaction (Blázquez & Feu, 2010; Ongallo, 2012). The trend is to make complaints and suggestions through the entity's social networks.

The medical service in a sports organization is vital since it is not known when first aid will be required for sports accidents or the monitoring and care of sports injuries. It is essential to have qualified personnel and the material and medical equipment for the care of users/athletes (Medina-Rodríguez, 2010; Yildiz, 2011). Cafeteria service or vending machines are usually concessioned to third parties, operating with minimal hygiene conditions, not offering nutritious food, inadequate physical spaces, and a lack of qualified personnel in care and service. Another aspect that has not been well valued by users is the quality-price ratio of food (Liu et al., 2009). Another aspect to consider is that the facilities must have large parking lots (Medina et al., 2015; Nuviala et al., 2010). Theses must have accessibility and inclusion spaces, which refers to all those measures aimed at facilitating access for people with a disability, whether it is physical, mental, or sensory (Blázquez & Feu, 2010).

The attitudes and skills that employees have to relate and apply their knowledge with customers within the same facility are decisive to achieve loyalty (Beigvand & Amirtash, 2014; Calabuig et al., 2012; Yildiz, 2011). Social interaction between employees and clients grows day-by-day and strengthens the bond between them, attributing significant importance to the different tangible elements (Kim & Trail, 2010). In summary, the perceived quality of service is an essential factor that can help sports center managers understand and improve their work and improve the efficiency of the service they offer. Therefore, it is essential to have valid and reliable tools to measure the quality perceived by users (Calabuig et al., 2012). In this sense, research on the quality of sports services is one of the main lines on which organizational philosophy is based (Morales-Sánchez and Gálvez-Ruiz, 2011).

References

Aznar, M. (2015). *Análisis de las actividades físicas y deportivas extraescolares en los centros de enseñanza secundaria de la ciudad de Zaragoza* [Tesis doctoral, Universidad Pablo Olavide]. https://dialnet.unirioja.es/servlet/tesis?codigo=101266

Beigvand, L., & Amirtash, A. (2014). Comparison of service quality between private and public municipal sports clubs of Tehran from customer's perspective based on the servaqual model. *Indian Journal of Fundamental and Applied Life Sciences, 4*(3), 1000–1003.

Bernal, A. (2013). *Fidelización de clientes en organizaciones deportivas: calidad, valor percibido y satisfacción como factores determinantes* [Tesis doctoral, Universidad Pablo Olavide, Sevilla]. https://dialnet.unirioja.es/servlet/tesis?codigo=62666

Blázquez, A., & Feu, S. (2010). Sistema de codificación para el análisis de los indicadores de calidad de las cartas de servicios en materia deportiva. *Revista Internacional De Ciencias Del Deporte, 19*(6), 112–127.

Boceta, M. (2012). *Calidad percibida, satisfacción y valor percibido por los usuarios de servicios prestados por el instituto municipal del deporte del ayuntamiento de Sevilla en centros deportivos de gestión directa. Segmentación de usuarios* [Tesis doctoral, Universidad Pablo Olavide]. https://dialnet.unirioja.es/servlet/tesis?codigo=111726

Calabuig, F., Burillo, P., Crespo, J., Mundina, J. J., & Gallardo, L. (2010). Satisfacción, calidad y valor percibido en espectadores de atletismo. *Revista Internacional De Medicina y Ciencias De La Actividad Física y El Deporte, 10*(40), 577–593.

Calabuig, F., Molina, N., & Núñez, J. (2012). Una aplicación inicial del modelo tridimensional de calidad de servicio en centros deportivos privados. *E-Balonmano. Revista De Ciencias Del Deporte, 8*(1), 67–81.

Calabuig, F., Quintanilla, I., & Mundina, J. (2008). La calidad percibida de los servicios deportivos: Diferencias según instalación, género, edad y tipo de usuario en servicios náuticos. *RICYDE. Revista Internacional De Ciencias Del Deporte, 4*(10), 25–43.

Camino, M., & García-Fernández, J. (2014). La percepción de calidad, valor y satisfacción de un club deportivo. La perspectiva de padres y deportistas adultos *e-balonmano. Com: Revista De Ciencias Del Deporte, 10*(2), 99–112.

Ceballos-Gurrola, O., Medina-Rodríguez, R. E., Juvera-Portilla, J. L., Peche-Alejandro, P., Aguirre-López, L. F., & Rodríguez-Rodríguez, J. (2020). Imagen corporal y práctica de actividades físico-deportivas en estudiantes de nivel secundaria. *Cuadernos De Psicología Del Deporte, 20*(1), 252–260.

Diario Oficial de la Federación DOF (2022). Ley General de Cultura Física y Deporte. Cámara de Diputados del H. Congreso de la Unión. https://www.diputados.gob.mx/LeyesBiblio/pdf/LGCFD.pdf

Dorado, A., & Gallardo, L. (2005). La gestión de la calidad a través de la calidad. INDE.

Elasri, A., Triadó, X. M., & Aparicio, P. (6 de junio de 2013). *Evolución de los factores de satisfacción de clientes en centros deportivos entre 1996 y 2013.¿ Cómo han cambiado las percepciones de los usuarios?*. In Descubriendo nuevos horizontes en administración, XXVII Congreso Anual AEDEM, España. https://dialnet.unirioja.es/servlet/articulo?codigo=4411766

Elasri, A., Triadó, X. M., & Aparicio, P. (2015). Customer satisfaction in municipal sports centres in Barcelona. Apunts. *Educación Física y Deportes, 119*, 109–117.

Flores Allende, G., Velarde Martínez, O., Cuevas Vázquez, E., & Pinto Chávez, J. (2019). Tipo de equipamiento en instalaciones deportivas de gestión municipal en el área metropolitana de Guadalajara (México) en RIASPORT. *La seguridad deportiva a debate* (pp. 67–78). Dykinson. https://vlex.es/vid/tipo-equipamiento-instalaciones-deportivas-842598250

Gambau i Pinasa, V. (2020). COVID-19: La crisis ha afectado a todos. *Revista Española De Educación Física y Deportes*, *429*, 15–18.

García, J., Vegara, J. M., López, G. F., & Díaz, A. (2016). Satisfacción de usuarios de servicios deportivos en orihuela (Alicante). *SPORT TK-Revista EuroAmericana De Ciencias Del Deporte*, *5*(1), 155–162.

García-Fernández, J., Cepeda, G., & Martín, D. (2012). La satisfacción de clientes y su relación con la percepción de calidad en centro de fitness: Utilización de la escala CALIDFIT. *Revista De Psicología Del Deporte*, *21*(2), 309–319.

Granero, A., Ruiz, F., García, M., Baena, A., & Gómez, M. (2008). Análisis del perfil sociodemográfico de senderistas y ciclistas que recorren el camino de Santiago. *Retos. Nuevas Tendencias De Educación Física, Deporte y Recreación*, *13*, 56–59.

Hernández, R., Fernández, C., & Baptista, P. (2014). *Metodología de la investigación* (6th ed.). McGraw-Hill.

Hernández-Cortés, P. L., Enríquez-Reyna, M. C., Leyva-Caro, J. A., & Ceballos-Gurrola, O. (2019). Apoyo social y autonomía para el ejercicio en espacios abiertos. Medición en adultas mayores de la comunidad. *Cuadernos De Psicología Del Deporte*, *19*(3), 243–253.

Imbroda, J. (2014). *Análisis de fidelización y la satisfacción del usuario de centros deportivos* [Tesis doctoral, Universidad de Málaga]. https://dialnet.unirioja.es/servlet/dctes?codigo=52832

INFOBAE. (2020). Así será la nueva normalidad al ir al gimnasio. Noticia https://www.infobae.com/america/mexico/2020/05/15/asi-sera-la-nueva-normalidad-al-ir-al-gimnasio/

Instituto Nacional de Estadística y Geografía [INEGI] (2022). *Módulo de práctica deportiva y ejercicio físico* (MOPRADEF). INEGI. https://www.inegi.org.mx/programas/mopradef/

Kim, Y. K., & Trail, G. (2010). Constraints and motivators: A new model to explain sport consumer behavior. *Journal of Sport Management*, *24*(2), 190–210.

Lara Rodríguez, L. M. (2020). Los muchos rostros del deporte y la perspectiva de género en Luis Manuel Lara Rodríguez, *Deporte y género. El margen desde los márgenes* (1st ed., Vol. 1, pp. 45–67). Universidad Autónoma de Ciudad Juárez/Universidad Autónoma del Estado de México.

Lara Rodríguez, L. M., & Juárez Lozano, M. (2020). Intervención socioeducativa desde el deporte en Ciudad Juárez. Experiencias, métodos y estrategias en Cely Celene Ronquillo Chávez, *Hacia la construcción de una nueva agenda educativa*. Colección Investigar, intervenir y evaluar en educación, (1st ed., Vol. 3, pp. 195–225). Universidad Autónoma de Ciudad Juárez.

Larson, B., & Steinman, R. (2009). Driving NFL fan satisfaction and return intentions with concession service quality. *Services Marketing Quarterly*, *30*(4), 418–428.

Leyra, B. (2019). Resizing Children's work: Anthropological notes on Mexican girls. In M. Rausky, & M. Chaves (Eds.), *Living and working in poverty in Latin America* (pp. 13–39). Palgrave Macmillan.

Liu, Y. D., Taylor, P., & Shibli, S. (2009). Measuring customer service quality of English public sport facilities. *International Journal of Sport Management and Marketing*, *6*(3), 229–252.

Macarro, J., Martínez, A., & Torres, J. (2012). Motives of practice physical activity and sport in Spanish adolescents at the end of their secondary education. *Journals of Research in Educational Psychology*, *10*(1), 371–396.

Martínez, L., & Martínez, J. A. (2007). Cognitive-affective model of consumer satisfaction. An exploratory study within the framework of a sporting event. *Journal of Business Research*, *60*(2), 108–114.

Martínez León, C. P. (2020). *Jóvenes y Deporte*. Boletín del Instituto Mexicano de la Juventud. IMJUVE.

Medina, R., Ceballos, O., Pérez, J., Medina, M., & Ramos, I. (2015). La gestión de la calidad en entidades deportivas. Dirección de publicaciones UANL.

Medina-Rodríguez, R. (2010). Opinión de los usuarios/deportistas acerca de los servicios ofrecidos por una entidad deportiva municipal. *Revista Mexicana De Investigación En Cultura Física y Deporte, 2*(2), 236–252.

Mestre, A. (2013). Componentes de la gestión deportiva: Una aproximación. *Revista De Educación Física, 2*(2), 1–19. https://revistas.udea.edu.co/index.php/viref/article/view/15775

Mondaca, F., Zueck, M. C., Mayorga-Vega, D., Flores, L. A., Benitez, Z. P., & Peinado, J. E. (2020). Composición e invarianza factorial del autoinforme de barreras para la práctica de ejercicio físico (ABPEF-m) en universitarios mexicanos deportistas. *Cuadernos De Psicología Del Deporte, 20*(2), 253–264.

Morales Sánchez, V., & Gálvez-Ruiz, P. (2011). La percepción del usuario en la evaluación de la calidad de los servicios municipales deportivos. *Cuadernos De Psicología Del Deporte, 11*(2), 147–154.

Morquecho-Sánchez, R., Morales-Sánchez, V., Ceballos-Gurrola, O., & Medina-Rodríguez, R. E. (2016). Cuestionario de evaluación de la calidad percibida en organizaciones de servicios deportivos universitarios (Qunisport V. Mx): Programa factor. *Revista Iberoamericana De Psicología Del Ejercicio y El Deporte, 11*(2), 271–277.

Moscoso-Sánchez, D. (2020). El contexto del deporte en españa durante la crisis sanitaria de la COVID-19. *Sociología Del Deporte, 1*(1), 15–19.

Niñerola, J., Capdevila, L., & Pintanel, M. (2006). Barreras percibidas y actividad física: El autoinforme de barreras para la práctica de ejercicio físico. *Revista De Psicología Del Deporte, 15*(1), 53–69.

Nuviala, R. (2013). *Juicios de valor de usuarios de servicios deportivos de tiempo libre de Andalucía* [Tesis doctoral, Universidad Pablo Olavide]. Repositorio Institucional - Universidad Pablo Olavide. https://rio.upo.es/xmlui/handle/10433/586

Nuviala, A., Grao-Cruces, A., Pérez-Turpin, J. A., & Nuviala, R. (2012). Perceived service quality, perceived value and satisfaction in groups of users of sports organizations in Spain. *Kinesiology, 44*(1), 94–103.

Nuviala, A., Tamayo, J. A., Iranzo, J., & Falcón, D. (2008). Diseño y validación de un instrumento de medida de la calidad de las organizaciones deportivas. *Retos. Nuevas Tendencias En Educación Física, Deporte y Recreación, 14*, 10–16.

Nuviala, A., Tamayo, J., Nuviala, R., González, J., & Fernández, A. (2010). Propiedades psicométricas de la escala de valoración de organizaciones deportivas EPOD. *Retos: Nuevas Tendencias En Educación Física, Deporte y Recreación, 18*, 83–87.

Nuviala, A., Tamayo, J. A., Nuviala, R., Pereira, E., & Carvalho, J. (2012). Predicción del abandono deportivo en la adolescencia a través del estudio de la calidad percibida. *Movimiento, 18*(1), 221–239.

Ongallo, C. (2012). *La atención al cliente y el servicio posventa*. Díaz de Santos

Pérez, I. (19 febrero de 2020). *Industria deportiva en México: afectada por la incertidumbre financiera*. EL MISTER. http://elmister.info/industria-deportiva-en-mexico-afectada-por-la-incertidumbre-financiera/

Reyes-Robles, M. (2018). *La satisfacción de clientes/deportistas y trabajadores en entidades deportivas como determinante de los servicios deportivos* [Tesis Doctoral, Universidad Autónoma de Nuevo León]. Repositorio institucional de la Universidad Autónoma de Nuevo León. http://eprints.uanl.mx/14637/

Reyes-Robles, M., Medina-Rodríguez, R. E., Ramírez-Siqueiros, M. G., López-Walle, J., & Ceballos-Gurrola, O. (2018). Satisfaction of an employee in a sports entity: Design and validation of a measerement scale. *Journal of Physical Education Research, 5*(1), 53–63.

Rial, J., Varela, J., Rial, A., & Real, E. (2010). Modelización y medida de La calidad percibida en centros deportivos: La escala QSport-10. *RICYDE. Revista Internacional De Ciencias Del Deporte, 6*(18), 57–73.

Román Miranda, A. L., Lezama Ruiz, N., & Maldonado Astudillo, J. P. (2020). Perspectiva del desarrollo empresarial *fitness* en Acapulco, México. *Inventio. La Génesis De La Cultura Universitaria En Morelos, 16*(38), 1–9. https://doi.org/10.30973/inventio/2020.16.38/4

Ruíz-Alejos, C. (2015). *Análisis de la calidad percibida, satisfacción, valor percibido e intenciones futuras de los usuarios de los servicios deportivos públicos gestionados por Logroño Deporte* [Tesis doctoral, Universidad de la Rioja]. https://dialnet.unirioja.es/servlet/tesis?codigo=46490

Sánchez, C., González, C. M., López, G. F., & Díaz, A. (2017). Satisfacción de clientes externos. Estudio de caso de una piscina cubierta. *SPORT TK-Revista Euroamericana De Ciencias Del Deporte, 6*(2), 81–88.

Sánchez-Hernández, R., Martínez-Tur, V., González-Morales, M., Ramos, J., & Peiró, J. M. (2009). Un análisis transnivel de las relaciones de la calidad de servicio y la confirmación de expectativas con la satisfacción de los usuarios. *Psicothema, 21*(3), 421–426.

Vegara, J. C., Quesada, V., & Blanco, I. (2011). Factores clave para la valoración de la calidad del servicio y satisfacción del cliente: Modelos causales, desarrollo y evolución. *Revista Virtual Universidad Católica Del Norte, 1*(35), 380–400.

Vernet, C. (8 de mayo de 2020). *El deporte profesional en México.* SCORE. https://scoredeportes.com.mx/?p=13237

Vila, I., Sánchez, C., & Manassero, M. (2009). Satisfacción percibida de los usuarios de las instalaciones deportivas municipales de Palma de mallorca. *Revista Iberoamericana De Psicología Del Deporte, 4*(1), 59–74.

Villafranco, G. (2016). *4 millones de mexicanos van al gimnasio (y prefieren correr que ser más fuertes).* Forbes. https://www.forbes.com.mx/4-millones-de-mexicanos-van-al-gimnasio-y-prefieren-correr-que-ser-mas-fuertes/.

Yildiz, S. (2011). An importance-performance analysis of fitness center service quality: Empirical results from fitness centers in Turkey. *African Journal of Business Management, 5*(16), 7031–7041.

Chapter 9

Impact of Products and Services Innovations on Consumer Behavior

The Portuguese Fitness Industry

Vera Pedragosa
Universidade Autónoma de Lisboa, Portugal

Jairo León-Quismondo
Universidad Europea de Madrid, Spain

Thiago Santos
Universidade Europeia, Portugal

Chapter Contents

Introduction	123
Innovation in the Fitness Industry	124
Consumers' Expectations	126
Consumers' Behaviors	127
Fitness Industry in Portugal	129
Case Analysis – GO Fit in Portugal	131
Conclusions and Managerial Perspectives	133
References	134

Introduction

The benefits of regular practice of physical activity are worldwide accepted through organizations (e.g., International Health, Racquet and Sportsclub Association, World Health Organization (WHO), American College of Sport Medicine, and Europe Active) and by the scientific community (Pedersen & Saltin, 2015; Siddiqui et al., 2010; Warburton, 2006). These works show positive evidence related to the reduction in mortality, diseases, and their prevention, resulting in an improvement in the quality of life, as well as in the physical and psychological well-being. The last Eurobarometer (European Commission, 2018) reports that, in 2017, more than 68% of the Portuguese did not perform any type of exercise or sport and 6% of the population do it rarely. When comparing these results with the data of physical activity levels collected by the National Health Survey (NHS) in

DOI: 10.4324/9781003388050-11

2019 (resident population aged ≥15 years), the levels are similar, showing stability in the value of the main indicators of physical activity and sedentary behavior (PNPAF, 2020). Thus, NHS data of 2019 reveal that 65% of the Portuguese population did not take part in any type of physical exercise (sports or leisure activities), with only 9% reporting being active at least 5 days per week.

In order to combat the pandemic of physical inactivity, the WHO has set as one of its main goals the global reduction of physical inactivity. For that purpose, a new global strategic action plan for 2018–2030 was launched (WHO, 2019). Alongside this global action plan, in Portugal, the National Programme for the Promotion of Physical Activity (PNPAF, 2020) is one of the priority health programs of the Directorate-General for Health (DGS). The PNPAF's mission is to generalize a physically active lifestyle as a sign of health and well-being, involving relevant social actors in citizen-centered initiatives and generating chains leading to increase the population's interest in regular physical activity practice and reduction of sedentary time. Despite the limitations in citizens' mobility and the quarantines, Portugal defined the practice of physical activity as one of the exceptions to the confinement measures, recognizing its importance for physical and mental health in this context.

The industry of fitness plays a crucial role in reducing and combating the level of inactivity in Portugal, allowing the regular practice of exercise in a particular type of facility: accredited spaces with specialized professionals. The same barometer mentions that people who exercise regularly usually do it in fitness facilities. This fact emphasizes the importance of this sector in the general panorama of sports products and services innovations in Portugal (European Commission, 2018). Since 2007, many studies (ACSM, 2021; Thompson, 2021) explore the world fitness worldwide trends every year. The first worldwide trend is online training and wearable fitness technology (WFT), whereas the first European trend is personal training and HIIT (high-intensity interval training) (Batrakoulis, 2019). For Portugal, the number 1 trend is the concern of having certified professionals (regarding to credibility of the service) and WFT reaches position 9 in the rank (Franco et al., 2021).

Innovation in the Fitness Industry

Innovation is a core activity for any kind of organization and comprises new processes and solutions for existing problems. Innovation includes changes in what is being offered to the world – innovation in products and services – and the ways it is being created and delivered –process innovation (Bessant et al., 2005). However, due to the complexity of this concept and the multidisciplinary nature of previous approaches, there is no consensus on its definition. Some authors have suggested that there are more than 60 possible definitions of innovation in the academic literature (Baregheh et al., 2009). Nevertheless, most of them include core elements such as the novelty in products or services, development of new ideas, new processes, or improvement (Baregheh et al., 2009; Bessant et al., 2005; Bustinza et al., 2018).

Impact of Products and Services Innovations   125

In business, innovation allows surviving in the current growingly competitive environment. In the last two decades, there has been an increasing interest in innovation within the management of sport and physical activity services (Ratten & Ferreira, 2016; Tjønndal, 2016, 2017). However, some authors suggest that although the theoretical framework of innovation is relatively new, the innovation phenomenon is nothing new to the sport (Tjønndal, 2017). Following Tjønndal (2017), different types of innovation could be adopted by sport organizations (Table 9.1).

One of the most common barriers to avoiding innovation is the fear of risk. Risk is inherent to innovative services (Herzenstein et al., 2007; Ratten & Ferreira, 2016). However, risk also exists when no change is performed. In other words, a sport center that stays as it is right now and only focuses on the present will drastically decrease its attractiveness and competitiveness in the upcoming years. For example, sport centers that are early adopters will adopt innovation before it has spread in the industry. In this case, those centers will take advance of the potential usefulness of innovations but might have to deal with risk since many customers will be innovation-averse. In the case of late adopters, they will implement innovations after it is common in their market, avoiding the risk of bad acceptance among customers but accepting the risk of being less impressive with their innovations since they will be seen as normal (Ratten, 2017).

Within the sports sector, the fitness industry is a benchmark for increasing adherence of society to regular physical activity. The last report by the International Health, Racquet and Sportsclub Association (IHRSA, 2020) states that, as of 2019, the number of health and fitness facilities worldwide is over 210,000 serving over 183 million members. Only in Europe, the number of fitness centers scales up to 63,644, with 64.8 million memberships (Europe Active, 2020). These numbers reflect the ubiquity of fitness centers and their reference as sports facilities, helping to sport promotion among society, thus increasing the adherence to physical activity (Cheung & Woo, 2016; Clavel et al., 2018; León-Quismondo et al., 2020b).

Table 9.1 Types of Sport Innovation

Types of sport innovation	Description
Technological	New ways of sport participation and new advances concerning organizational management of services
Commercial	New ways in which products or processes are marketed
Organizational	Projects that pursuit institutional or organizational change
Social	New solutions to complex social issues, pursuing to positively influence society
Community-based	New partnerships with local community groups to encourage working toward a common goal
Organizational	Projects that pursuit institutional or organizational change

Such a large number of fitness centers has generated a new reality in the fitness industry, where innovation plays a crucial role. First, it seems more than evident that there is no place in the market for providers whose offer is similar to the average offer of competitors. Instead, each provider should differentiate from others, adding value, following innovative solutions such as new services, new processes, or new structural organization. Second, the great variety in the offer has generated customers with a higher degree of experience and higher expectations. People who are willing to engage in physical activities in fitness centers have a solid background, have a higher knowledge of the characteristics of the service, can compare between them and, therefore, choose the one that best meets their needs. One of the most efficient ways of facing this situation is through innovation. As highlighted previously, the current scenario of high rivalry among centers requires innovative solutions for creating new opportunities and for avoiding the obsolescence of existing ones.

Consumers' Expectations

Every consumer has expectations related to what they think to happen with the fitness servicescape. One of the goals is having profitable fitness centers and a way to achieve this is through managing the expectations of consumers. In this regard, meeting the customer's expectations is crucial. The capacity of fitness centers to meet their customer expectations, and even exceed them, is very likely to result in a positive perception of quality, satisfaction, and positive behavior of consumer (Pedragosa & Correia, 2009). The knowledge of what consumers expect from fitness centers allows managers to identify (Gonçalves et al., 2016; Theodorakis et al., 2001).

Two different types of expectations toward services can be identified in consumers. First, they expect services to provide certain attributes and use these expectations to make judgments about service quality (Parasuraman et al., 1985). For instance, a fitness center that provides a wide variety of services compared to another is more likely to be perceived as a high-quality service provider. For instance, if the fitness center does not offer a parking lot, it will be perceived as a poor quality service compared to another that provides a parking lot, even if the range of activities offered is high. Second, consumers have expectations in every single encounter with the service. This forms feelings of satisfaction or dissatisfaction with the service (Chiu et al., 2021; Wong, 2004). These expectations are perceptual in nature. The feeling with the service is determined by consumers' perceptions of how the encounter with the service met their expectations, rather than by any other attributes provided by the service. For instance, if the fitness center provides a parking lot, but the only free parking space is far away from the entrance and a consumer misses the start of the class, the user is likely to feel dissatisfied with the perception of the car park lot service since their expectations were not met. Alternatively, if the consumer did not miss the start of their class activity, it is likely to have little or no impact on their satisfaction with the service. Satisfaction can be regarded as the outcome that emerges from the experience with the service, whereas service quality is concerned with the attributes of the service itself (Pedragosa, 2012).

The expectations can be influenced by six conditions: pass experience, consumer's needs, word-of-mouth, market communications, price, and image (Pedragosa & Correia, 2009). Consumers with previous experience in the service have more complex expectations than consumers without previous experience. Therefore, the higher the experience, the higher expectations for that service. The needs of the consumer are a natural trigger to raise the expectations and the reason to choose that service instead of another service. Word-of-mouth is the greater strength to influence the expectations and is considered the powerful machine to influence the purchases. Market communications, advertisements, advertising material, personal selling, and contracts are offers of explicit promises to consumers regarding the attributes of the services the organization will offer. As the promises are antecedent to the expectations, consumers use the promises to form their expectations. The price is considered by some to be key for influencing expectations as well as a perceived indicator of the level of quality of service delivered (for instance, a high level of service is expected in a high price center). Consumers' image of an organization is an important antecedent of expectations. A positive or negative view of the organization created by the image impacts what consumers expect.

Coye (2004) noted that expectations can be managed intentionally to increase, reduce, or highlight the initial expectations of the service. These results of expectations are disconfirmation, which occurs when there are differences between what is expected and what is actually received (positively or negatively) (Chiu et al., 2021). This is usually measured as the "gap" between expectations and performance (Burns et al., 2003). Pioneering work by Parasuraman et al. (1985) based on the disconfirmation paradigm identified that if service delivery meets consumer expectations (confirmation), then the service is considered to have an acceptable level of quality. If the service exceeds expectations (positive disconfirmation), then consumers perceive the service quality to be good. Alternatively, if the service does not meet the consumer's expectations, then the service quality is perceived as poor (negative disconfirmation). In order to provide services that are perceived to be of acceptable quality and to positively impact consumer behavior, it is necessary to confirm and exceed the expectations through the management of consumer expectations. The innovations of fitness products and services are a way to meet the expectations of consumers, through creating value comparing to the competition. Nowadays, innovations for fitness consumers are designed using technology that enhances their experience in fitness centers.

Consumers' Behaviors

The interactivity provided by the "tech" development is allowing consumers to have more control over their consumption experiences. If in the past the relationship between consumers and organizations was based on a one-way relationship (from the organization to consumers). There is currently a two-way interaction logic (from the organization to consumers and viceversa) that enables consumers to engage with an organization through both online and offline channels. This scenario tends to improve exclusive experiences adapted to consumer needs (Santos et al., 2019). Sports organizations have innovated by the creation of events and channels, which aim to get closer to their consumers. This relationship tends to engage them and increase their levels of interaction with organizations, to improve its value co-creation, innovation, and businesses (Gambetti & Graffigna, 2010; van Doorn et al., 2010; Vivek et al., 2012). Thus, cultivating a strong and stable relationship with consumers is crucial for the organizations, as those who engage with a brand tend to favor it, through the purchase and use of their products and services (Esch et al., 2006).

In this sense, consumers involved with brands and organizations represent an advantage in a dynamic and competitive market (Ernst et al., 2011). For example, 92.4% of consumers indicated their positive intention to consume a certain brand if they have a positive experience with their products or service. In addition, 93.9% would be available to recommend some brand, if they are satisfied with it (Javornik & Mandelli, 2012). As seen, consumer behavior is highly influenced by consumption experience (Tripathi, 2009). Thus, if the experience is positive, there is a set of effective behavior, such as: speaking positively about brands (Tripathi, 2009); sharing good perceptions about the products in the online and offline channels (Bergkvist & Bech-Larsen, 2010); or helping organizations in the innovation business processes (Hoyer et al., 2010). Thus, consumer behavior is not only centered on the purchase of the product but on the issues that can influence this decision-making process (Hollebeek, 2011).

The levels of consumer interactions with organizations depend on cognitive, affective, emotional, and behavioral characteristics (Hollebeek, 2011). The behavioral elements are based on consumers' actions toward their experiences with organizations (Vivek et al., 2012). Kumar et al. (2010) present four dimensions that seek to explain the value attributed by the consumer in the context of his consumption experience. The first dimension is the value of the consumer's continued experience with the brand – customer lifetime value. This dimension focuses on the idea that when creating a commitment to the brand, the consumer tends to spend more money in a time frame toward their favorite organization (Rust et al., 2004). The second dimension is the customer referral value and means the value given to the brand by the consumer and how sharing this value attracts other consumers (Chauhan & Pillai, 2013). Following Kumar and colleagues, the third dimension is the customer influence value, which refers to the motivation that the consumer has to assume before other consumers the reason for choosing the brand, product, or service (Kaltcheva et al., 2014). Finally, the fourth dimension is called customer knowledge value and concerns the contribution of the consumer in the stages of product and service development and innovations (Morris & Martin, 2000). Therefore, based on consumer experiences, behaviors, and information, the organizations tend to enhance their innovation process

(Ernst et al., 2011). What is sought as a result of this interaction is to increase the quality of products or services, the reduction of costs and risks in the production, and the effective marketing processes in order to increase brand value (Hoyer et al., 2010). Among all conditions, "tech" innovations have been identified as fundamental for the construction of more positive behavior in the consumer's relationship with organizations (Carlson & O'Cass, 2012; Mollen & Wilson, 2010). This is due, in part, to the significant increase in the quantity and quality of innovation tools (e.g., online channels, apps) managed or not by organizations to direct the information reproduced by the consumer.

In contrast, not all the innovation tools are always properly managed. Sharing information is often confusing, irrelevant, and tends not to materialize consumer engagement or positive behaviors toward the organizations. Certainly, engaged consumers are valuable assets, in such a way that they become the most fervent brand ambassadors and can guarantee the organization's sustained growth. It seems clear that these aspects are fundamental to the success of the sport organization. In this situation, different fitness centers try to involve their consumers through innovative processes that allow these organizations to sustain their position in the market, increasing the chances of surviving and adapting to new challenges in the fitness context (León-Quismondo et al., 2020b). This level of knowledge of its consumers has increased the fitness organizations' expertise in the control of consumer experiences and behaviors. For example, some studies consider consumer segmentation as pivotal to create good experiences in this market (León-Quismondo et al., 2020b; Tsitskari et al., 2017). Issues such as exercise motivation, sociodemographic characteristics, and different perceptions of consumer based on gender and age have been established in the previous studies, to better organize consumer experiences and consumer expectations (León-Quismondo et al., 2020a). Complementarily, the assessment of the effects of customer satisfaction, service quality, perceived quality, and loyalty are important strategies to maintain a positive level of consumer perception of the service in the fitness market (Chao, 2015; Tsitskari et al., 2017; Vieira et al., 2019).

Fitness Industry in Portugal

During the decade of 1980, Portuguese fitness was mainly influenced by the Fitness American practices. Since then, three periods of time can be defined (Gomes et al., 2017; Pedragosa, 2021): initial period (between 1980 and 1998); modern period (from 1998 until 2008); technological period (from 2008 until now). In the initial period, most of the gyms were essentially oriented to male members, and their offer was almost limited to a single exercise room for bodybuilding. In the modern period, the gyms (i.e., health clubs) started to offer several services as exercise room; group classes; spa; personal training; parking; restaurants; babysitting (Pedragosa, 2012), as well as the women interest becomes increased. In the technological period, after the crisis of 2008, news business models emerge beyond the conventional gyms, with innovations of products and services. Since then, the fitness industry in Portugal has become more complex. In 2019, Portugal is the home of 1,100 fitness centers serving 688,210 members, mostly women (57%). The global market represented 289,371 million euros (excluding Value Added Tax) (Pedragosa & Cardadeiro, 2020).

In 2020, the COVID-19 pandemic negatively impacted Portugal's fitness industry. The number of fitness centers decreased 30% to 800 and the number of members decreased 29% (491,355 members), mostly women (56%). The global market revenue decreased 42% with 167,408 million euros (excluding VAT) (Pedragosa & Cardadeiro, 2021). One of the biggest challenges of fitness centers is to generate positive consumer behaviors on members through the satisfaction with products and services that result in profitable business. To match this challenge, the fitness industry, after the 2008 crisis (technological period), started offering more than traditional gyms, doing by new product and service innovation: different business models; new prices segment; and high technology. Thus, the concept of fitness itself has been developing to wellness concept in order to satisfy the psychological needs besides physical ones (Pedragosa, 2012).

In Portugal, the market share of one-store fitness centers is 37%, whereas the chains (more than one fitness center) represent 63% of the market share. The innovations through new business models (fitness centers) have five categories: health clubs (or conventional gyms), personal trainer studios, CrossFit box, woman gyms, and fitness boutiques. The franchising business model increased from less than 1% (2018) to 9% in 2021 (Pedragosa & Cardadeiro, 2021). Most of them (78%) are health clubs that offer several services (a complete fitness offer) such as weight training equipment, cardiovascular equipment, group classes, functional training, swimming pool, racquet sports, ball sports, sauna/jacuzzi, spa and wellness, virtual classes, applications (apps), WFT, and outdoor classes. The second business model, personal trainer studios, represents 9%. These centers do not offer sports such as racquet sports, or other ball sports. Some of these centers or training studios can offer personal training, yoga, pilates, or electro-stimulation. The third business model, fitness boutique, gained representativeness since 2018, representing 6% in 2019 (i.e., 2% in 2018). This model offers similar services as the first business model without the ball-sports offer. The fourth business model, woman gyms, represents 4% and don't offer swimming pool, racquet sports, ball sports, sauna/jacuzzi, and spa and wellness. The fifth and last business model, CrossFit box, has common aspects with the second business model (i.e., personal trainer studios) and represents 2% of the market. The innovations that are present beyond the business models are the price segment. Three categories can be established: low-cost (i.e., equal or less than €29.90); middle-market (i.e., range between €29.90 and €55.00); premium (over €55.00). The average monthly fee in Portugal is €30.25 (with VAT). What's more, 36% of fitness centers have average monthly fees in the middle-market segment and 55% in low-cost (Pedragosa & Cardadeiro, 2021). The representativeness of the low-cost segment continues growing in the technological period (Figure 9.1).

Finally, the pandemic COVID-19 has led to a surge in technological innovations. The main technological innovations before COVID-19 were related to

Impact of Products and Services Innovations 131

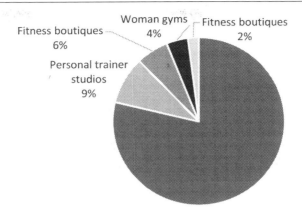

Figure 9.1 Fitness Business Models in Portugal 2020.

technological machines, applications (apps for easing the management of the facilities and group classes), and virtual classes at fitness centers (i.e., in hours with fewer members). The pioneers in Portugal were Fitness Hut and GO Fit. In pandemic crises COVID-19, the intensity of technology to meet expectations, satisfactions, and positive consumer behavior led to offering virtual classes at home (for instance, using Zoom), WFT (for instance, MYZONE represented by Portugal Gimnica), and On-demand (Les Mills On-demand). The applications refer to software developed for electronic devices such as smartphones, tablets, or watches that can be described in applications to fitness facilities management (Ferreira et al., 2021). The WFT are electronic devices that can be used as accessories for practical uses in fitness, such as: monitoring physical activity, counting steps taken, counting calories, training intensity, among other uses (Lunney et al., 2016). On-demand offers several services of fitness (for instance, record group classes) that members can use livery according to their needs. Normally, WFT and On-demand have a price to use. In Portugal, 66% of fitness centers have fitness applications, 65% of virtual classes, and 20% of WFT (Pedragosa & Cardadeiro, 2021).

Case Analysis – GO Fit in Portugal

The GO Fit is part of the group of companies that form Ingesport. It is a Spanish-settled company with more than 20 years of experience and chaired by Sáez Irigoyen, which bases its activity on the development and promotion of large sports complexes. Currently, GO Fit comprises 20 fitness facilities, operating between Spain and Portugal. Ingesport builds its fitness facilities based on a mixed model in which the Administration provides long-term public land and the company provides private investment and professional management. In this way, Ingesport works for private companies – hotels and real-estate companies – and for municipalities, providing sports advice and management of sports centers and ad hoc programs. The administrative concession scheme appears as an effective formula to turn a sector affected by the economic crisis into a profitable sector and to be able to build, operate, and maintain infrastructures and facilities in the area of health and sport and to guarantee the best value for money for citizens. The Administration cedes the land to the private investor in exchange for an annual fee with a time horizon of around 40 years, as they require a high investment. Concessions are awarded through a public tender, which may be at the initiative of the Administration itself or of the private company.

In Portugal, GO Fit opened its first store in 2015, in the district of Lisbon, called GO Fit Olivais. Later in 2015, GO Fit opened the second unit in the center of Lisbon, Go Fit Campo Grande. The company aims to ensure price, quality, accessibility, and sustainability, combining high public service performance and private profitability. GO Fit seeks to continue its expansion strategy in Portugal, even after the COVID-19 crisis. The GO Fit brought to Portugal excellence in innovation as a business model, price segment, and high technology offered to members. Regarding the business model, in accordance with the first category described in this chapter, GO Fit is considered a health club (or conventional gyms) with the highest number of services offered compared to all the other business models described: weight training equipment, cardiovascular equipment, group classes, functional training, swimming pool, racquet sports, ball sports, sauna/Jacuzzi, spa and wellness, virtual classes, applications (apps), WFT, and outdoor classes. Regarding price innovation, the GO Fit fits into the middle-market segment with an average monthly fee of about 40€. The Go Fit leads the market with a strong positioning directed to the family that allows this value to include father and mother and all the children up to 21 years old. In the fitness industry in Portugal, this concept of business versus price versus family has revolutionized innovation in the sector.

Finally, concerning innovation technology, GO Fit is considered a pioneer in Portugal with the offer of the latest generation fitness machines (i.e., Technogym) with internet access, TV, and synchronization of the system through the key and App. The key allows opening the car park, the turnstile, the locker, store the workout, and the member's biometric data. The App allows booking classes and checking their capacity, having access to pre-recorded classes (WFT), live online classes, and accessing to exclusive discounts for members (which rewards the number of times they access the App through points to exchange for brand merchandising products – a measure to increase attendance and consequently loyalty). All the fitness rooms have an extra 1,000 m², from the weight-training room to the group classrooms, including a bike room (i.e., stationary bikes) with the possibility of physical and virtual classes. The spaces in Portugal have an average of 8,000 m² per fitness facility, which is part of the 29% of fitness facilities that have more than 1,500 m² (Pedragosa & Cardadeiro, 2021).

GO Fit has an exercise and health lab for the production of scientifically validated training plans and group classes by GO Fit Lab. The GO Fit Lab is the research and innovation unit of GO Fit that includes a physiology lab located in one of the sports centers. Several health programs are developed in GO Fit Lab to ensure a scientifically proven quality product that meets the expectations of members and their families. Apart from the sustainability character of GO Fit centers, social responsibility is also present in its philosophy. A more active life is promoted through diverse programs: parish councils, kindergarten, schools, nursing homes, and athletes – with several actions that provide sport and physical activity for all. To sum up, the great revolution of GO Fit in Portugal is done through the offer of premium services, combining technological excellence (i.e., weight machines, diversity of classes, online classes, Key, App, WFT, etc.), with the offer of products and services scientifically proven through the GO Fit Lab, with a low price (i.e., for 40€, you can train four people from the same household). The brand activation of GO Fit is also revitalized through its own merchandising for sale or exchange of points in the clubs.

Conclusions and Managerial Perspectives

No organization can succeed without adapting to the current social needs and context. This chapter highlights the extreme importance of adapting, renewing, and developing new ideas. Innovation is a source of competitive advantage. In order to reach it, sport organizations are forced to adapt to the upcoming reality. The outcomes of innovation include a better position in the industry, leadership in the market, higher value, and, as a result, more satisfied customers. In Portugal, fitness centers are considered one of the benchmark providers of sports services. After the 2008 crisis and the later COVID-19 outbreak, the industry has become very demanding and only the leading brands managed to survive. Innovation plays a crucial role in brand leadership in the Portugal fitness industry, deployed in three main axons: different business models; new prices segment; high technology (Figure 9.2).

Consumers are increasingly sharing their impressions of their consumption experiences through uncounted online and offline channels. In this sense, the

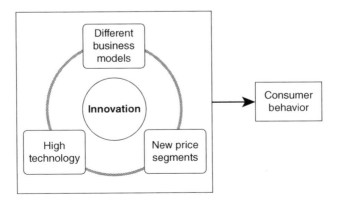

Figure 9.2 Innovation of Fitness Products and Services in Portugal.

empowerment of consumers within their consumption experiences becomes an important element that needs to be considered in the context of the sports industry. For example, García-Fernandez et al. (2020) consider that behavior patterns are specified in the way in which people invest their time and money, in their interests and their vital priorities, and are influenced by purchasing power, personality, motivation, or family history. In addition, these authors consider that the business model on the fitness sector is constantly being updated, and is mostly influenced, currently, by a technological-based service. All the evolution of service standards evidenced in this chapter and referred to in the literature on the context of fitness has called for more efficient management of the logic of technology and innovation and its applicability in sport, as well as the adaptability of the industry to this whole consumption scenario. This context is also extremely influenced by the challenges imposed by the pandemic experienced in the last year. This became an area of opportunity for fitness organizations that increase the number of virtual classes, develop massively fitness apps, and expanding their services in terms of equipment and technology (Myers et al., 2020).

In summary, the current chapter was driven by important research questions, including how the innovation perspective has an impact on one of the most promising markets in Ibero-American sports, the fitness in Portugal. Although the impact of innovation on consumer behavior is clear in the fitness industry and, specifically, in the Portuguese context, this case can also serve as a reference for other sport professionals, other than fitness.

References

ACSM (2021). *American College of Sports Medicine - ACSM's guidelines for exercise testing and prescription* (11th ed.). Wolters Kluwer.

Baregheh, A., Rowley, J., & Sambrook, S. (2009). Towards a multidisciplinary definition of innovation. *Management Decision*, 47(8), 1323–1339.

Batrakoulis, A. (2019). European survey of fitness trends for 2020. *ACSM's Health & Fitness Journal*, 23(6), 28–35.

Bergkvist, L., & Bech-Larsen, T. (2010). Two studies of consequences and actionable antecedents of brand love. *Journal of Brand Management*, 17(7), 504–518.

Bessant, J., Lamming, R., Noke, H., & Phillips, W. (2005). Managing innovation beyond the steady state. *Technovation*, 25(12), 1366–1376.

Burns, R. C., Graefe, A. R., & Absher, J. D. (2003). Alternate measurement approaches to recreational customer satisfaction: Satisfaction-only versus gap scores. *Leisure Sciences*, 25(4), 363–380.

Bustinza, O. F., Herrero, F. V., Gomes, E., Lafuente, E., Basáez, M. O., Rabetino, R., & Vaillant, Y. (2018). Product-service innovation and performance: Unveiling the complexities. *International Journal of Business Environment*, 10(2), 95–111.

Carlson, J., & O'Cass, A. (2012). Optimizing the online channel in professional sport to create trusting and loyal consumers: The role of the professional sports team brand and service quality. *Journal of Sport Management*, 26(6), 463–478.

Chao, R. F. (2015). The impact of experimental marketing on customer loyalty for fitness clubs: Using brand image and satisfaction as the mediating variables. *The Journal of International Management Studies*, 10(2), 52–60.

Chauhan, K., & Pillai, A. (2013). Role of content strategy in social media brand communities: A case of higher education institutes in India. *Journal of Product & Brand Management, 22*(1), 40–51.

Cheung, R., & Woo, M. (2016). Determinants of perceived service quality: An empirical investigation of fitness and recreational facilities. *Contemporary Management Research, 12*(3), 363–370.

Chiu, W., Cho, H., & Chi, C. G. (2021). Consumers' continuance intention to use fitness and health apps: An integration of the expectation–confirmation model and investment model. *Information Technology & People, 34*(3), 978–998.

Clavel, I., García-Unanue, J., Iglesias-Soler, E., Felipe, J. L., & Gallardo, L. (2018). Prediction of abandonment in Spanish fitness centres. *European Journal of Sport Science, 19*(2), 217–224.

Coye, R. W. (2004). Managing customer expectations in the service encounter. *International Journal of Service Industry Management, 15*(1), 54–71.

Ernst, H., Hoyer, W. D., Krafft, M., & Krieger, K. (2011). Customer relationship management and company performance—the mediating role of new product performance. *Journal of the Academy of Marketing Science, 39*(2), 290–306.

Esch, F., Langner, T., Schmitt, B. H., & Geus, P. (2006). Are brands forever? How brand knowledge and relationships affect current and future purchases. *Journal of Product & Brand Management, 15*(2), 98–105.

Europe Active. (2020). *European Health & Fitness Market Report 2020.* https://www2.deloitte.com/content/dam/Deloitte/de/Documents/consumer-business/European-Health-and-Fitness-Market-2020-Reportauszug.pdf

European Commission. (2018). *Special Eurobarometer 472 Report - Sport and Physical Activity.* https://www.europarc.org/wp-content/uploads/2020/01/Special-Eurobarometer-472-Sports-and-physical-activity.pdf

Ferreira Barbosa, H., García-Fernández, J., Pedragosa, V., & Cepeda-Carrion, G. (2021). The use of fitness centre apps and its relation to customer satisfaction: A UTAUT2 perspective. *International Journal of Sports Marketing and Sponsorship,* Vol. ahead-of-print No. ahead-of-print.

Franco, S., Rocha, R. S., Ramalho, F., Simões, V., Isabel, V., & Ramos, L. R. (2021). Tendências do fitness em Portugal para 2021 fitness trends in Portugal for 2021. *Cuadernos De Psicología Del Deporte, 21*(2), 242–258.

Gambetti, R. C., & Graffigna, G. (2010). The concept of engagement: A systematic analysis of the ongoing marketing debate. *International Journal of Market Research, 52*(6), 801–826.

García-Fernández, J., Gálvez-Ruiz, P., Grimaldi-Puyana, M., Angosto, S., Fernández-Gavira, J., & Bohórquez, M. R. (2020). The promotion of physical activity from digital services: Influence of e-lifestyles on intention to use fitness apps. *International Journal of Environmental Research and Public Health, 17*(18), 6839.

Gomes, R., Gustavo, N., Melo, R., & Pedragosa, V. (2017). PORTUGAL: A growing sport market in a dominant state model. In A. Laine, & H. Vehmas (Eds.), *The private sport sector in Europe. A cross-national comparative perspective* (pp. 269–285). Springer.

Gonçalves, C., Meireles, P., & Carvalho, M. J. (2016). Consumer behaviour in fitness club: Study of the weekly frequency of use, expectations, satisfaction and retention. *The Open Sports Sciences Journal, 9*(1), 62–70.

Herzenstein, M., Posavac, S. S., & Brakus, J. J. (2007). Adoption of new and really new products: The effects of self-regulation systems and risk salience. *Journal of Marketing Research, 44*(2), 251–260.

Hollebeek, L. (2011). Exploring customer brand engagement: Definition and themes. *Journal of Strategic Marketing*, *19*(7), 555–573.

Hoyer, W. D., Chandy, R., Dorotic, M., Krafft, M., & Singh, S. S. (2010). Consumer co-creation in new product development. *Journal of Service Research*, *13*(3), 283–296.

IHRSA. (2020). *The 2020 IHRSA Global Report*. https://www.ihrsa.org/publications/the-2020-ihrsa-global-report/

Javornik, A., & Mandelli, A. (2012). Behavioral perspectives of customer engagement: An exploratory study of customer engagement with three Swiss FMCG brands. *Journal of Database Marketing & Customer Strategy Management*, *19*(4), 300–310.

Kaltcheva, V. D., Patino, A., Laric, M. V., Pitta, D. A., & Imparato, N. (2014). Customers' relational models as determinants of customer engagement value. *Journal of Product & Brand Management*, *23*(1), 55–61.

Kumar, V., Aksoy, L., Donkers, B., Venkatesan, R., Wiesel, T., & Tillmanns, S. (2010). Undervalued or overvalued customers: Capturing total customer engagement value. *Journal of Service Research*, *13*(3), 297–310.

León-Quismondo, J., García-Unanue, J., & Burillo, P. (2020a). Service perceptions in fitness centers: IPA approach by gender and age. *International Journal of Environmental Research and Public Health*, *17*(8), 2844.

León-Quismondo, J., García-Unanue, J., & Burillo, P. (2020b). Best practices for fitness center business sustainability: A qualitative vision. *Sustainability*, *12*(12), 5067.

Lunney, A., Cunningham, N. R., & Eastin, M. S. (2016). Wearable fitness technology: A structural investigation into acceptance and perceived fitness outcomes. *Computers in Human Behavior*, *65*, 114–120.

Mollen, A., & Wilson, H. (2010). Engagement, telepresence and interactivity in online consumer experience: Reconciling scholastic and managerial perspectives. *Journal of Business Research*, *63*(9–10), 919–925.

Morris, R. J., & Martin, C. L. (2000). Beanie babies: A case study in the engineering of a high-involvement/relationship-prone brand. *Journal of Product & Brand Management*, *9*(2), 78–98.

Myers, K., Brown, M. B., Payne, S. C., & Rosney, D. M. (2020). The reinvention of the health and fitness industry during the coronavirus pandemic. *CommonHealth*, *1*(3), 121–131.

Parasuraman, A., Zeithaml, V. A., & Berry, L. L. (1985). A conceptual model of service quality and its implications for future research. *Journal of Marketing*, *49*(4), 41–50.

Pedersen, B. K., & Saltin, B. (2015). Exercise as medicine - evidence for prescribing exercise as therapy in 26 different chronic diseases. *Scandinavian Journal of Medicine & Science in Sports*, *25*(Suppl 3), 1–72.

Pedragosa, V. (2012). *Satisfação e fidelização em ginásios e health clubs: estudo das expetativas, das emoções e da qualidade [Satisfaction and loyalty in gyms and health clubs: study of expectations, emotions and quality]*. (Unpublished Doctoral Dissertation). Universidade de Lisboa.

Pedragosa, V. (2021). An overview of fitness in Portugal: Business models, attraction and building members' loyalty. In J. García-Fernández, & P. Gálvez-Ruíz (Eds.), *The global private health & fitness business: A marketing perspective* (pp. 25–31). Emerald Publishing Limited.

Pedragosa, V., & Cardadeiro, E. (2020). *Barómetro do fitness em Portugal*. Edições AGAP.

Pedragosa, V., & Cardadeiro, E. (2021). *Barómetro do fitness em Portugal*. Edições AGAP.

Pedragosa, V., & Correia, A. (2009). Expectations, satisfaction and loyalty in health and fitness clubs. *International Journal of Sport Management and Marketing*, *5*(4), 450–464.

PNPAF (2020). *Programa nacional para a promoção da atividade física*. Direção-Geral da Saúde.

Ratten, V. (2017). *Sports innovation management*. Routledge.

Ratten, V., & Ferreira, J. J. (2016). Sport entrepreneurship and innovation. In V. Ratten & J. J. Ferreira (Eds.), *Sport entrepreneurship and innovation* (pp. 1–12). Routledge.

Rust, R. T., Lemon, K. N., & Zeithaml, V. A. (2004). Return on marketing: Using customer equity to focus marketing strategy. *Journal of Marketing, 68*(1), 109–127.

Santos, T. O., Correia, A., Biscaia, R., & Pegoraro, A. (2019). Examining fan engagement through social networking sites. *International Journal of Sports Marketing and Sponsorship, 20*(1), 163–183.

Siddiqui, N. I., Nessa, A., & Hossain, M. A. (2010). Regular physical exercise: Way to healthy life. *Mymensingh Medical Journal, 19*(1), 154–158.

Theodorakis, N., Kambitsis, C., & Laios, A. (2001). Relationship between measures of service quality and satisfaction of spectators in professional sports. *Managing Service Quality: An International Journal, 11*(6), 431–438.

Thompson, W. R. (2021). Worldwide survey of fitness trends for 2021. *ACSM'S Health & Fitness Journal, 25*(1), 10–19.

Tjønndal, A. (2016). Sport, innovation and strategic management: A systematic literature review. *Brazilian Business Review, 13*(Special Issue), 38–56.

Tjønndal, A. (2017). Sport innovation: Developing a typology. *European Journal for Sport and Society, 14*(4), 291–310.

Tripathi, M. N. (2009). Customer engagement - key to successful brand building. *Vilakshan: The XIMB Journal of Management, 6*(1), 131–140.

Tsitskari, E., Tzetzis, G., & Konsoulas, D. (2017). Perceived service quality and loyalty of fitness centers' customers: Segmenting members through their exercise motives. *Services Marketing Quarterly, 38*(4), 253–268.

van Doorn, J., Lemon, K. N., Mittal, V., Nass, S., Pick, D., Pirner, P., & Verhoef, P. C. (2010). Customer engagement behavior: Theoretical foundations and research directions. *Journal of Service Research, 13*(3), 253–266.

Vieira, E., Ferreira, J. J., & São João, R. (2019). Creation of value for business from the importance-performance analysis: The case of health clubs. *Measuring Business Excellence, 23*(2), 199–215.

Vivek, S. D., Beatty, S. E., & Morgan, R. M. (2012). Customer engagement: Exploring customer relationships beyond purchase. *Journal of Marketing Theory and Practice, 20*(2), 122–146.

Warburton, D. E. R. (2006). Health benefits of physical activity: The evidence. *Canadian Medical Association Journal, 174*(6), 801–809.

WHO (2019). *Global action plan on physical activity 2018-2030: More active people for a healthier world*. World Health Organization.

Wong, A. (2004). The role of emotional satisfaction in service encounters. *Managing Service Quality: An International Journal, 14*(5), 365–376.

Chapter 10

Educational Quality in Physical Education during Covid-19 Pandemic

Raquel Morquecho Sánchez

Autonomous University of Nuevo León, México

María Fernanda León Alcerreca

Autonomous University of Nuevo León, México

Lina Guadalupe Sierra García

Autonomous University of Nuevo León, México

Erika Alexandra Gadea Cavazos

Autonomous University of Nuevo León, México

Alma Rosa Lydia Lozano González

Autonomous University of Nuevo León, México

Chapter Contents

Introduction	138
Education Quality Management	139
Quality Appraisal in Educative/Sportive Services	140
SERVQUAL Model in Physical Education	141
Origins and Structure of SERVQUAL Model	141
SERVQUAL Model Application in Sportive Organizations	143
Conclusion	144
References	145

Introduction

México was one of the most afflicted countries because of COVID-19, with one of the highest mortality rates around the world per 100.000 habitants. Since 11 March 2020, the health emergency was declared, in consequence the population was confined. The Mexican government and most countries ordained the closure of the educational institutions and the suspension of in-person classes in

DOI: 10.4324/9781003388050-12

every educational level as a measure to ease the pandemic effects. Because of this, online schooling acquired an unprecedented importance, marking a turning point in pedagogical practices and in every system all over the world. In addition, social, cultural, and economic inequalities were evidenced in over 180 countries hit by the COVID-19 pandemic (Bravo-García & Magis-Rodriguez, 2020). This teaching paradigm change has forced the institutions to search guides and references to adapt their process for their methodological framework for learning. The main challenge in educational systems in the last few months has been to keep the vitality of teaching and promote development of significant learnings. There have been two key allies for this challenge: teachers and virtuality (use of ICTs). This represented a defiance without precedents, as most of the teachers had to generate their own apprenticeship in order to work on virtual environments and at the same time, take responsibility to instruct their students to handle that kind of spaces (Bonilla-Guachamín, 2020).

Technology is changing the way to do things in every social scope and every level, even our ways of acting and thinking. The educational systems need to face the social, economic, and technological changes, adapting the actual teaching-learning circumstances. At this moment, schools in Mexico are oriented toward quality education models, where the student is the central axis in the teaching-learning process. Hence, the importance to implement rules, guidelines, and tools directed to assess the educational quality, regardless of the health contingency. The nature of this assessment is fundamentally on proving learning results, therefore standard instruments are used to help express the results in numeric values that are easy to compare. The education services sector is not free of the customer competition and offered quality. The quality of an educational center will be the sum of different factors, including the subject of Physical Education. Because of this, in this chapter, we talk about the SERVQUAL Model, which aims to assess the service quality and is validated for educational and sportive services.

Education Quality Management

Currently, the service quality has been consolidated as a necessary alternative to achieve an organization's success. The interest in quality obeys the many advantages offered by the philosophy to improve constantly, to boost the number of loyal users, to increase the attraction of new users, and to generate new opportunities for an organization's development (Pozo Muñoz et al., 2000). This is why in recent years, quality management defends itself as an active rule to upgrade the social position of every organization. Quality revolution is growing to become a management model that involves every social actor that intervenes in the organization processes. As a consequence, of the growing interest to include quality management systems in educational organizations, the main objective of this work is to analyze every dimension in quality service and how each one affects the sociocultural contexts, specifically in educational and sportive ambit, and also establish the importance of quality in physical education classes in our country during and after COVID-19. This analysis will use the SERVQUAL Model (Parasuraman et al., 1988) as reference.

Quality services become a decisive factor in the organizations' development (Parasuraman et al., 1985), thus it is essential to know and analyze its dimensions to be able to obtain continuous improvement of the service. Quality management is a universal concept and can be applied in practically every area in organization guidance and services, nevertheless, it has been accepted by every institutional level in educational services. In society, the educational quality is noticeable due to an institution's capability to shape respectable and competent citizens. This quality abounds in main aspects related to human and social development, efficiency, human resources requirements, and costs. Unlike other types of organizations, education is essential in every process, because it satisfies a determinate role in individual growth and countries improvement. Educational quality has evolved to a business philosophy, adapted to client/users satisfaction in a way that contributes to the continuous improvement of academic institutions and their programs; this satisfied the different types of institutional internal and external clients by providing the expectations they have, since these institutions need to be in a constant actualization of their user needs, referring as external client to the students and to professors, headmaster, and contact personal as an internal client.

Quality Appraisal in Educative/Sportive Services

The characteristics of the service, like universality, temporality, and heterogeneity, make necessary the adaptation of the management strategies, so for the consumer, the quality of a service is harder to evaluate than the quality of a tangible product. Therefore, understanding the service quality represents a real complication to sport managers as well as measurement counting with a series of dimensions realized as service features that were perceived as a personal user's judgement (Nuviala et al., 2008). Rial et al. (2010) suggest that carrying out a recurring, valid, and reliable evaluation of the perceived quality is not an easy job, since it implies to establish a previous model that contains every dimension and important elements of the service itself in different offer moments. Dorado and Gallardo (2005) and Dorado et al. (2006) point out a lack of studies in the context of sportive services that allow to determine which dimensions define the appreciation over the quality of the services offered in sports. On the other hand, the idea of educational service quality according to Morales-Sánchez et al. (2013) is that educational institutions provide a service with the aim of satisfying the needs and demands of the students, but the growing global competition led to an increase of the student expectations related to educational services quality. Service specifications usually do not guarantee by itself that the students' needs can be satisfied and this can happen if notable deficiencies exist in the organization system when providing and supporting a better quality process.

SERVQUAL Model in Physical Education

We will analyze some studies that have been done related to evaluation of Physical Education Area. Please note that out of the presented studies, only three take into the students' opinion to analyze the Physical Education Area. The rest do not consider the students point-of-view as an important measure, although as it has already been exposed that the educational community considered this a main element in educational center quality. SERVQUAL Model Applied to Physical Education During Social Confinement Due to COVID-19. The controversy around physical education in Mexico and what educational quality means both endow a fundamental and important topic in modern societies. Sports services targeted toward kids and teenagers who are amidst their physical, social, and emotional development ought to be closer to education in times of sanitary contingency. It is known that both physical activity and sports contribute to an improvement of physical and social capabilities in kids and teenagers, thus it has been included in various curricula, focusing completely on the student (cognitive, motor, and affective functions); thereby it is considered of high importance continuing this course while in social confinement.

The effectiveness of specific physical education programs has been previously demonstrated. However, that same effectiveness must also be evaluated taking into account its long-term results, thus successfully modifying collective behavior. While the younger generation advances through their school life, the support given by the school to their physical education slowly declines until it stops when they reach adulthood. Hence, young people must be guided to develop positive opinions toward physical activity as well as habits that fit in their daily lives; this can be achieved by teaching cognitive and behavioral strategies that facilitate the adoption of active lifestyles, therefore boosting individual responsibility focused on physical activity and increasing the probability that future generations are more physically active. It has been shown that cardiovascular ailments are the primary cause of premature death around the world. Henceforth, the prevention of sedentarism is a public health priority. Therefore, the development of physical activity habits must be one of the main objectives of the various health education policies where Physical Education has a main role, either in the context of in-person or online classes (Table 10.1).

Origins and Structure of SERVQUAL Model

Parasuraman et al. (1985) studies are referents in service quality management nowadays. These authors developed a conceptual model in 1985, basing in previous works of Groönroos (1978, 1982, 1984), which say that perceived quality of the service is the result of the comparison between the anterior expectations and the real performance of the discern service (Parasuraman et al., 1985; Parasuraman et al., 1988). The basis of this concept model has its origin in exploratory qualitative studies, based on valuing the main lines of perceived quality service

142 R.M. Sánchez, M.F.L. Alcerreca, L.G.S. García et al.

Table 10.1 Realized Investigations in "Assessment of Physical Education and Sports" Context

Study - Author - Year	Objective – Methodology
Armengol et al. (1996). *The situation of the teaching of Physical Education in Secondary Education*	This study makes a comparison between the public centers of the autonomous communities of Aragon and La Rioja, and Catalonia. It collects personal and professional data from teachers through a survey, the context in which they work.
Menéndez et al. (1996) *Physical education status Considerations from a case study*	They want to know the opinions that students, teachers, and parents have about physical education.
Chavarria (1998) *Situation of Physical Education in the educational system*	This study makes a diagnosis of physical education in the primary stage. For this, it focuses on the development and concretion of the curriculum, on the systematics of the entire evaluation process, on curricular modifications and adaptations of students with special educational needs in the centers analyzed.
Sáenz López (1999) *The importance of Physical Education in Elementary School*	The study analyzes the causes of the physical education subject as a secondary role; recently approved in the competitive examinations in the Andalusian Community.
Dalmau Torres (2004) *Analysis of the status of physical education in primary education*	This research aims to know the situation of Physical Education in the educational system of Logroño, analyzing the recognition of this subject in the elementary stage through the opinions of the groups that make up the school community: students, parents, and teachers.
Manzano et al. (2003) *Curriculum, sports, and physical activity in the school environment. The vision of physical education teachers in Andalusia*	The objective of the study is to know the status of physical education in Andalusian educational centers
De Knop et al. (2004) *The quality of Physical Education in Flemish schools*	This study tries to obtain an overview of the expectations that the students, physical education teachers, teachers of other areas, parents' association, and personalities from the world of sports have regarding the quality factors of school physical education.
González-Arévalo (2006) *The quality of the Physical Education area. The case of the centers that teach compulsory secondary education (ESO in Spanish) the city of Barcelona*	It intends to carry out an "X-ray" of the physical education area in secondary schools in the city of Barcelona by trying to describe how the physical education areas are organized and work, and determine the quality of the physical education area.
Morales-Sánchez et al. (2013) *Quality evaluation in the area of physical education in a secondary school and high school*	This work presents an adaptation of the SERVQUAL model to the field of secondary education, specifically to the area of physical education.

as a maladjustment between expectations and results perceptions. When we talk about expectations, it refers to the desires and the needs of the consumer. The perceptions are the beliefs related to obtaining service. In that way, a client perceives a high-quality service when the experience with the service equals or exceeds the initial expectations. On the other hand, the service will be catalogued with bad quality when the expectation can't be satisfied by the service experience. Parasuraman et al. (1988) indicated that it is necessary to diagnose the service before evaluating the quality by starting to analyze the perceptions of clients and users related to received service. The measure scale and the five dimensions that define the quality of a service are: tangible elements, reliability, empathy, capacity of response, and security, which have been significant elements for generalized use of this model as well as to study service quality.

There are five dimensions of quality service that are applicable to provide a general institution service: (a) *reliability:* defined as the benefit of promise service and established in time; (b) *capacity of response:* staff disposition to bring support and quick attention to users; (c) *security:* attention and skills given to the staff to inspire credibility and confidence; (d) *empathy:* ability to understand the client perspective; and (e) *tangible elements:* appearance of physical facilities, equipment, and personal and communication materials. In their final form, the SERVQUAL questionnaire has 22 items, half of these are designated to measure the level of the expectations according to consumers, whereas the last 11 items were designed to gauge the current perception of the given service by a private organization. This questionnaire is complemented with another question section that includes the most important inquiry, the general score in quality service in a 1 to 10 scale, from very poor to excellent quality. This question compares the general perception of the service regarding every particular aspect of it. The service quality is measured according to differences subtracting expectative scores to the corresponding perceptions points.

SERVQUAL Model Application in Sportive Organizations

According to Morales-Sánchez (2003),.SERVQUAL questionnaire is the consequence of many previous studies by Groönroos (1978, 1982, 1984). It's about one of the most used tools and has been applied in many different areas and contexts since its creation (Arunasalam et al., 2003; Lowndes & Dawes, 2001; Mundina et al., 2005). But also, the SERVQUAL Instrument has been criticized, mainly over two issues. The second issue refers to the factorial weights distribution of each one of the questionnaire dimensions. Initially, it hypothesized that every dimension of the service quality construction had the same value. The results found show that the SERVQUAL scale has a bidimensional structure: a factor known as mixed that groups the perceived effectiveness by the user, the needs satisfaction, previous experience and accessibility, and the understanding efficiency in professional superiority, speed and price service-associated terms, and another factor called tangible items that concern to the perceived quality of the service material resources, which doesn't mean that these findings override the original five-dimension questionnaire.

Morales-Sánchez (2003) in a study carried out in municipal sports organizations in Málaga, Spain, determines that according to the results of the analysis, this questionnaire is considered as a reliable and valid tool with a meticulous factorial structure since the parsimony indices are higher to 0.50, 0.69 to expectations scale and 0.68 for the perception scale. It also provides great utility information for the physical activity evaluation programs. The questionnaire enables to perform both a summative and a formative evaluation, the most used in physical activity ambit. In this sense, the SERVQUAL allows to determine the importance of the five dimensions in quality consumer perception. Also, it has other applications, such as comparing customer's expectations and perceptions overall, comparing the SERVQUAL of a company with the competence scores, considering the different consumer perception about quality, and evaluating the internal client perception related to quality.

The SERVQUAL questionnaire has been used in diverse educational area studies in many different scholarship levels, in physical education and different sports university and professional scopes (Gadea Cavazos et al., 2018; Hernandez-Mendo, et al., 2016; Morales-Sanchez & Correal (2003), Morales-Sánchez et al. (2005); Morales-Sánchez et al., 2009; Morales-Sánchez et al., 2013; Morquecho-Sánchez et al., 2016; Pérez-López et al., 2015). Also; in the investigations like Morales-Sánchez (2009), the latter adaptation that presented the SERVQUAL Model in the secondary teaching context, specifically in the physical education area. The variety of theories based on the paradigm of the appropriate approach to measure quality management in educational services seems clear since the SERVQUAL Model is an effective assessment mechanism to demonstrate the quality of a service in different organizational, institutional, and social ambit, in health areas and others. For this reason, educational services applying a process of continuous improvement, either in schooled or non-school modalities, have to firstly raise awareness among their most relevant staff about the importance of giving a full quality service.

Then, they need to measure quantitatively the perceived quality levels in the students, where they can identify the positive and negative bearings of the service in order to enhance the positive ones and diminish the negatives, and repeat this process constantly, always aspiring to achieve real and continuous improvement. However, given the subjectivity of services, our proposal to achieve more significant results that determine the impact, bye the application of validated measurement tools, as presented in this chapter, leading to both internal and external consumers such as professors, general staff, and students of every educational institution.

Conclusion

In conclusion, the importance of constant development applied to the quality of educational services, whether it may be in a scholarized environment or not, must raise awareness of the importance of providing quality service among all personnel

Educational Quality in Physical Education   145

composing an educational institution. Nevertheless, given the subjectivity of these services, we propose that, to achieve better results and to determine their impact, it is necessary to use models, instruments, and tools that show viable and trustworthy results, such as the one shown within this chapter. Even though the SERVQUAL Model has been the main reference for the majority of the studies done, it is insufficient for proper quality evaluation of educational and sports services. From our perspective, it is necessary to apply intervention programs between evaluations, as well as in various moments where these services are offered.

We suggest the importance of evaluating the quality of educational and sports services, the application of a quantitative methodology that evaluates the dimensions or principles of quality as well as the development of a qualitative methodology using mixed methods, and to advance with the continuous training of contact personnel (teachers) in the use and application of ICT'S (Information and Communication Technologies). Focusing on physical education in Mexico, not so long ago, different mechanisms of quality evaluation have been integrated, mainly within the private sector, and within recreational and sports-aimed institutions. It is to be noted that there is a necessity to know and apply more and better evaluation tools aimed to the educational sector with the goal of understanding improvement opportunities, applying strategies and enhancement actions related to new technologies as well as applying corrective actions with the goal of continuously optimizing educational services, specifically Physical Education in Mexico.

References

Armengol, C., Rexach, J., & Tamarit, M. (1996). La situación de la enseñanza de la educación física en las enseñanzas medias. In Ministerio de Educación y Cultura (Ed.), *Catálogo de investigaciones* (pp. 74–75). Ministerio de Educación y Cultura.

Arunasalam, M., Paulson, A., & Wallace, W. (2003). Service quality assessment of Workers' compensation health care delivery programs in New York State using SERVQUAL. *Health Marketing Quarterly, 21*(1–2), 29–64.

Bonilla-Guachamín, J. A. (2020). Las dos caras de la educación en el COVID-19. *CienciAmérica, 9*(2), 89–98.

Bravo-García, E., & Magis-Rodríguez, C. (2020). La respuesta mundial a la epidemia del COVID-19: Los primeros tres meses. Boletín Sobre COVID-19 Salud Pública y *Epidemiologia, 1*(1), 3–8.

Chavarria, X. (1998). *Situació de l'educació física en el sistema educatiu.* Ponencia presentada al Congrés de l'educació física i l'esport en edad escolar a la ciutat de Barcelona, Barcelona, España

Dalmau-Torres, J. M. (2004). Análisis del estatus de la Educación Física en la Enseñanza Primaria (Doctoral dissertation, tesis doctoral, Universidad de La Rioja.

De Knop, P., Theeboom, M., Huts, K., Van Hoecke, J., & De Martelaer, K. (2004). *The quality of school physical education in Flemish secondary schools.* Vrije Universiteit Brussel.

Dorado, A., & Gallardo, L. (2005). La gestión de la calidad: el compromiso de las organizaciones deportivas para el siglo XXI. Barcelona: Inde.

Dorado, A., Gambau, V., & Gallardo, L. (2006). La calidad en la gestión deportiva: Un valor en alza. In A. Fraile, & X. Pujadas (Eds.), *Culturas deportivas y valores sociales.*

Investigación social y deporte. Asociación Española de Investigación Social Aplicada al Deporte.

Gadea Cavazos, E., Morquecho-Sánchez, R., Pérez García, J., & Morales-Sánchez, V. (2018). Adaptación del cuestionario SERVQUAL para la evaluación de la calidad del servicio educativo en la asignatura de cultura física y salud en méxico. *Cuadernos de Psicología Del Deporte, 18*(3), 150–162.

Gonzales-Arévalo, C. (2006). *La Qualitat de l'àrea d'educació física. El cas dels centres que imparteixen l'educació secundària obligatòria de la ciutat de Barcelona*. Tesis Doctoral sin publicar, Universidad de Barcelona, Barcelona, España.

Groönroos, C. (1978). A service oriented approach to marketing for services. *European Journal of Marketing, 12*(8), 588–601.

Groönroos, C. (1982). *Strategic management and marketing in the service sector. Swedish School of Economics and Business Administration*. Helsingfors.

Groönroos, C. (1984). A service quality model and its marketing implications. *European Journal of Marketing, 18*(4), 36–44.

Hernández-Mendo, A., Blanco-Villaseñor, Á., Pastrana, J. L., Morales-Sánchez, V., & Ramos-Pérez, F. J. (2016). SAGT: Aplicación informática para análisis de generalizabilidad. *Revista Iberoamericana de Psicología del ejercicio y el deporte, 11*(1), 77–89.

Lowndes, M., & Dawes, J. (2001). Do distinct SERVQUAL dimensions emerge from mystery shopping data? A test of convergent validity. *Canadian Journal of Program Evaluation, 16*(2), 41–53.

Manzano, J. I., Sáenz-López Buñuel, P., Sicilia Camacho, A., Varela Domínguez, R., Cañadas Larrubia, J. F., Delgado Noguera, M. A., & Gutiérrez Delgado, M. (2003). *Currículo, deporte y actividad física en el ámbito escolar. La visión del profesorado de educación física en andalucía*. Serie Deporte y Documentación, 31. Instituto Andaluz del Deporte: Consejería de Turismo y Deporte.

Menéndez, M., Rodríguez, H., Cortés, N., Hernández, A., & Barbero, J. I. (1996). *Estatus de la educación física. Consideraciones a partir del estudio de un caso*. Pamplona. AEISAD.

Morales-Sánchez, V. (2003). *Evaluación psicosocial de la calidad en servicios municipales deportivos: Aportaciones desde el análisis de variabilidad*. SPICUM.

Morales-Sánchez, V. (2009). Evaluación de la calidad en organizaciones deportivas: Análisis de generalizabilidad. *Revista De Psicología General y Aplicada, 62*(1–2), 99–109.

Morales-Sánchez, V., Berrocal, M. A., Morquecho-Sánchez, R., & Hernández-Mendo, A. (2013). Evaluación de la calidad en el área de educación física en un centro de enseñanza secundaria y bachillerato. *Revista Iberoamericana De Psicología Del Ejercicio y El Deporte, 8*(2), 411–427.

Morales-Sánchez, V., & Correal, J. (2003). *La calidad en la gestión de los servicios deportivos*. In A. Hernández Mendo (Coord.), Psicología del Deporte (Vol. III): Aplicaciones 2 (pp. 81–101). Tulio Guterman.

Morales-Sánchez, V., Hernández Mendo, A., & Blanco Villaseñor, A. (2005). Evaluación de la calidad en los programas de actividad física. *Psicothema, 17*(2), 311–317.

Morales-Sánchez, V., Hernández Mendo, A., & Blanco Villaseñor, A. (2009). Evaluación de la calidad en organizaciones deportivas: Adaptación del modelo SERVQUAL. *Revista De Psicología Del Deporte, 18*(2), 137–150.

Morquecho-Sánchez, R., Medina-Rodríguez, R. E., Ceballos-Gurrola, O., & Morales-Sánchez, V. (2016). Cuestionario de evaluación de la calidad percibida en organizaciones de servicios deportivos universitarios (qunisport v.Mx): Programa factor. *Revista Iberoamericana De Psicología Del Ejercicio y El Deporte, 11*(2), 271–277.

Educational Quality in Physical Education 147

Mundina, J., Quintanilla, I., Sampedro, J., Calabuig, F., & Crespo, J. (2005). *Estudio de la calidad percibida y la satisfacción de los espectadores y los deportistas de los juegos mediterráneos almería 2005.* J. Mundina.

Nuviala, A., Tamayo, J. A., Iranzo, J., & Falcón, D. (2008). Creación, diseño, validación y puesta en práctica de un instrumento de medición de la satisfacción de usuarios de organizaciones que prestan servicios deportivos. *Retos. Nuevas Tendencias En EdUcación Física, Deporte y Recreación, 14,* 10–16.

Parasuraman, A., Berry, L., & Zeithaml, V. (1988). SERVQUAL: A multiple-item scale for measuring consumer perceptions of service quality. *Journal of Retailing, 64*(1), 12–40.

Parasuraman, A., Zeithaml, V. A., & Berry, L. L. (1985). A conceptual model of service quality and its implications for future research. *Journal of Marketing, 49*(4), 41–50.

Pérez-López, R., Morales-Sánchez, V., Anguera, M. T., & Hernández-Mendo, A. (2015). Evaluación de la calidad total en servicios municipales deportivos orientados a la población infantil: Aportaciones desde el análisis cualitativo con ATLAS. ti. *Cuadernos de psicologia del Deporte, 15*(1), 143–150.

Pozo Muñoz, C., Rebolloso Pacheco, E., & Fernandez Ramírez, B. (2000). Las actitudes de los estudiantes universitarios hacia sus profesores: Implicaciones para la mejora de la calidad docente. *Educational Psychology, 6*(1), 27–50.

Rial, J., Varela, J., Rial, A., & Real, E. (2010). Modelización y medida de La calidad percibida en centros deportivos: La escala QSport¬10. *Revista Internacional De Ciencias Del Deporte, 18*(6), 57–73.

Sáenz López, P. (1999). La importancia de la educación física en primaria. *Apunts. Educación Física y Deportes, 57,* 20–31.

Chapter 11

Innovation in Sport Centres
Accessibility and Adapted Sports Programmes

Zacarías Adame García
Centro de Estudios Universitarios Cardenal Spínola CEU
(Centre associated with the University of Seville), Spain

Alberto Nuviala Nuviala
Pablo de Olavide University, Spain

Jerónimo García-Fernández
Universidad of Seville, Spain

Nicolás Fernández Martínez
Centro de Estudios Universitarios Cardenal Spínola CEU
(Centre associated with the University of Seville), Spain

Chapter Contents

Introduction	148
Review of Literature	149
Method	151
Results	156
Discussion	159
References	161

Introduction

Physical activity is a fundamental tool to be incorporated into life habits if a harmonious and healthy development is to be achieved (Butzer et al., 2021). People with disabilities use physical activity and sport as a tool for rehabilitation and reintegration into an increasingly fair and inclusive society (D'Elia, 2021). However, not all sports centres have sufficient resources to accommodate people with disabilities, people who live with a higher risk of illness and who face more barriers when attending fitness facilities (Nikolajsen et al., 2021b). In view of this situation, many managers of sports facilities are currently concerned about the

DOI: 10.4324/9781003388050-13

accessibility situation of their gyms (Cereijo et al., 2019) and are trying to improve to adapt to the needs of the population in order to come closer to universal accessibility models (Arbour & Ginis, 2011). In this sense, people with disabilities are also more likely to miss out on opportunities to be physically active compared to other adults and children without disabilities and have more difficulties in selecting a wide range of adapted activities on offer (Shields & Synnot, 2016). For many of them, when pursuing goals of social relations and enjoyment of leisure and free time, barriers are left behind and what is important is a good system of physical activities that enable affective and peer relationships (Li et al., 2021).

Another fact that often aggravates the possibilities of participation in physical activities in gyms and sports centres is that, at present, non-disabled users do not show attitudes of affection and acceptance (Kissow, 2015). Their position towards disability is at least neutral and they make little effort to support the interests and needs of people with disabilities (Goering, 2015). It is not only architectural barriers that need to be highlighted. Employees of gyms, for example, beyond the built environment, lack the knowledge to be able to adapt their training sessions to the real needs of disabled users (Richardson et al., 2017a), although their desire to facilitate and adapt sport practice makes many people with disabilities continue in the different programmes of gyms (Nikolajsen et al., 2021a). In addition, the costs associated with adapted physical activity programme fees, and adapted transport as a form of mobility, are other common barriers to participation in physical activity (Jaarsma et al., 2019). A context is therefore pursued where more and more people with disabilities are going to sports centres for physical activity (Oh & So, 2022) and where health clubs promote and encourage activity programmes, pursuing healthy lifestyles, providing training and supervision and fostering interpersonal relationships (Butzer et al., 2021).

Therefore, the main objective of this chapter is to determine which are the accessibility elements in sports centres that influence the practice of physical-sports activities by people with disabilities. All of this is linked to discovering opportunities for innovation that can contribute to the different business models that exist in the industry of local sports centres. In short, the work is organised around five blocks. The first block is the introduction. The second is the theoretical foundation, where the theoretical framework and the current situation from which this research originates will be presented. The third section presents the methodology used, describing the sample of participants and the procedure for data collection and analysis. The fourth section presents the results of the research. The fifth and final section contains the discussion and conclusions reached as a result of this research.

Review of Literature

The presence of people with disabilities in today's society is well-known (Rodríguez & Ferreira, 2010), even more so when it comes to addressing their participation in physical activity and sport programmes. However, more controlled studies on participation in adapted activities are still needed (Yazicioglu et al., 2012), with sports centres being a very favourable practice space for this group (Richardson et al., 2017a). Thus, it is a concept that has evolved in recent years: handicap, impairment, disability, functional diversity and different abilities. In research, a review of the existing scientific literature shows that the most commonly used term is "disability" (Badia et al., 2011; Calder et al., 2018; Rimmer et al., 2017; Wicker & Breuera, 2014). Therefore, this term is used, with some nuances where other terminology is employed in the course of this chapter.

Sports centres, fitness centres or gyms can be ideal places for people with disabilities to engage in recommended levels of physical activity. However, they sometimes encounter barriers that cause accessibility problems: the built environment (Calder et al., 2018; Hansen et al., 2021; Ortega et al., 2021); material resources and specialised equipment (Calder & Mulligan, 2014; Calder et al., 2018; Richardson et al., 2017a); organisational aspects (Wicker & Breuera, 2014); qualification of technicians (Richardson et al., 2017a); safety (Rimmer et al., 2017); policy and ideological (Bonnell et al., 2021; Vasudevan et al., 2015); social environment (Arbour & Ginis, 2011); means of transport (Arbour & Ginis, 2009; Reklaitiene et al., 2016); cost of the sport programme (Rimmer et al., 2008); among others.

Participation in leisure activities has been identified as a factor that favours inclusion in the community and also contributes to a better quality of life (Badia et al., 2011). Some research findings show that participation in leisure activities is more determined by personal factors and perceived barriers than by factors related to the disability itself (Shapiro & Malone, 2016). It is of recognised interest to the fitness industry to detect needs and remove barriers so that people with disabilities can enjoy sport through the premise of universal accessibility (Fernández & Tejada, 2014). Sport managers and directors are the recipients of studies (Anderson et al., 2017) which reveal the importance of making progress in terms of adaptations in the search for inclusive practice, leading to improvements in the quality of life for customers with disabilities (Arbour & Ginis, 2011). In this sense, research on disability-specific sporting motives is of interest to understand the different levels of motivation (Anderson et al., 2017), both in those responsible for the creation of sport programmes and in the recipients of these activities, regardless of whether they are practised individually or collectively (Richardson et al., 2017b).

Specifically, with respect to Adapted Physical Activity (Pérez et al., 2012), the analysis of sport management curriculum standards requires that programmes and pathways prepare students to work in a "diverse sport management environment" (p. 54). People with disabilities in sport is a growing segment and sport management professionals need to be informed of these current trends and issues. Examining course content in relation to diversity (Pitts & Shapiro, 2017), specifically in disability sport, is an insight for researchers and managers to search for arguments in creating specialised training programmes for sport staffs. It is important to recognise that the emergence of adapted sport in our society is largely due to the Paralympic movement. From its media coverage, it has led to increased awareness of sport participation opportunities for people with disabilities and the adoption

Innovation in Sport Centres 151

of norms regarding exercise expectations, with evidence of the power of sport to boost confidence, self-efficacy and quality of life (Blauwet & Willick, 2012). When taken together – accessibility, disability rights and social integration – Paralympic sport has the power to transform the lives of those who participate and to further stimulate the expansion of opportunities available to the next generation of athletes with disabilities (Misener & Darcy, 2014), as well as promoting positive affective states such as feelings of joy, satisfaction, inspiration, excitement and enthusiasm (Shapiro & Martin, 2010).

On the other hand, recent research shows that sports services have to be adapted to the needs of users, thinking of customers with disabilities as future consumers of these sports services, although some of this research relating physical activity levels to accessibility in sports facilities and centres presents inconsistent results (Pouliou et al., 2019). In this sense, it is necessary to determine that sports facilities accessibility contributes to an increase in the practice of sport by people with and without disabilities, as all users benefit from it. According to routine health data, sport practice has a direct impact on health outcomes for those users who attend facilities with accessible sport spaces. This is irrespective of the individual characteristics of each user, such as gender, socio-economic or occupational characteristics. Along the same lines, some studies discover the innovative capacity of some cities to include accessibility elements in their facilities, predominantly those located outdoors, as it has been shown that future users of traditional sports facilities (indoor facilities), before becoming customers, can discover the benefits of practising sports in outdoor facilities in their daily environment (Asefi & Nosrati, 2020).

The solution is to offer opportunities for innovative integrated solutions that are based not only on the demand of the subjects but also on the inclusion policies of the managers of sports centres, as there is no document that responds to modern fitness centre design (Zhdanova et al., 2020).

Method

For the collection of data, three observers participated to check whether or not the accessibility measures and other variables under study were met in each of the sports centres. A total of 87 sports centres in the province of Seville (Spain) were visited from September 2020 to April 2021. For the description of the data sample, some initial data (Table 11.1, Figure 11.1) are presented, which will be supplemented in the following section. Accordingly, these are presented on the basis of the general characteristics of the centres visited, these being: size (m^2) (Table 11.1, Figure 11.1). The sports centres were chosen at random and based on the availability of the sports managers and directors to answer the questionnaire located on the observation instrument. The sample, municipalities with more than 25,000 inhabitants, was distributed as follows (Table 11.2, Figure 11.2). It is also interesting to know the age; number of years of management of managers and sports directors (Table 11.3); and number of clients (Figure 11.3). The average age

Table 11.1 Total Number of Sports Centres Visited by Size (m²)

Sizes (m²)	Visited centres	%
From 0 to 250	19	21.84
251 to 500	19	21.84
501 to 1,000	21	24.14
1,001 to 2,000	12	3.79
2,001 to 5,000	6	6.90
5,001 to 10,000	8	9.20
More than 10,000	2	2.30
Total	87	100

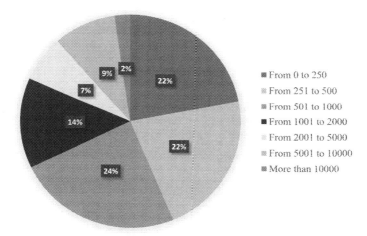

Figure 11.1 Sports Centres Studied According to Their Size.

Table 11.2 Total Number of Sports Visited Centres in Each of the Cities in the Province of Seville

Cities	Visited centres	%
Sevilla	26	29.89
Dos Hermanas	8	9.20
Coria del Río	9	10.34
La Rinconada	6	6.90
Écija	8	9.20
Carmona	4	4.60
Alcalá de Guadaíra	4	4.60
Utrera	9	10.34
Los Palacios y Villafranca	7	8.05
Camas	6	6.90
Total	87	100

Innovation in Sport Centres 153

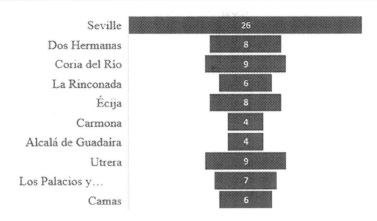

Figure 11.2 Total Sports Centres Visited in Each of the Cities in the Province of Seville.

Table 11.3 Total Number of Sports Centres Visited According to Managers and Director's Management Years

Management years	Visited centres	%
From 1 to 5	45	51.72
6 to 10	27	31.03
11 to 20	11	12.64
More than 20 years	4	4.60
Total	87	100

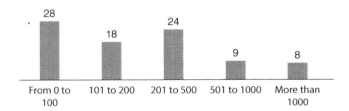

Figure 11.3 Sports Centres Studied According to Customer Census.

of the sports centres visited is 10.66 years, with the oldest centre being 35 years old and the youngest being 1-year-old. Asking the managers in sports directors about the number of years they have been managing their sports centre, we find this information in Table 11.3. The greatest seniority is 35 years and the lowest is 1 year, with the average number of years of management being 7.60 years. Looking at the total number of customers for each sports centre, we obtain the following graphic (Figure 11.3).

When visiting the sports centres, there are different business models, such as public sports centres, private sports centres, administrative concession, private gymnasium of less than 500 m², private gymnasium of more than 500 m², sports specialisation centre, personal training studio, social sports centre, private low-cost/low-price and premium/boutique (Table 11.4). Furthermore, out of the 87 centres observed, a total of 59 centres register customers with disabilities; with regard to the type of disability:

- Register of physically disabled customers: 58 sports centres.
- Register of visually impaired customers: 37 sports centres.
- Register of hearing-impaired customers: 37 sports centres.
- Register of customers with other disabilities: 50 sports centres.

Of the total number of centres observed, the following average values (Figure 11.4) were found with respect to the hiring regime of their workers. Analysing the sports facilities and spaces that the sports centres studied have, these are highlighted in Table 11.5.

The Observation Instrument includes a total of 119 variables, distributed and classified according to the following dimensions. A total of 16 variables relate to the dimension "Socio-demographic data and general characteristics of the sports centre". For the dimension "Main sports facilities", 18 variables were included. In addition, "Managers' profiles" was considered important, so eight items were included for this dimension. The dimension "Accessibility elements of the sports centre" contained a total of 20 variables, the same number of variables as for the dimension "Inclusion policies". Finally, "the offer of adapted physical activities" by each sports centre was a dimension containing a total of 37 variables.

For the collection of information, different visits were planned to be made by the three observers. Each of them visited different sports centres, chosen at random, from those existing in the districts of the province of Seville. Prior to the

Table 11.4 Total Number of Sports Centres Visited by Business Model

Business model	Visited centres	%
Public	11	12.64
Private	76	87.36
Administrative concession	6	6.90
Private gymnasium of less than 500 m²	8	9.20
Private gymnasium of more than 500 m²	17	19.54
Sports specialisation centre	12	13.79
Personal training studio	11	12.64
Social sports centre	5	5.75
Low-cost/Low-price	2	2.30
Premium/Boutique	2	2.30
Other	13	14.94
Total	87	100

Innovation in Sport Centres 155

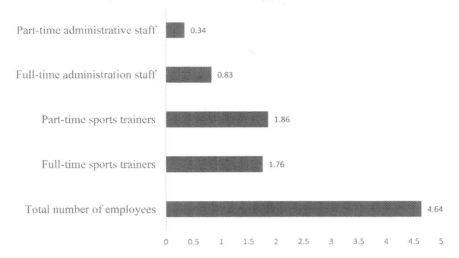

Figure 11.4 Average Values Over the Total Number of Employees for Each Sports Centre.

Table 11.5 Percentage of Sports Facilities that Have the Total Number of Centres Investigated

Type of sports facility	Total number of centres with such a facility	%
Sports hall	7	8.05
Paddle	25	28.74
Outdoor pool	7	8.05
Indoor pool	3	3.45
Other water areas	5	19.54
Multisports courts	17	19.54
Athletics	2	2.3
Fitness area	61	70.11
Cardio area	57	65.52
Cyclo Indoor hall	24	27.59
Group activity room	61	70.11
Covid Room	22	25.29
Social area	17	19.54
Play area	15	17.24
Games library	4	4.6
Nursing	20	22.99
Training classroom	12	13.79
Other sports facilities	19	21.84
Total	87	

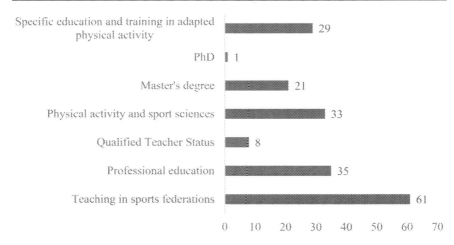

Figure 11.5 Academic Education of the Sports Centre Managers.

visits to the sports centres, telephone appointments were arranged with the managers and directors of the facilities. These professionals were previously informed of the development of the study and gave their informed consent. Permission was sought for access to public and private facilities. Visiting hours for some facilities could be modified due to certain pandemic conditions (Covid-19). The data obtained were processed with SPSS 25.0 software and descriptive statistics were found. The counts have given valuable information on the total number of centres visited and the averages have made it possible to observe differences in the trend of the data presented.

Results

Regardless of the type of adapted activity carried out by the sports centres observed, Table 11.6 shows the total number of centres that carry out adapted activities according to the target group (physical, hearing, visual). In this table, it can be seen that the adapted activities most frequently offered by sports centres are: personal training (20), racquet sports (17), group exercises (16) and weight training and cardio activities (16). On the other hand, the activities least offered are: PANE (1), aquatic activities (3) and individual sports (5). Regarding sports centres that hold sports events exclusively for people with disabilities, and according to the promotion of inclusive activities in which disabled and non-disabled customers have a normal experience in each sports centre, a total of 38 centres organise sports events of which they all organise activities aimed at people with physical disabilities, 23 centres organise activities for the visually impaired and 22 for the hearing impaired. A total of 78 centres promote inclusion in the activities that they offer. In addition, for the profile of sport managers and directors, they

Innovation in Sport Centres   157

Table 11.6 Total Number of Centres that Offer Activities Adapted for Each Group

Type of activities adapted	Centres offering these activities	Adapted for disabled customers		
		Physical	Visual	Hearing
Aquatic activities	3	3	2	1
Group exercises	16	13	11	9
Physical activities in the natural environment (PANE)	1	0	0	1
Cyclo indoor	7	6	4	3
Weight training and cardio activities	16	15	6	7
Personal trainings	20	19	12	8
Swimming	3	3	3	1
Racquet sports	17	16	1	8
Team sports	8	7	4	4
Individual sports	5	5	2	1
Other physical activities and sports	6	5	1	3

were asked about their academic background, including a question on whether they have a background in adapted physical activity (Figure 11.5).

To the question: "Do you have specific training in adapted physical activity?" A total of 29 managers (33%) answered in the affirmative. Of these 33%, a total of 18 (more than 50%) were found to have a family member with a disability. For the accessibility items, the data obtained are presented in general terms (Figure 11.6). This graph shows that the variable most frequently observed in the visits to the different sports centres is: "accessible entrances and exits"; while the variable least observed is: "adapted indicators in Braille". The managers of the sports centres comment that the accessibility elements are related to the demand of the customers of their centre. While "accessible entrances and exits" are part of the state regulations to be complied with by all sports centres, "Braille indicators" will depend on the real needs of the customers of each sports centre, with some managers indicating that these indicators are not always necessary as the visually impaired sportsperson is always accompanied by a family member or by a monitor of the sports centre. Regarding the inclusion policies of the managers and directors of the sports centres, they were asked about: the training, experience and professional skills of the sports technicians in terms of adapted physical activity; about the current specific training of the sports technicians and the managers themselves; as well as other items that are presented in Table 11.7.

Managers of sports centres, as a whole, attach great importance to knowing how to adapt training depending on the customer disability (98.85%). When recruiting for a job, they attach more importance to the fact that the candidate sports technicians have specific training in adapted physical activity (94.25%) than to

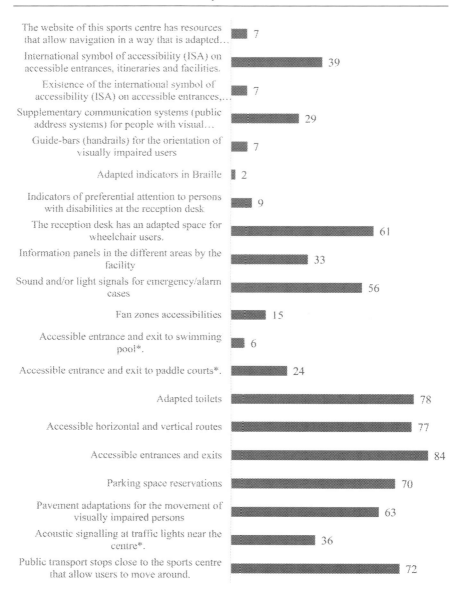

Figure 11.6 Accessibility Facilities Present in the Sports Centres Visited. "*" refers to Sports centre features.

Innovation in Sport Centres 159

Table 11.7 Inclusion Policies of Managers and Directors of Sports Centres

Inclusion policy questions	*Managers answering in the affirmative*	*%*
It is important for sports coaches to have specific training in physical activity for people with disabilities.	82	94.25
It is considered important for sports coaches to have had previous experience in working with people with disabilities.	75	86.21
Sports coaches should know how to adapt training depending on the disability of the customers.	86	98.85
Educational programmes on adapted physical activity should be part of the curriculum for sports centre technicians.	84	96.55
It is important for reception staff to have knowledge of sign language.	57	65.52
As a sport manager/director, you are currently undertaking or have undertaken educational programmes in recent months in the management of adapted activities.	40	45.98
Your level of knowledge of adapted physical activity is sufficient for the position you hold.	71	81.61
Are you aware of the existence of any sportsperson with a disability who stands out in your sports centre (Paralympic athletic)?	12	13.79
A worker in your sports centre has a disability.	28	32.18
From your viewpoint, it can be affirmed that your school can be considered as an inclusive school.	74	85.06

the experience in working with people with disabilities (86.21%). Regarding the knowledge that the reception staff should have about sign language, the importance decreases in the number of affirmative answers (65.52%); a fact that may be related to what was commented on in Figure 11.6 regarding the real demand of customers with disabilities present in the sports centres. The existence of high-level (Paralympic) athletes is low (13.79%), as well as the percentage of centres in which people with disabilities work (32.18%). Finally, a high percentage of centres (85.06%) are considered by their managers as inclusive or adapted centres.

Discussion

Taking into account that more than half of the sports centres visited have dimensions between 0 and 1,000 m²; highlighting that the average age of these centres exceeds 10 years; and that the sports directors who are in charge of the management of these centres have an average of more than 7 years of service, it can be concluded that most of the sports facilities have elements that facilitate accessibility for clients with disabilities, the public sports centres (business model) being the ones with the greatest number of accessible variables. With regard to the formative profile of managers, it should be noted that more than a third have specific training in adapted physical activities, a fact that can be explained by the number of managers (half of those mentioned above) who have family members with disabilities. As stated in Emir Öksüz and Brubaker (2020), the importance given by professionals in the sector to training in adapted physical activity may depend on, among other variables, the fact that they belong to and are linked to this group because they have family members with disabilities.

Most of the centres visited have no more than 500 users on average. Considering the different business models that exist, private centres and their different modalities stand out as sports centres that respond positively to collaborating in those research, although it has also been possible to obtain a suggestive sample of public centres that represent the population under study. Almost all the centres visited have a specific register of users with disabilities, with physically disabled customers being the most abundant. Visually and hearing-impaired customers also represent an important part of disabled users, with other disabilities such as: intellectual disability and other disorders and difficulties (Down's syndrome, autism, developmental disorders, attention deficit and hyperactivity disorders, etc.) also standing out. For these groups, the sports centres offer adapted activities. Almost all of the centres visited are considered inclusive centres in which users with disabilities can practice and use the different sports services in an inclusive environment, in which people with and without disabilities coexist, with group activities, the racket sports and the weight training and cardio activities being the most outstanding activities in this respect.

In this sense, it is necessary to ensure that spaces and facilities are accessible, incorporating innovation systems that allow users a renewed and inclusive experience for each of the physical activity programmes that are demanded (Fragala-Pinkham & Miros, 2020). Some innovation solutions involve the elimination of those barriers that prevent users from enjoying and practising the activities offered by the different sports centres. In this study, the accessibility elements with the highest scores were: "Accessible entrances and exits", "Adapted toilets" and "Accessible horizontal and vertical routes". In addition, it should be noted that a high percentage of centres have "Parking space reservations", "Pavement adaptations for the movement of visually impaired persons" and "Public transport stops close to the sports centre that allow users to move around". On the other hand, accessibility elements that received lower scores and that could be improved are related to the centres' websites, as they do not include software or resources that allow navigation for people with disabilities (especially visual impairment); the existence of the ISA (International Symbol of Accessibility); and adapted Braille indicators. In relation to the latter, some innovative experiences are along the lines of including these accessibility elements even if there is no real demand for them in the centre, since if future users with disabilities are aware of the existence of these resources, their expectations as future consumers of sports services may increase (Pussadu et al., 2020; Ratten & Ferreira, 2017).

To conclude, the profiles of the managers of the sports facilities visited are closely related to their inclusion policies. This point is confirmed by the fact that almost all interviewees attach importance to the fact that sports coaches have specific training in physical activity and consider it important that they have had previous experience in working with people with disabilities. These interviewees have higher education in physical activity and sport; university education; and, many of them, training in sports federations.

The limitations encountered in carrying out this work have been the availability of the sports managers and directors, as many of them had little time to assist us complete the observation instrument. Another limitation that can be pointed out is related to the refusal of some centres to collaborate for the simple fact of not having users with disabilities. Few centres refused to take part in the study, but some did not participate due to their data privacy policy. In the near future, the characteristics of users with disabilities in relation to their demands and needs for adapted sports practice can be investigated and compared with the results obtained in this study. It is of great importance to investigate what modifications should be made to the materials and facilities of sports centres so that, in an innovative way, users with disabilities can enjoy a pleasant and long-lasting experience when practising their daily sport.

This study opens up new horizons in terms of innovation, sports management and accessibility. In order to innovate, among other aspects, it will be necessary to consider the opinion of users with disabilities, as they are the ones who can contribute improvements to the existing sports system. Institutions must collaborate in the creation of public sports programmes that serve as a mirror for private entities which, in turn, must improve in the adaptation of material resources and spaces, according to the needs and demands of users. Currently, in the scientific literature reviewed, there is no evidence of studies regarding the motives or reasons why managers of sports centres do not respond, in some cases, to the real demand that exists in terms of adapted physical activity. It can be affirmed that the innovative character of this work lies in including the aforementioned variables in order to help identify the profiles of the managers. In short, new scenarios are opening up in which to investigate the motivations that lead people with disabilities to visit sports centres and what adaptations these centres should implement in their services, innovating in their activity programmes, to make the lives of these sportspeople more enjoyable and satisfying.

References

Anderson, C., Grant, R. L., & Hurley, M. V. (2017). Exercise facilities for neurologically disabled populations - perceptions from the fitness industry. *Disability and Health Journal*, *10*(1), 157–162.

Arbour, K. P., & Ginis, K. A. (2009). The relationship between physical activity facility proximity and leisure-time physical activity in persons with spinal cord injury. *Disability and Health Journal*, *2*(3), 128–135.

Arbour, K. P., & Ginis, K. A. (2011). Universal accessibility of "accessible" fitness and recreational facilities for persons with mobility disabilities. *Adapted Physical Activity Quarterly, 28*(1), 1–15.

Asefi, A., & Nosrati, A. G. (2020). The spatial justice in the distribution of built outdoor sports facilities. *Journal of Facilities Management, 18*(2), 159–178.

Badia, M., Orgaz, B. M., Verdugo, M. A., Ullán, A. M., & Martínez, M. M. (2011). Personal factors and perceived barriers to participation in leisure activities for young and adults with developmental disabilities. *Research in Developmental Disabilities, 32*(6), 2055–2063.

Blauwet, C., & Willick, S. E. (2012). The Paralympic movement: Using sports to promote health, disability rights, and social integration for athletes with disabilities. *PM&R, 4*(11), 851–856.

Bonnell, K., Michalovic, E., Koch, J., Pagé, V., Ramsay, J., Gainforth, H. L., & Sweet, …, S. N. (2021). Physical activity for individuals living with a physical disability in Quebec: Issues and opportunities of access. *Disability and Health Journal, 14*(3), 101089.

Butzer, J., Virva, R., Kozlowski, A., & Cistaro, R. (2021). Participation by design: Integrating a social ecological approach with universal design to increase participation and add value for consumers. *Disability and Health Journal, 14*(2), 101006.

Calder, A. M., & Mulligan, H. F. (2014). Measurement properties of instruments that assess inclusive access to fitness and recreational sports centers: A systematic review. *Disability and Health Journal, 7*(1), 26–35.

Calder, A., Sole, G., & Mulligan, H. (2018). The accessibility of fitness centers for people with disabilities: A systematic review. *Disability and Health Journal, 11*(4), 525–536.

Cereijo, L., Gullón, P., Cebrecos, A., Bilal, U., Santacruz, J. A., Badland, H., & Franco, M. (2019). Access to and availability of exercise facilities in Madrid: An equity perspective. *International Journal of Health Geographics, 18*(1), 15.

D'Elia, F. (2021). Inclusion in physical and sport education for special movement needs. *Conference: Journal of Human Sport and Exercise - 2021 - Autumn Conferences of Sports Science.*

Emir Öksüz, E., & Brubaker, M. D. (2020). Deconstructing disability training in counseling: A critical examination and call to the profession. *Journal of Counselor Leadership and Advocacy, 7*(2), 163–175.

Fernández, M., & Tejada, A. (2014). Accesibilidad universal en la edificación, el urbanismo y el transporte: Accesibilidad y edificación. Edificación de uso público. *Revista Científica Sobre Accesibilidad Universal, 4*, 19–32.

Fragala-Pinkham, M. A., & Miros, J. (2020). Community resources: Sports and active recreation for individuals with cerebral palsy. *Cerebral Palsy, 10*, 2507–2518.

Goering, S. (2015). Rethinking disability: The social model of disability and chronic disease. *Current Reviews in Musculoskeletal Medicine, 8*(2), 134–138.

Hansen, R. K., Larsen, R. G., Laessoe, U., Samani, A., & Cowan, R. E. (2021). Physical activity barriers in Danish manual wheelchair users: A cross-sectional study. *Archives of Physical Medicine and Rehabilitation, 102*(4), 687–693.

Jaarsma, E. A., Haslett, D., & Smith, B. (2019). Improving communication of information about physical activity opportunities for people with disabilities. *Adapted Physical Activity Quarterly, 36*(2), 1–17.

Kissow, A. M. (2015). Participation in physical activity and the everyday life of people with physical disabilities: A review of the literature. *Scandinavian Journal of Disability Research, 17*(2), 144–166.

Li, J., Zeng, B., & Li, P. (2021). The influence of leisure activity types and involvement levels on leisure benefits in older adults. *Front Public Health*, 9, 659263.

Misener, L., & Darcy, S. (2014). Managing disability sport: From athletes with disabilities to inclusive organisational perspectives. *Sport Management Review*, 17, 1–7.

Nikolajsen, H., Richardson, E. V., Sandal, L. F., Kristensen, B., & Troelsen, J. (2021a). Fitness for all: How do non-disabled people respond to inclusive fitness centres? *BMC Sports Science Medicine Rehabilitation*, 13(1), 81.

Nikolajsen, H., Sandal, L. F., Juhl, C. B., Troelsen, J., & Juul-Kristensen, B. (2021b). Barriers to, and facilitators of, exercising in fitness centres among adults with and without physical disabilities: A scoping review. *International Journal of Environmental Research and Public Health*, 18(14), 7341.

Oh, A., & So, W. Y. (2022). Assessing the needs of people with disabilities for physical activities and sports in South Korea. *Healthcare*, 10(2), 265.

Ortega, I. D., Hernández, M. A., Cervantes, C. M., & Rodríguez, L. F. (2021). Accesibilidad al entorno físico en instalaciones de acondicionamiento para personas con discapacidad física: Una revisión integradora. *Revista Ciencias De La Salud*, 19(1), 1–21.

Pérez, J., Reina, R., & Sanz, D. (2012). La actividad física adaptada para personas con discapacidad en españa: Perspectivas científicas y de aplicación actual. *Cultura, Ciencia y Deporte*, 7(21), 213–224.

Pitts, B. G., & Shapiro, D. R. (2017). People with disabilities and sport: An exploration of topic inclusion in sport management. *Journal of Hospitality, Leisure, Sport and Tourism Education*, 21(Part A), 33–45.

Pouliou, T., Lowe, S., & Higgs, G. (2019). Assessing the health impacts of adults' participation in sports: Investigating the role of accessibility to sport facilities. *International Journal of Population Data Science*, 4(3).

Pussadu, S., Paopun, N., & Pornapiraksakul, K. (2020). Satisfaction Factors of Fitness Center Users in Bangkok and Metropolitan Areas. *6th Regional Conference on Graduate Research Theme "Creating a Unified Foundation for the Sustainable Development" 23 August 2020. Sripatum University*, 743–752.

Ratten, V., & Ferreira, J. (2017). Entrepreneurship, innovation and sport policy: Implications for future research. *International Journal of Sport Policy and Politics*, 9(4), 575–577.

Reklaitiene, D., Pozeriene, J., & Ostaseviciene, V. (2016). The accessibility for people with disabilities - new challenge and possibilities for fitness and recreation services development. *Transformations in Business and Economics*, 15(2), 699–708.

Richardson, E. V., Smith, B., & Papathomas, A. (2017a). Disability and the gym: Experiences, barriers and facilitators of gym use for individuals with physical disabilities. *Disability and Rehabilitation*, 39(19), 1950–1957.

Richardson, E. V., Smith, B., & Papathomas, A. (2017b). Collective stories of exercise: Making sense of gym experiences with disabled peers. *Adapted Physical Activity Quarterly*, 34(3), 276–294.

Rimmer, J. H., Padalabalanarayanan, S., Malone, L. A., & Mehta, T. (2017). Fitness facilities still lack accessibility for people with disabilities. *Disability and Health Journal*, 10(2), 214–221.

Rimmer, J. H., Wang, E., & Smith, D. (2008). Barriers associated with exercise and community access for individuals with stroke. *Journal of Rehabilitation Research and Development*, 45(2), 315–322.

Rodríguez, S., & Ferreira, M. (2010). Diversidad funcional: Sobre lo normal y lo patológico en torno a la condición social de la dis-capacidad. *Cuadernos De Relaciones Laborales*, 28(1), 151–172.

Shapiro, D. R., & Malone, L. A. (2016). Quality of life and psychological affect related to sport participation in children and youth athletes with physical disabilities: A parent and athlete perspective. *Disability and Health Journal*, 9(3), 385–91.

Shapiro, D. R., & Martin, J. J. (2010). Athletic identity, affect, and peer relations in youth athletes with physical disabilities. *Disability and Health Journal*, 3(2), 79–85.

Shields, N., & Synnot, A. (2016). Perceived barriers and facilitators to participation in physical activity for children with disability: A qualitative study. BMC *Pediatrics*, 16, 9.

Vasudevan, V., Rimmer, J. H., & Kviz, F. (2015). Development of the barriers to physical activity questionnaire for people with mobility impairments. *Disability and Health Journal*, 8(4), 547–556.

Wicker, P., & Breuera, C. (2014). Exploring the organizational capacity and organizational problems of disability sport clubs in Germany using matched pairs. *Sport Management Review*, 17(1), 23–34.

Yazicioglu, K., Yavuz, F., Goktepe, A. S., & Tan, A. K. (2012). Influence of adapted sports on quality of life and life satisfaction in sport participants and non-sport participants with physical disabilities. *Disability and Health Journal*, 5(4), 249–253.

Zhdanova, I. V., Kayasova, D. S., Kuznetsova, A. A., & Kalinkina, N. A. (2020). Basics of architectural typology of modern fitness centers. *IOP Conference Series: Materials Science and Engineering*, 775(1), 012063.

Part III

Innovations in Sports Events

Chapter 12

Innovative Management Model and Multiplatform Distribution Content

The Liga Nacional de Basquete and Novo Basquete Brasil

Ary José Rocco Júnior

University of São Paulo, Brazil

Guilherme Buso

Genius Sports, Brazil

Chapter Contents

Introduction	167
Liga Nacional de Basquete (LNB) – Innovation and Evolution	170
Novo Basquete Brasil and Its Sub-products	174
Communication, Disruption and Innovation	177
Managerial Perspectives	179
References	182

Introduction

Brazil, officially Federative Republic of Brazil, is the largest country in South America and Latin America region, on both territorial extension and population. It is the fifth largest country on territorial area (8,510,295.91 km^2) and the sixth on population (O Globo, 2019) (with over 210 million inhabitants). In the American continent, Brazil is the only country that speaks mainly Portuguese and is the biggest lusophone country in the planet (Central Intelligence Agency, 2008). The country is also one of the most multicultural and ethnic diverse nations, as a consequence of the strong immigration deriving from several places in the world. By its current Constitution, proclaimed in 1988, Brazil is a presidential federative republic, formed by the union of 26 states, the Federal District (Brasilia) (Constituição da República Federativa do Brasil, 1988), and 5,570 cities (O Globo, 2013). Economically, the Brazilian GDP (Gross Domestic Product) is the 12th largest in the world and the eighth on Purchasing Power Parity (Fundo Monetário Internacional, 2020). According to the World Bank Group, Brazil is a recent industrialized

DOI: 10.4324/9781003388050-15

country and, thanks to its regional and international influence, is ranked as an emergent global power (World Bank, 2011).

On the sport perspective, regarding the geopolitical importance of the country, Brazil hosted, in the past ten years, two of the main sports events in the planet – the 2014 FIFA World Cup and the 2016 Olympic and Paralympic Games in Rio de Janeiro. These two events, among several other international competitions, have taken Brazil to the highest point within the international sports scenario, placing sport as one of the top priorities in the country's agenda; fully adding Brazil to the global sport industry context; and bringing to the country a wide amount of modern and innovative products and services. In order to host 3,429,873 fans that attended 64 matches during the 2014 FIFA World Cup, for instance, the country invested US$4.5 billion for either refurbishing or building 12 soccer arenas, which were later known as the stages of the "Cup of the Cups" (Rocco Junior & Mazzei, 2018). The competition presented an average of 53,591 spectators per game, the second largest attendance in history, and the arenas' occupancy rate average was 98.4%, way above FIFA's expectation (Rocco Junior & Mazzei, 2018). Approximately 3.2 million tickets were sold to regular fans in all games of the tournament (Rocco Junior & Mazzei, 2018), and, besides the global aspect of the competition, that points out the Brazilian fans' interest in sports events. Meanwhile, the 2016 Olympic Games in Rio highlighted the hospitality and interest of the Brazilian people for the biggest festival of the world of sports, even though the Games costed to Brazil 51% more than its initial budget, reaching the number of US$4.58 billion in expenses (McCarthy, 2016). On 10 September 2016, for example, the Olympic Park, the most important venue built for both the Olympics and Paralympics, hosted approximately 167,000 fans for the Paralympics competitions (G1, 2016). That was an even bigger audience than the highest number of people that attended an Olympic day. On 7 August 2016, during the Olympic Games, 157,000 people visited the Olympic Park in Rio de Janeiro (G1, 2016).

Since 2018, on the public point of view, the Special Secretary of Sport, an administrative body attached to the Ministry of Citizenship, has been responsible for developing and implementing social inclusion activities through sports in a national level, with the perspective of ensuring free access to physical activities, quality of life and human development to the Brazilian population, and also, ensuring political development and national incentive to high performance sport (Ministério da Cidadania, 2020). On an executive and structural point of view, the sport in Brazil is organized, on its diverse competitive games, by national sport confederations, being the main governing body responsible for regulating the entire structure: The Brazilian Olympic Committee (*Comitê Olímpico Brasileiro* – COB). Since Brazil is a federative republic country, each national sport confederation is formed by the association of state federations from their respective sports. Thus, the federations of each state are instituted by sports entities (clubs) that practice the sport related to the same federative unity.

In brief, the sport structure in Brazil is a mix of public and private organizations. The private organizations – Olympic committee, national confederations, state federations and clubs – are, mainly, well-structured, within an associative system, most of the times are financed with public resources and have their main leaders elected for three or four-year mandates. The major Brazilian sports organizations are, consequently, associative entities of private entitlement. Thereby, the majority of these organizations' administrators perform their duties on a temporary basis (determined period) and on a voluntary matter (without an effective paid working contract). Even though Brazil presents a rate of 45.9% on population sedentarism (Diesporte, 2015), which means, people who do not take any type of physical exercise, Brazilians are passionate about sports, specially soccer, considered a national love and the most important sport, which has helped promote the country overseas.

Basketball, the object of this study, was, until the late 1980s, the second most popular sport in the country, following only soccer, according to Brazilians. Currently, a research conducted by the consultancy company, Deloitte (2011), basketball was ranked as the fifth most popular sport according to Brazilians' preference, also being indicated by 16% of the 732 respondents as their favorite sport. Basketball, on this Deloitte research (2011), was ranked behind soccer (78%), volleyball (46%), swimming (24%) and tennis (19%).

Most recently, in 2019, IBOPE Repucom (2019), an important research institute in the country, showed that basketball occupied, on that year, the third place among Brazilian sports preferences. The growth of the sport, in few years, was a result of big innovative strategies that we will describe later on this academic piece. Two years earlier, in 2017, IBOPE Repucom also pointed out that Brazil had 31 million people confirming they were basketball fans. From this portion, 13 million were recognized as "core fans" and three million as basketball participants (IBOPE Repucom, 2017). The same institute, in 2020, released a combined social media ranking among the Brazilian sports confederations (Facebook, Twitter, Instagram, YouTube and TikTok). The Brazilian Basketball Confederation (*Confederação Brasileira de Basketball* – CBB), responsible for organizing sport in the country, was placed in October/2020 in 10th place, with a total of 187,102 followers, behind the Confederations of Soccer, Volleyball, Jiu-Jitsu, Athletics, Futsal, Water Sports, Judo, Rugby and Handball (IBOPE Repucom, 2020).

On a sports point of view, Brazilian basketball has achieved several international titles. The Men's National Team, for instance, collected on its record important achievements such as three Olympic bronze medals (1948 London, 1960 Rome and 1964 Tokyo Olympics), two World Championship titles (1959 Chile and 1963 Brazil), six Pan-American Games gold medals (1971 Cali, 1987 Indianapolis, 1999 Winnipeg, 2003 Santo Domingo, 2007 Rio de Janeiro and 2015 Toronto) and 18 South American tournament titles. The Women's National Basketball Team has also reached important titles, such as a silver medal in the 1996 Atlanta Olympics and a bronze medal in the following games, in 2000 Sydney, a World Championship title in Australia (1994), four Pan-American Games gold medals (1967 Winnipeg, 1971 Cali, 1991 Havana and 2019 Lima) and 26 South American tournament titles.

In Brazil, as it was mentioned before, basketball is planned, organized and controlled by the CBB, the most important governing body within the sport, responsible for the organization and authorization of events and representation of athletes in Brazil (CBB, 2020). The organization is affiliated to FIBA (International Basketball Federation) and to the Brazilian Olympic Committee (COB). On the official website, CBB presents its strategic principles. The organization affirms that its mission is "to lead the process of development of Brazilian basketball among its affiliated entities, clubs and athletes, throughout the national territory, seeking to reestablish as the second most popular sport in Brazil, representing the sport with excellence and expressive results on international competitions" (CBB, 2020). CBB's vision is "to be a worldwide reference in management model emphasized by governance, conformity, transparency, results, financial sustainability and basketball popularity" (CBB, 2020). The CBB values, according to the official website, are "honor, ethics and transparency, inclusion, teamwork, positive attitude and pursuit for excellence" (CBB, 2020).

Although the situation is quite stable now, Brazilian basketball faced, in the late 2000s, "a chaotic period, defined by several disputes between the clubs and the Confederation, court lawsuits, which resulted to an unfinished Men's National Championship for Clubs in 2008" (LNB, 2018). This situation, which damaged the image of Brazilian basketball, began to change on 1 August 2008, with the creation of the National Basketball League (*Liga Nacional de Basquete* – LNB), object of this chapter, guided by these words: "rebirth, innovation and evolution" (LNB, 2018).

Liga Nacional de Basquete (LNB) – Innovation and Evolution

The CBB was founded in 1933, in the city of Rio de Janeiro, the country's capital by then. During that year, some clubs adopted soccer's professionalism and created several specialized sports organizations in the country. That was how the Brazilian Basketball Federation was born, on 25 December 1933. A few years later, on 26 December 1941, the organization changed its name to CBB (CBB, 2020). Since the foundation until 2021, CBB has had eight presidents, elected by the state federations and their affiliated clubs. One of CBB's attributions, determined on the original by-law, was the organization of the Men's National Championship for Clubs. So, in 1965, CBB created the *Taça Brasil de Basquete* (Brazil Basketball Cup), the first official national tournament of basketball in the country, and also, a competition which would designate its champion as the club to represent Brazil in the Men's South American basketball tournament, a competition recognized by FIBA.

From 1965 to 1989, *Taça Brasil de Basquete* had always been organized by CBB being the biggest clubs' basketball competition in the country. In 24 years of its existence, eight different clubs had won the tournament and qualified to the South American competition representing Brazil. *Taça Brasil* was usually hosted in a single city, previously nominated by CBB, having their games played within a few days. The host city club would play against various state champions of the tournaments organized by each local federation. In 1990, the CBB changed the name of *Taça Brasil* to Men's National Basketball Championship, with a more organized playing format, adding more games throughout the season and having the teams playing home and away matches within a two-round system (regular season) and the final fixtures on a playoff series (quarter finals, semifinals and finals). This championship was played on that format until the end of 2008.

The 2000s represented a dark period for men's Brazilian basketball. The biggest sport stars in the country, such as forwards Oscar Schmidt and Marcel de Souza, both gold medalists with the National Team at the 1987 Indianapolis Pan-American Games, were retired from the courts. After decades on the top of international basketball scenario, the Brazilian Men's National Team did not qualify for three consecutive Olympic Games: Sydney 2000, Athens 2004 and Beijing 2008. In the clubs' competition sphere, the national championships, yet managed by CBB, were deteriorating even more (LNB, 2018). Problems with CBB inefficient management ended up affecting not only both the Men's and Women's National Teams, but also the main clubs' competitions in the country. For that reason, in 2005, one of the biggest Brazilian basketball legends, Oscar Schmidt, gathered 38 clubs in order to launch an independent league from CBB, the *Nossa Liga de Basquete* – NLB (Our Basketball League) (LNB, 2018).

Without CBB's official approval, the "Oscar League", as it was later remarked, lost its power and relevance among the traditional and prestigious basketball clubs. Some of them had athletes playing for the National Team and others had acquired qualification for international competition, so they could not risk to lose legitimacy within the regulations of FIBA. Nevertheless, NLB managed to finish its 2005–2006 season. However, without the presence of important teams, media support and CBB's authorization, the league did not continue its activities on the following year (LNB, 2018). Brazilian basketball clubs' competitions were in such a rough point that, in 2006, the National Championship did not reach an end. The final series was cancelled by a court decision. Two years later, Brazilian basketball suffered once again by juridical disputes and another clash among clubs from the state of Sao Paulo and the CBB (Globoesporte.com, 2020).

CBB's poor management and two disorderly national competitions (2006 and 2007), the clubs from the state of Sao Paulo were united, refused to compete on the 2008 National Championship, organized by the Confederation, and created the *Supercopa* (Supercup), which was later considered the predecessor of the NBB (*Novo Basquete Brasil* – New Brazilian Basketball) (Globoesporte.com, 2020), the object of this study. As mentioned before, the 2006 National Basketball Championship was cancelled before the end of the final series competed by two big Sao Paulo teams, Franca and COC/Ribeirão Preto (NSC Total, 2008). A disagreement among the CBB and the Brazilian Basketball Clubs Association (*Associação de Clubes de Basquete do Brasil* – ACBB), an independent league created by the Sao Paulo state most important teams, who were completely unsatisfied with CBB's latest decisions related to media rights share and a few clubs' nominations to represent the country on international competitions, led to a rupture among these parts (NSC Total, 2008). Therefore, in 2008, Brazilian fans watched two national competitions for clubs – the Championship organized by CBB, without the Sao Paulo teams; and the *Supercopa*, an independent tournament competed by eight clubs from the same state, out of the CBB's organizational extent (LNB, 2018).

Without relevant international results and an environment full of disputes among clubs, state federations and the CBB, the basketball scenario in the country, around the 2000s, especially in 2008, was chaotic. All of it was the result of a conservative, traditional and outdated management and political mentality. Various attempts of solving CBB's management and political problems have been taken, with no success, such as the *Nossa Liga de Basquete* (NLB) and *Supercopa*. At this moment, in mid-2008, top leaders among some of the most important basketball clubs in the nation decided to join forces and create the National Basketball League (LNB), founded on 1 August that year. The goal of the new sport entity, of course, was to take basketball back to the second place as the most popular sport in the country, following soccer (LNB, 2018). The new league, LNB, created its own competition, the New Basketball Brazil (*Novo Basquete Brasil* – NBB), to replace the former CBB's National Championship, and it was fully organized and managed by its own founding clubs and new league's participants. Based on most modern and innovative world's sport management model, following the steps of the biggest basketball league in the planet, the NBA (National Basketball Association), the Brazilian teams were audacious in order to develop a new management model within the national sports scenario and started seeing basketball as a product (Santos, 2014).

Anne Tjønndal, a researcher at Norwegian University of Science and Technology (NTNU), points out that "the most common innovation in sports are the changes described as improvement, renovation or 'new ideas'" (Tjønndal, 2018). According to Smith and Stewart (2010), "sport innovation usually assumes the form of a type of service because it owns single associated elements to an intense emotional experience and high level of social interaction compared to other sectors". Tjønndal (2018) also proposes a typology for sport innovation, which initially could be divided into these respective aspects: technological change, institutional, entrepreneurship, social issues, management and leadership, anti-ethic innovation, emergence of new sports and market influential change.

In the Brazilian sport context in the end of the 2000s, the foundation and development of the LNB fitted to almost every type of innovation presented by the Norwegian researcher. LNB's creation, thus, could be categorized at that moment, and according to Tjønndal (2018) typology, as: social innovation (when sports organizations, groups or individuals are confronted with social issues that require new and creative solutions); technological (that occurs through technological advances); commercial (when businesses are involved into sports changes); community (that involves social responsibility and entrepreneurship, in which individuals and sports organizations create partnerships with local communities in order to encourage work toward a common goal); and organizational (when sports organizations and governmental institutions seek for institutional change projects) (Tjønndal, 2018).

The creation of the *LNB*, on its essence, represented an organizational innovation as it brought a new management model to basketball clubs in the country, and also, to one of the main clubs' competitions in the Brazilian sports scenario. Within the typology proposed by Tjønndal (2018), "the sports organizations – the clubs – sought for an institutional project change". Winand et al. (2013) also declare that "on an organizational level, innovation is defined as an adoption of an idea or new behavior to the organization". The authors discuss that, on an organizational point of view, "the changes led by new practices within the organizations are relevant, as well as the elements that led to the adoption of new practices". Thereby, innovation is considered a subset of organizational change (Damanpour & Aravind, 2012), which leads organizations to transfer their current practices to forthcoming ones (Nadler & Tushman, 1997).

In 2008, the concept of a sports league was not – and still is not nowadays – very familiar in the country, because all of the competitions have been managed by state federations and national federations for decades (LNB, 2018). So, LNB was born from an idea on its management model not very common in Brazil, which every decision is debated and decided, exclusively, by the teams that are part of the league, as it occurs in the NBA, NFL (National Football League), Premier League and so many other prominent and successful leagues around the world (LNB, 2018). With LNB's rise, the 21 clubs founders started to be the direct responsible, without any interference from CBB, for organizing the championship, negotiate sponsorship deals, media rights, competition rules and any other aspects related to the league's concern on and off the court (LNB, 2018). LNB became a single voice representing the clubs (LNB, 2018), naturally occupying the gap left by the CBB. The foundation of LNB, an innovation within Brazilian sports system, a contrast to the traditional and obsolete CBB, which had been until that point responsible for organizing the Men's National Basketball Championship, the most important competition for clubs in the country, led to induce an adoption of new practices that spread through all of the organizations that had a relationship with Brazilian basketball sports system.

Carrying serious political and management issues with an obsolete vision of basketball both in the country and internationally, the CBB, in the mid-2000's, could not offer a prosperous environment to clubs in order to attract sponsors, media coverage, fans, consumers, therefore, contributing directly to the low technical level of men's basketball competitions in Brazil. The management issues at CBB, based on the traditional model of federations association, ended up to culminate, eight years later, in 2016, to a suspension of all Brazilian National Teams and clubs, both Men and Women, senior and youth squads, for all international competitions. The CBB was banned for outstanding payments toward FIBA and other accusations (Costa, 2016).

Novo Basquete Brasil and Its Sub-products

With the creation of LNB, driven, among other things, by the inability of the CBB to organize the Men's National Basketball Championship, the clubs that joined forces to build LNB felt the necessity of redesigning their main product, the competition among the most important basketball teams in the country. That is when the old and obsolete National Basketball Championship turns into New Basketball Brazil (*Novo Basquete Brasil* – NBB), a name that was chosen to symbolize a new era of the sport in the country (LNB, 2018). More than a simple name change, NBB needed to represent, both in a concrete and symbolic way, the upcoming changes that were, in fact, happening in Brazilian basketball around the late 2000s. Thus, NBB rises within the concept that Tjønndal (2018) names as commercial innovation, "when businesses are involved in creating changes in sport". LNB, through its main product, NBB, needed to be necessitated to show Brazilian basketball ecosystem that this new management model, in fact, was transforming, with creativity and innovation.

The development of NBB, within the context of LNB's rise, moves toward what Ratten (2018), one of the most important researcher in the area of sports innovation, pointed out as "the role of sports innovation in society". According to the author, sports innovativeness involves the creation of viable ideas that can potentially be profitable in long term. The role of sports innovation in society has changed due to realization that continuous transformation is important. This is a result of the dynamic nature of sport and the role of economic, environmental, institutional, social and technological change. Innovations can help an organization increase their revenues from new products or services but it might take a while for consumers to accept them. In order to evaluate the acceptance of new products, it is useful to analyze their usefulness or originality to consumers (Ratten, 2018).

The emerge of NBB was the result, on its essence, of the dynamic of Brazilian basketball, which presented unsupplied necessities from an outdated and political management model, on the part of CBB, in one of its main products, the Men's National Basketball Championship. The competition, created in 1990, was not attending the economical, institutional, social and technological necessities of the clubs, neither of the sponsors of the competition, the athletes and fans. In a short period of time, the new product, more adequate to the current Brazilian basketball environment, proved to be a great success among all the stakeholders involved in the process of creation and development. Sports innovation involves the process of creating new behaviors, products or services that are valued in the marketplace. Newness in sport is a feature of the industry as there are new sports being developed that bridge the old and the new. The first successful application of a new sports practice helps increase viewership and sports participation but marketing its innovativeness is an important component (Ratten, 2018).

LNB and NBB have already born with an innovative vision, for both Brazilian and South American standards, in terms of marketing and communications strategies. Obviously, the process of NBB's creation was not that simple. The clubs that founded the LNB needed to convince CBB that all the changes occurring within the new championship management were crucial to the rebirth of Brazilian basketball. However, one final step was still necessary in order to officially initiate LNB's activities: the CBB's approval (LNB, 2018). CBB's endorsement was necessary so NBB would finally be recognized as the official men's senior competition for clubs in Brazil, all the teams would be allowed to represent the country in the international tournaments and the athletes would be able to join the National Teams on all the official FIBA events (LNB, 2018). It was a tough and delicate situation, since CBB had to give up one of its main products, the Men's National Championship. Beyond that, previous attempts, such as the LNB one, for instance, failed mostly because they lack CBB's recognition and approval. However, unlike the previous attempts, the environment created by LNB made CBB comprehend that conflict among the teams' interests and CBB would damage Brazilian basketball's image even more.

Non-profit sports organizations, like sports federations, are being encouraged to adapt to the expectations of their stakeholders and individual member satisfaction and attraction of new members represent the main objectives. Given the growing number of commercial sports providers and the popularity of unorganized sports activities, it is crucial for sports federations to implement new services to retain and attract members. The adoption of new services to satisfy its members must be considered an innovation (Winand et al., 2013). Thus, organized by LNB and approved by the CBB, the first edition of NBB was launched on 15 December 2008, at Esporte Clube Pinheiros, in Sao Paulo city, with 15 teams. With an innovative management for the Brazilian standards, but following the sports world tendencies, as it can be observed by the successful model of the NBA, the biggest basketball league in the world, LNB and NBB improved fast and made a big contribution to the sport in order to attract sponsors, investors, media and, especially, fans' attention.

Since its creation, the LNB have always pursued for innovation. During all these years, several competitions, always built as products, were developed to attend the expectations and necessities of both Brazilian and Latin American basketball ecosystems. The main competition organized by LNB, the NBB, is competed in a regular season format, with home and away games among all the teams, and its final round, as it happens on most of the basketball leagues in the world, is played on a playoffs system. Since its first edition, in 2008, NBB has been recognized by FIBA as the official Men's Brazilian First Division Basketball Championship for clubs. Another important product designed by LNB on the first season, in 2008–2009, was the NBB's All-Star Game, a sport and entertainment event organized each year by the LNB, bringing together all the best athletes of the NBB. This product is inspired on the NBA All-Star Game (LNB, 2018). The entire event, that is a mix of sport and entertainment, is based on individual contests (Slam Dunk Competition, three-point Challenge and Skills Challenge) and a regular match, the All-Star Game, the main attraction

(LNB, 2018). Usually, the players that are chosen to participate on the event are picked by the teams' coaching staff members, athletes, media and national basketball legends. The fans can also be part of the voting process by selecting the starting line-up of the All-Star teams through an online election at the LNB's website (LNB, 2018).

LNB has also created the *Torneio Interligas de Basquetebol* in 2010, a friendly competition among both professional leagues in Brazil (LNB) and in Argentina (*Asociación de Clubes de Básquetbol*), organization responsible for the Men's National Championship in the country. This tournament had three editions, between 2010 and 2012, and returned to the competition calendar in 2019 (LNB, 2018). In 2011, as the teams demonstrated a concern with social innovation, when sports organizations, groups or individuals are confronted with social issues that require new and creative solutions (Tjønndal, 2018), LNB created the Olympic Development League (*Liga de Desenvolvimento Olímpico* – LDO), which later was transformed into the Basketball Development League (*Liga de Desenvolvimento de Basquete* – LDB). The LDB is a tournament competed by young athletes under-20 from teams that belong to the NBB and other clubs from all over the country (Lancelivre.com, 2011). In 2018, in order to enhance even more the LDB, the LNB created the *Taça Interligas de Desenvolvimento*, a single-game tournament that brings both the Brazilian and Argentinian Development Leagues' champions (Gazeta Esportiva, 2018). In 2014, LNB created another championship, the Golden League (*Liga Ouro*). In order to fortify and integrate more clubs to the league, the LNB designed the *Liga Ouro* as an access division to the NBB. In 2018, the Brazilian league presented another innovation to the basketball community called the Super 8 Cup, a one-game playoff series with the top eight teams in the first round of the season, that offers to the champion a spot in the next FIBA Basketball Champions League Americas, the most important competition for clubs in Latin America (LNB, 2018).

All these innovative products designed by LNB throughout time have been crucial to the organization in order to attract the attention of sponsors, media companies, investors, athletes and fans, and other basketball stakeholders. The exact dimension of what LNB has done with the creation of NBB can be analyzed on the first edition of the NBB Finals, at HSBC Arena, in Rio de Janeiro, when almost 16,000 fans attended the Game 5 of the series (LNB, 2018). Besides that, the LNB attracted the attention of the NBA and announced a groundbreaking partnership in December 2014. Since the 2014–2015 season, the LNB has shared knowledge and experiences with the NBA in several areas of management, basketball operations, finance, commercial, marketing, communications and entertainment, aiming to offer a better product to the fans and partners in the country (Meio & Mensagem, 2014). This partnership was the first agreement between the NBA and another local league in the world (LNB, 2018). The Brazilian basketball, unlike what happened in the 2000s, regained its respect worldwide. In 2012, in the Olympic Games in London, the Men's National Team returned to the competition, after 16 years of absence.

Communication, Disruption and Innovation

As it has been described before, in the first years of its history, LNB faced a big challenge of rebuilding men's Brazilian basketball reputation by creating a strong and competitive league. For that reason, the organization had to innovate within Brazilian sports market, with a new concept of sport competition and, mostly, management, with clubs administrating the organization collectively, within a collaborative and cooperative system among all the participants. In order to succeed with this new model, a series of initiatives and strategies, on various management areas of a sport organization, allied with a series of new and innovative products, were accomplished. Nevertheless, since its beginning, one of the most creative and innovative LNB areas was communication, always considered as a priority within the organization. "Take basketball to a larger number of people and show the fans a new image, that things have completely changed, was imperative" (LNB, 2020). In 2008, when LNB was created, *TV Globo*, the largest media and entertainment company in Brazil, became the media rights owner of the NBB (LNB, 2018). In addition to the media rights of the competition, *TV Globo* evolved into a truly partner of the league, promoting various initiatives with the sports entity.

The partnership with the NBA, in accordance with the vast experience of the American sport organization, emphasized the innovation elements that had already been present within both management and communications aspects of the LNB: the culture of collective management over the individual; the need for communicational strategies in order to engage fans; and the innovative concept of providing fans and arena attendants a full entertainment experience. With LNB's development, since its foundation in the end of 2008, the communication department has been in a frequent transformation. From the initial content distribution model, having *TV Globo* as its main partner, the LNB passed to adopt, in consequence of the maturity of the organization's management and the growth of their products, a new content distribution supported on a multiplatform model, extremely innovative and disruptive, based on both traditional media outlets and social media platforms (LNB, 2020).

Ratten (2018) points out the fact that innovations, while helping build competitive advantage, can also increase uncertainly due to the time spent on development. Market pressure to innovate means that it can be difficult to estimate its potential usefulness in the market-place. This is especially evident in sport where market acceptance is crucial for the innovations long-term performance. Many sports organizations have a non-profit or amateur status, which means they are not set up to adapt quickly. This means that while some sports innovations are produced in an amateur context, the trend is for profit-oriented organizations to commercialize the technological innovation. In 2008, when LNB was founded, the Brazilian sports environment was uncertain and full of amateur organizations, illustrated by the ideas of Ratten (2018). Besides, in the initial years of the LNB, technological advents, such as social media platforms and streaming services, were not even a reality on sports and entertainment businesses. However, as the author affirms, on the other hand, the Brazilian sports market, especially following the expectations on both the 2014 FIFA World Cup and the 2016 Summer Olympics in Rio de Janeiro, was yearning for innovations around these type of technologies and communication solutions. Ratten (2018) also affirms that an example of technological innovation in sport is Facebook, which is adding more live sports games streaming to its services. Live streaming of football has been popular for Facebook and provided an innovation growth opportunity for the social networking website. Live streaming sport events is popular because of the large audience it attracts (Ratten, 2018). However, because the broadcast rights for most sports events are under contract, Facebook has to look for alternative entry points. That was exactly what happened to the LNB. With the growth of the NBB, the entity's communication necessities increased and the league felt the importance of change its own initial mentality and start working on producing and distributing a better quality content of its main product, the NBB (LNB, 2020).

Having its media rights exclusively owned by *TV Globo* until the end of the 2017–2018 season, the LNB executed its first live streaming game of the NBB championship, an innovative moment within Brazilian sports business, only in 2014, when a game of that season, São José against Palmeiras, was streamed on the LNB's website (LNB, 2020). After a successful experience with the first streamed game, the LNB accomplished more than 40 live games with an online distribution on the following season – 2014–2015 (LNB, 2020). In 2016, when Facebook announced its own streaming services, the Facebook Live, the LNB became the first Brazilian sports organization to stream a live game on this social media, demonstrating all of its innovative capacity, with the *Liga Ouro* (second division tournament) five-game Finals series in 2016. On the 2016–2017 season, the LNB reinforced its pioneering and innovative essence by announcing the first streaming contract with Facebook in Brazil, with 30 NBB exclusive games on the platform (LNB, 2020). After the end of a 10-year contract with *TV Globo*, the LNB pulled out one of the biggest innovation moves in Brazilian sports by adopting the multiplatform model of content production and distribution for the games of the 11th NBB season, the main Brazilian men's basketball competition among clubs. The matches of the 2018–2019 season were exhibited on six different media partners: four TV networks (one free-to-air national TV – Band – and three paid TV channels – ESPN, Bandsports and Fox Sports) and two streaming social media platforms (Facebook and Twitter) (Folha de São Paulo, 2018).

This unprecedented model, as it was mentioned before, for sports content distribution in the country, allowed NBB to cover more than 75% of its regular season and playoffs games going live on at least one of its six partners. As part of the strategy, the games were distributed to each media outlet following the weekdays: Facebook (Mondays), ESPN (Tuesdays), Twitter (Wednesdays), Bandsports (Thursdays), Fox Sports (Fridays) and Band (Sundays). During the playoffs, some games were shared by more than one network (Folha de São Paulo, 2018). More than the adoption of an innovative concept of multiplatform distribution, the LNB took the responsibility of producing, in an appropriate and customized style to each platform, the NBB games throughout the season, guaranteeing a high standard production on every single game by developing a single visual identity and the same equipment quality to all the games (IstoÉDinheiro, 2018). Illustrating the ideas of Ratten (2018), another technological tool that highly contributed to the multiplatform distribution of the games' highlights on the social media platforms was the usage of WSC Sports. The software works with AI (artificial intelligence) analyzes and cuts videos of in-game plays automatically by an integration with the live stats.

Before 2019, the communications department of the LNB used to take more than 12 hours to edit the highlights or condensed videos of the NBB games. During night events, the videos could only be published on social media or sent to media partners on the next day. After the partnership with WSC Sports, this editing procedure became automatic and the videos are ready to be posted within 10 minutes. The software is integrated with the in-game live stats, "play-by-play" and the broadcast (in the 2019–2020, all the games are live on at least one media outlet). With this collected data, WSC Sports can automatically cut the plays of every single game of the league and the small clips are storage in a database. The 3-minute highlights and the 10-minute condensed game videos are all edited and published automatically, being supervised by a human just for precaution. Practically, all the official streamed and broadcasted games of the season have been analyzed by the program, which also allows the users to select plays by athlete, teams, play style or even the quality of the plays (classified by one to five stars) (UOL Esporte, 2020). For that reason, the LNB are allowed to produce tailormade and exclusive content to its own clubs, athletes and media partners. With a single click, player highlights, teams' best plays and all the games' condensed videos are done in a matter of minutes. Some examples of the type of content that are produced by NBB's communications teams are Top 10 Plays, Dunks, Assists and Blocks from each month of the competition, King of the Month (player's performance), All-NBB Team of the Week, are all kinds of videos that can be generated to the basketball ecosystem, in a unique and innovative model of content production and distribution (LNB, 2020).

With a strong championship and a valued brand, the innovative way that LNB thought and worked the production and dissemination of its own content are the new reality of sports in the country and it is a successful case of other organizations. The slogan created for the 2018–2019 season reflects, in an objective way, the current stage of the competition in Brazil: #VcNuncaViuNadaIgual (You Have Never Seen Anything Like It) (LNB, 2020).

Managerial Perspectives

After the conclusion of both Olympic and Paralympic Games in Rio de Janeiro, the "golden decade" of Brazilian sports came to an end. There was a positive expectation on the legacy of this decade to Brazilian sports, but it simply turned into a political promise from the ones who brought both of the events to the country, such as national governors and sports entities like the IOC (International Olympic Committee) and FIFA (International Federation of Association Football). Their main concern was the commercial value instead of the sport legacy of these events toward Brazilian sports future. A good portion of the main sports organizations in the country, for example, the Brazilian Olympic Committee (COB), the CBB and other national confederations, clubs and sports associations, experience a new moment with sponsorship withdrawal, inefficient management, governance, transparency and corruption issues, and also financial unsustainability (Mazzei & Rocco Junior, 2017).

One of the most neglected aspects of the investments made for the megaevents in Brazil was the legacy on sports management to the country. Various news throughout the most important media companies in Brazil, after both the 2014 World Cup and the 2016 Olympic Games, showed a real dimension of how the management of sport in the country, on different sports organizations, still had inefficiency and amateurism issues (Rocco Junior & Bastos, 2019). "Former president of the Brazilian Aquatic Sports Confederation (*Confederação Brasileira de Desportes Aquáticos* – CBDA) and two directors are arrested" (Folha.com, 2017a), "Most of the sports' sponsorship deals disappear after the Olympics in Rio" (Folha.com, 2017b), "Six months after Rio 2016, medalists lose sponsors and reveal sports crisis" (Globo.com, 2017) and "President of the Brazilian Olympic Committee, Carlos Arthur Nuzman, is arrested for fraud" (Gazeta Esportiva, 2017) are some examples of news that have affected the management of the main sports organizations in the country.

The inefficiency and management problems within Brazilian sports are not restraint to the national confederations of some sports only. The issues of entities that regulate and administrate sports in the country are also present on the main sports clubs (Rocco Junior & Bastos, 2019). As it is possible to notice by the headlines presented above, after the 2014 World Cup and both 2016 Olympic and Paralympic Games in Rio, the management of sports organizations in Brazil did not benefit from any of these huge international sports events. It was quite the opposite. The megaevents ended up by evidencing the management issues of most of the sports entities in the country, with various problems of administrative incompetence and inefficiency toward the relationship with athletes, coaches, fans, sponsors, media and Brazilian society in general (Rocco Junior & Bastos, 2019).

On the other hand, as it was mentioned before, the megaevents hosted in Brazil showcased to the country, especially to the Brazilian sports universe, the biggest innovations existent in the global sports industry. Large events, such as the World Cup and the Olympic Games, are a great stage to launch new and innovative technologies, services and products to the sports market. Brazil has been invaded, during these megaevents, by social, technological, communitarian and organizational innovations (Tjønndal, 2018). In order to cite just one example, within the context of this study, Sprinklr, a technology company that offers solutions for managing social experience to costumers, did a research on the most commented topics during the 2016 Rio Olympics and found that, during the event, out of 41,901,928 mentions about the Games on social media, 550,000 cited the official sponsors of the event (Digitalks, 2016). The tool also analyzed the countries that interacted more on social media about the topic: United States was the first, with over 614 thousand interactions, followed by Brazil, in second, with 158.3 thousand, and United Kingdom in third place, with 100.8 thousand mentions (Digitalks, 2016).

Another study conducted by Brazilian sports newspaper "Lance!" showed that the 2016 Rio Olympic Games were, on a digital point of view, the most interactive within social media, with more than 131 million people using social platforms and a total of 916 million interactions (Cordeiro, 2016). Facing this scenario, allied to what has been written previously, the rise of the LNB has represented a truly innovation within Brazilian sports organizations management model. The management system based on the unity of the clubs, within a cooperative and collaborative structure, is unique in the country. Combined with the innovative management system, the professional vision, which places Brazilian basketball and its products as business, is completely innovative to national sports organizations reality. Some of them are contaminated by amateurism and little commitment with sports, economic and financial results.

The LNB's innovative management model, followed by the success obtained by the basketball organization, can and should serve as an inspiration to other sport clubs and associations in the country, especially, to those amateur sports organizations that have lost interest from fans, participants and commercial and media partners throughout the years. This is the biggest management implication, to the Brazilian sports organizations, induced by all the innovative management actions created by LNB within Brazilian sports market.

The LNB's innovative management model brought to the organization an Innovation Virtuous Cycle (Figure 12.1). The innovative management led to the development of products, with emphasis to the NBB, which has had a wide business vision, with commercial and economical value and has generated new resources to the entity. With a favorable environment to the development of sports business resulted by the megaevents hosted in Brazil, the LNB found the ideal conditions to the usage of technology in new activations and innovative projects, as it has been mentioned in this study. The innovative adoption of a multiplatform content distribution strategy, within the Brazilian sports scenario, among other actions, is a result of this process and the business vision of LNB, which has been implanted by the innovative management model developed by the organization.

The technology, within LNB's innovative management process, demanded investments, such as the partnership with WSC Sports, that allowed an increase of highlight videos of the championship by using an AI editing software. This investment helped not only the League but also the associated clubs which are now able to create new and modern content and share them with the fans in order to create a bigger engagement on social media platforms. The basketball organization, with this innovative, creative and pioneering way of using technology for communications purposes, within the multiplatform concept, currently is the second largest Brazilian sport organization on number of social media followers, only behind the

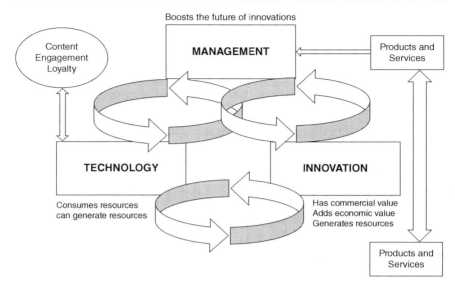

Figure 12.1 Innovation Virtuous Cycle (LNB).

Brazilian Football Confederation (CBF). LNB has 724,000 followers on Facebook, 267,000 on Instagram, 145,000 on Twitter, 50,000 on YouTube and 116,000 on TikTok (Ibope Repucom, 2020).

Other results of the innovative and strategic actions of LNB must also be taken into consideration. The final game of the 11th NBB season (2018–2019), among Flamengo and Franca, set the historical record of fans following a live streaming on the NBB Facebook page. The game had more than 367,000 viewers and a peak of 22.106 simultaneous users (O Tempo, 2021). During the five games of the final series, more than 1,276 million fans watched them live on Facebook, with 76,000 interactions and an average of 15,214 reactions per match (O Tempo, 2021). Therefore, the LNB can be, in an innovative way, a versatile content producer that works with its main product, the NBB, in diverse platforms and with an adequate language to each public, generating interaction and engagement among the fans. An example of success that, hopefully, can be followed by other sports organizations in Brazil and Latin America markets.

References

CBB. (2020). *Missão, Visão e Valores*. https://www.cbb.com.br/missao-visao-e-valores
Central Intelligence Agency. (2008). *Geography of Brazil in the World Factbook*. https://www.cia.gov/library/publications/the-world-factbook/geos/br.html.

Constituição da República Federativa do Brasil. (1988). *Constituição da República Federativa do Brasil de 1988*. http://www.planalto.gov.br/ccivil_03/constituicao/constituicao.htm

Cordeiro, L. (2016). *Brasil soma 916 milhões de interações no Instagram na Rio 2016*. https://www.bitmag.com.br/2016/08/brasil-soma-916-milhoes-de-interacoes-no-instagram-na-rio-2016/

Costa, G. (2016). *Fiba suspende o Brasil de torneios: "falta de controle total do basquete"*. https://www.uol.com.br/esporte/basquete/ultimas-noticias/2016/11/14/fiba-suspende-confederacao-brasileira-de-basquete.htm?cmpid=copiaecola

Damanpour, F., & Aravind, D. (2012). Managerial innovation: Conceptions, processes and antecedents. *Management and Organization Review*, 8(2), 423–454.

Deloitte. (2011). *Muito Além do Futebol – Estudo sobre esportes no Brasil*. Deloitte.

Digitalks. (2016). *Jogos Olímpicos registram mais de 40 milhões de menções nas redes sociais*. https://digitalks.com.br/indicadores-do-mercado/jogos-olimpicos-registram-mais-de-40-milhoes-de-mencoes-nas-redes-sociais/

Diesporte. (2015). *Diagnóstico Nacional do Esporte*. Ministério do Esporte.

Folha de São Paulo. (2018). *Sem Globo e com transmissão multiplataforma, NBB chega à 'adolescência'*. https://www1.folha.uol.com.br/esporte/2018/10/sem-globo-e-com-transmissao-multiplataforma-nbb-chega-a-adolescencia.shtml

Folha.com. (2017a). *Ex-presidente da Confederação Brasileira de Desportes Aquáticos (CBDA) e outros dois dirigentes são presos*. https://www1.folha.uol.com.br/esporte/2017/04/1873160-pf-prende-presidente-da-confederacao-de-natacao-e-outros-4-dirigentes.shtml

Folha.com. (2017b). *Maioria dos esportes vê patrocínio sumir após os Jogos do Rio*. https://www1.folha.uol.com.br/esporte/2017/03/1865706-maioria-dos-esportes-ve-patrocinio-sumir-apos-os-jogos-do-rio.shtml

Fundo Monetário Internacional. (2020). *World Economic Outlook Database*. https://www.imf.org/en/Publications/WEO/weo-database/2020/October/weoreport?c=512=PPPGDP,&sy=2020&ey=2020&ssm=0&scsm=1&scc=0&ssd=1&ssc=0&sic=0&sort=country&ds=.&br=1

G1. (2016). *Parque Olímpico registra recorde de público neste sábado*. http://g1.globo.com/rio-de-janeiro/paralimpiadas/noticia/2016/09/parque-olimpico-registra-recorde-de-publico-neste-sabado.html

Gazeta Esportiva. (2017). *Presidente do Comitê Olímpico Brasileiro (COB), Carlos Arthur Nuzman é preso acusado de fraude*. https://www.gazetaesportiva.com/mais-esportes/presidente-do-cob-carlos-arthur-nuzmane-preso-acusado-de-fraude/.

Gazeta Esportiva. (2018). *Paulistano bate Quimsa e conquista a Taça Interligas de Desenvolvimento*. https://www.gazetaesportiva.com/mais-esportes/basquete/paulistano-bate-quimsa-e-conquista-taca-interligas-de-desenvolvimento/

Globo.com. (2017). *Seis meses após a Rio 2016, medalhistas perdem apoio e esbarram na crise do país*. https://ge.globo.com/olimpiadas/noticia/seis-meses-apos-a-rio-2016-medalhistas-perdem-apoio-e-esbarram-na-crise-do-pais.ghtml

Globoesporte.com (2020). *Precursora do NBB, Supercopa completa 12 anos; troféu foi último de Hélio Rubens no Franca*. https://globoesporte.globo.com/sp/ribeirao-preto-e-regiao/basquete/noticia/precursora-do-nbb-supercopa-completa-12-anos-trofeu-foi-ultimo-de-helio-rubens-no-franca.ghtml

IBOPE Repucom. (2017). *Sponsorlink – pesquisa esporte 2017*.

IBOPE Repucom. (2019). *Sponsorlink – pesquisa esporte 2019*.

IBOPE Repucom. (2020). *Ranking Digital 2020 das Confederações Esportivas Brasileiras*.

IstoÉDinheiro. (2018). *NBB começa sua 11ª temporada com transmissões multiplataformas.* https://www.istoedinheiro.com.br/com-gestao-empresarial-e-novo-modelo-de-transmissao-multiplataforma-nbb-atinge-maturidade-em-sua-decima-primeira-temporada/

Lancelivre.com. (2011). *NNB lança Liga de Desenvolvimento Olímpico na segunda, em São Paulo.*

LNB. (2018). *LNB: 10 anos de inovação.* https://lnb.com.br/noticias/lnb-10-anos-de-inovacao/

LNB. (2020). *O modelo multiplataforma.* https://lnb.com.br/noticias/como-o-nbb-passou-de-uma-assessoria-de-imprensa-para-o-modelo-de-distribuicao-multiplataforma/

Mazzei, L. C., & Rocco Junior, A. J. (2017). Um ensaio sobre a Gestão do Esporte: Um momento para a sua afirmação no Brasil. *Revista de Gestão e Negócios do Esporte (RGNE), São Paulo, 2*(1), 96–109.

McCarthy, N. (2016). *The Massive Costs behind the Olympic Games.* https://www.statista.com/chart/5424/the-massive-costs-behind-the-olympic-games/

Meio & Mensagem. (2014). *NBA e NBB confirmam parceria.* https://www.meioemensagem.com.br/home/marketing/2014/12/10/nba-e-nbb-confirmam-parceria.html

Ministério da Cidadania. (2020). *Secretaria Especial do Esporte.* https://www.gov.br/cidadania/pt-br/noticias-e-conteudos/esporte/

Nadler, D. A., & Tushman, M. L. (1997). *Competing by design: The power of organizational architecture.* Oxford University Press.

NSC Total. (2008). *Basquete brasileiro ganha nova liga nacional.* https://www.nsctotal.com.br/noticias/basquete-brasileiro-ganha-nova-liga-nacional

O Globo. (2013). *Com 5 novos municípios, Brasil agora tem 5.570 cidades.* https://oglobo.globo.com/brasil/com-5-novos-municipios-brasil-agora-tem-5570-cidades-7235803.

O Globo. (2019). *Brasil é ultrapassado pelo Paquistão e cai para 6° no ranking de países mais populosos do mundo.* https://oglobo.globo.com/sociedade/brasil-ultrapassado-pelo-paquistao-cai-para-6-no-ranking-de-paises-mais-populosos-do-mundo-23742238.

O Tempo. (2021). *Basquete que deu liga.* https://lnb.com.br/noticias/evolucao-do-nbb-no-cenario-esportivo-ganha-destaque-no-jornal-o-tempo/

Ratten, V. (2018). *Sports innovation management.* Routledge.

Rocco Junior, A. J., & Bastos, F. C. (2019). Gestão e governança nas entidades esportivas brasileiras após os Jogos Olímpicos Rio-2016. In K. Rubio (Ed.), *Do pós ao neo Olimpismo: Esporte e movimento olímpico no século XX.* Editora Laços Képos.

Rocco Junior, A. J., & Mazzei, L. C. (2018). *Os Estádios e Arenas do Futebol Brasileiro e o legado da Copa do Mundo 2014: o padrão FIFA, o consumidor do esporte e o entretenimento. Sarapuí.* OJM Casa Editorial.

Santos, R. (2014). *6 anos de NBB - da criação ao sucesso.* http://globoesporte.globo.com/sportv/blogs/especial-blog/blog-do-renatinho/post/6-anos-de-nbb-da-criacao-ao-sucesso.html

Smith, A. C., & Stewart, B. (2010). The special features of sport: A critical revisit. *Sport Management Review, 13*(1), 1–13.

Tjønndal, A. (2018). Sport innovation: Developing a typology. *European Journal for Sport and Society, 14*(2), 291–310.

UOL Esporte. (2020). *NBB não precisa mais de humanos para editar melhores momentos; entenda...* https://www.uol.com.br/esporte/basquete/ultimas-noticias/2020/01/30/nbb-nao-precisa-mais-de-humanos-para-editar-melhores-momentos-entenda.htm?cmpid=copiaecola

Winand, M., Vos, S., Zintz, T., & Scheerder, J. (2013). Determinants of service innovation: A typology of sports federations. *International Journal of Sport Management and Marketing*, *13*(1/2), 55–73.

World Bank. (2011). *Country and lending groups*. http://web.archive.org/web/20110318125456/http://data.worldbank.org/about/country-classifications/country-and-lending-groups#Upper_middle_income.

Chapter 13

Innovative Promotions to Attract Non-Resident Spectators

A Case Study in Portugal

Maria José Carvalho

Faculdade de Desporto da Universidade do Porto & CIFI²D, Portugal

Marisa Sousa

Faculdade de Desporto da Universidade do Porto & CIFI²D, Portugal

Celina Gonçalves

Universidade da Maia, Instituto Politécnico de Bragança & CIDESD, Portugal

---

Chapter Contents

Introduction	186
Review of Literature	189
Method	191
Instrument and Procedures	191
Data Analyses	192
Results	192
Discussion	195
Conclusion	198
References	199

Introduction

Portugal, officially designated as the Portuguese Republic, is a sovereign democratic State, located in South-West Europe (Iberian Peninsula). Its territory is bordered by Spain to the North and East and by the Atlantic Ocean to the West and South, where two autonomous regions – Azores and Madeira – are located. Administratively, it is divided into 308 municipalities, subdivided into 3,092 parishes, and its capital is Lisbon. The official currency is the euro and the Portuguese political system is a semi-presidential republic with a head of government – the Prime Minister – and a head of state – the President of the Republic. Portugal became independent in 1143. In the 15th century, it began its maritime expansion, thus creating an overseas empire that lasted from 1415 to 1975. In 1910, the monarchy

DOI: 10.4324/9781003388050-16

was replaced by a republican regime. In 1933, a dictatorship was instituted, ruling the country until 25 April 1974. In 1976, a new constitution was adopted (by a Constitutional Assembly elected by universal suffrage), which provided for a wide range of fundamental rights – civil, economic, cultural, political, and social – and ensured a democratic, multi-party regime based on the dignity of the human person and the people's free will.

Portugal became a member of the United Nations on 14 December 1955 and joined the European Union (EU) on 1 January 1986. It is also a member of several other international and regional organizations, namely the Council of Europe, North Atlantic Treaty Organization (NATO), the Organization for Economic Cooperation and Development (OECD), and the Community of Portuguese Speaking Countries (CPLP). It is also a part of the Schengen area.

In 2019, the resident population in Portugal was 10,286 million, of which 5,430 million were women (52.8%) and 4,856 million were men (47.2%), continuing the trend over the years of the resident population being composed mostly of women. The number of people under 15 years of age makes up 13.6% of the population (1,402 million) (INE, 2021a), a figure that reflects the low birth rate of 1.42, while the minimum level of generational replacement in the most developed countries is 2.10 (INE, 2021b). In 2019, the Gross Domestic Product (GDP) per capita expressed in Purchasing Power Parities (PPP) in Portugal was 79% of the EU average, ranking 16th among the euro area countries. In 2019, the GDP *per capita*, at constant prices, was €25,299 (INE, 2021c).

Currently, we are in the 22nd Constitutional Government of the Portuguese Republic (Decree-Law n. 169-B, 2019) and the ministry responsible for Physical Education and Sport of the whole population is the Ministry of Education and Sport. This Ministry is responsible for formulating, conducting, implementing, and evaluating the national policy for the education system, within the preschool, basic, and secondary education as well as the extra-school education. The same Ministry is also in charge of the national youth and sport policy, and also for interplay between the national education policy and the national vocational training policy, within the scope of national policies for promoting the qualification of people. The Minister of Education supervises and oversees the Portuguese Institute for Sport and Youth, I. P. (IPDJ, in Portuguese), the organization responsible for implementing an integrated and decentralized policy for the areas of sport and youth, in close cooperation with public and private entities, namely sport bodies, youth and student associations, and local authorities.

The last Eurobarometer on sport and physical activity (CE, 2018) shows that 74% of the Portuguese population "never" or "rarely" does physical exercise or practice sport, and both Portuguese women and men are far from the European averages, ranking the fifth most sedentary country. However, women perform worst (78% of women, 68% of men), with around three out of four women "never" or "rarely" doing physical exercise or practicing sport. In performance sport, the Portuguese team attending the last Olympic Games (on Rio de Janeiro in 2016) showed a 68% male participation and 32% female participation, which also demonstrates a sporting reality with great progress toward gender equality in sport. In relation to sporting practice, only football has competitions that are recognized as professional: we are talking about the I and II Men's Leagues, each having 18 sporting societies in competition. Therefore, football is where the most significant part of the Portuguese sport industry is and hence our research investment on events of this nature, i.e. concerning football as a professional sport, as we shall see throughout this chapter.

Nowadays the organization of events, specifically sport events, has increased in the last decades in Europe, and Portugal followed this trend. This increase in sport events organization leads to the study of sport events over the past decades, since they generate positive and negative impacts (Sanz et al., 2012). Some major studies (e.g., Gratton et al., 2000) show the economic importance of events through the analysis of their economic impact in host cities. However, most of the economic impact studies aim to gain public support and subsidies to host the events than to produce academic contributions (Dixon et al., 2012). On the one hand, most of the economic impact research seems to be focused on the impact of mega events, as the events at international level (e.g., Baade & Matheson, 2004; Matheson, 2006; Porter & Fletcher, 2008; Preuss, 2007; Tien et al., 2011). On the other hand, the great difficulty in analyzing the economic impact of small events (Barajas et al., 2012) is described. Thus, the literature on small events seems to be scarce (Carvalho et al., 2018). Despite this, in the last few years, the focus starts to be moving to smaller events (Carvalho et al., 2018; Coates & Depken, 2011; Gibson et al., 2012; Matheson, 2006; Taks et al., 2013, 2011; Veltri et al., 2009; Wilson, 2006).

Sport events provide a great opportunity for the marketing strategies development in the clubs and host cities (Goldblatt, 2000). Considering that spectators play a major role in sport events, the analysis of their behavior has taken on a growing role in academic research (Allan et al., 2007; Amy, 2007; Lera-López & Rapún-Gárate, 2005; Lera-López et al., 2012; Trail et al., 2003). Knowing the factors that influence the people's decisions to attend the games is crucial for sport organizations to involve and attract more spectators to this phenomenon. This involvement will increase not only the reputation of teams and clubs, but also the entrance revenues and others, such as the income from the bars or merchandising in the official shops, generating direct and indirect benefits to sport organizations (Biscaia et al., 2010). The analysis of consumption patterns of spectators, thus, becomes crucial to understand and target those who participate in sport events, particularly non-resident spectators because they are those who bring "new money" for the city (Crompton, 2006; Crompton et al., 2001; Gratton, 2005).

Sport has acquired great importance in many facets of social and economic life, not only as an economic urban regeneration agent for cities and regions but also as wealth creation agent, through the "sport tourism" and in terms of social engineering, to promote inclusion, self-fulfillment, and development of communities (Hassan & Connor, 2009). Specifically regarding to host an event, the literature has underlined numerous benefits as the improvement of the city image (Dwyer et al., 2005), the poverty alleviation and job creation, the marketing benefits, and the infrastructure development (Saayman & Rossouw, 2008; Saayman & Saayman, 2012; Thomson et al., 2013). The idea that sport events promote economic development is rooted in intuition that, the consumption of hundreds of thousands or even millions of people who attend the games, generates several economic benefits (Sandy, 2004). Particularly football as a sport modality supports this idea of economic development, since its importance in our society is visible (Gómez-Bantel, 2015).

Although the economic impact of sport events has been widely studied (Baade et al., 2008; Gibson et al., 2005; Gratton et al., 2006; Huang et al., 2014; Lamla et al., 2014; Preuss, 2004; Wilson, 2006), the analysis of the costs incurred by the spectators has been neglected (Mak, 2004). In fact, the economic impact research on small-scale sport events seems to be scarce, because usually the literature has focused on the impact of mega-events such as the Olympic Games or the FIFA World Cup (e.g., Baade & Matheson, 2004; Matheson, 2006; Porter & Fletcher, 2008; Preuss, 2007; Tien et al., 2011). However, recently the smaller events start to have increased attention (e.g., Coates & Depken, 2011; Daniels & Norman, 2003; Matheson, 2006; Mondello & Rishe, 2004; Taks et al., 2011, 2013; Veltri et al., 2009; Wilson, 2006). Considering the gap in the specialized literature concerning the analysis of consumption patterns of non-resident spectators of small sport events, those carried out by the Portuguese professional soccer clubs participating in Liga NOS, the aim of this case study was to analyze the profile and consumption patterns of non-resident spectators who attend the games of Liga NOS in the city of Paços de Ferreira.

Review of Literature

The organization of events, specifically sport events, has increased in the last decades in Europe, and Portugal followed this trend. This increase in sport events organization leads to the study of sport events over the past decades, since they generate positive and negative impacts (Sanz et al., 2012). Some major studies (e.g., Agha, 2013) show the economic importance of events through the analysis of their economic impact in host cities. However, most of the economic impact studies aim to gain public support and subsidies to host the events than to produce academic contributions (Dixon et al., 2012). The economic impact is a concept widely studied in the literature. According to Lee (2001), the economic impact of a sport event is a net economic change in a host community that results from spending attributed to the sport event. Usually, the economic impact of sport event is measured by the input stream trace of "new money" in the city or region which can be directly attributed to the event. This "new money" is defined by Crompton (2006) as the consumption generated by the sport event occurred in the region. This "new money" can be estimated by the consumption generated by the spectators, and to measure the economic impact of these agents, we should assign "new money" to one of the following categories: ticketing, accommodation, food and beverage, local transportation, and shopping (Gratton, 2005).

Using the consumption made by resident spectators during sport events for estimation of the impact analysis has generated much discussion in two schools of thought (Crompton, 1995, 2006; Preuss et al., 2007). The economic impact studies determine the profitability of an investment for a territory and its inhabitants (Barajas et al., 2016) and are pointed to as an appropriate methodology for accessing what is essentially a major source of the benefits of a special event (Crompton, 2006). However, a deeply study about the profile and consumption patterns of football spectators should be broader than analyzing the economic impact of hosting an event at a specific location. Sport events are considered catalysts of economic and tourism growth in the places that perform, existing a great opportunity for the development of marketing strategies for the clubs and for host cities (Goldblatt, 2000; Li & Jago, 2013), because the collection and dissemination of qualified information about the spending of spectators will help event organizers to demonstrate the economic benefits which they produce in the communities, and improve understanding of the consumption pattern of spectators. Allen (2007) describes that a successful marketing strategy comes from a better understanding of consumers and their needs. Thus, marketing begins with the needs and human desires (Kotler, 2012). These two concepts permeate the marketing decision-making, because from them it is formed the marketing strategy in which the company will determine what will be its market.

The sport marketing has received a growing attention due to the involvement of consumers. People are motivated to get involved in sport by several reasons: economic, political, tourism, static, social, community, collective volunteering, among other reasons (Fedrizzi et al., 2017; Hallmann & Zehrer, 2017; Österlind, 2016). Therefore, the sport marketing manager must identify the characteristics that attract the spectators and participants to sport (Ratten, 2011), in order to better understand how they identify themselves with the sport, and, target them more effectively (Ratten 2011). The creation of profiles that include information on actual expenditure, as well as socio-demographic characteristics and travel behavior of different types of spectators, provides to organizers valuable information that can be used to identify products and services that complement the desires of spectators at sport events (Hinch & Higham, 2001). Thus, the spectators' consumption patterns are important for the acquisition of data required for marketing segmentation and policymaking (Wilton, 2006). According to this author, the identification of the characteristics and behavior of specific target markets are vital for the development of effective and efficient marketing strategies for clubs and the cities hosting the events. Therefore, the segmentation of the sport market became popular as a strategy for organizations, to define the most appropriate consumers (Ratten 2011). The market segmentation consists of distributing the market into groups of potential buyers, who have similar needs and desires, perceptions of values, or buying behaviors (Churchill, 2005).

However, the evaluation of expenditure incurred by sport spectators can be a challenging task since several indicators are used to estimate their costs. Examples of those indicators are: the number of viewers and their daily consumption; the types of spectators and types of events; the duration of the trip and the cost at the event location (Mules & Dwyer, 2005). To estimate this cost at the event location, are usually applied questionnaires, during the events (Mules & Dwyer, 2005). The demographic points such as gender, age, education, income, geographic proximity, and football practice could be important to this formation to know the profile and consumption patterns of spectators who attend sport events. These variables import to the clubs and sport event organizers for that observe the possible improvements in the management and the relation with the client, spectator. The gender and age are present in several papers which present data from the participants and corroborate with a perspective of spectator pattern and the attendance of sport events is growing (Khale, 2001; Sobral, 2015; Zhang et al., 2003). Education, income, geographic proximity, and football practice are some of the variables that bring information, but also that confirm that studies about sport events impact, are centered in economics. These variables are usually used to show the contributions and to analyze the impact these events on the host community, supporting that it is necessary to carry out more research in different contexts to analyze the differences according to the regions or cities in which it takes place (Barajas et al., 2016; Parra et al., 2014). Understanding non-resident spectators of small football clubs and how their participation in these events contributes to the development of cities will be an innovative tool to support strategic marketing decisions in sport in cities. In this sense, the aim of this study is to analyze the profile and consumption patterns of non-resident spectators of Liga NOS.

Method

Futebol Clube of Paços de Ferreira (FCPF) is a professional football club based in the city of Paços de Ferreira (Portugal), with more than 60 years of history. The club has participated in the main professional football league in Portugal for ten consecutive seasons. The club is recognized internationally, particularly in Portuguese-speaking African countries and in Europe for its participation in European competitions (Europa League (2007/2008 and 2009/2010) and Champions League (2013/2014)). The sample was constituted by 343 non-resident spectators who were randomly selected during five matches of Liga NOS in the city of Paços de Ferreira. Majority was male (79%) and only a few (21%) were female, with total average age of 36 years. At the level of education, half of the sample was secondary education (49%), followed by higher education (29%) and attend basic education (22%). At the level of income, the most part earning between €500 and €1,000 (42%) followed by who gain over €1,000 (35%) and the income under €500 (23%).

Instrument and Procedures

A validated questionnaire (Preuss et al., 2007) was adapted to the Portuguese reality (Quintal et al., 2016) and was applied. The questionnaire comprises four dimensions: (i) spectator profile analysis; (ii) spectator consumption patterns; (iii) spectator behavior; and (iv) spectator opinion of local conditions. With a 95% significance level and the error margin set at 5%, 343 non-resident spectators were randomly selected during five matches of Liga NOS in the city of Paços de Ferreira. Specifically, the questionnaire was applied to non-resident spectators in the city of Paços de Ferreira from January to May 2016. The participants were explained about the objectives of the research as well as the possible implications that could arise because of it. To preserve the identity of the respondents, the questionnaire was anonymous and was putted in a box by the respondent in the end of the filling.

Data Analyses

The data was analyzed through the SPSS Statistics 22.0 software, using descriptive, nonparametric tests (Wilcoxon-Mann-Whitney) and linear regression (ANOVA). First, a descriptive analysis was made to the sample using frequency tables and the mean and standard deviation. Then, the internal consistency of the different dimensions was analyzed to measure the different groups of items reliability, by Cronbach's alpha (α) coefficient.

Nonparametric tests were used to compare the distributions of ordinal variables in two or more independent samples. Thus, the Wilcoxon-Mann-Whitney test was used in the case of two independent samples and the Kruskal-Wallis test in the case of more than two independent samples. In the latter case, when rejecting the null hypothesis, Dunn's multiple comparison tests were performed to identify which groups had significant differences and linear regression was performed too.

Results

The spectator analyzed was mostly male, with a medium age of 36 years old. Half had completed secondary education, followed by those with higher education. Regarding monthly income, most had between €500 and 1,000, followed by those with over €1,000.

Concerning to the geographic proximity, more than 66% spectators travel between 16 and 45 km for the match. Analyzing the results regarding the football practice, the spectators are mostly distributed among "never practiced" (30.9%) and "practiced it always" (40.5%).

Was intended to measure the interest of respondents in sport (particularly football) and their degree of involvement with other international football leagues besides Liga NOS. Was found a relationship between *playing football* and *following football matches in international leagues*. Specifically, was obtained a correlation between *soccer practice* and *following football matches in international leagues* (0.435; p = 0.01). Regarding the expenditures dimension, the results demonstrate that a non-resident spectator spends an average of €25 in the city (food and drink – €10.82; shopping – €1.76; accommodation – €0.44; ticket to the game – €12.37). In this event, the spectators brought to the city of Paços de Ferreira an increase of

Innovative Promotions to Attract Non-Resident Spectators 193

Table 13.1 Linear Regression of Spending from Spectators

	Not standardized coefficients		Standardized coefficients	t	Sig.
(Constant)	2.552	2.493		1.024	.307
Time in the city	2.157	.455	.241	4.741	**.000**
Monthly income	2.028	.425	.276	4.773	**.000**
Gender	-.838	1.224	-.035	-.684	.494
Education level	-1.004	.737	-.075	-1.362	.174
Age	.011	.044	.015	.257	.798

€8,703. Either in average or total spectators' expenditure, it was observed that the categories with higher values are *Ticket to the game* and *Food and Drink*. The variables that have the greatest influence on the average spending from spectators, was *Time in the city* (p = .000) and *Monthly income* (p = .000) (Table 13.1).

To analyze the correlation between spending from spectators with the variables – gender, education level, and monthly income – the adequate nonparametric tests were conducted. The results showed that in the categories *Food and Drink* (p = .001) and *Ticket to the game* (p = .031), there are significant differences in the spending of both genders, with men having a higher average order than women. Thus, men spend more than women. The hypothesis that the distribution of expenditures among education levels in the various categories is the same was evaluated by nonparametric Kruskal-Wallis test. The results showed no significant differences between expenditures and the educational level of non-resident spectators. The hypothesis that the distribution of expenditure among the monthly income levels is the same was evaluated by nonparametric Kruskal-Wallis test and the results. In the case of the category *Food and Drink* (p = .000), a comparison by peers have been made and a significant difference in the distribution of expenditure occurs between the following performance levels: less than €500 – between €1000 and €1499; less than €500 – between €1500 and €2249; less than €500 – between €2250 and €2999; between €500 and €999 – between €2250 and €2999. In the case of the category *Accommodation* (p = .029), the low number of observations make it difficult to analyze the data. In summary, the results showed that in the categories *Food and Drink* and *accommodation*, there are significant differences in expenditures between the levels of income. Regarding the spectator behavior, the descriptive statistics of evaluated variables are presented in Table 13.2. Was aimed to understand the intentions and motivations of spectators regarding to the event and the city.

It was found that 84.8% of respondents visited the city of Paços de Ferreira because of the game. Around 46.1% of respondents had arrived less than ten minutes to the city of Paços de Ferreira, thus less than half of the non-resident spectators turn out not to visit the city center before the games. On the other hand, 14.3% visited the city at least for 60 minutes before going into the surrounding of the stadium. In relation to the arrival, the results showed that most respondents went

Table 13.2 Descriptive Statistics of Spectator Behavior Variables

Variable	Frequency	Percentage (%)
Plans to visit the city (n = 343)		
No	291	84.8%
Yes	52	15.2%
Visit the city with the intention of watching the game (n = 343)		
No	16	4.7%
Yes	327	95.3%
Time in the city (n = 343)		
−10 minutes	158	46.1%
11–30 minutes	87	25.4%
31–60 minutes	49	14.3%
+61 minutes	49	14.3%
Overnight stay in the city (n = 343)		
No	330	0.3%
Yes	13	1.7%
Intention of future visit (n = 343)		
No	33	9.6%
Unlikely	12	3.5%
Don't know	25	7.3%
Likely	83	24.2%
Yes	190	55.4%
City recommendation (n = 343)		
No	19	5.5%
Unlikely	11	3.2%
Don't know	57	16.6%
Likely	48	14%
Yes	208	60.6%

to the surroundings of the stadium with more than 60 minutes beforehand to start the game. Regarding the overnight stay in the city, the results suggest that a minority of respondents spent the night in the city and four were staying in a hotel and nine with relatives or friends. Concerning to intention to a future visit and recommendation of the city, 55.4% of respondents intend to do so in the next years, and 24.2% considered "likely" to happen. In relation to the recommendation of city of Paços de Ferreira, 60.6% of non-resident spectators would certainly recommend the city to other people and only 5.5% would not recommend at all. Regarding to visit the city, the results suggest that 95.3% respondents visited the city with the intention of watching the game and only a minority (4.7%) was already in the city for other reasons, and the match constitutes a secondary intention.

Concerning to opinion of local conditions, the two issues of this dimension intended to assess the opinion of non-resident spectators in relation to the stadium "Capital do Móvel" and the city of Paços de Ferreira. The results showed that there is a lack of knowledge about the stadium. In fact, it is undergoing renovation works during this sport season, so it is reasonable that most of respondents have a lack of knowledge regarding to it. The results also show that respondents generally have a good opinion about Paços de Ferreira city, being the Restaurants and Commerce, the categories most highly rated by respondents.

Discussion

The purpose of this case study was to analyze the profile and consumption patterns of non-resident spectators of small events. Most spectators that participated in this case study were male, indicating that men consider sport more than women, already described in literature (Charleston, 2009) and verified in some other studies (e.g., Correia & Esteves, 2007; Fernandes et al., 2013; Sobral, 2015). However, the female assistance rate confirms the declining trend of gender differences in attendance of sport events (Cunningham & Kwon, 2003). This highlights the importance of defining marketing strategies to attract more women to these events (Khale, 2001).

The spectators' large age range obtained in this case study was similar to Zhang et al. (2003) investigation. Additionally, most spectators under 49 years old obtained seem to suggest that football games include several characteristics that appeal for spectators during the most active phases of their lives, maintaining interest for a long time. These results corroborate Desbordes et al. (1999) and Sobral (2015) studies, which also demonstrated the decrease of interest in sport events with aging. Additionally, the diffusion of this game via television may also have contributed to the older spectators who prefer to watch the game in the comfort of their homes. Regarding to the level of education of spectators, these results are similar to Portuguese average level of education and to other results obtained on Portuguese spectators (e.g., Biscaia et al., 2010; Carvalho et al., 2018). The monthly income analysis showed a medium salary of non-resident spectators, with the majority answering a monthly income below €1,000, slightly above the Portuguese average income (approximated €950). These results are also in line with literature (Carvalho et al., 2018; Santos, 2011). The geographic proximity results obtained confirm some other studies' results found in the literature. For instance, Pan and Gabert (1997) and Santos (2011) also obtained 95.8% of spectators traveling less than 50 km and taking 30–60 minutes from home to the stadium. Our results seem to also be explained by the fact of the analyzed club being a small and more regional Portuguese Club.

Most economic impact studies of sport events analyze the spectators' expenditures during the event, in the city where the event takes place. Gratton (2005) proposed as main categories of expenses in events: the ticket to the game, accommodation, food (food and drink), local transport, and shopping. In this case study, the local transport is not analyzed, since the results obtained revealed that respondents' spectators used their own car to travel to and within the city of Paços de Ferreira. Our case study found higher values in spectators' expenditure in *Ticket to the game* and *Food and Drink* dimensions. Similar results were also obtained by Kelley et al. (2014) in the National Hockey League games. The results regarding the category of *Ticket to the game* obtained in this study seem to be a necessary condition to watch the game. On the other hand, the spending in the *Food and Drink* seems to be explained by the fact of being forbidden to enter into stadiums with food or drinks, but also because usually food and drink are more expensive inside the stadiums. Regarding this specific category, also Barajas et al. (2016) point *Food and Drink* as one of the expected spending of spectators' expense. The lower spending values obtained in *Accommodation* category were expected, since more than 65% of respondents' spectators travelled less than 50 km to watch the game. Thus, the event organizers should encourage the non-resident spectators to spend at least one night in the event city, increasing their expenditure, and consequently the amount of "new money" in the city. In fact, it is described in the literature that the spectators who stay one or more nights in the event host city spent more money and increase the benefits to the local community and city (Gibson et al., 2012).

In trying to identify which variables have the greatest influence on the average spending from spectators, our results indicate that the *time in the city* and *monthly income* are variables that positively influence the average spending of respondents' spectators. In fact, if spectators spend more time in the city, their average spending will increase (Cannon & Ford, 2002; Gibson et al., 2012). Literature also refers that the demographic from spectators is significantly related to the average spending (Cannon & Ford, 2002). Regarding *monthly income*, it is expected that people who earn more also spend more. Our results also showed that in the categories *Food and Drink* and *Ticket to the game*, there are significant differences in the spending of both genders: men spend more than women. Regarding *Ticket to the game* category, the lower spending of women can be explained by some marketing campaigns designed to raise women more often to soccer stadiums. Regarding *Food and Drink*, the higher spending by men can be explained by the higher consumption during the games by men (e.g., beer).

Regarding the hypothesis that the distribution of expenditures among education levels in the various categories are the same, the results showed no significant differences between expenditures and the educational level of non-resident spectators. These results are supported by previous study such as Cannon and Ford (2002), which found that the educational level of a spectator does not affect the way they apply their money. Likewise, Lera-López et al. (2012) study confirms this evidence. Individuals with low-level education are likely not to spend money on sport attendance, but once the consumption decision is taken, educational level has no effect on the amount of money spent. Concerning to the hypothesis that the distribution of expenditure among the monthly income levels is the same, the results showed that in the categories *Food and Drink* and *accommodation*, there are significant differences in expenditures between the levels of income. The spectators with higher monthly income levels spend more than those who have a lower level of income. These results are similar as Dixon et al. (2012) results, which concluded that the spectator with higher monthly income spend more money at the event.

When considered the spectator behavior, we found that majority of respondents visited the city of Paços de Ferreira because of the game. These results demonstrate the influence of sport events for the host cities, and in this case, the importance to the city to host these football games. These results show that without the event, people would not visit or spend their money in the city (Agha, 2015). Thus, considering these results, the political leaders of Paços de Ferreira city and the organizers of this type of events should always promote this type of sport events, aiming to increase the visits of tourists or spectators to the city, increasing the amount of "new money" that is also brought to the city. The results obtained in relation to the arrival seem to show that spectators give greater importance to the following situations: *to make sure that they did not lose the beginning of the game; eat and drink; meet friends; enjoy the atmosphere; and lastly avoid the traffic*". This data is important because it allows to understand how spectators will go beforehand into the surrounding of the stadium and enable the clubs to potentiate the supply of goods and services in the surrounding of the stadium.

According to Cannon and Ford (2002), the longer the spectators are in the city, the greater will be their spending, thus, it is essential to create mechanisms to attract spectators to spend more time in the host city before and after the game. In Paços de Ferreira city, specifically the stadium, it is in an almost desert location of local commerce. Thus, it is essential to create more infrastructures to the supply of goods and services in the surrounding of the stadium. The low number of persons staying in the city is explained by the proximity of the city of Paços de Ferreira with the main motorways of the north of Portugal, which allows non-resident spectators to return home after the game, quickly and safely. In addition, there is very limited accommodation offer in the city, which may also limit the permanence of the spectators in the city. These results corroborate the study of Allan et al. (2007), which concluded that the number of non-resident spectators who stayed overnight in host cities was very low.

Concerning to intention to a future visit and recommendation of the city results obtained, they are similar to those found by Wicker et al. (2012) where 76.9% of spectators said they intended to visit the city in the near future. The collected data show that there is a high recommendation rate of the city by non-resident spectators to their family and friends, corroborating the results obtained by Chen and Funk (2010). Also, these authors found that most of all studied respondents indicated an interest in revisiting the city. Regarding to visit the city, the results suggest that most respondents visited the city with the intention of watching the game. This data is associated with the fact that sport events were a great recreational opportunity for people; this is confirmed in the study of Elias (1985), which states that sport events are social occasions where spectators are free from the stresses of day-to-day. Concerning to the good opinion of respondents about Paços de Ferreira city, the Restaurants and Commerce categories were the most highly rated by respondents, similarly to other Dixon et al. (2012) study where spectators tend to value restaurants and commerce of the cities during their visits.

Conclusion

Considering the aim of the study was to analyze the profile and consumption patterns of non-resident spectators of Liga NOS in FCPF games, this case study can provide clues to understand the typical Portuguese football spectator, in small events, and develop strategies to keep them in cities longer by promoting local tourism. There is a growing consensus among sport marketing researchers around the idea that the improvement of smart marketing and its planning should be the main objectives of sport organizations. This means that those responsible for sport marketing must carry out activities that encourage positive approaches in planning future activities (Ratten 2011). Although good marketing communication is essential, the results of this case study suggest that most marketing strategies should focus on the target audience, which, in this study, includes male audiences aged between 20 and 40 years, with a monthly income close to the Portuguese national average.

Regarding the female audience attending small football matches, the female attendance rate confirms the declining trend of gender differences in participation in sporting events. This highlights the importance of defining marketing strategies to attract more women to these events, implementing strategies with complementary experiences to the event to attract women (e.g., getaway, relaxation, socialization, exploration, prestige, beaches, mountains, shopping, weather ...) reducing the differences between the sexes. Thus, marketing campaigns aimed at raising women more to football stadiums must be reinforced. Length of stay in the city and monthly income are variables that positively influence the average expenditure of spectators. Thus, it is essential that clubs and cities develop mechanisms that allow spectators to arrive earlier in the city during daytime matches. The option of tickets with a stay package and/or associated with complementary activities or events in the gastronomic, traditional, and cultural or commercial areas could be used to keep spectators in the city longer (Figure 13.1).

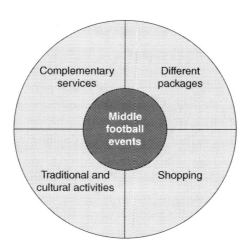

Figure 13.1 Increasing Tourism in Cities Organizing Middle Football Events.

The results of the present case study also show that football is a sport that manages to capture the attention not only of practitioners but also of those who have never practiced it. Furthermore, there is a strong relationship between the practice of sport and the monitoring of football matches in the various media, demonstrating the great involvement of people with the sport. The moderate relationship obtained between playing football and watching international league matches may mean that Portuguese spectators prefer to follow more competitive football leagues than less competitive ones like the Portuguese ones. Other initiatives that should be adopted by clubs or by the city are, for example, the creation of a club museum to be visited before the games, a fan zone for entertainment, a tourist and gastronomic itinerary to visit the city of Paços de Ferreira, or even the creation of a package including transport, lunch, and ticket to the game. Regarding the economic impact, public agencies and the club must increase the dissemination and promotion of the main services offered by the city through the various means of communication, in order to maximize the economic impact of sporting events.

The present case study seems to bring innovative ideas to small soccer sporting events. These ideas are important for the development of the sport, for the development of tourism in the cities where these events take place and considered important for the analysis of the expenses of future spectators. Even considering that these results are context-specific, the results obtained can be generalized to similar sporting events of Liga NOS, in Portugal. However, it would be interesting to carry out similar analyses in other clubs, as well as in other cities, trying to understand if the profile and consumption patterns of non-resident spectators are similar in central and southern Portugal. The replication in other sports, such as basketball, volleyball, futsal, among others, will be interesting to increase and enhance tourism. It could also be interesting to propose a qualitative method with sporting event managers trying to know if they consider the cities where the events take place, the experience to make the spectator get involved, commit, and spend time in the city. In summary, the present case study allowed us to identify the profile and consumption patterns of non-resident spectators who watch the Futebol Clube Paços de Ferreira football championship matches in Liga NOS, offering suggestions to improve the performance of sport managers through the definition of management and marketing strategies to keep spectators in cities longer and attract new fans.

References

Agha, N. (2013). The economic impact of stadiums and teams: The case of minor league baseball. *Journal of Sports Economics, 14*(3), 227–252.

Agha, N. (2015). A theoretical comparison of the economic impact of large and small events. *International Journal of Sport Finance, 10*(3), 103–121.

Allan, G., Dunlop, S., & Swales, K. (2007). The economic impact of regular season sporting competitions: The Glasgow old firm football spectators as sports tourists. *Journal of Sport & Tourism, 12*(2), 63–97.

Allen, J. (2007). *Organização e gestão de eventos [Organization and management of events].* Editora Campus.

Amy, S. (2007). Spectator profiles and economic impact of the 2009 US Women's Open. *Thunderbird International Business Review*, 49(5), 630–631.

Decree-Law no. 169-B/2019 of 3 December approving the organisation and functioning regula-tions of the 22nd Constitutional Government. Accessed on 7 February 2021, available at https://dre.pt/application/conteudo/126869983

Baade, R., Baumann, R. W., & Matheson, V. (2008). Assessing the economic impact of college football games on local economies. *Journal of Sports Economics*, 9(5), 628–643.

Baade, R. A., & Matheson, V. A. (2004). The quest for the Cup: Assessing the economic impact of the World Cup. *Regional Studies*, 38(4), 343–354.

Barajas, A., Coates, D., & Sanchez-Fernandez, P. (2016). Beyond retrospective assessment. Sport event economic impact studies as a management tool for informing event organiza-tion. *European Research on Management and Business Economics*, 22(3), 124–130.

Barajas, Á, Salgado, J., & Sánchez, P. (2012). Problemática de los estudios de impacto económico de eventos deportivos. *Estudios de Economía Aplicada*, 30(2), 441–461.

Biscaia, R., Correia, A., & Rosado, A. (2010). Sociodemographic profile and motives of basketball spectatores. *Revista Brasileira de Ciências do Esporte*, 32(2–4), 199–216.

Cannon, T. F., & Ford, J. (2002). Relationship of demographic and trip characteristics to visitor spending: An analysis of sports travel visitors across time. *Tourism Economics*, 8(3), 263–271.

Carvalho, M. J., Sousa, M., Paipe, G., Bavaresco, G., & Felipe, J. L. (2018). Economic im-pact of 11th Douro Valley Half Marathon. *Physical Culture and Sport Studies and Research*, 78(1), 41–49.

CE. (2018). *Special Eurobarometer 472 Sport and physical activity*, accessed on 12 February 2021, available at https://ec.europa.eu/commfrontoffice/publicopinion/index.cfm/survey/getsurveydetail/instruments/special/surveyky/2164

Charleston, S. (2009). The English football ground as a representation of home. *Journal of Environmental Psychology*, 29(1), 144–150.

Chen, N., & Funk, C. D. (2010). Exploring destination image, experience and revisit in-tention: A comparison of sport and non-sport tourist perceptions. *Journal of Sport & Tourism*, 15(3), 239–259.

Churchill, G. (2005). *Marketing: Criando valor para os clientes*. Saraiva.

Coates, D., & Depken, C. A. (2011). Mega-events: Is Baylor football to Waco what the Super Bowl is to Houston? *Journal of Sports Economics*, 12(6), 599–620.

Correia, A., & Esteves, S. (2007). An exploratory study of spectator's motivation in foot-ball. *International Journal of Sport Management and Marketing*, 2(5–6), 572–590.

Crompton, J. L. (1995). Economic impact analysis of sport facilities and events: Eleven sources of misapplication. *Journal of Sport Management*, 9(1), 14–35.

Crompton, J. L. (2006). Economic impact studies: Instruments for political shenanigans? *Journal of Travel Research*, 45(1), 67–82.

Crompton, J. L., Lee, S., & Shuster, T. J. (2001). A guide for undertaking economic impact studies: The Springfest example. *Journal of Travel Research*, 40(1), 79–87.

Cunningham, G. B., & Kwon, H. (2003). The theory of planned behaviour and intentions to attend a sport event. *Sport Management Review*, 6(2), 127–145.

Daniels, M., & Norman, W. (2003). Estimating the economic impacts of seven regular sport tourism events. *Journal of Sport & Tourism*, 8(4), 214–222.

Desbordes, M., Ohl, F., & Tribou, G. (1999). *Marketing du sport*. Económica Publisher.

Dixon, A. W., Backman, S., Backman, K., & Norman, W. (2012). Expenditure-based seg-mentation of sport tourists. *Journal of Sport & Tourism*, 17(1), 5–21.

Dwyer, L., Forsyth, P., & Spurr, R. (2005). Estimating the impacts of special events on an economy. *Journal of Travel Research, 43*(4), 351–359.

Elias, N. (1985). *A Busca da Excitação* (DIFEL Ed.). Lisboa.

Fedrizzi, V. L. P., Mendes, B. C., & Schliemann, M. (2017). Tourism of events in Campos do Jordão: CJCVB strategies to attract events. *Revista De Turismo Contemporâneo, 5*, 55–70.

Fernandes, N., Correia, A., Abreu, A., & Biscaia, R. (2013). Relationship between sport commitment and sport consumer behavior. *Motricidade, 9*(4), 2–11.

Gibson, H. J., Kaplanidou, K., & Kang, S. J. (2012). Small-scale event sport tourism: A case study in sustainable tourism. *Sport Management Review, 15*(2), 160–170.

Gibson, H., McIntyre, S., MacKay, S., & Riddington, G. (2005). The economic impact of sports, sporting events, and sports tourism in the UK. The Dream™ Model. *European Sport Management Quarterly, 5*(3), 321–332.

Goldblatt, J. (2000). A future for event management: The analysis of major trends impacting the emerging profession. In J. Allen, R. Harris, L. K. Jago & A. J. Veal (Eds.), *Events Beyond 2000: Setting the Agenda* (pp.1–8). Australian Centre for Event Management.

Gómez-Bantel, A. (2015). Football clubs as symbols of regional identities. *Soccer & Society, 17*(5), 1–11.

Gratton, C. (2005). *The economic impact of sport tourism at major events*. Elsevier Butterworth-Heinemann.

Gratton, C., Dobson, N., & Shibli, S. (2000). The economic importance of major sports events: A case-study of six events. *Managing Leisure, 5*(1), 17–28.

Gratton, C., Shibli, S., & Coleman, R. (2006). The economic impact of major sports events: A review of ten events in the UK. *Sociological Review, 54*(2), 41–58.

Hallmann, K., & Zehrer, A. (2017). Event and community involvement of sport event volunteers. *International Journal of Event and Festival Management, 8*(3), 308–323.

Hassan, D., & Connor, S. O. (2009). The socio-economic impact of the FIA World Rally Championship 2007. *Sport in Society, 12*(6), 709–724.

Hinch, T. D., & Higham, J. E. S. (2001). Sport tourism: A framework for research. *International Journal of Tourism Research, 3*(1), 45–58.

Huang, H., Mao, L. L., Kim, S. K., & Zhang, J. J. (2014). Assessing the economic impact of three major sport events in China: The perspective of attendees. *Tourism Economics, 20*(6), 1277–1296.

INE. (2021a). PORDATA. Accessed on 25 May 2021, and available at https://www.pordata.pt/Portugal/Popula%C3%A7%C3%A3o+residente+total+e+por+grandes+grupos+et%C3%A1rios-513

INE. (2021b). PORDATA. Accessed on 25 May 2021, and available at https://www.pordata.pt/Portugal/Popula%c3%a7%c3%a3o+residente++m%c3%a9dia+anual+total+e+por+sexo-6

INE. (2021c). PORDATA. Accessed on 25 May 2021, and available at https://www.pordata.pt/Portugal/Indicadores+de+fecundidade+%c3%8dndice+sint%c3%a9tico+de+fecundidade+e+taxa+bruta+de+reprodu%c3%a7%c3%a3o-416

Kelley, K., Harrolle, M. G., & Casper, J. M. (2014). Estimating consumer spending on tickets, merchandise, and food and beverage: A case study of a NHL team. *Journal of Sport Management, 28*(3), 253–265.

Khale, L. (2001). The social values of fans for men's versus women's university basketball. *Sport Marketing Quarterly, 10*(2), 156–162.

Kotler, P. (2012). *Administração de marketing*. Pearson Education.

Lamla, M. J., Straub, M., & Girsberger, E. M. (2014). On the economic impact of international sport events: Microevidence from survey data at the EURO 2008. *Applied Economics*, 46(15), 1693–1703.

Lee, S. (2001). A review of economic impact study on sport events. *Sport Journal*, 4(2), 1–6.

Lera-López, F., Ollo-López, A., & Rapún-Gárate, M. (2012). Sports spectatorship in Spain: Attendance and consumption. *European Sport Management Quarterly*, 12(3), 265–289.

Lera-López, F., & Rapún-Gárate, M. (2005). Sports participation versus consumer expenditure on sport: Different determinants and strategies in sports management. *European Sport Management Quarterly*, 5(2), 167–186.

Li, S., & Jago, L. (2013). Evaluating economic impacts of major sports events – a meta-analysis of the key trends. *Current Issues in Tourism*, 16(6), 591–611.

Mak, J. (2004). *Tourism and the economy: Understanding the economics of tourism*. University of Hawaii Press.

Matheson, V. (2006). Is smaller better? A comment on "comparative economic impact analyses" by Michael Mondello and Patrick Rishe. *Economic Development Quarterly*, 20(2), 192.

Mondello, M., & Rishe, P. (2004). Comparative economic impact analyses: Differences across cities, events and demographics. *Economic Development Quarterly*, 18(4), 331–342.

Mules, T., & Dwyer, L. (2005). Public sector support for sport tourism events: The role of cost-benefit analysis. *Sport in Society*, 8(2), 338–355.

Österlind, M. (2016). Sport policy evaluation and governing participation in sport: Governmental problematics of democracy and health. *International Journal of Sport Policy and Politics*, 8(3), 347–362.

Pan, D. W., & Gabert, T. E. (1997). Factors and differential demographic effects on purchases of season tickets for intercollegiate basketball games. *Journal of Sport Behavior*, 20(4), 447–464.

Parra, C., Calabuig, M., AñóSanz, V., Ayora, P., & Núñez, P. (2014). The impact of a medium-size sporting event: The host community perceptions. *RETOS-Neuvas Tendencias En Educacion Fisica, Deporte y Recreacion*, 26(3), 88–93.

Porter, P., & Fletcher, D. (2008). The economic impact of the Olympic Games: Ex ante predictions and ex poste reality. *Journal of Sport Management*, 22(4), 470–486.

Preuss, H. (2004). Calculating the regional economic impact of the Olympic Games. *European Sport Management Quarterly*, 4(4), 234–253.

Preuss, H. (2007). The conceptualization and measurement of mega sport event legacies. *Journal of Sport & Tourism*, 12(3–4), 207–228.

Preuss, H., Seguin, B., & O'reilly, N. (2007). Profiling major sport event visitors: The 2002 Commonwealth games. *Journal of Sport & Tourism*, 12(1), 5–23.

Quintal, G., Paipe, G., Carvalho, M., & Felipe, J. (2016). Strategic tool to estimate the consumption patterns of non-residents spectators at sporting events (Liga NOS): Adaptation to Portuguese reality. *Brazilian Business Review*, 13(Special Ed), 102–120.

Ratten, V. R. (2011). International sport marketing: Practical and future research implications. *Journal of Business & Industrial Marketing*, 26(8), 614–620.

Saayman, M., & Rossouw, R. (2008). The economic value of the 2010 Soccer World Cup. *Acta Commercii*, 8(1), 1–14.

Saayman, M., & Saayman, A. (2012). The economic impact of the Comrades Marathon. *International Journal of Event and Festival Management*, 3(3), 220–235.

Sandy, R. (2004). *The economics of sport: An international perspective*. Palgrave Macmillan.

Santos, L. (2011). *Qualidade, Satisfação e Lealdade dos Espectadores de Futebol*. Unpublished Master Thesis, Universidade Técnica de Lisboa, Lisboa, Portugal.

Sanz, V. A., Moreno, F. C., & Camacho, D. P. (2012). Impacto social de un gran evento deportivo: El gran premio de europa de fórmula 1. *Cultura, Ciencia y Deporte, 7*(19), 53–65.

Sobral, J. (2015). *A percepção dos adeptos de futebol em relação aos investimentos dos patrocínios sobre as organizações desportivas*. Unpublished Master Thesis, Instituto Português de Admistração de Marketing, Porto, Portugal.

Taks, M., Green, B., Chalip, L., Kesenne, S., & Martyn, S. (2013). Visitor composition and event-related spending. *International Journal of Culture, Tourism and Hospitality Research, 7*(2), 132–147.

Taks, M., Kesenne, S., Chalip, L., Green, B. C., & Martyn, S. (2011). Economic impact analysis versus cost benefit analysis: The case of a medium-sized sport event. *International Journal of Sport Finance, 6*(3), 187–203.

Thomson, A., Schlenker, K., & Schulenkorf, N. (2013). Conceptualizing sport event legacy. *Event Management, 17*(2), 111–122.

Tien, C., Lo, H. C., & Lin, H. W. (2011). The economic benefits of mega events: A myth or a reality? A longitudinal study on the Olympic Games. *Journal of Sport Management, 25*(1), 11–23.

Trail, G. T., Fink, J. S., & Anderson, D. F. (2003). Sport spectator consumption behavior. *Sport Marketing Quarterly, 12*(1), 8–17.

Veltri, F., Miller, J., & Harris, A. (2009). Club sport national tournament: Economic impact of a small event on a mid-size community. *Recreational Sports Journal, 33*(2), 119–128.

Wicker, P., Hallmann, K., & Zhang, J. J. (2012). What is influencing consumer expenditure and intention to revisit? An investigation of marathon events. *Journal of Sport & Tourism, 17*(3), 165–182.

Wilson, R. (2006). The economic impact of local sport events: Significant, limited or otherwise? A case study of four swimming events. *Managing Leisure, 11*(1), 57–70.

Wilton, J. J. (2006). Collecting and using visitor spending data. *Journal of Travel Research, 45*(1), 17–25.

Zhang, J. J., Pennington-Gray, L., Connaughton, D. P., Braustein, J. R., Ellis, M., Lam, E. T., & Williamson, D. (2003). Understanding women's professional basketball game spectators: Sociodemographics, game consumption, and entertainment options. *Sport Marketing Quarterly, 12*(4), 228–243.

Chapter 14

Success Factors in Sporting Events through IPA Approach

The Case of an International Horse Show Jumping

Jairo León-Quismondo
Universidad Europea de Madrid, Spain

Pablo Burillo
Universidad Europea de Madrid, Spain

Thiago Santos
Universidade Europeia, Portugal

Álvaro Fernández-Luna
Universidad Europea de Madrid, Spain

Chapter Contents

Introduction	204
The Industry of Sport Events	206
Impacts and Legacies	208
Understanding Spectators' Experience	208
Sport Events Evaluation	209
Measures and Tools	209
Importance-Performance Analysis (IPA)	210
A Case Analysis	212
Discussion	217
References	219

Introduction

Spain is one of the countries with the largest number of international sporting events in the world. Since the 1982 World Cup, passing through the milestone of the Barcelona 92 Olympic Games, Spain has gained importance in the international sports scene as a possible venue for international championships in any sporting discipline. Among the factors that have made this situation possible are:

DOI: 10.4324/9781003388050-17

the professionalization of competitions, federations, clubs, and organizing companies; the creation of infrastructures with capacity for a large number of spectators; and, finally, the development of tourism as one of the main drivers for the development of the Spanish economy. Madrid is the capital of Spain and the most populated city in the country, with 3,334,730 inhabitants, of which 6,779,888 in the metropolitan area (Spanish Statistical Office, 2021). One of the main reasons for travelling to Madrid is attending sporting events, both as primary and secondary objectives on a particular trip (Nishio et al., 2016).

Concerning international sporting events, Madrid has hosted two UEFA Champions League finals in the 2010–2020 decade, as well as other events such as the Karate World Championship in 2018 or the semi-finals of the World Championship "League of Legends" in 2019 (La Vanguardia, 2019b). Within this international dimension, we can highlight the recurring sporting events that have chosen the city of Madrid as the stable host city of international circuits. Within this type of events, we can highlight the Mutua Madrid Open, a Masters 1000 tournament belonging to the ATP circuit held in Madrid from 2009 to the present time; and the Longines Global Champions Tour, held at the Club de Campo Villa de Madrid (Madrid Country Club) since 2013 (Diario Gol, 2013; Longines Global Champions Tour, 2021).

In this chapter, the chosen event is an international horse show jumping event celebrated in Madrid, Spain, as part of a larger international championship. It is the most important equestrian circuit in the world. Considered the "Formula 1" of equestrianism, the tournament was created in 2006 by an Olympic medallist and currently includes venues such as Doha, Saint Tropez, Cannes, Monaco, London, Berlin, City of Mexico, and New York (BSJA, 2009). The event is a show jumping competition with an obstacle height of 1.60 meters. The Madrid event includes other jumping competitions with lower heights and prizes, as well as the King's Cup of horse-jumping on the same weekend. The event venue is the Club de Campo Villa de Madrid SA, an institution created in 1936, currently a property of the Madrid City Council and the General Direction of Heritage State, and managed by a municipal company (Club de Campo Villa de Madrid, 2013). Additionally, the same organizing company also manages other events of the circuit.

To understand the dimension of this event and its importance, it is mandatory to briefly set the context of equestrianism in Spain. Currently, horse riding is practiced weekly by 0.5% of the Spanish population, 1.3% have practiced it at least once a year, and 0.7% do so once a month. Overall, horse riding practitioners are 2.4% of the total sports practitioners in Spain (43.3% of the population), and this percentage is considerably higher among those under 24 years old (5.9%). In the competitive sports field, the Royal Spanish Equestrian Federation has 52,405 federated members, being 1.3% of the federated athletes in the Spanish territory. The federation members are mostly women (36,756 women vs. 15,649 men). Likewise, the highest number of federative licenses are found in the regions of Catalonia (8,339) and Andalusia (6,087). Finally, in Spain, 107 high-level athletes were recognized by the High Spanish Sports Council (Consejo Superior de Deportes,

CSD), participating in 275 international competitions in 2019, obtaining seven medals. It is also necessary to emphasize that horse riding is included as an official discipline within the educational sport qualifications at different levels (Ministry of Culture and Sports, 2020).

Among horse riding events, dressage and show jumping are the two most popular disciplines. Around them, there is an entire industry that currently generates more than 300,000 million euros and 2 million jobs worldwide (La Vanguardia, 2019a). In Spain, according to the only study published so far, carried out in 2013, the equestrian sector has an impact of 5,303 million euros and generates 61,247 direct jobs (Daemon Quest - Deloitte, 2013). However, these data refer to the sector as a whole, where the impact of contests (103 million euros), clubs (622 million euros), and equestrian shows (20 million euros). Regarding sporting events, the impact of Madrid Horse Week is notable, which is another reference event that includes the World Cup of Dressage, the Masters Cup, the World Cup of Show jumping, and an International Championship of two-star jumping (CIS2*), together with a scientific congress and the "horse room". In this case, the impact, according to the organizers, was 32 million euros, with a total of 45,000 attendees in 2019 (La Vanguardia, 2019a). This background proves the importance of holding an international horse how jumping event in Madrid, Spain. This chapter focuses on the 2019 edition of the tournament, held between 21 and 23 May 2019, which had 16,322 attendees and generated 689 direct and indirect jobs. Thus, this show jumping event is a great example, which offers a line-up of food trucks, enlivened with live music, more than 40 exhibitors, a market with exclusive products from the best artisan brands –including jewellery, shoes, and glasses, among others – enough toiletries, and a children's area with rides and a pony park.

In this sense, the continuous evaluation of the services and the general event management, and the application of organizational improvements based on the results, becomes crucial. An example is the research carried out by the Universidad Europea Sports Management Research Group both in the Mutua Madrid Tennis Open (from 2016 to 2019) and in the Longines Global Champions Tour (2019) (Universidad Europea, 2020). Once the context of the equestrian industry in Spain and the main sporting events held in the Capital of Spain have been addressed, the following sections of this chapter deal with the experience of the spectators and innovative ways of evaluation of these events.

The Industry of Sport Events

Nowadays, sports event management is one of the fields that contribute more to the development of the sports phenomenon worldwide. From a community sports event to the highest competitive level that involves the best athletes in the world, sports events have attracted an increasing number of people, brands, and media interest.

Chappelet and Parent (2015) propose a set of parameters that combinates help to understand the different types of events and categorization, which allows to understand different levels of sports event management. As seen in Table 14.1, depending on the size, temporal characteristics, financial objectives, and sporting characteristics, sports events can be different levels of requirement and consequent management. For example, hosting sports megaevents requires that sports organizations, hosts cities, and/or countries incur a wide range of costs, such as candidate fees, marketing expenses, urban restructuring, renovation of sports facilities, and construction of the new ones (Biscaia et al., 2017; Horne, 2007; Sant & Mason, 2015).

On the other hand, events of lesser magnitude compared to sports megaevents (e.g., larger sports events) can make use of the local resources decreasing costs, public investment, and using pre-existing sports facilities, which tends to impact a greater possibility of management efficiency in the event and consequent benefit to the community (Daniels & Norman, 2003; Malchrowicz-Mośko & Poczta, 2018; Schulenkorf & Schlenker, 2017). This whole scenario, although promising, has raised some constraints concerning the business models explored by the sports organizations through the events, as well as the process that host organizations and/or communities developed in order to guarantee a real assessment of the promotion of sports culture, or some positive impact (e.g., economic or social) that derives from these events (Chalip, 2006).

Table 14.1 Parameters to Categorize Sport Events

Parameters	Definitions
Size	Consider a number of participants, number of revenues, budget, or number of spectators and television/online viewers.
Spatial characteristics	Related to the place where the event is accomplished, outdoors or indoors places, public or private arenas, competitions can occur in different venues or in one venue simultaneously or not.
Temporal characteristics	Related to the duration and/or the periodicity of the event and the competition calendar.
Sporting characteristics	Related with the number of sports in the event, the level of competition (e.g., mass-participation sport, elite), and the popularity of the sport (e.g., football in Europe, baseball in the USA).
Financial objectives	An event can be organized with the aim of enhancing financial support for the development of a particular sport, or, for profit, through promotion, entertainment, ticket sales, and sponsor investment.
Renown	Help to measure the capacity of resonance of the event (local, regional, national, or international) in terms of image and fame of the event (i.e., number of participants, spectators, sponsors, and media coverage).

Impacts and Legacies

In recent years, interest in the impacts and legacies of sports events has grown exponentially (Biscaia et al., 2017; Thomson et al., 2019). Conceptually, legacies of sports events are related to "planned and unplanned, positive and negative, tangible and intangible structures created for and by a sports event that remain longer than the event itself" (Preuss, 2007, p. 211). Already the notion of sports events impacts is linked to the contextual indicators generally used to describe some change in a parameter in the host community (e.g., economic, sociocultural, and environmental) caused by the event (Preuss, 2015). Understanding the impact and legacy of a sports event is essential, and it can represent a central source of the potential value of the event (Chalip, 2006). Still, recent examples, such as the 2014 FIFA World Cup in Brazil and the numerous protests before and during the event focusing on the cost of the new stadiums (Grohmann, 2018), raise the question of how and whether target consumers and the host community perceive and evaluate the value of hosting a sporting event (Santos et al., 2016).

In this regard, it is crucial to understand the factors that contribute to increasing the perceived value of the event for consumers and the host communities. For example, previous studies suggest that a positive perception of the standard of service quality at sports events is a critical issue for the hosts (Ko et al., 2011), this is due to the fact that a positive perception of service quality in the event impacts positively on the perceived value of the event from consumers and/or the host community (Cronin et al., 2000; Yoshida et al., 2013). On the other hand, cities or places that have lower levels of human development and a lower approval rate of hosting the event tend to have a lower perception of service quality and the impact of the event on the community (Santos et al., 2016). In line with this idea, Vargo and Lusch (2012) consider that the value creation process is not related only to consumption. Thus, sports events often represent a complex experience and, therefore, examining consumers' perceptions of the service experience and its subsequent value can provide useful information, leading to improvements in future organizations at these and other similar events.

Understanding Spectators' Experience

From the sports consumers' point of view and based on their experiences, a significant paradigm shift has also been noted regarding the consumption of sports events (Biscaia et al., 2017). In the past, participating in the event was considered a main part of the interaction between organizations and consumers. Nowadays, the investment in consumers experiences "in" and "through" of the event has been evidenced as a fundamental factor to understand the global consumers' experience and, consequently, to engage consumers, connecting them in a personal and memorable way with the event (Frew & McGillivray, 2008). In this respect, previous studies (Biscaia et al., 2017; Cronin et al., 2000) consider that understanding the level of consumers' satisfaction with the event could allow to improve their experience and consequently impact the possibility of positive word-of-mouth and future event recommendations (Santos et al., 2016). In addition, from the sports events emerge a wide range of emotions that may impact the desire to return to consuming the event (Biscaia, 2016; Martin et al., 2008). Complementarily, the positive association between the perception of the experience with the service, the emotions felt in the experience with the event, and the satisfaction of participating in the event tends to favor the future behavioral intentions of the consumers (Ko et al., 2011). It can be said that a good consumer experience impact is a fundamental measure to understand the future actions of consumers in relation to participate in the future sports events (Biscaia, 2016).

Sport Events Evaluation

Sports events are experiences with no physical products. Some authors consider the success of a sporting event depends on the spectator's perceptions of the provided service quality during the event celebration (Calabuig-Moreno et al., 2016). The complexity lies in the great variety of nature of different sporting events. For instance, the differences in venues, spectators, duration, and sport modalities make highly complex their evaluation. Although the number of evaluation tools has indeed increased, the proliferation of sporting events has been much faster than the development of measures and tools.

Measures and Tools

There is an increasing number of tools and scales to measure the perceptions of sporting event attendees. One of the most widely extended instruments is SERV-QUAL (Parasuraman et al., 1985) (Table 14.2). Despite SERVQUAL is one of the most cited instruments on service quality, some authors have concerned about the unnecessary assessment of the expectations. Their inclusion is not considered fundamental for some authors since they (1) increase the length of the questionnaire, (2) reduce the predictive reliability of the performance in the scale, and (3) make it less accessible and less easy to understand the analysis and interpretation of the results. Consequently, some other derived models appear, such as SERVPERF (Cronin & Taylor, 1992), which eliminate the items about expectations, or

Table 14.2 Five Dimensions of SERVQUAL, Number of Items, and Description

Dimension	No. of items	Description
Reliability	5	The accuracy of the company performing the service
Assurance	4	To inspire courtesy, trust, and confidence
Tangibles	4	It includes the physical evidence of the service
Empathy	5	To provide personal attention to customers
Responsiveness	4	It concerns the readiness of the employees

210   J. León-Quismondo, P. Burillo, T. Santos et al.

Table 14.3 Main Traditional Models for Measuring Sporting Events

Model	Authors	No. dimensions	Name dimensions
SERVQUAL	Parasuraman et al. (1985)	5	Reliability, assurance (security), tangibles, empathy, and responsiveness
SERVPERF	Cronin and Taylor (1992)	5	Reliability, assurance (security), tangibles, empathy, and responsiveness
TEAMQUAL	McDonald et al. (1995)	5	Tangibles, responsiveness, reliability, assurance (security), and empathy
SPORTSERV	Theodorakis et al. (2001)	5	Reliability, assurance (security), tangibles, empathy, and responsiveness
EVENTQUAL	Calabuig-Moreno et al. (2010)	4	Accessibility, personnel, tangibles, and complementary services

SPORTSERV (Theodorakis et al., 2001), that shares four of the five dimensions with SPORTQUAL.

Other models suggest the inclusion of diverse dimensions in their scales, as for TEAMQUAL model (McDonald et al., 1995), or the development of *ad-hoc* tools (Kelley & Turley, 2001; Zhang et al., 2005). In 2010, a specific scale named EVENTQUAL (Calabuig-Moreno et al., 2010) was developed for measuring the perceived service quality of sporting events spectators. Thus, the various measures and tools unquestionably contribute to enriching the scientific background on the assessment of sporting events (Table 14.3). However, after the analysis of the event, a clearer road map (i.e., clearer strategies) is needed. This would make easier the interpretation and implementation of strategies by non-scientific agents: the managers of sporting events.

Importance-Performance Analysis (IPA)

The aforementioned tools are almost equally effective. However, effective tools with simpler interpretation are required. In this regard, the importance-performance analysis (IPA), developed by Martilla and James (1977), is a useful tool for measuring the experience in any kind of organization. IPA measures the respondents' judgments on the importance and performance of different service attributes: first, it assesses the expectations or importance of a set of service attributes and, second, it measures the perceived performance of the same set of attributes. Thus, IPA allows performing a simple but effective diagnosis of organizations.

The IPA is graphically represented on a matrix named IPA matrix. It consists of two axes. The y-axis represents the level of importance, whereas the x-axis depicts the level of performance. The traditional IPA matrix is divided into

Success Factors in Sporting Events 211

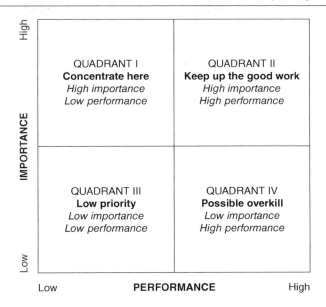

Figure 14.1 Traditional Importance-Performance Analysis (IPA) Matrix.

four equally sized squares (Figure 14.1). This way four different quadrants are obtained: concentrate here, low priority, keep up the good work, and possible overkill (Figure 14.1).

The latest approaches (Ábalo et al., 2006) introduce the idea of *discrepancy*, which refers to the difference between performance and importance. In this line, the *line of discrepancy* changes the traditional model, represented in the IPA matrix as a 45-degree line, and connecting those points with the same level of importance and performance. All the elements in the discrepancy line are iso-rating or iso-priority attributes (Bacon, 2003) and, following Levenburg and Magal (2005), are optimal points in the IPA matrix. All the points over the discrepancy line would have a negative discrepancy, whereas all the points below the discrepancy line would have a positive discrepancy. A negative discrepancy is related to levels of dissatisfaction, whereas a positive discrepancy is related to levels of satisfaction (Table 14.4). Based on the idea of discrepancy, a new approach to IPA emerges. The same four strategies continue but their representation in the IPA matrix is slightly different (Figure 14.2).

As previously highlighted, the interesting part of the IPA is that offers clear and straight strategies to every attribute of the service that is analyzed. This is unquestionably one of the strong points of this tool. Despite the IPA was originally developed as a marketing managerial tool, its use has spread across different fields of knowledge (Table 14.5).

In the sports scope, the IPA is still an innovative method. Currently, some promising research has started to check its benefits for the sports sector

Table 14.4 Relationship between Discrepancy and Satisfaction or Dissatisfaction

Discrepancy	Representation	Satisfaction/ dissatisfaction	Strategy
Negative	Over the discrepancy line	Dissatisfaction	Concentrate here
Positive	Below the discrepancy line	Satisfaction	Keep up the good work, low priority, or possible overkill
No discrepancy	In the discrepancy line	No satisfaction nor dissatisfaction	Optimal point

(Table 14.6). Although there is not a consistent background of IPA in the sports industry, as soon as its popularity increases, its potential to evaluate the perceived quality of these services or events will also increase.

A Case Analysis

A validated questionnaire based on IPA (Martilla & James, 1977) was designed for a horse show jumping event settled in Madrid, Spain. The questionnaire design and validation were performed in Spanish. An initial literature review allowed to determine the most useful information to collect in a sporting event (Alcaraz et al., 2009; Burillo et al., 2012; Elasri et al., 2015; Nuviala et al., 2013). An initial draft of service attributes was developed. Afterward, the number of initial items was reduced and, later, reviewed by a panel of experts (four PhD university professors with research expertise of more than five years in sporting events). The panel of experts offered their individual opinion about the adequacy of each item. After

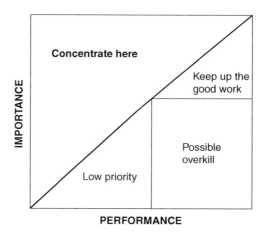

Figure 14.2 New Importance-Performance Analysis (IPA) Matrix.

Success Factors in Sporting Events 213

Table 14.5 Previous Work on IPA Related to Different Fields of Knowledge

Field of knowledge	Previous work
Tourism	Chu and Choi (2000); Deng (2007); Evans and Chon (1989); Go and Zhang (1997); Hudson (1998); Sever (2015); Wade and Eagles (2003); Ziegler et al. (2012)
Education	Alberty and Mihalik (1989); Ford et al. (1999); Hanssen and Mathisen (2018); Nale et al. (2000); O'Neil and Palmer (2004); Ortianu et al. (1989)
Healthcare	Ábalo et al. (2007); Dolinsky and Caputo (1991); Hawes and Rao (1985); Yavas and Shemwell (2001)
Food	Aigbedo and Parameswaran (2004); Sampson and Showalter (1999); Tontini and Silveira (2007)
Banking	Joseph et al. (2005); Matzler et al. (2003); Yeo (2003)

reaching the agreement, the final version comprises 10 items for the importance scale (α = 0.760) and the same 10 elements for the performance scale (α = 0.831). Every participant valued on a 5-point Likert scale, the level of importance of the 10 attributes, as well as the level of performance of the same 10 attributes.

A study was conducted on a sample of 367 spectators from an international horse show jumping in Madrid, Spain, in 2019. The research context is the aforementioned in the introduction of this chapter. Participants were aged between 18 and 89 years (M = 39.01 years; SD = 13.89). Most of them were men (61%), had a monthly household income between €2,500 and €4,999 (42.10%), were passionate about horse show jumping (38.15%), and had attended similar events previously (53.10%). A previously trained group of researchers distributed questionnaires personally. The contact with participants was either during the sporting event or when leaving the venue. All of them were informed about the research objectives and they accepted to participate voluntarily. The analysis was performed with IBM SPSS 23.0 Statistics software (IBM Inc., Chicago, IL, USA), setting the critical level of significance at p <0.05. The descriptive data are described as mean and standard deviation. Kolmogorov Smirnoff analysis showed a non-normal behavior of variables. Therefore, nonparametric tests were performed. Wilcoxon test was used for inference analysis in comparisons between importance and performance,

Table 14.6 Previous Work on IPA in the Sports Scope

Field of knowledge	Previous work
Outdoor recreation	Tarrant and Smith (2002)
Fitness centers	León-Quismondo et al. (2020); Polyakova and Mirza (2016); Rial et al. (2008); Yildiz (2011); Zamorano-Solís and García-Fernández (2018)
Sport organizations / sport clubs	Arias-Ramos et al. (2016); Martínez-Caro et al. (2014); Serrano-Gómez et al. (2014)
Sporting events	Parra-Camacho et al. (2020)

Table 14.7 IPA Results in an International Horse Show Jumping

Items	Importance			Performance			D
	M	SD	Rank	M	SD	Rank	
1. Event environment	4.58	0.65	2	4.49	0.72	3	−0.09*
2. Comfort in the facilities	4.43	0.72	5	4.24	0.83	5	−0.19**
3. Additional activities	4.02	0.97	8	3.94	0.99	8	−0.08
4. Commercial area	3.88	1.06	10	3.95	1.00	7	0.08
5. Variety of F&B stalls	4.07	0.97	7	3.87	1.10	9	−0.20**
6. Waiting time (queues) in F&B area	4.24	1.01	6	3.65	1.25	10	−0.59**
7. Ticket prices	3.95	1.08	9	3.96	1.07	6	0.02
8. Quality of competitions	4.54	0.70	4	4.47	0.76	4	−0.07
9. Quality of horsemen/horsewomen	4.55	0.74	3	4.52	0.75	2	−0.03
10. Organization of the event	4.68	0.60	1	4.59	0.71	1	−0.10**
Global Mean	4.29	-	-	4.17	-	-	−0.22

Annotations: M = mean; SD = standard deviation; Rank = ranking; D = discrepancy; *p <0.05; **p <0.01.

while Spearman test was applied for correlational analyses. The sociodemographic variables considered were gender and previous attendance to this kind of event. Regarding IPA model, the data interpretation was based on Ábalo et al. (2006).

Table 14.7 includes the 10 attributes analyzed and shows the IPA results for each of them. The mean score of Importance was 4.39 out of 5, while the mean score of Performance of the same attributes was 4.17 out of 5. As the level of Importance is higher than the level of Performance – with a discrepancy of −0.22 points – it can be confirmed that the general perception of the spectators of this event was related to levels of dissatisfaction. Regarding the discrepancy values obtained (D), Figure 14.3 shows that the commercial area of the facilities (Item 2; D = 0.08) and the price of tickets (Item 7; D = 0.02) are the only two elements related to

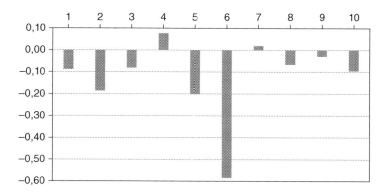

Figure 14.3 Discrepancies of the Analyzed Attributes.

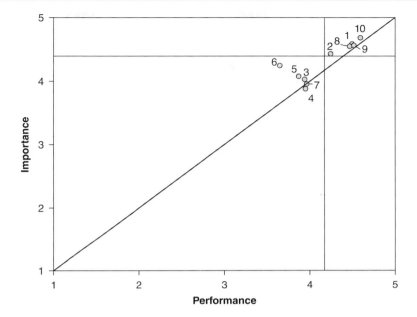

Figure 14.4 IPA Matrix – General Results.

levels of satisfaction since they present positive discrepancies. The rest of the elements are related to dissatisfaction levels, highlighting the waiting time (queues) in the food and beverages area (Item 6; D = −0.59), since it is the attribute with the most negative discrepancy among all the elements analyzed. The Importance-Performance matrix (Figure 14.4) and its expanded view (Figure 14.5) allows classifying these elements into "Concentrate here" (eight elements) and "Low priority" (two elements).

For Concentrate Here, all the elements that are located above the discrepancy line are related to levels of dissatisfaction and, consequently, must be improved. A greater distance of the element with the discrepancy line translates into a higher probability of leading to greater dissatisfaction. Therefore, the waiting time in the food & beverages area (Item 6) is the element that requires the most attention since its importance is considerably higher than the user's perceived performance. The variety of food & beverage stalls (Item 5) is in the same situation, although with a lower level of priority, as is the comfort in the facilities (Item 2). Furthermore, those elements that remain above the discrepancy line and closer to it are in a third priority level (Items 1 and 10) and in a fourth priority level (Items 3, 8, and 9).

On the other hand, the elements located below the discrepancy line are related to levels of satisfaction. In this specific case, both the commercial area in the venue (Item 4) and the ticket prices (Item 7) are low-priority items, without requiring specific attention.

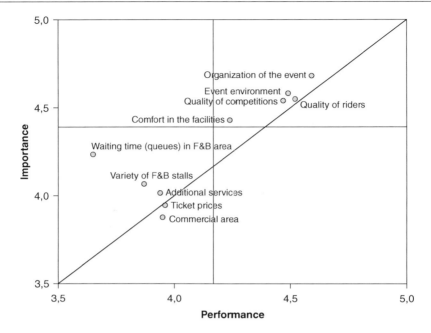

Figure 14.5 IPA Matrix – Expanded View.

A summary of the recommended actions to be carried out by the organizer of the event is exhibited in Table 14.8. Taking into account a more detailed analysis, according to the sociodemographic profile of the spectators, the results showed statistically significant differences based on gender and previous attendance at similar events (Table 14.9). On the one hand, the spectators who had not attended any international horse show jumping event previously stated that the atmosphere and the additional activities of the event were more important, compared to those who

Table 14.8 Summary of Recommended Actions to Be Carried Out by the Organizer

Item	Element	Classification	Priority Level
6	Waiting time (queues) in F&B area	Concentrate here	1
5	Variety of F&B stalls	Concentrate here	2
2	Comfort in the facilities	Concentrate here	2
10	Organization of the event	Concentrate here	3
1	Event environment	Concentrate here	3
3	Quality of horsemen/horsewomen	Concentrate here	4
8	Quality of competitions	Concentrate here	4
9	Additional activities	Concentrate here	4
7	Ticket prices	Low priority	5
4	Commercial area	Low priority	5

Success Factors in Sporting Events 217

Table 14.9 Significant Differences in the Importance of the Analyzed Attributes

Items	Women		Men		
	M	DT	M	DT	D
Comfort in the facilities	4.31	0.77	4.50	0.67	0.19*
Quality of competitions	4.67	0.58	4.46	0.76	0.21**
Items	Previous attendance		First attendance		
	M	DT	M	DT	D
Additional activities	3.91	1.03	4.15	0.87	0.24*
Quality of competitions	4.70	0.53	4.37	0.82	0.33**
Quality of horsemen/ horsewomen	4.68	0.60	4.41	0.84	0.27**
Organization of the event	4.74	0.54	4.62	0.65	0.12*

Annotations: M = mean; SD = standard deviation; D = mean differences; *p <0.05; **p <0.01.

had attended previously. On the other hand, those who had already attended similar events indicated that the quality of the competitions, horsemen/horsewomen, and the organization of the event was more important to them. In addition, these spectators also showed a better Performance in these elements of the event, so their satisfaction is higher than their level of expectation. Based on gender, the results reveal that men give more importance to comfort in the facilities and women give more importance to the quality of the competition.

Discussion

This chapter highlights the need of taking a proactive approach to the assessment of sporting events. This chapter deals with an innovative assessment method for market adaptation, IPA, which allows setting different levels of priority with associated managerial strategies. The successful implementation of strategies enables a growth of the interest and demand from spectators, leading to financial sustainability of sporting events, growth of revenue, and ensuring its continuity over several years. This is considered a virtuous circle of innovation (Figure 14.6). In the case of the analyzed horse show jumping, different levels of priority have been established, thus allowing the managers to meet the organizations' strategic priorities. In this specific case, the food and beverage service, the organizational aspect, comfort, and event environment are the factors that lead to success. By ensuring the proper work of these elements, the event leads to higher perceived quality and, consequently, leads to a more financially sustainable event in future years (Figure 14.7).

Although the IPA can be successfully applied in sporting events, this model is not limited to them. Other sport services could benefit from this tool, as well as other services from different fields or other countries. In that case, a scale adaptation should be conducted previous to the start of the formal analysis. It should be noted that, when conducting IPA in diverse countries, the cultural heritage,

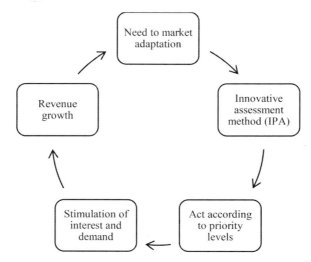

Figure 14.6 Virtuous Circle of Innovation in Sporting Events through IPA Approach.

customs, and the product/service life cycle are of great importance. The pace of change in the sports environment has unquestionably increased during the last three decades. Innovative assessing methods, such as IPA, are essential for adapting to the continuous change of the sports industry and for reaching appropriate levels of service.

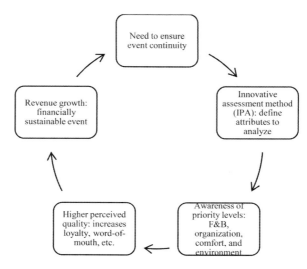

Figure 14.7 Virtuous Circle of Competitive Advantage of the Sporting Event Described in the Case Analysis.

References

Ábalo, J., Varela, J., & Manzano, V. (2007). Importance values for Importance–Performance analysis: A formula for spreading out values derived from preference rankings. *Journal of Business Research, 60*(2), 115–121.

Ábalo, J., Varela, J., & Rial, A. (2006). El análisis de importancia-valoración aplicado a la gestión de servicios. *Psicothema, 18*(4), 730–737.

Aigbedo, H., & Parameswaran, R. (2004). Importance-performance analysis for improving quality of campus food service. *International Journal of Quality & Reliability Management, 21*(8), 876–896.

Alberty, S., & Mihalik, B. J. (1989). The use of importance-performance analysis as an evaluative technique in adult education. *Evaluation Review, 13*(1), 33–44.

Alcaraz, N., Soriano, C., López, A., Rosa, D., Magraner, L., Porcar, R. M., Such, M. J., Sánchez, J. J., & Prat, J. M. (2009). *Factores de éxito desde la perspectiva del usuario en instalaciones deportivas, de ocio y salud en Comunidad Valenciana.*

Arias-Ramos, M., Serrano-Gómez, V., & García-García, O. (2016). ¿Existen diferencias en la calidad percibida y satisfacción del usuario que asiste a un centro deportivo de titularidad privada o pública? Un estudio piloto. *Cuadernos De Psicología Del Deporte, 16*(2), 99–110.

Bacon, D. R. (2003). A comparison of approaches to importance-performance analysis. *International Journal of Market Research, 45*(1), 55–71.

Biscaia, R. (2016). Revisiting the role of football spectators' behavioral intentions and its antecedents. *The Open Sports Sciences Journal, 9*(1), 3–12.

Biscaia, R., Coreia, A., Santos, T., Ross, S., & Yoshida, M. (2017). Service quality and value perceptions of the 2014 FIFA world cup in Brazil. *Event Management, 21*(2), 201–216.

BSJA. (2009). *Global Champions Tour kicks off in Arezzo.* https://web.archive.org/web/20090403213749/http://www.bsja.co.uk/international/news/global-champions-tour-kicks-off-in-arezzo

Burillo, P., Sánchez-Fernández, P., Dorado, A., & Gallardo, L. (2012). Global customer satisfaction and its components in local sports services. A discriminant analysis. *Journal of Sports Economics & Management, 2*(1), 16–33.

Calabuig-Moreno, F., Crespo-Hervàs, J., Prado-Gasco, V., Mundina-Gómez, J., Valantine, I., & Stanislovaitis, A. (2016). Quality of sporting events: Validation of the Eventqual scale. *Transformations in Business & Economics, 2*(38), 21–32.

Calabuig-Moreno, F., Mundina-Gómez, J., & Crespo-Hervàs, J. (2010). Eventqual: Una medida de la calidad percibida por los espectadores de eventos deportivos (Eventqual: A measure of perceived quality of sporting event spectators). *Retos, 18*(2), 66–70.

Chalip, L. (2006). Towards social leverage of sport events. *Journal of Sport & Tourism, 11*(2), 109–127.

Chappelet, J.-L., & Parent, M. M. (2015). The (wide) world of sports events. In M. M. Parent, & J.-L. Chappelet (Eds.), *Routledge handbook of sports event management* (pp. 1–19). Routledge.

Chu, R. K. S., & Choi, T. (2000). An importance-performance analysis of hotel selection factors in the Hong Kong hotel industry: A comparison of business and leisure travellers. *Tourism Management, 21*(4), 363–377.

Club de Campo Villa de Madrid. (2013). *History of the Club.* https://www.ccvm.es/en/node/8543

Cronin, J. J., Brady, M. K., & Hult, G. T. M. (2000). Assessing the effects of quality, value, and customer satisfaction on consumer behavioral intentions in service environments. *Journal of Retailing, 76*(2), 193–218.

Cronin, J. J., & Taylor, S. A. (1992). Measuring service quality: A reexamination and extension. *Journal of Marketing, 56*(3), 55–68.

Daemon Quest - Deloitte (2013). *Study of the impact of the equestrian sector in Spain.* Deloitte.

Daniels, M. J., & Norman, W. C. (2003). Estimating the economic impacts of seven regular sport tourism events. *Journal of Sport & Tourism, 8*(4), 214–222.

Deng, W. (2007). Using a revised importance-performance analysis approach: The case of Taiwanese hot springs tourism. *Tourism Management, 28*(5), 1274–1284.

Diario Gol. (2013). *Madrid hosts the most important equestrian circuit in the world.* https://www.diariogol.com/hemeroteca/madrid-acoge-el-circuito-de-hipica-mas-importante-del-mundo_431786_102.html

Dolinsky, A. L., & Caputo, R. K. (1991). Adding a competitive dimension to importance-performance analysis. An application to traditional health care systems. *Health Marketing Quarterly, 8*(3–4), 61–79.

Elasri, A., Triadó, X. M., & Aparicio, P. (2015). La satisfacción de los clientes de los centros deportivos municipales de Barcelona. *Apunts Educación Física y Deportes, 119*, 109–117.

Evans, M. R., & Chon, K. S. (1989). Formulating and evaluating tourism policy using importance-performance analysis. *Journal of Hospitality & Tourism Research, 13*(3), 203–213.

Ford, J. B., Joseph, M., & Joseph, B. (1999). Importance-performance analysis as a strategic tool for service marketers: The case of service quality perceptions of business students in New Zealand and The USA. *Journal of Services Marketing, 13*(2), 171–186.

Frew, M., & McGillivray, D. (2008). Exploring hyper-experiences: Performing the fan at Germany 2006. *Journal of Sport & Tourism, 13*(3), 181–198.

Go, F., & Zhang, W. (1997). Applying importance-performance analysis to Beijing as an international meeting destination. *Journal of Travel Research, 35*(4), 42–49.

Grohmann, K. (2018). *IOC struggles to find thirst for 2026 Winter Games after another withdrawal.* Reuters. https://www.reuters.com/article/olimp-inverno-dificuldade-idBRKCN1NL28I-OBRSP

Hanssen, T. E. S., & Mathisen, T. A. (2018). Exploring the attractiveness of a Norwegian rural higher education institution using importance-performance analysis. *Scandinavian Journal of Educational Research, 62*(1), 68–87.

Hawes, J. M., & Rao, C. P. (1985). Using importance - performance analysis to develop health care marketing strategies. *Journal of Health Care Marketing, 5*(4), 19–25.

Horne, J. (2007). The four 'knowns' of sports mega-events. *Leisure Studies, 26*(1), 81–96.

Hudson, S. (1998). Measuring service quality at tourist destinations: An application of importance performance analysis to an Alpine Ski Resort. *Journal of Travel & Tourism Marketing, 7*(3), 61–77.

Joseph, M., Allbright, D., Stone, G., Sekhon, Y., & Tinson, J. (2005). Importance-performance analysis of UK and US bank customer perceptions of service delivery technologies. *International Journal of Financial Services Management, 1*(1), 66–88.

Kelley, S. W., & Turley, L. (2001). Consumer perceptions of service quality attributes at sporting events. *Journal of Business Research, 54*(2), 161–166.

Ko, Y. J., Zhang, J., Cattani, K., & Pastore, D. (2011). Assessment of event quality in major spectator sports. *Managing Service Quality: An International Journal, 21*(3), 304–322.

La Vanguardia. (2019a). *The horse industry, a business beyond elite competition.* https://www.lavanguardia.com/deportes/20191201/471994222782/la-industria-del-caballo-un-negocio-mas-alla-de-la-competicion-de-elite.html

La Vanguardia. (2019b). *The "League of Legends" world championship lands tomorrow in Madrid.* https://www.lavanguardia.com/vida/20191025/471180632522/el-campeonato-mundial-de-league-of-legends-desembarca-manana-en-madrid.html

León-Quismondo, J., García-Unanue, J., & Burillo, P. (2020). Service perceptions in fitness centers: IPA approach by gender and age. *International Journal of Environmental Research and Public Health, 17*(8), 2844.

Levenburg, N. M., & Magal, S. R. (2005). Applying importance-performance analysis to evaluate e-business strategies among small firms. *E-Service Journal, 3*(3), 29–48.

Longines Global Champions Tour. (2021). *The Best in Show Jumping.* https://www.gcglobal-champions.com/en-us/lgct/about

Malchrowicz-Mośko, E., & Poczta, J. (2018). A small-scale event and a big impact—is this relationship possible in the world of sport? The meaning of heritage sporting events for sustainable development of tourism—experiences from Poland. *Sustainability, 10*(11), 4289.

Martilla, J. A., & James, J. C. (1977). Importance-performance analysis. *Journal of Marketing, 41*(1), 77–79.

Martin, D., O'Neill, M., Hubbard, S., & Palmer, A. (2008). The role of emotion in explaining consumer satisfaction and future behavioural intention. *Journal of Services Marketing, 22*(3), 224–236.

Martínez-Caro, E., Martínez-Caro, E., & Díaz-Suárez, A. (2014). La calidad del servicio en los clubes de fútbol base de la región de Murcia. Una aplicación del análisis de importancia-satisfacción. *SPORT TK: Revista EuroAmericana De Ciencias Del Deporte, 3*(1–2), 33–40.

Matzler, K., Sauerwein, E., & Heischmidt, K. (2003). Importance-performance analysis revisited: The role of the factor structure of customer satisfaction. *The Service Industries Journal, 23*(2), 112–129.

McDonald, M. A., Sutton, W. A., & Milne, G. R. (1995). TeamQUAL: Measuring service quality in professional team sports. *Sport Marketing Quarterly, 4*(2), 9–15.

Ministry of Culture and Sports. (2020). *Sports Statistics Yearbook 2020.* Ministry of Culture and Sports.

Nale, R. D., Wathen, S. A., & Barr, P. B. (2000). An exploratory look at the use of importance-performance analysis as a curricular assessment tool in a school of business. *Journal of Workplace Learning, 12*(4), 139–145.

Nishio, T., Larke, R., van Heerde, H., & Melnyk, V. (2016). Analysing the motivations of Japanese international sports-fan tourists. *European Sport Management Quarterly, 16*(4), 487–501.

Nuviala, A., Grao-Cruces, A., Tamayo, J. A., Nuviala, R., Álvarez, J., & Fernández-Martínez, A. (2013). Diseño y análisis del cuestionario de valoración de servicios deportivos (EPOD2). *Revista Internacional de Medicina y Ciencias de La Actividad Física y del Deporte, 13*(51), 419–436.

O'Neil, M. A., & Palmer, A. (2004). Importance-performance analysis: A useful tool for directing continuous quality improvement in higher education. *Quality Assurance in Education, 12*(1), 39–52.

Ortianu, D. J., Bush, A. J., Bush, R. P., & Twible, J. L. (1989). The use of importance-performance analysis for improving the quality of marketing education: Interpreting faculty-course evaluations. *Journal of Marketing Education, 11*(2), 78–86.

Parasuraman, A., Zeithaml, V. A., & Berry, L. L. (1985). A conceptual model of service quality and its implications for future research. *Journal of Marketing, 49*(4), 41–50.

Parra-Camacho, D., Añó, V., Ayora, D., & González-García, R. J. (2020). Applying importance-performance analysis to residents' perceptions of large sporting events. *Sport in Society, 23*(2), 249–263.

Polyakova, O., & Mirza, M. T. (2016). Service quality models in the context of the fitness industry. *Sport, Business and Management: An International Journal*, 6(3), 360–382.

Preuss, H. (2007). The conceptualisation and measurement of mega sport event legacies. *Journal of Sport & Tourism*, 12(3–4), 207–228.

Preuss, H. (2015). A framework for identifying the legacies of a mega sport event. *Leisure Studies*, 34(6), 643–664.

Rial, A., Rial, J., Varela, J., & Real, E. (2008). An application of importance-performance analysis (IPA) to the management of sport centres. *Managing Leisure*, 13(3–4), 179–188.

Sampson, S. E., & Showalter, M. J. (1999). The performance-importance response function: Observations and implications. *The Service Industries Journal*, 19(3), 1–25.

Sant, S.-L., & Mason, D. S. (2015). Framing event legacy in a prospective host city: Managing Vancouver's Olympic bid. *Journal of Sport Management*, 29(1), 42–56.

Santos, T. O., Correia, A., Biscaia, R., Araújo, C., Pedroso, C. A. M., Stinghen, F. M., Azevêdo, P. H., Molleta, S. R., Costa, V. T., & Menezes, V. G. (2016). A qualidade da copa do mundo da FIFA Brasil 2014 nas cidades-sede. *Movimento*, 22(2), 611–624.

Schulenkorf, N., & Schlenker, K. (2017). Leveraging sport events to maximize community benefits in low- and middle-income countries. *Event Management*, 21(2), 217–231.

Serrano-Gómez, V., Rial, A., Sarmento, J. P., & Carvalho, M. J. (2014). Análisis de importancia valoración (IPA) Como herramienta de diagnóstico en la gestión de clubes de golf. *Revista Intercontinental De Gestão Desportiva*, 4(1), 86–98.

Sever, I. (2015). Importance-performance analysis: A valid management tool? *Tourism Management*, 48, 43–53.

Spanish Statistical Office. (2021). *Population by provincial capitals and sex*. https://www.ine.es/jaxiT3/Datos.htm?t=2911

Tarrant, M. A., & Smith, E. K. (2002). The use of a modified importance-performance framework to examine visitor satisfaction with attributes of outdoor recreation settings. *Managing Leisure*, 7(2), 69–82.

Theodorakis, N., Kambitsis, C., & Laios, A. (2001). Relationship between measures of service quality and satisfaction of spectators in professional sports. *Managing Service Quality: An International Journal*, 11(6), 431–438.

Thomson, A., Cuskelly, G., Toohey, K., Kennelly, M., Burton, P., & Fredline, L. (2019). Sport event legacy: A systematic quantitative review of literature. *Sport Management Review*, 22(3), 295–321.

Tontini, G., & Silveira, A. (2007). Identification of satisfaction attributes using competitive analysis of the improvement gap. *International Journal of Operations & Production Management*, 27(5), 482–500.

Universidad Europea. (2020). *Economic and Social Impact of Longines Global Champions Tour 2019. Private Report*. Universidad Europea.

Vargo, S. L., & Lusch, R. F. (2012). The nature and understanding of value: A service-dominant logic perspective. *Review of Marketing Research*, 9, 1–12.

Wade, D. J., & Eagles, P. F. J. (2003). The use of importance-performance analysis and market segmentation for tourism management in parks and protected areas: An application to Tanzania's national parks. *Journal of Ecotourism*, 2(3), 196–212.

Yavas, U., & Shemwell, D. J. (2001). Modified importance-performance analysis: An application to hospitals. *International Journal of Health Care Quality Assurance*, 14(3), 104–110.

Yeo, A. Y. C. (2003). Examining a Singapore bank's competitive superiority using importance-performance analysis. *Journal of American Academy of Business*, 3(1/2), 155–161.

Yildiz, S. M. (2011). An importance-performance analysis of fitness center service quality: Empirical results from fitness centers in Turkey. *African Journal of Business Management*, 5(16), 7031–7041.

Yoshida, M., James, J. D., & Cronin, J. J. (2013). Value creation: Assessing the relationships between quality, consumption value and behavioural intentions at sporting events. *International Journal of Sports Marketing and Sponsorship*, 14(2), 51–73.

Zamorano-Solís, S., & García-Fernández, J. (2018). El análisis de importancia-valoración según género y permanencia: El caso de los centros de fitness. *Materiales Para La Historia Del Deporte*, 16, 24–35.

Zhang, J. J., Lam, E. T. C., Connaughton, D. P., Bennett, G., & Smith, D. W. (2005). Development of a scale to measure spectator satisfaction toward support programs of minor league hockey games. *International Journal of Sport Management*, 6(1), 47–70.

Ziegler, J., Dearden, P., & Rollins, R. (2012). But are tourists satisfied? Importance-performance analysis of the whale shark tourism industry on Isla Holbox, Mexico. *Tourism Management*, 33(3), 692–701.

Chapter 15

Key Strategic and Innovative Decisions That Explain the Success of the Valencia Marathon

Ramón Llopis-Goig
Universidad de Valencia, Spain

Juan L. Paramio-Salcines
Universidad Autónoma de Madrid, Spain

Chapter Contents

Introduction	224
Sport Events Industry and City Marathons	225
Political and Socioeconomic Context of Valencia	228
Strategy in Action	231
Participants' Feedback for Improvement	234
Conclusion	239
Acknowledgments	240
References	240
Appendix I	244

Introduction

As many other cities at global level, since the early 21st century, the city of Valencia, Spain's third largest city with over 800,000 inhabitants and one of the leading destinations for national and international visitors, has embarked on a long-term strategy to use sport-related projects to promote significant economic, urban, social, tourist, and sporting changes in the city. To name a few, Valencia's recent experience with major sport events includes the 2007 and 2010 America's Cup, the 2008 World Indoor Athletic Championship, the Formula One Grand Prix urban circuit, Valencia Tennis Open ATP 500, and, in our case, a second-order mega event, the Marathon of Valencia – renamed Marathon Valencia Trinidad Alfonso (MVTA) since 2014 (Llopis Goig, 2012; Paramio-Salcines, 2014). Looking in perspective, the inaugural Popular Marathon of Valencia, organized by a local athletic club, *Sociedad Deportiva Correcaminos* (SDC), was held on 29 March 1981, attracting roughly 800 runners with the aim of promoting local athletics (Lastra, 1984). Since then, and over the last four decades, the MVTA has evolved and grown, as part of the overall strategy to use sport

DOI: 10.4324/9781003388050-18

events envisaged by the 2010 *Sport Strategic Plan of Valencia* (Fundación Deportiva Municipal de Valencia, 2011), to become one of the leading marathons worldwide. The race has also been valued for its potential to promote direct economic benefits and knock-on effects to position the race as a major tourist product as well as to promote Valencia as a *City of Running*.

Most previous research studies on the Valencia Marathon have been directed to evaluate the economic, tourist, social, and sporting impacts of the race on the city, the sizeable increase in the participation, and the post-marathon evaluation of a range of innovative and quality services provided to runners over the latest editions – see annual studies by the Instituto Valenciano de Investigaciones Económicas (IVIE, 2017, 2018, 2019, 2020; Parra-Camacho et al., 2021). Recently, academic research has examined the management process to improve the operation of the five most relevant marathons in Spain, including the Valencia Marathon (García-Vallejo et al., 2020). However, less is known about what key strategic and innovative decisions have been critical to explain the success of this benchmark race over the years.

The next section extends previous work (Llopis Goig, 2012; Paramio-Salcines, 2014; Paramio-Salcines et al., 2017) to examine related literature on the relationships between the sport event industry, city marathons, and their impacts on the cities and their citizens that host these races. The following section provides some background information on the political and socioeconomic context of the city of Valencia and the Valencia Marathon. Bringing together literatures on corporate strategy and sport management, the authors outline the main strategic and innovative actions which will explain the evolution over the last four decades as well as the economic, tourist, and sporting outcomes of the MVTA. It concludes by incorporating the main findings and the managerial implications of the study. The chapter draws on documentary analysis of academic and professional publications and reports from Valencia City Council, event organizers, and local research economic groups such as the IVIE.

Sport Events Industry and City Marathons

The study of all types of sport events, including mega events, hallmark events, and community events, has significantly proliferated in the sport management and tourism literatures over the last four decades. Hosting or bidding for sport events is not a new phenomenon. Entering the 21st century, as Smith (2012) pointed out, we are in a new era of sport events characterized by globalization. Urban leaders continue to value sport events for their potential to generate a diversity of direct and indirect sporting and non-sporting benefits (as well as, in some cases, negative effects) to the host nation or city (Ferguson & O'Connor, 2018; Gratton & Henry, 2001; Gratton et al., 2006; Müller, 2015a; Smith, 2012). Within this literature, there are also some critical authors regarding the strategic use of sport events by cities and nations (Matheson, 2012; Zimbalist, 2015). Several authors have addressed the evolution in size and the relevance of the sport event industry and the tourism market at global level. Both industry sectors have enjoyed unprecedented growth as well as becoming highly competitive markets (Heere et al., 2019).

The preponderance of research has focused on the assessment of the effects as well as sport and non-sport legacies of mega sport events on the countries or cities that have hosted them (Roche, 2000, 2017; Smith, 2012; Zimbalist, 2015; see also Thomson et al., 2019 for a systematic review of sport events legacy literature since the early 2000s). Beyond mega events, there is an emerging literature relating to the role and impact (and legacies) of other types of sport events on the process of reimaging cities, such as the 2007 and 2010 America's Cup in Valencia (Llopis Goig & García Alcober, 2012), hosting stages of the Tour of France (Heere et al., 2019; Paramio-Salcines et al., 2017) and not least, city marathons as we will examine below. As Thomson et al. (2019) and others have examined, research on city marathons is also expansive since 2000 onward parallel to the growth and intense competition between city marathons and other road races at international level. A growing body of research claims that city marathons seem to play an increasingly significant role, contributing to the economic, urban, tourist, social, and sporting effects on those cities that host the race (e.g., Coleman, 2004; Coleman & Ramchandani, 2010; Gratton et al., 2006; Huang et al., 2015; Miller & Washington, 2017; Parra-Camacho et al., 2021; Shipway & Jones, 2008; Wicker et al., 2012). As part of event sport tourism, city marathons have become a niche market, attracting large numbers of runners from outside the host city (Gibson et al., 2012; Heere et al., 2019; Miller, 2012; Miller & Washington, 2017; Paramio-Salcines et al., 2017; Wicker et al., 2012).

Despite this progress, there is no clear consensus among academics about precisely defining what type of event a marathon represents and what factors are required to classify one marathon as *major*. From the practitioner's perspective, the Abbott World Marathon Majors organization values six of the largest and most renowned marathons worldwide on the basis of the sporting performance, level of participation, economic impact, and other indicators. Based on the TCS New York City Marathon, Paule-Koba (2020) describes city marathons as a *recurring event* that happens on a regular (annual) time frame (in this case the first Sunday of November), understood as the "easiest" type of event to execute because it occurs consistently. Martin and Hall (2020) consider the criteria of sporting performance to describe a city marathon as a world marathon major when the world's elite long-distance runners come together to compete. By this definition, those authors coincide with the ranking of the six most significant marathons as proposed by the Abbott World Marathon Majors organization (Abbott World Marathon Majors, 2020). From a sociological perspective, Roche (2017) differentiates between (first order) mega events, special events, hallmark, and community types (see also Roche, 2000). Notwithstanding, and considering the complexity and variability of types of events in the second phase of modernization, Roche suggests that we should expand this typology by including second-order mega events. Following Roche, we initially classify the Valencia Marathon as a second-order mega event.

Most studies on the managerial aspects, impacts, and legacies of marathons on cities that hosted them are based mainly on the US (Fickenscher, 2006, 2011; Martin & Hall, 2020; Miller & Washington, 2017), Britain (Coleman, 2004; Coleman & Ramchandani, 2010; Gratton et al., 2006; (Suozzo, 2006) Shipway & Jones, 2008), Germany (Wicker et al., 2012), China (Huang et al., 2015; Qiu et al., 2020), and some recent contributions relating to Spanish cities (Alemany-Hormaeche et al., 2019; García-Vallejo et al., 2020; Parra-Camacho et al., 2021; Pedrosa Carrera, 2016). The preponderance of existing literature has evaluated those races as purely economic phenomena. As part of the historical expansion of what is valued as the leading marathons worldwide, the New York Road Runners, who are the organizers of the New York Marathon since the 1970s, have commissioned several studies to measure the economic, tourist, social and participation impacts on the city of New York (New York Road Runners, 2020). In relation to this benchmark race, Fickenscher (2006) estimated that the race brought $188 million to New York in 2006, while five years, the race increased the economic impact to $340 million, drawing 2 million spectators and more than 45,000 runners (Fickenscher, 2011).

From a comparative perspective, it has been reported that in 2011, ING New York marathon brought $340 million to New York, Boston Marathon brought $95 million to Boston, and Bank of America Chicago Marathon had an economic impact of $80 million (Miller, 2012). Beyond the US, Gratton et al. (2006) valued the London Marathon as a major event due to the huge economic impact (estimated at £1.2 million from participant spending) on the city. In a follow-up study on the Virgin London Marathon, Coleman and Ramchandani (2010) estimated that this leading marathon brought £27.1 million into the London economy (£13.1 million from spectators, £9.5 million from runners, £6.9 million from bednights in London hotels and guest houses, £6.3 million from the catering industry, and £1.6 million from organizers net spend).

In addition to the economic impacts on host cities, Miller (2012) and Miller and Washington (2017) have consistently pointed out that marathon races have also become major tourist destinations. Focusing on the US context, Running USA stated, "cities are embracing marathons for the economic upswing. One of the benefits of a marathon of any size is that bring people to your city, it showcases your city, it brings people back" (in Miller & Washington, 2017, p. 277). However, there are limitations to what we currently know about city marathons (García-Vallejo et al., 2020; Thomson et al., 2019; Wicker et al., 2012). In a quest to understand the profile and expenditure of runners at marathons, different scholars have started to examine those factors. Wicker et al. (2012), for example, have studied the key driving factors that influence consumer expenditure of marathon runners and their intention to revisit three marathon events in Germany (Cologne, Bonn, and Hanover). Similarly, tourism scholars, Huang et al. (2015) used the Shanghai International Marathon in China to add a new perspective as represents the image congruence between marathons and host cities. Martin and Hall (2020) have specifically explored the impact of the New York City Marathon on the city hotel demand after Hurricane Sandy in 2012 which contributed to the cancellation of the race. In Spain, this literature has recently expanded, by incorporating some studies such as García-Vallejo et al. (2020) which examined five marathons in Spain (Barcelona, Madrid, Malaga, Sevilla, and Valencia) from the management perspective after identifying the main organizational areas and how to maximize the planning and management of those races.

Parra-Camacho et al. (2021) focused particularly on the social impact of Valencia Marathon from the residents' perceptions, while Pedrosa Carrera (2016) analyzed the management factors at the 2015 Zurich marathon in Seville. As the study of Wicker et al. (2012), Alemany-Hormaeche et al. (2019) examined the segmentation of runners and the level of satisfaction of those runners in the 2016 Palma de Mallorca Marathon. In this debate, many authors have underlined the importance of developing strategic capabilities to perform as well as evaluating critical factors of success in business (Johnson et al., 2017) and in the management of events and facilities (Schwarz et al., 2017). As Foster et al. (2016) note, creation and innovation play a more important role to help the events and event managers to evolve from being a national (or local) event to an international orientated event as the MVTA represents. In this process, García-Vallejo et al. (2020), Newland (2020), Yoshida et al. (2013), and others argue that event concept innovations, co-creation, and associated management issues have not yet been extensively studied. These concepts will be examined in the case of the MVTA. Beforehand, we will look at the political and socioeconomic context of the city of Valencia and the MVTA.

Political and Socioeconomic Context of Valencia

As Fox et al. (2014) recommended in doing research on events, it is critical to analyze the political and socioeconomic context of the event itself to shed light of the policy implications of the event. With the new political scenario in Spain after the Francoist period, the city of Valencia, a traditionally agrarian and provincial city, has become the capital of the Spanish autonomous region the *Comunitat Valenciana*. Since the early 1990s, it could be argued that this was the beginning of a sea-change in the transformation of the city to become an economic center and major tourist destination, with an important role in hosting major sport events as we will explain later (Ajuntament de Valencia, 1987; Del Romero Renau, 2010; Prytherch & Boira-Maiques, 2009; Rius-Ulldemolins & Gisbert, 2019; Rius-Ulldemolins et al., 2015; Salom Carrasco & Pitarch Garrido, 2017).

In the case of the Marathon of Valencia, it is relevant to note that since the first democratic Council elections in 1979 to present times, the political control of the city can be examined in three distinct periods: first, from 1979 to 1991, with the municipal government in hands of a social democrat political party (*Partido Socialista*); second, from 1991 to 2015, with a conservative party (*Partido Popular*) in the local institutions; and third, from 2015 to nowadays, with a coalition of left-wing and Valencian nationalist political parties (*Compromís, Partido Socialista, València en Comú*). In the first period, the municipal government controlled urban politics, with three different mayors, in a period during which local councils gradually increased their powers in relation to culture, education, health, urban planning, and sport, but with limited resources to address local needs. In the second period, under the leadership of mayor Rita Barberá, the city saw a gradual reorientation of the role of the Valencia City Council from what can be understood as a managerial city – with the previous socialist government being a direct provider of local services – to a more entrepreneurial city – aiming to promote local capital accumulation – as Amendola (1997), Hall and Hubbard (1998), and Harvey (1990) conceptualize as a trend in postmodern urban politics and planning.

Prytherch and Boira-Maiques (2009) describe the Valencia approach as a new neo-liberal agenda. As previously stated, this reorientation of local politics began to take shape in the early 1990s, when the symptoms of industrial decline began to be evident and growth in the tourism sector was seen as an alternative, for which, the city was not prepared despite the city's coastal location. Prior to the democratic period, the city of Valencia had a low-profile tourism industry, in part caused by a neglect of artistic heritage and very few tourist attractions. Influenced by the success of Barcelona with the 1992 Olympic Games, it was at this point that the city began to build high-profile urban projects, located in the final section of the old riverbed of the Turia River, which would help to redefine the image of the city as an attractive tourist destination. After flash floods of Valencia in 1957, urban leaders decided to divert the Turia River and to use its bed as a road. However, mass demonstrations by residents brought about a change in this initial plan. In 1981, the transformation of the Turia riverbed, known as Jardin del Turia Park, started to become a central urban park with more than 110 hectares and a length of 9 km. The urban park is one of the largest of its kind in Spain and combines a provision of public sport facilities, auditoriums, high-profile cultural buildings, and recreational areas, linked to athletic events and mass participation (Bosch Reig, 2011). Other Spanish cities such as Seville and Madrid followed suit with this urban and sport event-led strategy to promote their own urban renewals and change their respective city's image. Seville hosted the 1992 World Expo and made a bid for the 2004, 2008, and 2012 Olympic Games, while Madrid was nominated officially as the "*European City of Culture*" in 1992; it made bids for the 2012, 2016, and 2020 Olympic Games (Brunet, 1994; Smith, 2012).

Key characteristics of the greater involvement of the Valencia Council in urban politics involve giving more significance to local economic development by building mega buildings, most of them designed by "starchitects" – as Roche (2017) describes those international architects involved in mega projects – promoting prestigious sport and cultural events and not least, the development of partnerships between the Council and local business (Del Romero Renau, 2010; Prytherch & Boira-Maiques, 2009; Rius-Ulldemolins & Gisbert, 2019; Rius-Ulldemolins et al., 2015; Salom Carrasco & Pitarch Garrido, 2017). In this case, although some of the projects developed in the city of Valencia had begun in the previous decade, it is at the beginning of the 1990s when two essential infrastructure projects for the city began to be promoted: the City of Arts and Sciences and the Congress Palace, both designed by two authentic "starchitects", namely Santiago Calatrava and Norman Foster, respectively. Both cultural infrastructures are two of the main landmarks that the city uses in their tourist promotion. The third period commenced in 2015, with the coming to municipal power of a coalition of left-wing and Valencian nationalist political parties under the leadership of mayor Joan Ribó. The decline of the Partido Popular, after 25 years in control of local politics, contributed decisively to this third period, as well as the suspicion of corruption that had arisen in recent years regarding the conservative party in different territorial areas of the country. The promotion of major events as an economic development strategy began to be questioned by the political forces of the opposition given that the effects of the Great Recession that began in 2008 still ravaged Valencian society.

These shifts in the political culture of the city from 1979 to nowadays have also been reflected in the local sport policy. During the 1980s and 1990s, the municipal governments sport policy favored the building of a network of sport facilities, with the promotion of mass participation as part of the *"Sport for All"* movement. As in other Spanish cities, the city's Sport Department (*Fundación Deportiva Municipal Valencia*) was created on 10 April 1981. At the beginning of the 21st century, the municipal government found that sporting events could be used to promote economic development and local tourist (see Llopis Goig & García Alcober, 2012 for a much detail description of the portfolio of events hosted in Valencia from the early 1990 to 2007). The municipal government concluded that the city needed an event that would attract media attention and promote it as a tourist destination; the America's Cup, one of the most important sporting mega events in the world, was a perfect fit for those objectives.

The Valencia City Council took on the challenge of organizing the 32nd and 33rd edition of the America's Cup in 2007 and 2010 and hosted other major sporting events, such as a Formula One Grand Prix, run on the streets of the city, and the Open Tennis 500 tournament, which also contributed to the overall international recognition gained through the America's Cup (Del Romero Renau, 2010). In the transition from the first to the second decade of the 21st century, the municipal government began to understand the fit and potential of the Valencia Marathon in its overarching economic and tourist development strategy. The Valencia City Council then proposed to the race organizers, SDC, to join forces with the aim of making this event more recognized globally. The race organizers accepted the challenge and after the approval, in the first quarter of 2011, of the *Valencia Sports Strategic Plan*, implemented and prepared changes that ultimately led to an extraordinary transformation in the management and more important, to the internationalization of the event.

At the time of writing, the coalition in place of left-wing and Valencian nationalist political parties has undertaken a clear reorientation of urban and economic development policies. It must be said, however, that the change was already in motion because of the Great Recession (2008–2015). In the case of the Formula One Grand Prix, the last race was held in 2012. The economic impact from the races did not meet initial projections and, subsequently, the Valencian regional government had to assume the losses caused by the organization of the event. In the case of the Open Tennis 500, the organizers wanted to stop staging the event in Valencia due to what they perceived as a lack of interest from the regional government. This stance has also been ratified with the current coalition in the city of Valencia. Even the legacy of the America's Cup did not seem entirely safe a few years after its celebration. A study carried out in 2013 (Parra-Camacho et al., 2016) indicated that even though citizens recognized that this mega event had contributed to promoting the city as a tourist destination and had increased its international prestige, its celebration had ultimately generated more negative than positive effects (see also Del Romero Renau & Trudelle, 2011).

The general rolling back of municipal policies aimed at urban transformation and the development of infrastructure projects and sporting events has not been an obstacle to the growth and international recognition of the Valencia Marathon. It cannot be denied that the growth in the practice of running seen in Europe since the beginning of the 21st century – what Scheerder et al. (2015) have called the second wave of running – has positively influenced the growth of the MVTA. As with any other sporting event, the recent success of the MVTA is to a large extent the result of well-executed long-term strategic planning and management process; an area that will be analyzed in more detail in the following section.

Strategy in Action

The planning of a city marathon is a crucial part of a long-term strategic management process (Coleman, 2004; Coleman & Ramchandani, 2010; Foster et al., 2016; García-Vallejo et al., 2020; Huang et al., 2015; Paule-Koba, 2020; Wicker et al., 2012). In this process, it is also important that urban leaders as well as organizers and managers of events such as the MVTA need to take strategic decisions. Those decisions have also affected operational decisions linked to the evolution in size, status, race location, timelines, and legacies of a city marathon in its progression toward its status today as, arguably, one of the major marathons worldwide. As Foster et al. (2016, p. 222) note "at the creation stage it defines the concept, the plan to get to a successful event, and its governance". These authors also argue that to understand the evolution and expansion of an event as the MVTA EDP represents, creation plays an important role. Not least, one of the keys to successful event management is effective leadership, which must facilitate all stages in the event lifecycle (Schwarz et al., 2017).

The Marathon Popular de Valencia emerged in 1979 when a group of local runners set up the club SDC with the mission to promote popular athletic events and to boost local athletics. Like the New York City Marathon when a group of running enthusiastic launched the race in 1970, in Valencia, a local couple, Miguel Pellicer and Angelita Carrasco, were key in setting up the abovementioned club (Lastra, 1984) (see also appendix). Two years later, the idea of running a marathon became a reality when the club, as the event rights holders, organized officially on 29 March 1981, the first edition, known at this time as *Marathon Popular de Valencia*. Interestingly, the first Valencia Marathon which attracted 800 runners coincides with the first London Marathon which attracted 7,055 runners. Not surprisingly, planning, managing, and executing the first edition was not extremely successful as it only attracted approximately 800 amateur runners. In this case, it is important to say that there was (and still is) a compatibility of the city marathon with the athletics culture in the city since the 1980s. This running culture started to flourish in this decade with the setting up of several local athletic clubs, including SDC, which were involved in the management of other races.

This growth in local athletics coincides with the beginning of the mass race movement in Spain in the 1980s after the political transition from the Francoist period to a new social democratic system. In this phenomenon, the first Marathon Popular de Valencia was officially held three years later than other marathons in Spanish cities, including Marathon Popular de Madrid (April 1978), Barcelona (March 1978), and San Sebastian (October 1978). Running emerged as one of the most popular sport activity in the 1960s in many countries. Coincidentally with the "*Sport for All*" philosophy promoted officially by the Council of Europe in 1966 (Paramio-Salcines et al., 2018), the Spanish government launched the same year their first "*Sport for All*" campaign under the slogan *Contamos Contigo* (Counting on you) to increase sports participation rates. At that time, sports participation rate in the whole country was quite low (12 percent in 1968) (Puig et al., 1985). One of the phenomena that emerged at that time was the boom in urban runners.

Much like the New York City Marathon, the Valencia Marathon has been organized –and continues to be, along with other local athletics races – by SDC since 1981. In the following year (1982), one of the first strategic decisions taken by the organizers was to shift the official time schedule of the marathon from March to February, a decision which had been operative for over three decades until the organizers decided in 2011 to move the timeline of the race to November. This decision is vital in explaining the current success of the Valencia Marathon; not only did it allow the Valencia Marathon to distance itself from the calendar dates of the other top marathons in Spain – for example, in Madrid, Barcelona, and Seville – but also the new date was more appealing for prospective participants, due to the better race-day temperatures and the timing in the preparation stage. The decision, which was a result of the *Strategic Sport Plan of Valencia*, was made in collaboration between the Fundación Deportiva Municipal and SDC; and it was approved in 2011 (Cervera et al., 2011). As noted by the then Valencia Mayor, Rita Barberá, the aim of this document was

> to lay out the guidelines that will help us to face the constant challenge of the future, our future as a sport city, through an infrastructure of sports services that can meet our own internal needs, but that is also appealing to those outside the city and gives a good image of Valencia.
>
> (Fundación Deportiva Municipal de Valencia, 2011, p. 5)

Although Valencia Council was valued as the driving force of the *Strategic Sport Plan of Valencia*, this document brought together not only City Council representatives but also probably most importantly, it incorporated the views of local business companies, higher education institutions, tourist representatives, and many local organizations. Following the recommendations of the *Strategic Sport Plan of Valencia*, those groups started to develop some strategic and innovative projects to increase sports participation in the city, the tourist industry and relevant to our case, to develop the concept of Valencia as a "City of Sport" (Cervera et al., 2011; Estelles-Miguel et al., 2017). Valencia was internationally recognized as *European Capital of Sport* in 2011, due to the long-term promotional development of sport for all, building of public sport facilities, the setting of innovative projects, and not least, to the planning and management of large portfolio of sport events. Equally important has been to see the range of unique elements that came to signify the MVTA as a winning business product. As part of this process, SDC – who is both MVTA rights holder and organizer – has been year by year taking some strategic and innovative decisions – from the time schedule, location of the starting and finish line of the race at the *City of Arts and Sciences* complex in the center of the city, types of sponsorships developed over the last decades, or the latest concept of the marathon as an entertainment event – that could go to explain the success of MVTA (see also the appendix I which summarizes a selected list of key decisions over a long-time frame).

Considering the hyper competition from different city marathons at national and international levels, it is critical to examine the distinctive organizational decisions, resources, human management, numbers of runners, sponsors, and services provided that make MVTA better or at least similar to any other major marathon's organizations, not only from the perspective of the organizers but also from that of the runner (Newland, 2020; Parra-Camacho et al., 2021; Paule-Koba, 2020). As in other major marathons cases where main sponsors give support and the name to those marathons (e.g., BMW Berlin Marathon, Bank of America Chicago Marathon, or Virgin Money London Marathon (now renamed as the TCS London Marathon), we could speculate that another pivotal decision has been the arrival of an important sponsor, the Foundation Trinidad Alfonso, run by one of the main businessmen in Spain, Juan Roig. Even though in 2011 and 2012, Divina Pastora, an insurance company, became the official sponsor of the marathon, the turning point came in 2012 when Foundation Trinidad Alfonso became one of the sponsors. This collaboration started with the contribution of this local foundation to the Half Marathon Valencia. This collaboration increased one year later, in 2013, when Foundation Trinidad Alfonso became the main sponsor. As part of this agreement, the Marathon Valencia took on the title it is known by currently.

As the event organizers asked themselves why everybody wants to organize the Valencia Marathon, it is important to explain what the critical success factors are that contribute to understand the evolution of the MVTA as a world class marathon. To this end, we have considered relevant, as Foster et al. (2016) and

Johnson et al. (2017) suggest, to compare the level of competence of MTVA with the other six major city marathons to identify those critical factors. Following the steps suggested by Johnson et al., we have identified the following performance standards that give at the time of writing the MVTA a competitive advantage over its main counterparts. These factors may be: (1) the current location of the start-line and finishing-line of the MVTA in the City of Arts and Science Centre, designed by Santiago Calatrava, the international architect born in Valencia. This architectural complex is ranked as Valencia's principal landmark. This decision can be considered an important organizational innovation; (2) the continual improvement and range of services provided to runners before, during, and after the race which has been recognized with the Platinum Label Road Race in 2020; (3) the sponsorship of the Foundation Trinidad Alfonso with a strong corporate reputation in the city and in Spain; and (4) the sporting performance of elite men and women runners over the last decade has been one of the benchmark factors to improve the MVTA's international reputation and to drive the growth of tourism. As an example, on 6 December 2020 (the last edition under the effects of the COVID-19 pandemic), two Kenyans runners, Evans Chebet, crossed the finish line with the astonishing time of 2 hours 3 minutes, the sixth fastest time of the whole history of any male marathon runners. Peres Jepchirchir finished the race in 2 hours 17 minutes 16 seconds, the fifth fastest time of any female marathon runner. On the same day, another Kenyan runner, Kibiwott Kandie, broke the world record at the Valencia Half marathon at 57 minutes 32 seconds.

Participants' Feedback for Improvement

As Table 15.1 shows the MVTA men's race fastest time is the third in the marathon ranking after the Virgin London Money Marathon and BMW Berlin Marathon and the women's race fastest time is the second after the Virgin London Money Marathon. Because of the sporting performance of both male and female runners, the World Athletics, the international governing body for the sport of athletics, has recognized MVTA as a "World Athletics Platinum Label" (World Athletics, 2021), a recognition that has only be awarded to a few major marathons. The sporting performance in all races run by SDC has contributed to the attraction not only of the top distance runners, but also to increase mass participation. This finding was in line with previous studies on marathons and outstanding performance.

From the participation perspective, the race has evolved from being a local event with roughly 800 runners in 1981, to become an international event in December 2019, prior to the COVID-19 pandemic, with 25,546 runners. This growth of mass participation has also contributed to situate MVTA at the top of ranking of mass participants in city marathons in Spain (García-Vallejo et al., 2020; Parra-Camacho et al., 2021; Statista, 2019), the fourth in Europe, only after two of the world marathons majors such as London and Berlin, and not least Paris and the seventh at global level, after the six world majors (IVIE, 2020). As Table 15.2

Table 15.1 Comparative Data between the Abbott World Marathon Majors and the Marathon of Valencia Trinidad Alfonso (2019 Race Prior to the COVID-19 Pandemic) and Best Men's and Women's Records All Time

	Month	First edition	Largest field-runners	Men's record	Women's record	Estimated spectators	Race Organizer	WA Label
Tokyo Marathon	March	2007	35,460	2:03:58	2:17:45	1 million	Tokyo Marathon Foundation	Platinum
Boston Marathon	September	1897	35,868	2:03:02	2:19:59	Half million	Boston Athletic Association	Platinum
Virgin London Money Marathon	October	1981	42,549	2:02:37	2:17:01	750	London Marathon Events Limited	Platinum
BMV Berlin Marathon	September	1974	46,983	2:01:39	2:18:11	1 million	SCC EVENTS GmbH	Platinum
Bank of America Chicago Marathon	October	1977	45,932	2:03:45	2:14:04	1.7 million	Bank of America Chicago Marathon	Platinum
TCS New York City Marathon	November	1970	53,520	2:05:06	2:22:31	+1 million	New York Road Runners	Platinum
Marathon Valencia Trinidad Alfonso EDP	December	1981	25,546	2:03:00	2:17:16	200,000	S.D. Correcaminos	Platinum

Source: Adapted from Abbott World Marathon Majors (2020) and reviewed from all seven marathons official websites

Table 15.2 Evolution in the Number and Share of Participants at the MVTA EDP and 10K According to Their Origin (2011–2019)

	2011	2012	2013	2014	2015	2016	2017	2018	2019
MVTA EDP	6,732	9,013	11,300	13,350	16,682	19,095	19,242	22,101	25,546
10K	1,100	6,121	7,800	8,012	8,547	8,970	8,876	9,225	7,043
From Spain	7,063	12,886	15,743	17,415	20,149	20,694	20,951	22,083	21,354
Valencia	*4,282*	*8,085*	*10,497*	*10,989*	*11,905*	*11,634*	*10,666*	*9,674*	*8,846*
Rest of Spain	*2,781*	*4,801*	*5,246*	*6,426*	*8,244*	*9,060*	*10,285*	*12,409*	*12,508*
From overseas	769	2,248	3,357	3,946	5,080	7,371	7,167	9,243	11,235
Total	7,832	15,134	19,100	21,362	25,229	28,065	28,118	31,326	32,589
	2011	2012	2013	2014	2015	2016	2017	2018	2019
MVTA EDP	86.0%	59.6%	59.2%	62.5%	66.1%	68.0%	68.4%	70.6%	78.4%
10K	14.0%	40.4%	40.8%	37.5%	33.9%	32.0%	31.6%	29.4%	21.6%
From Spain	90.2%	85.1%	82.4%	81.5%	78.9%	73.7%	74.5%	70.5%	65.5%
Valencia	*54.7%*	*53.4%*	*54.9%*	*51.4%*	*47.2%*	*41.4%*	*37.9%*	*30.9%*	*27.1%*
Rest of Spain	*35.5%*	*31.7%*	*27.5%*	*30.1%*	*32.7%*	*32.3%*	*36.6%*	*39.65*	*38.4%*
From overseas	9.8%	14.9%	17.6%	18.5%	20.1%	26.3%	25.5%	29.5%	34.5%
Total	100%	100%	100%	100%	100%	100%	100%	100%	100%

Source: IVIE (2020, p. 23) and previous reports from IVIE

Key Strategic and Innovative Decisions 237

shows, the number of participants in the Valencia Marathon has quadrupled in the last decade, from 6,732 in 2011 to 25,546 in 2019. If the participants in the 10K – a race introduced in 2011 to bring more runners closer to the marathon and to incentivize marathoners' companions to participate in the race – are added to this tally, a total figure of 32,589 athletes is reached compared to the 7,832 in 2011.

Participation from individuals from outside Spain has grown extraordinarily in the same period, going from 769 participants in 2011 to 11,235 in 2019 – and they came from a total of 101 countries – meaning that their presence as a percentage of total participants has gone from 9.8 percent to 34.5 percent. The number of Spanish runners from outside Valencia has also seen a tremendous growth, going from 2,781 in 2011 to 12,508 in 2019, although their percentage weight among total participants has only grown three percentage units, going from 35.5 percent to 38.4 percent. With 72.9 percent of runners coming from other parts of Spain and outside of Spain, the MVTA itself has become a significant sport tourism product. Regarding this relationship between performance in sport events and the intention to revisit the city of the marathon, this finding was in line with previous studies by Gholipour et al. (2020). In our case, the outstanding performance at the Valencia Marathon can drive as one of the direct effects the growth of tourism to the city of Valencia. This is also seen in the studies carried out in recent years by the IVIE, in which it is concluded that the income generated by the activities that revolve around the celebration of the Valencia Marathon are much greater than the expenditures of the host organization.

The latest report (IVIE, 2020) estimated that the expenses incurred in organizing the race amounts to €5,406,657, while the income generated by the money spent in Valencia by runners and their companion amounts to €22,803,199 (see Table 15.3). Taking into account the expenditure that is susceptible to general economic impact, the aforementioned report indicates that, for every euro spent in organizing the event, €4.2 more is generated through tourist spending. This is a clear example of the multiplier effect and the ultimate positive financial impact the event has on the Valencian economy. According to the event typology developed by the United Kingdom Sport, the MVTA is a clear example of a "competitor-driven event" as most of expenditure is led by spending of runners. The evolution of the impacts of the Valencia Marathon on production, income, and employment can be found in Table 15.3. The IVIE estimates the 2019 Valencia Marathon generated €52,052,098 in terms of production value (sales), €15,877,835 in terms of income (added value), and created 524 new jobs. Lastly, the experience of participating in the race is highly valued by the runners themselves. According to data from a survey conducted among participants of the 2019 edition, runner's satisfaction reached a score of 8.9 out of 10 (IVIE, 2020, p. 31). This study also revealed how loyal the runners were to the race, with 42.3 percent of the runners being returning participants and with 98.6 percent of them saying they would, likely or with complete certainty, recommend the race to other runners.

Table 15.3 2019 Economic indicators of the Marathon Valencia in the City of Valencia (In Euros)

	2011	2012	2013	2014	2015	2016	2017	2018	2019
Total expenditure of the organizers	1,047,950	1,233,191	1,382,642	2,000,841	3,066,331	3,884,205	4,330,191	4,896,964	5,406,657
Total expenditure of the participants	1,422,650	5,938,903	8,044,108	10,410,944	17,346,649	13,692,022	20,403,415	17,952,872	22,803,199
Total impact on production	4,791,845	13,780,401	18,008,961	22,604,053	35,751,902	30,312,569	43,152,036	42,799,467	52,052,098
Total impact on income	1,871,684	4,261,713	5,439,659	6,818,068	10,634,389	9,508,163	13,029,947	13,333,898	15,877,835
Total impact on employment	51	140	186	257	408	350	431	429	524

Source: IVIE (2020, pp. 22-25)

Conclusion

The purpose of this study was to examine and evaluate the key success factors and milestones that might account for the evolution of a community city marathon race 40 years ago to situate the MVTA at the top of ranking of participants in city marathons in Spain, the fourth marathon in Europe, only after two of the world marathons majors such as London and Berlin, and not least Paris and the seventh at global level, after the six world majors. If the Flora London Marathon (renamed as Virgin Money London Marathon and more recently as the TCS London Marathon) took over 20 years to achieve its current stature as a world marathon major, the Valencia Marathon has come an amazingly longer way (40 years) since its first race in March 1981, coincidentally the same day as the first London Marathon, to become a second-order mega event.

The analysis carried out has allowed us to identify those factors that have contributed to the growth of the MVTA over the last ten years. Although the purpose of this study was not of a comparative nature, we have come to current competitive advantages of the MVTA against the six world's renowned marathons. Among them, we must refer the adoption of a mostly urban course, with its start-line and finishing-line of the MVTA in the City of Arts and Science Centre complex. This change has contributed to strengthening both the audiovisual spectacular nature of the race and not least, the level of satisfaction experienced by runners. Another key element in this process has been the decision to shift the celebration date of the race to autumn (November/December), which has allowed to separate it from the date of other major Spanish marathons, to enable people to enjoy a better weather condition and to place the race with a better alignment in the international marathons calendar.

With the arrival of the Foundation Trinidad Alfonso as the main sponsor to the race in 2013, the race has grown in relevance after incorporating some critical innovative factors along the way as well as the ongoing improvement to offer new products to enhance the runner experience; both factors could explain the success of the event. The latest factor has finally produced an extraordinary growth in terms of runners' participation, economic impact, and sport performance. The recognition of MVTA as "World Athletics Platinum Label" by World Athletics – the international governing body for athletics – is self-evidence. The factors mentioned above might be extremely relevant – as Wicker et al. (2012) identified in the German marathons – on the intention of runners to revisit Valencia and to the Valencia Marathon.

Our study allows us to point out some managerial implications about the characteristics of those sports events that could be considered most advantageous for host cities. A decade later after Valencia City Council's strategy to use large-scale cultural infrastructures and sport mega events, described by Rius-Ulldemolins and Gisbert (2019) as "The Calatrava Model", to promote the economic growth and to develop the tourist attraction, the MVTA EDP has remained the benchmark sport event in Valencia. The effects of the Grand Recession and the change in urban governance strategy promoted by new left-wing coalition since 2015 have contributed to abandon "The Calatrava Model". As the case of the city of Valencia shows, the urban development strategy has also had risks. To avoid what Müller (2015b) described as "the megaevent syndrome", Matheson (2012) recommends local authorities hosting regular small sport events which can be more beneficial for cities than hosting mega events, which are episodic and usually only seen once in a lifetime for host cities. On this issue, public investment in infrastructures and security is minimal as well as the cost related to sport facilities and accommodation for participants and organizers; issues that are common in our case study.

Parallel to the growth of the MVTA has favored the growth of local athletics and to promote the culture of running in the city of Valencia. Among others key decisions, it is worth noting the launching of an annual local circuit of races, the launching of a local circuit for local runners known as 5K Circuit Jardin del Turia or the platform Valencia City of Running, which brings together different races held in the city. The factors mentioned above show the potential of the MVTA to promote economic, tourist, social, sporting, and symbolic effects on the city of Valencia and their residents; case that might inspire other cities in South America and other parts of the world. In future studies, it might be relevant to explore the dynamic aspects of the key success factors of city marathons such as the case of MVTA, considering that other city marathons at national and international level can imitate or supersede those offered at the MVTA.

Acknowledgments

The authors would like to thank the Instituto Valenciano de Investigaciones Económicas (IVIE) for giving us permission to use their data on the impacts of the Marathon Valencia Trinidad Alfonso in the city of Valencia over the years as well as we really appreciate the comments from staff from the Abbott World Marathon Majors organization.

References

Abbott World Marathon Majors. (2020). *About us. Abbott World Marathon Majors are leading and growing a community of marathon runners around the globe.* https://www.worldmarathonmajors.com/about

Ajuntament de Valencia (1987). *La Valencia de los noventa. Una ciudad con futuro.* Ajuntament de Valencia.

Alemany-Hormaeche, M., Rejón-Guardia, F., & García-Sastre, M. A. (2019). Analysis and segmentation of sports events' participants: The marathon course in Palma de Mallorca. In A. Artal-Tur, M. Kozak, & N. Kozak (Eds.), *Tourist in tourist behavior. New products and experiences from Europe* (pp. 17–34). Springer.

Amendola, G. (1997). *La ciudad postmoderna.* Celeste Ediciones.

Bosch Reig, I. (2011). El Parque del Turia. Pulmón verde, deportivo y cultural de Valencia. In Ajuntament de Valencia (Ed.), I Congreso Europeo de Infraestructuras Deportivas *(1st European Conference on Sports Facilities)* (pp. 100–107). Ajuntament de Valencia.

Brunet, F. (1994). *Economy of the 1992 Olympic games.* Centre d' Estudies Olympics.

Cervera, L., Cerezo, R., Rosa, D., & Orts, E. (2011). Valencia 2010 Plan Estratégico del Deporte. In Ajuntament de Valencia (Ed.), I Congreso Europeo de Infraestructuras Deportivas *(1st European Conference on Sports Facilities)* (pp. 202–215). Ajuntament de Valencia.

Coleman, R. (2004). Flora London marathon 2000 –the economic legacy. *Journal of Hospitality and Tourism Management, 10,* 51–73.

Coleman, R., & Ramchandani, G. (2010). The hidden benefits of non-elite mass participation sports events: An economic perspective. *International Journal of Sports Marketing & Sponsorship, 12*(1), 19–31.

Del Romero Renau, L. (2010). Dos décadas de urbanismo-espectáculo en españa. Los grandes eventos Como motor de cambio urbano. *Boletín De La Asociación De Geógrafos Españoles, 53,* 309–327.

Del Romero Renau, L., & Trudelle, C. (2011). Mega events and urban conflicts in Valencia, Spain: Contesting the new urban modernity. *Urban Studies Research, 1,* 1–12.

Estelles-Miguel, S., Juarez Tarraga, A., Palmer Gato, M. E., & Albarracin Guillem, J. M. (2017). Municipal sport management: Practical application in the city of Valencia. In M. Peris-Ortiz, J. Álvarez-García, & M. Del Rio-Rama (Eds.), *Sports management as an emerging economic activity. Trends and best practices* (pp. 293–308). Springer.

Ferguson, K., & O'Connor, S. (2018). Sport event management. In D. Hassan (Ed.), *Managing sports business. An introduction* (2nd ed.) (pp. 561–588). Routledge.

Fickenscher, L. (2006). Marathon brings NYC $188 million. *Crain's New York Business.* New York, 22, 41, 1.

Fickenscher, L. (2011). Marathon makes big strides. *Crain's New York Business.* New York, 27, 42, 1.

Foster, G., O'Really, N., & Dávila, A. (2016). *Sports business management. Decision making around the globe.* Routledge.

Fox, D., Gouthro, M. B., Morakabati, Y., & Brackstone, J. (2014). *Doing event research: From theory to practice.* Routledge.

Fundación Deportiva Municipal de Valencia. (2011). *Plan estratégico del deporte de Valencia (Valencia strategic plan for sport).*

García-Vallejo, A., Albahari, A., Año-Sanz, V., & Garrido-Moreno, A. (2020). What's behind a marathon? Process management in sports running events. *Sustainability, 12*(15), 1–18.

Gholipour, H. F., Arjomandi, A., Marsiglio, S., & Foroughi, B. (2020). Is outstanding performance in sport events a driver of tourism? *Journal of Destination Marketing & Management, 18,* 100507.

Gibson, H., Kaplanidou, K., & Kang, J. (2012). Small-scale event sport tourism: A case study in sustainable tourism. *Sport Management Review, 15*(2), 160–170.

Gratton, C., & Henry, I. P. (Eds.) (2001). *Sport in the city. The role of sport in economic and social regeneration.* Routledge.

Gratton, C., Shibli, S., & Coleman, R. (2006). The economic impact of major sports events: A review of ten events in the UK. *The Sociological Review, 54*(S2), 41–58.

Hall, T., & Hubbard, P. (Eds.) (1998). *The entrepreneurial city. Geographics of politics, regime and representation.* John Wiley & Sons Ltd.

Harvey, D. (1990). *The Condition of Postmodernity.* Blackwell.

Heere, B., Wear, H., Jones, A., Breitbarth, T., Xing, X., Paramio Salcines, J., Yoshida, M., & Derom, I. (2019). Inducing destination images among international audiences: The differing effects of promoting sport events on the destination image of a city around the world. *Journal of Sport Management, 33*(6), 506–517.

Huang, H., Lunhua Mao, K., Wang, J., & Zhang, J. J. (2015). Assessing the relationships between image congruence, tourist satisfaction and intention to revisit in marathon tourism: The Shanghai international marathon. *International Journal of Sports Marketing &Sponsorship, 16*(4), 46–66.

Instituto Valenciano de Investigaciones Económicas (IVIE). (2017). *36 Maratón Valencia Trinidad Alfonso EDP 2016. Impacto Económico y Valoración de los Corredores*. IVIE. https://www.ivie.es/es_ES/ptproyecto/impacto-de-la-36-maraton-valencia-trinidad-alfonso/

IVIE. (2018). *37 Maratón Valencia Trinidad Alfonso EDP 2017. Impacto Económico y Valoración de los Corredores*. IVIE. https://www.ivie.es/es_ES/ptproyecto/impacto-de-la-37-maraton-trinidad-alfonso/

IVIE. (2019). *38 Maratón Valencia Trinidad Alfonso EDP 2018. Impacto Económico y Valoración de los Corredores*. IVIE. https://www.ivie.es/es_ES/maraton-valencia-2018-genera-37-euros-gasto-turistico-euro-invertido-organizacion/

IVIE. (2020). *39 Maratón Valencia Trinidad Alfonso EDP 2019. Impacto Económico y Valoración de los Corredores*. IVIE. https://www.ivie.es/es_ES/ptproyecto/impacto-economico-del-39-maraton-trinidad-alfonso-valencia/

Johnson, G., Whittington, R., Scholes, K., Angwin, D., & Regnér, P. (2017). *Exploring strategy. Text and cases* (11th ed.). Pearson.

Lastra, T. (1984). *Historia del Club Correcaminos*. https://www.correcaminos.org/wp-content/uploads/2019/05/Texto-historico-Toni-Lastra-enero1984.pdf

Llopis Goig, R. (Ed.) (2012). *Megaeventos deportivos. Perspectivas científicas y estudios de caso*. Editorial UOC.

Llopis Goig, R., & García Alcober, M. P. (2012). La America's Cup regresa a Europa. Impacto Económico de la 32ª America´s Cup en la sociedad anfitriona. In R. Llopis Goig (Ed.), *Megaeventos deportivos. Perspectivas científicas y estudios de* caso (pp. 155–174). Editorial UOC.

Martin, J., & Hall, J. (2020). The impact of the New York City marathon on hotel demand. *Economies, 8*(4), 89.

Matheson, V. (2012). Efectos de los principales megaeventos deportivos en las economías locales, regionales y nacionales. In R. Llopis Goig (Ed.), *Megaeventos deportivos. Perspectivas científicas y estudios de* caso (pp. 53–73). Editorial UOC.

Miller, R. (2012) Marathons. In *Sports marketing 2012* (pp. 422–423). Richard K. Miller & Associates.

Miller, R., & Washington, K. (2017). *Leisure business market research handbook 2017-2018* (6th ed.). Richard K. Miller & Associates.

Müller, M. (2015a). What makes an event a mega-event? Definitions and sizes. *Leisure Studies, 34*(6), 627–642.

Müller, M. (2015b). The mega-event syndrome: Why so much goes wrong in mega-event planning and what to do about it. *Journal of American Planning Association, 81*(1), 6–17.

New York Road Runners. (2020). *New York Road Runners 2018-2019 impact report*. https://www.nyrr.org/About

Newland, B. L. (2020). Designing the event experience. In T. J. Aicher, L. Newland, & A. L. Paule-Koba (Eds.), *Sport facility and event management* (pp. 125–145). Jones & Barnett Learning.

Paramio-Salcines, J. L. (2014). Sport and urban regeneration. In I. Henry, & L. Ko (Eds.), *Routledge handbook of sport policy* (pp. 275–288). Routledge.

Paramio-Salcines, J. L., Prieto, J., & Llopis-Goig, R. (2018) Managing sporting access and participation: An international perspective. In D. Hassan (Ed.) *Managing sport business: An introduction* (2nd ed.) (pp. 152–176). Routledge.

Paramio-Salcines, J. L., Ruiz Barquín, R., & Baena Arroyo, J. (2017). Identidad urbana y el turismo de eventos deportivos: El grand depart tour de francia 2015 (Identity of cities and event sport tourism: The grand depart tour de France 2015). *Cuadernos De Turismo, 40*(40), 489–520.

Parra-Camacho, D., Aguado, S., & Alguacil, M. (2021). El impacto social de un evento deportivo mediano recurrente: El caso del maratón de Valencia. *Cultura, Ciencia y Deporte, 16*(50), 553–562.

Parra-Camacho, D., Añó, V., Calabuig, F., & Ayora, D. (2016). Percepción de los residentes sobre el legado de la America's cup. *Cuadernos De Psicología Del Deporte, 16*(1), 325–338.

Paule-Koba, A. L. (2020). Bidding and planning for different events. In T. J. Aicher, B. L. Newland, & L. Paule-Koba (Eds.), *Sport facility and event management* (pp. 105–124). Jones & Barnett Learning.

Pedrosa Carrera, M. J. (2016). Zurich Maratón Sevilla 2015. La ciudad como objetivo (Zurich Seville City marathon. The city as a target). *Journal of Sports Economics & Management, 6*(2), 112–125.

Prytherch, D., & Boira-Maiques, J. V. (2009). City profile: Valencia. *Cities, 26*(2), 103–115.

Puig, N., Martínez del Castillo, J., & Apunt, G. (1985). Evolución de las campañas de deporte para todos en españa (1968-1983). *Revista De Investigación y Documentación Sobre Las Ciencias De La Educación Física y Del Deporte, 1*, 59–104.

Qiu, Y., Tiau, H., Zhou, W., Lin, Y., & Gao, J. (2020). 'Why do people commit to long distance running': Serious leisure qualities and leisure motivation of marathon runners. *Sport in Society, 23*(7), 1256–1277.

Rius-Ulldemolins, J., & Gisbert, V. (2019). The costs of putting Valencia on the map: The hidden side of regional entrepreneurialism, 'creative city' and strategic projects. *European Planning Studies, 27*(2), 377–395.

Rius-Ulldemolins, J., Hernández i Martí, G. M., & Torres, F. (2015). Urban development and cultural policy "White elephants": Barcelona and Valencia. *European Planning Studies, 24*(1), 61–75.

Roche, M. (2000). *Mega-events and modernity*. Routledge.

Roche, M. (2017). *Mega-events and social change*. Manchester University Press.

Salom Carrasco, J., & Pitarch Garrido, M. D. (2017). Análisis del impacto en el turismo de la estrategia de desarrollo urbano basado en megaproyectos. El caso de la ciudad de Valencia (analysis of the impact on tourism of the megaproject-based urban development strategy. The case of the City of Valencia). *Cuadernos De Turismo, 40*, 573–598.

Scheerder, J., Breedveld, K., & Borgers, J. (2015). Who is doing a run with the running boom? The growth and governance of one of Europe's most popular sport activities. In J. Scheerder, K. Breedveld, & J. Borgers (Eds.), *Running across Europe. The rise and size of one of the largest sport markets* (pp. 1–27). Palgrave Macmillan.

Schwarz, E. C., Westerbeek, H., Liu, D., Emery, P., & Turner, P. (Eds.) (2017). *Managing sport facilities and major events* (2nd ed.). Routledge.

Shipway, R., & Jones, I. (2008). The greatest suburban event. An insider's perspective on experience at the 2007 flora London marathon. *Journal of Sport & Tourism, 13*(1), 61–77.

Smith, A. (2012). *Events and urban regeneration. The strategic use of events to revitalise cities*. Routledge.

Statista. (2019). *Main marathons in Spain in 2019, by number of runners who finished the race*. Statista.

Suozzo, A. (2006). The Chicago Marathon. University of Illinois Press.

Thomson, A., Cuskelly, G., Toohey, K., Kennelly, M., Burton, P., & Fredline, L. (2019). Sport event legacy: A systematic quantitative review of literature. *Sport Management Review, 22*(3), 295–321.

Wicker, P., Hallman, K., & Zhang, J. J. (2012). What is influencing consumer expenditure and intention to revisit? An investigation of marathon events. *Journal of Sport & Tourism, 17*(3), 165–182.

World Athletics. (2021). Year's deepest fields gather for Valencia marathon and half marathon. https://www.worldathletics.org/competitions/world-athletics-label-road-races/news/valencia-marathon-and-half-marathon-preview-2

Yoshida, M., James, J. D., & Cronin, J. Jr. (2013). Sport event innovativeness: Conceptualization, measurement, and its impact on consumer behavior. *Sport Management Review, 16*(1), 68–84.

Zimbalist, A. (2015). *Circus maximus. The economic gamble behind hosting the Olympics and the World Cup*. Brooking Institution Press.

Appendix I

Selected list of key decisions that explain the evolution of the Valencia Marathon to a second-order Mega-Event

Greatest milestones in the history of Valencia Marathon

1979	Establishment of the *Club Sociedad Deportiva Correcaminos* (SDC)
1981	The first edition of the Valencia Marathon (Marathon Popular de Valencia)
1986	The Valencia Marathon incorporated into the Association of International Marathons and Distance Races (AIMS).
1988	Valencia is awarded to host the Spanish Marathon Championship (also in 1993 and 2000 editions)
1989	The Valencia Marathon adopts a new, mostly urban, course.
1995	The system of compensating finishers is established (also applied in the 1996 edition and abandoned in 1997)
2005	The creation of the popular Racing Circuit of Valencia.
2010	Paco Borao (President of the *Sociedad Deportiva Correcaminos* since 2005) becomes the president of AIMS. He has been reelected in 2014 and 2018.
2011	Approval of *The Valencia Strategic Plan for Sport*. The race date is moved to the fall and the 10K race is added to the event. The start and finish lines are moved to the Ciudad de las Artes y las Ciencias. Divina Pastora becomes the main sponsor of the event.
2013	After becoming a sponsor in 2012, the Fundación Trinidad Alfonso becomes the main sponsor of the event and contributes to building the race brand (MVTA).

2014	The City Council of Valencia and the Fundación Trinidad Alfonso create the Valencia City of running organization, which brings together different races held in the city (four of them holding "World Athletics certification").
2015	The launching of the 5K Circuito Jardin del Turia in the old riverbed of the Turia River
2016	Recognition of the marathon as Gold Label Road Race (World Athletics).
2020	Recognition of the marathon as Platinum Label Road Race (World Athletics). An unexpected issue as the health restrictions caused by the COVID-19 pandemic required a critical decision by the organizers. Consequently, the 40th edition of the 2020 MVTA was limited to elite-level runners only.

Source: Own elaboration based on different official sources

Chapter 16

Ecuador as a Destination for International Events

A Case Study of Oceanman in Manta

E. Su Jara-Pazmino

University of West Georgia, USA

Universidad San Francisco de Quito, Ecuador

Simon M. Pack

St. John's University, USA

Chapter Contents

Introduction	246
Sport Structures in Ecuador	247
Case Analysis: Oceanman Manta 2021	249
Background of the Case	249
The Event Organizer, Sara Palacios	249
The Oceanman Franchise	250
Oceanman in Manta, Ecuador, 2021	251
Sara Palacios, Event Organizer	251
Mario Alava, Athletic Director of Manta Municipality	254
Highlights from Traditional and Social Media Outlets	254
Conclusions and Managerial Perspectives	255
References	257

Introduction

Ecuador, a country of just over 17 million, is located on the northwest coast of South America (World Bank Group, 2018). The country gets its name from the Equator, which crosses just 26 km from the capital city of Quito. Ecuador is also well known for its Galapagos Islands, which inspired Charles Darwin's Theory of Evolution. With over 280,000 km², Ecuador is roughly the size of the state of Colorado in the United States. The countries that border Ecuador are Colombia to the north, Peru to the south and east, while the Pacific Ocean lies to the west. As previously mentioned, one of the most notable areas is the province that includes the Pacific archipelago of the Galapagos Islands.

Ecuador has three different regions: the coastal plain, the Sierra inter-Andean central highlands, and the Amazon jungle. The western coastal area borders the

DOI: 10.4324/9781003388050-19

Pacific Ocean and it is estimated that 98% of the native forest has been eliminated in favor of cattle ranching and other agricultural production including banana, cacao, and coffee plantations, which have been the main exporting products for decades. The forest fragments that still survive include tropical dry forest, tropical wet forest, tropical moist evergreen forest, premontane cloud forest, and mangrove forest. These forest remnants are considered the most endangered tropical forests in the world. The main cities on the coast are Guayaquil and Manta. Guayaquil is the biggest city with nearly 2 million residents and it is home to the chief port in the country. The Guayas River is navigable for the greater part of its course and a traditional open water competition has been organized in this river since 1923 in celebration of the city's independence.

On the other hand, Manta is one of the most important cities for business and tourism on the Pacific Coast of Ecuador. With a population of around 300,000, Manta has been exploding with new growth recently. Manta has an international airport and an important military base, which was used by the US Air Force from 1999 to 2009. Given the city's location along the Pacific Coast of Ecuador, water sports and tourism are very significant to the local economy. Surfing in Ecuador is very popular because of a year-round steady climate. Manta was the host city for the 2004 Bodyboarding World Cup and the 2018 South American Windsurfing Championships. Manta also has some of South America's most breathtaking beaches including *El Murcielago, Barbasquillo, Santa Marianita,* and *San Lorenzo.*

Each of Ecuador's regions has different factors that affect its climate. The first part of the year is generally the wet season and the second half of the year is the relatively dry season. Both the Coast and Amazon are warm, with small temperature variations among the seasons, and more differences between day and night. The average daytime high temperatures range from 84 to 91°F (29–33°C) with nighttime lows falling between 68 and 75°F (20–24°C). Throughout Ecuador, variation in rainfall primarily determines seasons.

Ecuador has also attracted immigrants from Colombia and Peru after Ecuador adopted the US dollar as its national currency in 2000. Ecuador is the eighth largest economy in Latin America with major exports such as crude oil and derivatives, shrimp, bananas, coffee, cut flowers, cocoa to destinations such as the United States, Chile, Peru, Colombia, and Russia. It is important to note that the service sector accounts for about half of Ecuador's gross domestic product, with transportation and tourism making up the bulk of the industry. Tourism has become an economic mainstay for Ecuador and, as such, has created an enormous economic potential for the country and for the inclusion of sporting events as a byproduct of the tourism industry.

Sport Structures in Ecuador

Government involvement in sport in Ecuador follows the Latin American regional model, where government and policy has been justified under three rationales: (1) sport as a vehicle to build social cohesion, (2) economic development, and

(3) fostering international cooperation (Bravo et al., 2016). Grix and Carmichael (2012) noted that the government allocates large sums of money because sport is seen intrinsically as a benefit for all of society. It is believed that elite athletes will inspire and contribute toward an increase in the number of participants involved in sport and physical activity, which will help create a farm system of future elite athletes. Government involvement in and subsidization of sport in Latin America occurs on a large scale but this involvement has also created complex bureaucracies that operate at national, state, and local levels (Bravo et al., 2016). Government has a profound understanding of the opportunities associated with hosting a wide array of medium-sized sporting events, especially as a means to boost tourism.

In Ecuador, as is the case in much of Latin America, the "association" or "club" model of governance is the predominant feature and most operate as non-profit civil associations that often require some form of government support (Bravo et al., 2016). Therefore, the government in Ecuador has been deeply involved in the finance, infrastructure, governance, and management of the sport industry through the creation of governmental agencies such as the Ministry of Sport, which functions under the following four pillars: (1) quality of service, (2) leisure, (3) networks, and (4) prevention. At the heart of quality of service, the government aims to promote elite athletes and the professionalization of sport. From the leisure perspective, the government intends to promote the use of leisure time for exercise with the purpose of improving quality of life, multiculturalism, and inclusion for all citizens. As the previous two areas are refined and formalized, the government must endeavor to network and encourage the association athletes to participate in competitive teams and with recreational purposes. Lastly, the government has a duty to promote sport to prevent a multitude of ailments, which result from a sedentary life style. While the government's support is evident in the sport industry in Ecuador, private sector involvement and support remains irregular.

Soccer, also known as most in Latin America as "fútbol", is Ecuador's national sport. The national team has enjoyed success in regional competitions and in the World Cup. Other popular sports are basketball, volleyball, ecua-volley (a variant of volleyball played in Ecuador), track and field, weight lifting, and swimming. Other traditional sports include bullfighting, handball, fishing, and mountaineering. Ecuador's Olympic participation began at the 1924 Summer Games in Paris and its first Olympic medal was Jefferson Perez's gold from the 1996 Games in the 20 km walk. Most recently, Ecuador has successfully hosted international competitions such as the 2014 Adventure Race World Championship, the Huairasinchi Adventure Race (an endurance event), the 2016 Galapagos CAMTRI Sprint Triathlon American Cup, the Ironman 70.3 Ecuador from 2015 to 2019, and the Oceanman Manta 2021 open water swimming competition. These events have successfully promoted sport tourism in Ecuador and have shown the local government that international sport events produce a positive economic impact for the local community. It is undeniable that COVID-19 has affected all industries around the world and in Ecuador, there were three different states of emergency declarations with restrictions on movement, social gatherings, and travel. These

Ecuador as a Destination for International Events 249

declarations spanned the period from March 2020 to May 2021. The pandemic has worsened the economic and political situation in Ecuador; however, the natural resources that the country provides are favorable for sport competitions and remain unique to the region.

Case Analysis: Oceanman Manta 2021

Due to the exploratory nature of this case study on the first Oceanman hosted in Manta, Ecuador, the researchers analyzed information from multiple sources. An integrative interpretation of information (Ghauri & Gronhaug, 2005) from semi-structured interviews with the event organizers, local authorities, traditional and social media data, and the information from the Oceanman organization were all sources of data for this case study. The leading research question of this case study relates to the factors that influenced the event manager's decision-making process while planning and executing the Oceanman in Manta, Ecuador, for the first time. Based on this inquiry, it is important to mention the background of the two entities in charge of organizing this international event, Sara Palacios, the local event organizer, and the Oceanman organization.

Background of the Case

The Event Organizer, Sara Palacios

A native of Quito, Ecuador, Sara Palacios, also known as "Sara de Mar" participated in competitive swimming from a young age in local and national competitions. As she grew older, she learned about the open water competitions, and in 2003, she represented Ecuador in the South American Open Water Joao Pessoa. In 2018, Sara became the first South American woman to swim across the English Channel. In order to understand the importance of this event, in comparison more people have summited Mount Everest than finished the English Channel swim (Fox-Sowell, 2018). Sara went on to complete the Triple Crown of Open Water Swimming, which is a marathon swimming challenge consisting of three historically important swims: The English Channel, 20.5 miles between England and France; the Catalina Channel, 20 miles between Santa Catalina Island and the California mainland; and the Swim Around Manhattan, 28.5 miles circumnavigating the Manhattan Island in New York City. The World Open Water Swimming Association (WOWSA) has certified Sara's many accomplishments. Sara's next challenge is the Moloka'i Channel as part of the Oceans Seven, which is a marathon swimming challenge consisting of seven open water channel swims and is the equivalent of the Seven Summits mountaineering challenge. It includes the North Channel, the Cook Strait, the Moloka'i Channel, the English Channel, the Catalina Channel, the Tsugaru Strait, and the Strait of Gibraltar. In addition to her athletic pursuits in the water, Sara is owner of Aguas Abiertas Ecuador (AAE), a company that serves to increase the awareness of open water swimming and to

250 E.S. Jara-Pazmino and S.M. Pack

promote high-quality open water competitions in Ecuador. Sara and AAE's CEO, Diego Egas, decided to create a partnership with the Spanish Oceanman franchise in order to host the first Oceanman in Ecuador in 2021.

The Oceanman Franchise

Oceanman started in 2015 as the first global open water swimming race franchise. The franchise has expanded in Europe and America, reaching more than 1,000 swimmers per event. This is the only global international Open Water Swimming event series. Oceanman is a premier event brand with high-quality standards in terms of competing distances, image, communication and media, competition rules and regulations, and safety measures. The values that lead the franchise are strength, adaptation, courage, and resistance – all the qualities that athletes need to be successful in this type of race. An important part of the athlete experience is to create engagement before, during, and after the event. The communication campaign focused on the destination, including launch announcement, workshops, race ambassadors, and celebrity contributors. The events also include exclusive, quality, informative, and entertaining content through videos that go beyond the race itself. Storytelling that shows Oceanman understands the competitors and is well-positioned to accompany them along the way. The interviews with sport personalities and endorsers create user response and engagement with the audience. The social media communication channels, Facebook, Instagram, Twitter, and YouTube, show strong metrics that provide Oceanman with an important platform (Table 16.1).

The main target market for the Oceanman swimming competitions are athletes between the ages of 30 and 45 followed by those in their 20s. There is a 10% participation rate for those between the ages of 15 and 19 and a 5% rate for those 45 and older. Participants of the Oceanman events are mostly in the middle socioeconomic class with a small percent in the upper class. The structure of the event presents five distances which are Sprint (1–2 km), Half Oceanman (3–5 km), Oceanman (6–14 km), Oceankids (500–800 m), and Oceanteam (3 × 500 m–3 × 1,500 m).

Table 16.1 Social Media – Metrics of Oceanman Franchise in May 2021

Instagram	Facebook	YouTube	Twitter
• 14K followers – 100% organic • 2,000 likes range per post • Reach of over 6,000 per week • Average weekly impact 70.000	• 101K followers – 98% organic • 240 M Video Views • 240K range per post on FB • 33K interaction in a post • Total reach over 800,000 people • 95% of reach "non-followers"	• 1.3 K Subscribers • 203,606 views	• 3,290 Followers • 3,500 Tweets

Competitors are allowed to wear a wetsuit only in water that is below 75 degrees Fahrenheit. The competitors are organized among 33 categories based on age, gender, and one for those with various disabilities. There were 23 competitions scheduled in 2021, among which 5 were hosted in Europe, 4 in the Americas, and 14 in the Middle East. The event hosted in Manta is the first time the event was hosted in Ecuador.

Oceanman in Manta, Ecuador, 2021

In order to gain a deeper understanding of the factors that influenced the decision-making process of event manager Sara Palacios, in the planning and executing of the Oceanman Manta 2021, the researchers used a qualitative research method. As detailed by Yin (2003), "an exploratory case study is an empirical inquiry that investigates a contemporary phenomenon within its real-life context, especially when the boundaries between phenomenon and context are not clearly evident" (p. 13). In addition, Yin mentioned that a case study relies on multiple sources of evidence, with data needing to converge in a triangulating fashion. In this case study, the researchers performed semi-structured interviews with the event organizer, Sara Palacios, and a representative from the Manta local government, Mario Alava. Obtaining information from these two different stakeholders' perspectives provided the researchers with important information that outlines Ecuador's potential to become an international sport event destination. In addition to the interviews, the researchers also analyzed the event information from the Oceanman organization and publications from traditional and social media sources.

Sara Palacios, Event Organizer

During the interview, Palacios pointed out that there is a lack of knowledge about open water swimming competitions in the country and the production of events of this kind. In order to prepare for the crossing of the English Channel, Sara mentioned that she had to travel to Peru and Bolivia in order to participate in open water competitions. There is only one other Ecuadorian swimmer, Galo Yepez, that has crossed the English Channel in 1997, and 21 years later, Sara was the second Ecuadorian to achieve this impressive feat.

While preparing for her open water swimming competitions, Palacios identified an opportunity to host open water competitions in Ecuador. There are impressive natural resources along the coast and lakes in Ecuador, however, there is a lack of sport management professionals that can plan and execute high-quality events. Another positive factor that makes Ecuador an ideal destination for International sporting events is the use of the US dollar as the official currency, which makes it easier for all stakeholders to maintain a commercial exchange. The need to organize these kinds of events drove Palacios to search for a brand that would support her goal to promote and organize swimming marathon events. As a result of her search, she found the Spanish franchise Oceanman that is already established in

Europe, Asia, and Africa. On the other hand, the franchise was looking to expand to new locations in Americas, especially to tourist destinations that would motivate the Oceanman participants to compete in various events during the year. Ecuador fits the profile and Manta provides the infrastructure requirements in order to host the first Oceanman in Latin America.

The partnership was established and the date was set for May 2020 but unfortunately, COVID-19 forced the postponement of the event to 2021. Oceanman Manta 2021 was to be a leader in the production of events in the Americas with Oceanman competitions scheduled for 2022 in destinations such as Chile, Colombia, Argentina, and the United States. Palacios mentioned, that based on the current economic indicators in Ecuador, the possibility to host an international event is not favorable. Latin America has been known for adverse conditions for the promotion of sport and entertainment events including violence and corruption, political unrest, and market size and population purchasing power. Sara Palacios mentioned, "If we go by the book we would never promote any sporting event like this in Ecuador. However, we live here and that is our reality. Those are the cards that we have been dealt, and it is not fair that big sporting and entertainment events have not been able to be hosted here in Ecuador". When planning and executing the event Sara focused on the opportunities that the country offered and prepared a contingency plan against foreseeable risks.

The lack of open water swimming events challenged Palacios to plan and execute sporting events in this discipline. Her main goal, as the event organizer, is to produce high-quality events in Ecuador. As a secondary goal, Palacios seeks to educate athletes and fans on the ins and outs of marathon swimming. In reference to the type of competition that Sara wants to promote she mentioned, "We want to promote the athlete experience where the event will provide top customer service, coaching clinics, speakers, and other elements to produce a top experience". The athlete experience seeks to create a community around the competition and the sport. Past participants would be able to motivate the participation of more athletes in future Oceanman competitions.

The goal is to have an annual Oceanman competition in Ecuador. In the first edition, the majority of participants are locals and about 10% of participants are international. There were 500 registered participants, which for the first edition of any Oceanman competition is a great number. The goal is to increase the number to 1,000 participants in the future, which would be similar to other Oceanman competitions in Mexico and Italy. Palacios stated, "the idea is to challenge the participants to compete every year and achieve personal goals, in addition to motivating them to participate in other destinations of the Oceanman as well". Currently, the other open water swimming competitions are: (1) Travesia San Vicente Bahia, a 2 km distance and an average number of 400 participants, (2) Lago San Pablo, a 4 km race which is the most traditional race in Ecuador and has about 180 participants, and (3) Cuicocha, which has a lower temperature and usually hosts less than 100 participants. The event that sets a high bar for Oceanman is the Ironman which is not a marathon swim event, however, it serves as a reference for a high-quality sporting event that serves close to 2,000 participants.

Palacio's plan is to promote a yearly event at least for 5 years. She identified the majority of athletes participating in the first edition are locals, which shows that there is a good market to put on this event. The bulk of the athletes are registered for the short distance, 2 km race. Sara mentioned, "we will encourage them to participate next year in the 5km race and the following year in the 10km race. We also lost about 10% of our international participants due to COVID, however we remain positive and expect them to come for next year's event". Oceanman has set up various races in amazing destinations so the participants that traveled to Mexico this year, might be motivated to travel to Ecuador next year. In her attempt to educate athletes and fans about marathon swimming, Palacios commented, "I am finishing an Open Water Coaching course and I would like to guide women and men to cross the English Channel. I did not have a guide in my journey, I had to learn everything from zero". At the moment, Diego Egas, the CEO of AAE and who is responsible for all the logistics involved in the races, has learned and knows more about Open Water races than anybody in the country. Therefore, AAE has the "know-how" and they want to share that knowledge with more athletes competing in the sport.

In the decision-making process of finding a host city for the event, Palacios and Egas searched various cities in Ecuador, however, Manta was the only city that had all the franchise requirements in regard to hotel capacity and conference facilities. Manta is seeking to be known as the Sports Capital of Ecuador and Latin America. The local municipality is committed to providing support to private organizations such as AAE and the Oceanman organization to put on successful international sporting events, which bring positive economic impact to the city.

Private, corporate sponsorships in Ecuador are very difficult to obtain, usually driven by personal connections. The lack of knowledge about the sport and the event creates an event more difficult scenario to help obtain the support and the trust necessary to establish sponsorships. A lot of companies do not want to risk investments in new events or new athletes. They want to have evidence of their success before they compromise their resources. In an effort to secure more sponsorships for these kinds of events in the future, Palacios is eager to analyze the economic impact study done by the local municipality as well as the handling of social media outlets that would show private corporations the potential benefits of sponsoring an Oceanman event. In the area of marketing, the Oceanman franchise establishes a brand manual, which outlines the logo usage and general do's and don'ts of hosting the event. Requirements include a press conference before the event, high-quality pictures from the event, and other information for future promotion. Nevertheless, AAE has a lot of freedom to establish their own strategy and is responsible for handling social media outlets and also coordinating the information from the official webpage with Oceanman. Additionally, Palacios plans to take advantage of the natural resources of Ecuador, the coast, lakes, and rivers, and produce more events in an economically sustainable way. Palacios would like

Mario Alava, Athletic Director of Manta Municipality

The Municipality of Manta has been guided by Athletic Director Mario Alava since the beginning of 2019. During the interview with Alava, he mentioned, "our action plan is based on two main goals, the first is to use sports as a tool to transform society". He mentioned that the municipality will not invest in training elite athletes, but on the other hand, the budget has been distributed to various projects targeting at-risk youth, older adults, and people with disabilities. Starting in 2019, the public policy for the municipality of Manta was to focus on changing the current situation of many youth which are being affected by obesity, drugs, gang violence, and domestic violence.

For the second goal, Alava commented, "we also want to attract sporting events to the city. We identify the positive economic impact that sport events bring to the city of Manta, not only for the area of sports but also for tourism, restaurants, hotels, and other local businesses". He mentioned that in the past the city successfully hosted international events such as Ironman Ecuador 70.3, as well as the Gran Fondo New York (GFNY). Besides these international competitions, Alava mentioned that they are also hosting events in surfing, boxing, triathlon, and many other sports. The Municipality of Manta and its public administrators identified a great opportunity in supporting private organizations to promote big sporting events. Alava commented, "we have all the necessary infrastructure, an airport, hotel system, and transportation. We also conducted economic impact studies that show the positive impact that hosting sporting events has for our city's economy". In order to encourage more private organizations to promote events in Manta, the Athletic Department of the Municipality of Manta has created an effective and efficient process for collaboration with permits and other regulations that private organizations have to approve before executing their event. Alava commented that they seek to maintain this level of public policy as they attempt to transform Manta into the Sport Capital of Latin America. The municipality has worked toward this goal since 2019 and they also had to face big challenges during COVID-19, however at the moment, they feel confident that their process will continue to bring successful sporting events to the city of Manta.

Highlights from Traditional and Social Media Outlets

According to the Gran Fondo de New York, Manta is a city considered "The Gateway of the Pacific", characterized by providing the best experience of nature, beaches, adventure sports, and nightlife. It is the first tourist, maritime, and fishing port of Ecuador of great importance for Ecuadorian foreign trade. Manta has a tourist charm, for its magnificent beaches, located in the heart of the city. It is important to notice that the message of Oceanman is not just about competition but also about creating and contributing to a community. Pablo Verdu, writer for El Mundo, points out that Fermin Egido, director of the Oceanman sport franchise, identified the need to mix sport, adventure, and tourism as one of the keys to success. Egido mentioned, "we take swimmers to idyllic and exotic places where a person cannot swim alone. It is not just about doing exercise in one of the most beautiful places in the world, additionally it should be a cultural experience due to the activities that are taking place parallel to the competition. Egido explained that Oceanman is already a community that has decided to use its free time traveling and swimming.

It is important to note that Oceanman Manta had to be postponed for almost a year due to COVID-19. Nevertheless, Palacios and Egas were able to maintain the interest and the excitement for all the participants through a press conference to establish new dates for the event. Additionally, the newly created Oceanman Ecuador's social media attracted thousands of Instagram followers, as well as others to the various social media platforms such as Facebook and Twitter. Based on the success of Oceanman Manta in 2021, the event has been renewed for 2022 and the hopes of the organizers is that it will be an annual stop on the Oceanman circuit.

Conclusions and Managerial Perspectives

After analyzing the information previously presented in the case study of the first edition of the Oceanman in Manta, Ecuador, we identified the factors that influenced the event manager's decision-making process. Palacios set out to promote open water swimming competitions in Ecuador as well as to educate the stakeholders of the sporting event on how to provide a high-quality event experience for the participants. Her vision was in spite of the economic and social indicators obtained after a Strengths, Weaknesses, Opportunities, and Threats (SWOT) analysis of the country which outlined many challenges that the event managers would have to face in order to produce a high-quality event. The event managers also focused on the opportunities outlined in the previous analysis, the natural resources that Ecuador offers such as amazing beaches, lakes, rivers, temperate weather conditions, and a navigable local currency. Figure 16.1 illustrates the process that event manager Sara Palacios followed in order to produce the Oceanman Manta 2021.

Event managers also identified the lack of maturity in the market and the need to seek support from a bigger organization in order to secure the "know-how" of event production. After securing the support from an internationally successful brand such as Oceanman, then the event organizers sought the support from the local government. It is not typical in South American cities to have an established process to support the production of sporting events. However, Manta and the local municipal administrators proved to be poised and ready to support a public-private collaboration to host a high-quality sport event. Based on previous experience, the local municipality seeks to attract private organizations that will produce

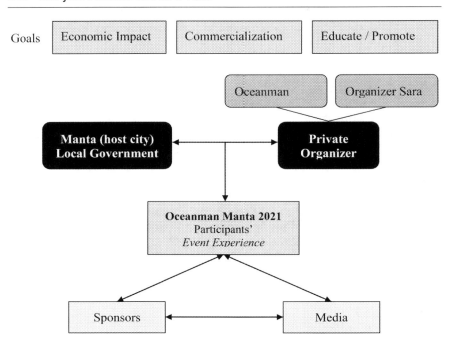

Figure 16.1 Functional Structure for the Organization of Oceanman Manta 2021.

international sport events which in turn will bring positive economic impact to the city of Manta.

It is important to mention that the goals from the franchise and the local government aligned in obtaining economic benefit as well as promoting tourism. The commercialization of sport is widely documented and Mark McCormack defined it in the "Golden Triangle" (Futterman, 2016). McCormack, the owner and former chief executive of International Management Group (IMG), was the first to realize that within the golden triangle of sport, sponsorships, and media lay vast wealth, just waiting to be tapped. Based on the data collected for this case study, the researchers identified the lack of sponsorships and a weak media impact of the Oceanman Manta 2021. It is understandable that the media content available to promote the event was very limited since this was the first edition and therefore moving forward into the second edition of the Oceanman Manta, it is imperative to strengthen the impact that the event has in traditional media and social media in order to increase the chances of getting better support from sponsors. Once again, we can prove that the "Golden Triangle" is the best way to commercialize and monetize a sport event. Future research should focus on strategies to increase the media impact of the event in 2022 and beyond and for the growth of similar events in the Manta and other parts of Ecuador in the future based on this model of public-private partnership and cooperation.

References

Bravo, G., Lopez de D'Amico, R., & Parrish, C. (2016). *Sport in Latin America: Policy, organization, management*. Routledge, Taylor & Francis Group. https://doi.org/10.4324/9781315797649

Fox-Sowell, S. (2018). The Mount Everest of Open Water Swims. News @ Northeastern. Retrieved from https://news.northeastern.edu/2018/07/25/the-mount-everest-of-open-water-swims/

Futterman, M. (2016). *Players: The story of sports and money, and the visionaries who fought to create a revolution*. Simon and Schuster.

Ghauri, P., & Gronhaug, K. (2005). *Research methods in business studies: A practical guide*. Pearson.

Grix, J., & Carmichael, F. (2012). Why do governments invest in elite sport? A polemic. *International Journal of Sport Policy*, 4(1), 73–90. https//doi.org/10.1080/19406940.2011.627358

World Bank Group. (2018). Ecuador Systematic Country Diagnostic. World Bank, Washington, DC. Retrieved from http://hdl.handle.net/10986/30052

Yin, R. K. (2003). *Case study research: Design and methods* (3rd ed.). Sage.

Chapter 17

Sport Events as a Catalyst for Economic, Sociocultural, Tourism and Environmental Sustainability in Portugal

Mário Coelho Teixeira

University of Évora, Portugal
Center for Advanced Studies in Management and Economics (CEFAGE)

Agamenon Carvalho Júnior

University of Évora, Portugal

André Dionísio Sesinando

University of Évora, Portugal

Chapter Contents

Introduction	258
Theoretical Background	260
Method	261
Results and Discussion	263
Background Characteristics	263
Consumption Behaviour	266
Environmental Analyses	268
Hypothesis Validation	269
Conclusion	269
References	271

Introduction

Sport is a cultural manifestation with enormous potential in bringing people, cultures and nations closer together (García-Fernández et al., 2022), either by stimulating sociability or by conveying a sense of identity, of belonging, of being part of and inclusion (Reis et al., 2022). Considering this premise on the importance of sport as a driving factor for societies in the most diverse dimensions (Teixeira & Ribeiro, 2016), this study aims to analyse and assess the possible impacts associated with the holding of a high-profile sport event in the city of Lisbon, the Portuguese capital, in relation to economic, sociocultural and environmental sustainability development, while trying to understand its direct interaction with the

DOI: 10.4324/9781003388050-20

promotion of local tourism and socioeconomic development in the region where the event takes place.

The hosting of sports events worldwide has grown substantially in the last decade (Vassiliadis et al., 2021), not only leveraged greater tourist flows but also because citizens are increasingly open and awake to the need to adopt more active and healthy habits of regular sports practice (Figueira & Teixeira, 2020). However, there is an urgent need to study the potential of this type of event that brings together thousands of participants to not only promote sport and sports practice but also to take the opportunity to boost local tourism and economic activity (Barandela et al., 2018; Mortazavi, 2021; Pereira et al., 2015). The sustained management of sport requires more and more qualified professionals in sport management (Sesinando & Teixeira, 2021; Teixeira et al., 2022), to better understand if in fact this type of events produces direct effects on local and national tourism and cultural promotion, while assessing its potentiality to generate greater interest in participating not only for the sports aspect but also in a sustainable and environmentally friendly tourism and cultural aspect (Djaballah et al., 2015; Gholipour et al., 2020).

In this sense, we have designed an investigation aimed to understand and explore the 4th edition of the Half Marathon of the Discoveries in Lisbon (Portugal) in relation to its economic, sociocultural and sustainability potential and impact. The data was collected using a questionnaire survey directed at participants of the event and allowed the analysis of several indicators. After analysing the answers, it was possible to validate a total of 590 answers. This study is divided into five parts, the first part being related to the introduction, objectives and hypotheses of the study. The second part related to the literature review, where the existing state-of-the-art is addressed in general terms. The third part related to the research methodology, which contains information on the sample, techniques and procedures used, as well as the structure of the questionnaire. The fourth part related to the presentation, analysis and discussion of results. Finally, the fifth part of the work corresponds to the main conclusions of the study, as well as some of its limitations and future suggestions, ending with the references used in the preparation and support of this research.

Sport, in its multiple aspects, has been considered in recent decades as a very important factor in the development of societies in general (Sesinando et al., 2022; Teixeira, 2019), and as an enabler of local, regional or even national economic and social development (Sesinando et al., 2023; Taks et al., 2014). The sports product presents increasing value and attractiveness as a tourist factor of interest (Rojas-Méndez et al., 2019), and as such, this study aimed to analyse a sport event held in the city of Lisbon, the capital of Portugal, to better understand the possible economic, social and sustainability impacts as the main objective of the study. On the other hand, and no less importantly, it is also the aim of the research to specifically analyse and identify the direct impacts on local development, while trying to understand the added value for the sustainable development of local tourism, based on the opinion of the national and international participants themselves present at this event. To find concrete answers that help us understand the phenomenon under study, as well as the proposed objectives, four hypotheses were defined with the purpose of assessing some of the variables under investigation. The hypotheses of this study are:

H_1 – The participation of national and international citizens in the event enhances the local economic impact on the city of Lisbon;

H_2 – It is possible to verify the loyalty of the national and international participants to the event because of their participation in previous editions;

H_3 – The event under study presents a recurrent growth rate in number of participants when compared with previous editions;

H_4 – There is an explicit concern of the organisation responsible for the event with the environment, adopting concrete measures of preservation and environmental responsibility during the event.

Theoretical Background

According to Dionisio (2009), "the importance of sport in modern societies has grown significantly in recent decades, both through the increase of its practice and the increase of its demand as a show, live or through the media". Following the same line, Teixeira (2009, p. 24), states that "while politics, religion, nationality and culture divide people, sport unites individuals, offering a learning of positive values such as teamwork, solidarity and accountability". The sport events, similarly, to other types of events, are characterised for being an event duly organised by a responsible entity, which may occur in the most diverse contexts and in the most diverse aspects, in which the sport component serves as a basis for the whole event, i.e., there is the effective practice of a certain modality and/or modalities as a purpose of its realisation/organisation. According to Madeira et al. (2007, p. 27), a sport event can be characterised according to its "intangibility, inseparability, variability and perdurability", i.e., "events are essentially subjective experiences, difficult to measure, where practitioners and spectators are an integral part of the event". These types of events traditionally generate high participation rates, are held in specific locations depending on their purpose and can be designated as small, medium and large or even mega-events depending on the number of participants taking part (Vassiliadis et al., 2021).

Quilende (2018) states that the typology of events is defined according to the nature of the activities that are carried out, i.e., they can be sport, cultural, social, ecological, leisure, entertainment, among others (Vassiliadis et al., 2021). According to Madeira et al. (2007, pp. 19–20), "events may be classified according to size and scale (…) being the most common categories the mega-events, branded events and large-scale events". These may also be classified according to the specific sector in which they are inserted and may be public, sporting or touristic events. Events may also be characterised according to the place where they are held, i.e., they may be local, regional, national or global (international). Several authors have different ways of distinguishing and characterising event typology but broadly speaking, the vast majority shares this general view on event typology.

The event under study held its first edition in 2013, in the city of Lisbon and consists of an urban running event with three different routes, i.e., participants can choose the 21 km or 10 km running event and can also choose the 5 km walking option. The event takes place as already mentioned in the city of Lisbon, but it has a particularity that distinguishes it from the others in that it is closely linked not only to the history of Portugal but also by the route that allows participants to run a route in the middle of the historical area of the city, while passing by monuments, statues and historical icons of Portugal. This is an event with a competitive edge, but also a family event, thus allowing families or groups of friends to participate without having to have a merely competitive spirit. Lisbon City Hall has been one of the main partners of the event, which, right from its first edition, earned the designation of "Quality Road Race" event with five stars awarded by the Running for all European Athletics organisation.

The definition of tourism, according to several authors, can be translated as an activity carried out in periods in which one or more individuals are absent from their place of residence, and may have several motivations such as business, leisure or participation in sociocultural activities. As Melo (2019, p. 244) states, according to the World Tourism Organization, tourism is of such relevance that it "acts as a driver for the socio-economic development of nations worldwide and is a major source of wealth for developing countries". In the same direction, Marujo and Carvalho (2010), citing Marujo (2008), state that "tourism is currently one of the most important phenomena from the political, economic, environmental and socio-cultural point of view. It is no longer seen solely as a synonym for leisure and has come to assume a role as a social agent in the societies in which it develops".

Melo (2019, p. 252), citing Weed and Bull (2009), refers "sports tourism is a social, economic and cultural phenomenon arising from the unique interaction between activities, people and places". According to the same author (p. 252), now quoting Hinch and Higham (2004), they "define sport tourism as sport-based travel, out of one's place of residence, for a limited period, where sport is characterised by a unique set of rules, where competition is related to physical skills and playful nature". Carvalho and Lourenço (2009, p. 125) state that "sports tourism does not emerge from any rupture with sport or tourism, but from a multidisciplinary methodological approach between these two phenomena, (…) what is happening is that the sport phenomenon has grown in a sense that has made sport need to use the services and knowledge of tourism". The participation of tourists in sports activities or contexts can also be grouped into the following typology: sports tourism, sports show tourism and other sports tourism contexts (Carvalho & Lourenço, 2009).

Method

This section presents the universe and sample under study, as well as the methods and techniques used in data processing, the procedures for data collection and the type of instrument used, and its structure. The Half Marathon of the Discoveries in

Lisbon, which served the purpose of this research, took place in Portugal in 2016 and registered a total number of 5,774 people enrolled. However, a total of 5,307 people participated thus representing the universe of the study. In this sense, and once the universe under study was constituted, 2,771 questionnaires were applied, corresponding to a total of 52.0% of the effective participants and which were divided by type of participation, that is, 959 participants in the 10 km race, 2,638 participants in the main 21 km race and 1,710 participants in the 5 km walking race. In total, and after applying the instrument for data collection, we obtained 590 validated responses, i.e., 21.3% of the total sample.

The study followed a deductive approach, in which the analysis and interpretation of the data are of a descriptive quantitative nature, and data of primary origin was thus collected. Considering the size of the sample under study and the possible difficulty in collecting data in this type of event, we decided that the best solution would be to use a mixed type of questionnaire, since its structure includes open response and multiple-choice questions, with a total of 37 questions, 8 open responses and 29 multiple choices. The instrument was structured based on the methodology used in an international research project conducted within the scope of the International Research Network in Sport Tourism (IRNIST) organisation and made available via Google Forms platform. The IRNIST project aims to deepen knowledge and analysis of sustainability and the study of possible economic, sociocultural and environmental impacts of sport events.

Considering that the main objective of this research focuses on the analysis and observation of the possible impacts of a major sport event in the city of Lisbon in the economic, sociocultural and environmental dimensions and to obtain rigorous data that would allow us to have a broad statistical spectrum, the questionnaire survey used was directed to all participants of the event. During the design phase of the research model, we realised that to evaluate the cause-effect relationship, it would be necessary to survey and collect information from the main stakeholders to ascertain the real contribution to local economic development and impact through the holding of a sport event. In this sense, the questionnaire is divided into five parts, in which 37 questions were structured, as previously mentioned. The first part of the questionnaire corresponds to the sociodemographic variables, which allowed characterising the sample under study, i.e., variables such as gender, age, nationality, among others. Then, the second part is related to information about the participants' place of residence and travel distance to the event, the way they travelled and participation in previous editions. The third part concerns the social component, i.e., if the participants were alone or accompanied and the type of existing kinship, and if there was the need to stay overnight in the region of the event (Lisbon) due to participation in the event. The fourth part of the questionnaire concerns the economic component, that is, the intention was to identify the costs of travel, accommodation, food, among others and lastly, the fifth part of the questionnaire intended to ascertain the frequency of participation in this type of tourism-sports event, the degree of satisfaction in particular with participation in the event under study, with special attention to the opinion of participants on environmental issues, i.e., concern for sustainability and preservation of the environment.

Once the instrument for data collection had been identified, as well as the most viable solution for structuring and providing access to it in the simplest, quickest and most effective way, it was necessary to collect the participants e-mail address contacts from the organisation. In this sense, and after making the organiser (*Xistarca*) aware of the purpose of the research and the objectives, 2,771 email contacts were provided, which corresponds to 52.0% of the total number of participants (5,307). After that we started by sending the questionnaires directly to the participants through the Mailchimp platform. The data were processed using the statistical programme SPSS v.24 and the Excel programme was also used to graphically diagram the data collected.

Results and Discussion

The event of study, as previously mentioned, was the Half Marathon of the Discoveries, which has been held in the city of Lisbon, in Portugal, since 2013. In its fourth edition, we took the opportunity to explore some economic, social and sustainability variables that allowed us to better understand the dimension of the event itself, as well as characterise a part of the participants in various dimensions. Since its 1st edition, the level of participation has gradually increased as we can see in Table 17.1, except for 2016, when there was a small decrease in the total number of registrants, still higher than the 2nd edition. Regarding the number of participants when compared with the gender, it is possible to verify that the participation has increased in both genders. This type of running event tends to be mostly constituted by male participants, however, it is possible to verify with great emphasis that there is a percentage of growth in the female gender when compared with previous editions. Table 17.2 demonstrates the percentage growth of participants by gender and edition of the event.

Background Characteristics

In relation to the results obtained with this research, and according to the data collected through the sample of 590 participants in the event, we will now present the descriptive analysis based on the sociodemographic characteristics of the

Table 17.1 Number of Registrations by Edition of the Event

No. of editions	No. of registrations	% Annual growth
1st edition (2013)	4,166	-
2nd edition (2014)	4,557	9.4%
3rd edition (2015)	5,738	26.0%
4th edition (2016)	5,307	-7.5%

264 M.C. Teixeira, A.C. Júnior and A.D. Sesinando

Table 17.2 Number of Registrations per Edition in the Event According to Gender

Event editions and gender type		No. of registrations	Annual growth %
1st edition (2013)	Male	3,298	-
	Female	868	-
2nd edition (2014)	Male	3,448	4.5%
	Female	1,109	27.8%
3rd edition (2015)	Male	4,048	17.4%
	Female	1,690	52.4%
4th edition (2016)	Male	3,726	-7.9%
	Female	1,581	-6.4%

sample which is represented in Table 17.3. The sample under study comprises a total of 590 participants, of which 450 are male and 140 are female, representing 76.3% and 23.7%, respectively, of the total number of respondents. Regarding nationality, as expected, most of the participants are Portuguese, with a total of 575 participants (97.5%), while the remaining 15 participants (2.5%) are from 6 different countries. In what concerns the country of residence, most of the participants live in Portugal, with a total of 579 participants (98.1%), while the remaining 11 participants (1.9%) are from 5 different countries. Regarding the age of the participants, there is a great diversity of participants with regarding their age, but that the majority are aged between 31 and 50 years. Regarding the marital status and no. of children, the great majority of the participants are married, with a total of 294 elements (49.8%) and have 2 children, with a total of 206 elements (34.9%). Regarding the Academic Qualifications and Employability status, most of the participants have qualifications at degree level, corresponding to 310 elements (52.5%) and are employed, corresponding to 477 elements (80.8%). Regarding the area of residence of the participants, it was possible to observe that the great majority of them live outside the municipality of Lisbon, corresponding to 373 elements (63.2%), while 217 elements, corresponding to 36.8% live in this municipality. Of the total number of non-residents in the municipality of Lisbon, we found that 215 participants, corresponding to 57.7%, live in the municipalities bordering the city of Lisbon, which we may call residents in the region of *Lisboa e Vale do Tejo*. The remaining 158 participants not residing in the municipality of Lisbon (42.3%) live outside these municipalities. In relation to participation in previous editions, and according to the data collected, it was possible to verify that the great majority of respondents participated for the first time in this event, corresponding to a total of 352 elements (59.6%), while 238 practitioners had already participated in previous editions (40.4%). Finally, we intended to ascertain the level of displacement between the area of residence and the location of the event, to ascertain the distance covered by participants to attend the day of the event. In this sense, we found that most participants travelled less than 20 km to participate in the event, corresponding to 54.4%.

Sport Events as a Catalyst 265

Table 17.3 Sociodemographic Characteristics of the Sample

Variables		No. of registrations	Frequency %
Nationality	Portuguese	575	97.5%
	Spanish	1	0.2%
	French	1	0.2%
	German	1	0.2%
	Brazilian	9	1.5%
	English	2	0.3%
	Irish	1	0.2%
Country of residence	Portugal	579	98.1%
	France	2	0.4%
	Brazil	4	0.7%
	Belgium	2	0.4%
	USA	1	0.2%
	United Kingdom	1	0.2%
Age	<30 years old years old	74	17.5%
	31–40 years old	196	33.2%
	41–50 years old	216	36.6%
	51–60 years old	84	14.2%
	>60 years old	20	3.4%
Marital status	Single	159	26.9%
	Married	294	49.8%
	Union in Fact	93	15.8%
	Divorced	41	6.9%
	Widow(er)	3	0.6%
No. of children	0	195	33.1%
	1	140	2.7%
	2	206	34.9%
	3	43	7.3%
	4	4	0.7%
	5	2	0.3%
Type of qualifications	Basic education	12	2.0%
	Secondary education	153	25.9%
	Bachelor's degree	310	52.5%
	Master's degree	101	17.1%
	Doctorate	14	2.5%
Employability situation	Employee	477	80.8%
	Self-employed	69	11.7%
	Unemployed	14	2.4%
	Retired	15	2.5%
	Another	15	2.5%
Participation in past editions	Yes	238	40.4%
	No	352	59.6%
Distance between the residence and the venue	<20 km	321	54.4%
	21–40 km	172	29.2%
	41–100 km	44	7.5%
	101–200 km	14	2.4%
	>200 km	39	6.6%

Consumption Behaviour

To get to know the participants better, we tried to find out more about their consumption habits and Table 17.4 shows the consumption pattern based on participation in the event. Regarding the participants travel expenses to the event, the vast majority spent €10, corresponding to 45.3% of the total number of participants. It was also possible to observe that a very significant number of participants

Table 17.4 Participant's Consumption Behaviour during the Event

Variables		No. of registrations	Frequency %
Travel expenses	€0	191	32.2%
	€10	267	45.3%
	€20	63	10.7%
	€30	14	2.4%
	€40	8	1.4%
	€50	17	2.9%
	€60	6	1.0%
	>€61	24	4.1%
Food expenses	€0	432	73.2%
	€10	70	11.9%
	€20	27	4.6%
	€30	20	3.4%
	€40	8	1.4%
	€50	6	1.0%
	€60	3	0.5%
	>€61	24	4.1%
Accommodation expenses	€0	558	94.6%
	€10	-	-
	€20	6	1.0%
	€30	6	1.0%
	€40	4	0.7%
	€50	4	0.7%
	€60	2	0.3%
	>€61	10	1.7%
Duration of stay in Lisbon	0	529	89.7%
	1–2	48	8.1%
	3–4	5	0.9%
	>5	8	1.3%
Souvenirs expenses	€0	565	95.8%
	Up to €30	15	2.5%
	Up to €60	4	0.7%
	Up to €90	2	0.3%
	>€91	4	0.7%
Miscellaneous expenses	€0	492	83.4%
	Up to €30	75	12.7%
	Up to €60	8	1.4%
	Up to €90	2	0.4%
	Up to €120	7	1.2%
	>€121	5	0.9%

claimed not to have had any expenses with travel, i.e., 191 elements, corresponding to 32.2% of the sample. Regarding the food expenses, most participants stated that they had not spent any money on food, a total of 432 elements, corresponding to 73.2% of the sample. On the other hand, the remaining participants had various expenses with food. Regarding the accommodation expenses, we found that almost all the participants claimed not to have had any need for accommodation expenses, a total of 558 of the participants and corresponding to 94.6% of the sample. Only a small part of the participants claimed to have had accommodation expenses. Regarding other types of expenses, such as souvenirs or other expenses, and to better understand the possible local economic impact of holding and participating in this event, most participants said they had not incurred any additional expenses in the event and travel to the city of Lisbon.

In relation to the sociocultural analysis of the study, this aimed to assess and analyse whether the participants of the event were travelling alone or accompanied, who accompanied them and whether they took the opportunity to do more than the sport activity, taking advantage of the visit to the city of Lisbon from a tourist perspective. In this sense, the data collected shows that most of participants were accompanied by other people, corresponding to 423 participants, while 167 participants went alone to the event. Table 17.5 demonstrates the distribution of participants according to whether they were accompanied when travelling to the event. In relation to the number of companions of each participant, it was possible to verify that most participants were accompanied by between one and two people as we can see according to the total number of companions they brought to the venue.

Regarding the type of companion, the great majority of the 423 participants were accompanied by friends, corresponding to 217 participants (51.2%), while 102 participants were accompanied by their family (24.0%). The remaining were accompanied by members of their teams, coaches, work colleagues, among others. Regarding participation in other cultural activities in the municipality of Lisbon, most participants stated that they had not participated in any additional activities or visits. Only a small part of the total number of participants stated having taken the opportunity to participate in cultural activities, recreational activities, going to the cinema, visiting relatives, among others. From a tourism perspective, and when asked if they liked the city of Lisbon and if they would return only for

Table 17.5 Number of Participants with and without Companions at the Event

Variables		No. of registrations	Frequency %
No. of participants with accompanying persons	Alone	167	28.4%
	Accompanied	423	71.6%
No. of accompanying persons	0	167	28.4%
	1–2	267	45.2%
	3–4	92	15.6%
	>5	64	10.8%

tourism, 440 participants said yes, they would return to the city only for tourism, corresponding to 74.6% of the total sample. On the other hand, 150 participants stated that they do not intend to return on tourism and that they did not like the city, corresponding to 25.4% of the participants. Finally, and when questioned about a future participation in a sport event in the city of Lisbon, 579 participants stated that they would participate in future events, corresponding to 98.1% of the sample, while only 11 participants answered that they do not intend to participate in a sport event in the city of Lisbon again (1.9%).

Environmental Analyses

In relation to environmental analysis, the aim of the study was to analyse and evaluate whether the event respected and implemented environmental combat and prevention measures. In this sense, and through the opinion of participants, we tried to obtain feedback on their experience at the event at this level. The organisation immediately took some measures to preserve the environment, such as online registration, digital registration of participation and the provision of litter bins at various locations during the event, among others. In this sense, when asked about their opinion on whether the organisation had taken measures to preserve the environment, 455 participants, corresponding to 77.1% of the sample, said yes, that the organisation had taken such measures. The remaining 135 participants, corresponding to 22.9%, answered that the organisation had not taken measures respecting the concern for the environment.

Regarding the participation in the event, the objective was to analyse and evaluate the global experience of the participants in different dimensions. Most of the participants responded that their trip to Lisbon was essentially due to their participation in the event, corresponding to 422 elements (71.5%), while the remaining 168 respondents (28.5%) stated that this was not the main reason for their participation in the event. Regarding the participants level of satisfaction, it was possible to see that most participants assessed the experience as very satisfactory, with a total of 219 elements (37.1%), followed by participants who said they were satisfied, with a total of 206 elements (34.9%) of the sample.

As regards the reasons for attending this event, most participants stated that the main reason for attending the event was that the venue was relatively close to their place of residence, i.e., 258 participants corresponding to 43.7% of the sample. A large percentage of participants (33.7%) replied that the reason for attending the event was the quality of the organisation. It should also be noted, since it is a relevant factor given the typology of the event, that only 12 participants, corresponding to 2.0%, stated that the main reason for participating in the event was the practice of sports, while 9 participants referred that it was related to the tourist offer, corresponding to 1.5% of the total sample. Following the main reason for attending the event, we tried to analyse the feeling of loyalty to the event by asking about the possibility of participating in future editions. Most participants stated that yes, they intend to participate in the event again, corresponding to

Sport Events as a Catalyst   269

568 participants (96.3%), while only 22 participants do not intend to participate again (3.7%).

Hypothesis Validation

In terms of hypothesis validation, according to the data obtained, it is possible to verify that the participation in this event did not potentiate significant expenses in the local economy, since most participants did not spend any amount on food, accommodation or various additional expenses. In this sense, and due to the data obtained, it was not possible to validate this hypothesis. According to the data collected, it was possible to see that only 238 participants (40.4%) had participated in previous editions and that the majority of the 352 participants surveyed (59.6%) in this 4th edition was participating in the event for the first time. Considering that it was only possible to reach a total of 590 participants in relation to the 2,771 questionnaires sent out, we believe that we do not have sufficient data to allow us to accurately assess whether there is loyalty on the part of participants in relation to previous editions. The data collected only allow us to affirm that there is a continuous adhesion of new participants in each new edition of this event. In this sense, we are not allowed to verify this hypothesis based on the available data.

According to the data collected, it was possible to verify a gradual increase in the number of participants in this event since its 1st edition. The 2nd edition of the event grew by 9.4% compared to the 1st edition, while the 3rd edition had a very significant growth of 25.9%. However, the following edition, which served as the basis for this research, had a decrease of -7.5%, which led to a lower participation compared to the previous event. In this sense, the hypothesis was not validated since it does not present a growth rate compared to previous years. Regarding the organisations concern in adopting environmental preservation and care measures during the event, the participants were categorical in stating that the events organisation showed additional concern in this area. Of the total respondents, 77.1% responded positively when asked about these issues, while only 22.9% responded negatively. In this sense, and according to the hypothesis formulated, it is possible to state that it was successfully verified.

Conclusion

This research aimed to analyse and evaluate the impacts of a sport event in relation to the economic, sociocultural and environmental sustainability dimensions, as well as its contribution to local tourism development. The sample involved in this study included 590 participants, which is not unremarkable, however, and in view of the total number of participants, it turned out to be not very representative. Regarding the analysis and interpretation of the results obtained, there was an increase in the number of participants in the first three editions, and in the last edition, there was a decrease in participation of around −7.5%. The participants continue to be mainly male, but there has been a gradual increase in the participation of female participants since the first edition of this event. Most participants are Portuguese and live in Portugal, mainly aged between 31 and 50 years. In general, they have a university degree and are employed. Regarding the participation in previous editions, it was found that the majority participated in the event for the first time. Regarding the economic analysis and the possible impacts of holding this event, the data collected helps to conclude that there was no significant positive impact. The fact that most of the participants are national citizens and that they live near the venue of the event inhibits the propensity for additional spending on food, accommodation, among others. There was in fact some spending among participants in local commerce due to their presence at the event, but it was not significant enough to be considered as having a high impact on local development.

On the other hand, if we consider the potential of the event in relation to the number of people involved, we verify that there are reasons to believe in a possible change of this scenario. This is because the adoption of joint strategies between the various agents linked to tourism and sports, through marketing and advertising techniques in the tourist-sports and cultural promotion in various platforms, may enhance the propensity for a greater adhesion not only to the event itself, but to the entire cultural and tourist experience that can be promoted and coupled to a sports event. The low availability and interest in spending additional money during the event may be associated with the short distance between the place of residence and the venue of the event, but also the lack of partnerships and/or opportunities for post-event activities that could promote a longer stay in the city, thus promoting and boosting the local economy and sustainable tourism. Regarding the sociocultural analysis of the event, it was possible to conclude that there are positive impacts. First, the fact that the event name is associated with a historical moment in Portugal, which arouses interest and curiosity in the theme, but also, and no less importantly, the fact that the event takes place in the historical centre of the magnificent city of Lisbon. The location of the event in this city rich in cultural heritage promotes local tourism, while at the same time making Portuguese culture better known to a wide range of national and international participants. The opportunity for participants to socialise and exchange knowledge and experiences makes this type of event a highly sociable element and a promoter of local development.

Finally, and regarding the analysis of environmental sustainability, the data collected shows that measures were defined by the event organisation to combat environmental preservation before, during and after the event. In this sense, we can state that there was no negative impact with the holding of this event in the city of Lisbon. The measures taken by the organisation included the placement of several rubbish bins along each route, as well as in the specific places for hydration and near the start and finish line. Toilet areas were also made available and, at the end of the event, Lisbon City Hall itself provided full support in the general cleaning of the area where the event took place. The registration process can also be considered as environmentally friendly, as it was an exclusively online procedure, thus avoiding the excessive use of paper. The only negative point, or one that may have created some less environmentally friendly impact, concerns the fact that the holding of these events forced the temporary reorganisation of traffic in the vicinity, with the same being shifted to other areas. This reorganisation tends to generate greater traffic flows and congestion in certain locations, giving rise to a greater concentrated pollution load. In short, this is an event that generates a great impact if we consider the importance of sport in improving general well-being, as well as promoting healthier living habits. However, when the economic, sociocultural and environmental dimensions are considered, we can see that the measures taken have not had a significant impact on the promotion of tourism, culture and the development of the local economy. Portugal has been a destination of choice for tourism, as has the city of Lisbon, so we believe that the conditions are in place to better promote this type of event in national territory, reinforcing international promotion as well.

In the present research, the greatest difficulty was reaching the largest possible number of participants through email address contacts. The registration by email or the provision of the email was not a mandatory component in the platforms for registration in the event, which made direct contact difficult. The fact that several registrations were made by team also did not allow differentiating and reaching more participants. However, it was possible to achieve a sample that allowed us to obtain elucidative data, considering the purpose of the study. In the future, and to facilitate and promote the opportunity for participants to be able to share their experience and contribute to the study and development of this type of experience, it is essential to obtain various forms of contact. Participants should be informed of any studies underway so that they too may contribute to the improvement of processes and to a better socioeconomic understanding of the impacts associated with the holding of this type of event.

On the other hand, we see the importance of a greater dynamics between the various agents involved, to promote unique opportunities associated with the participation in this type of events, such as, for example, offers of accommodation and meals with exclusive and inviting prices that enhance not only the experience in the sporting event but also the direct contribution to the local economy. This synergy should be carried out not only in Portugal, but also abroad, where we can generate interest and curiosity in tourists. In relation to sustainability and preservation of the environment, it is important that the impacts of sporting events continue to be assessed not only to promote sport associated with the environment but also in the importance of its preservation, thus making Portugal the centre of tourist interest where sport, healthy habits and care for the environment act as a key element in a policy of sustainable development of tourism, with sport as a focus of interest and curiosity.

References

Barandela, J., Fernández, P., Álvarez, M., & Alonso, A. (2018). Economic valuation of a medium-sized sporting event: Impact of the Spanish Swimming Championship. *Journal of Physical Education and Sport, 18*(3), 1349–1355.

Carvalho, P. G., & Lourenço, R. (2009). Turismo de prática desportiva: Um segmento do mercado do turismo desportivo. *Revista Portuguesa De Ciências Do Desporto*, 9(2), 122–132.

Dionisio, P. (2009). *Casos de sucesso em marketing desportivo*. Livros d'Hoje.

Djaballah, M., Hautbois, C., & Desbordes, M. (2015). Non-mega sport events social impacts: A sensemaking approach of local governments' perceptions and strategies. *European Sport Management Quarterly*, 15(1), 48–76.

Figueira, T. M. N., & Teixeira, M. R. C. (2020). Políticas públicas de desporto: Promoção de desportos náuticos na área metropolitana de lisboa. *Motrivivência*, 32(62), 1–19.

García-Fernández, J., Grimaldi-Puyana, M., & Bravo, G. A. (2022). *Sport in the Iberian Peninsula: An introduction*. In J. García-Fernández, M. Grimaldi-Puyana, & G. A. Bravo (Eds.), Sport in the Iberian Peninsula: Management, Economics and Policy. Routledge.

Gholipour, H. F., Arjomandi, A., Marsiglio, S., & Foroughi, B. (2020). Is outstanding performance in sport event a driver of tourism? *Journal of Destination Marketing & Management*, 18(1), 100507.

Hinch, T. D., & Higham, J. E. (2004). *Sport Tourism Development*. Channel View Publication.

Madeira, B., Caetano, J., Rasquilha, L., & Santos, R. (2007). Gestão de *marketing de eventos desportivos*. Plátano Editora.

Marujo, M. N. (2008). Turismo e comunicação. RV Editores.

Marujo, M. N., & Carvalho, P. (2010). Turismo, planeamento e desenvolvimento sustentável. *Turismo & Sociedade*, 3(2), 147–161.

Melo, S. (2019). Desporto e turismo: Práticas e viagem. In A. Correia, & R. Biscaia (Eds.), *Gestão do desporto, compreender para gerir* (pp. 243–280). Faculdade de Motricidade Humana.

Mortazavi, R. (2021). The relationship between visitor satisfaction, expectation and spending in a sport event. *European Research on Management and Business Economics*, 27(1), 100132.

Quilende, M. (2018). *A importância do marketing em eventos desportivos*. Obnósis Editora.

Reis, R., Neto, S., Teixeira, M., & Telles, S. (2022). *Stadiums x covid-19: A new way to twist*. In M. Pinho, M. A. Schueda, & D. R. Brosculin (Org.), Principles and Concepts for development in nowadays society (pp. 852–856). Seven Editora.

Rojas-Méndez, J. I., Davies, G., Jamsawang, J., Sandoval Duque, J. L., & Pipoli, G. M. (2019). Explaining the mixed outcomes from hosting major sporting events in promoting tourism. *Tourism Management*, 74(1), 300–309.

Sesinando, A., & Teixeira, M. (2021). Recursos humanos, liderança, e gestão do desporto: A importância da formação no desenvolvimento desportivo municipal. *Anais Do 11° Congresso Internacional Do Conselho Regional De Educação Física Da 7ª Região (Con-CREF7)*, 1(1), 28–38.

Sesinando, A. D., Segui-Urbaneja, J., & Teixeira, M. C. (2022). Professional development, skills, and competences in sports: a survey in the field of sport management among public managers. *Journal of Physical Education and Sport*, 22(11), 2800–2809.

Sesinando, A. D., Urbaneja, J. S., & Teixeira, M. C. (2023). *Liderança e Motivação na Gestão do Desporto: Conceitos e implicações práticas na administração local*. Atena Editora.

Taks, M., Green, B. C., Misener, L., & Chalip, L. (2014). Evaluation sport development outcomes: The case of a medium-sized international sport event. *European Sport Management Quarterly*, 14(3), 213–237.

Teixeira, M. (2009). *Portugal, poder local e desporto*. Grifos.

Teixeira, M. (2019). *Gestão do Desporto – Desenvolvimento Desportivo Regional e Municipal*. MediaXXI.

Teixeira, M. C., Rijo, V. A., & Sesinando, A. D. (2022). Sports management research: analysis of scientific development in Portugal (2008-2017). *Journal of Physical Education*, 33(1), e-3353.

Teixeira, M. R. C., & Ribeiro, T. M. P. (2016). Sport policy and sports development: Study of demographic, organizational, financial and political dimensions to the local level in Portugal. *The Open Sports Sciences Journal*, 9(1), 26–34.

Vassiliadis, C. A., Mombeuil, C., & Fotiadis, A. K. (2021). Identifying service product features associated with visitor satisfaction and revisit intention: A focus on sports events. *Journal of Destination Marketing & Management*, 19, 100558.

Weed, M., & Bull, C. (2009). *Sports Tourism: Participants, Policy and Providers*. Routledge.

Chapter 18

Beach Volleyball Management in Brazil
Reflections on the Modality's Autonomy

Fernando Marques d'Oliveira
Rio de Janeiro State University, Brazil

Silvio Costa Telles
Rio de Janeiro State University, Brazil
Rio de Janeiro Federal University, Brazil

Luiz Carlos Nery
Rio de Janeiro State University, Brazil

Mário Coelho Teixeira
Évora University, Portugal
Center for Advanced Studies in Management and Economics (CEFAGE)

Chapter Contents

Introduction	274
Contextualizing the Field – Beach Volleyball: from Invention to Spectacularization	275
Method	278
Results and Discussion	285
Fortaleza Metropolitan Region	286
João Pessoa Metropolitan Region	287
Vitória Metropolitan Region (Grande Vitória)	289
Rio de Janeiro Metropolitan Region (Grande Rio)	290
Conclusion	291
References	292

Introduction

From its creation to the current times, beach volleyball has been showing a significant growth in the global scenario in terms of competitive sports practice and was one of the sports that took the least amount of time to enter the official program

DOI: 10.4324/9781003388050-21

of the Summer Olympic Games. Throughout this process, Brazil became one of the world's strongest powerhouses in this sport, earning hundreds of international prizes and making it strategic for the Brazilian Olympic Committee (COB) in winning Olympic medals for the country. In the Rio de Janeiro 2016 edition of the Olympic Games, Brazil achieved the Olympic championship in the men's competition and the women achieved the Olympic vice-championship. The model that was adopted by Brazilian beach volleyball and is used to this day has shown to be successful regarding the titles and profits achieved for financial backers and sponsors. It has, in fact, become a reference for the national confederations for other sports and even those from other countries. As stated by Pizzolato (2004), "the modality's management is seen as an example of action for the field's professionals. The CBV is seen as the best and most structured confederation currently active in Brazil".

Throughout the beach volleyball regulation process and the sport's subsequent incorporation as an Olympic sport, priority was given to the creation of official regulations that aimed to guide its competitive practice, allowing the athletes to participate in official competitions without needing to be tied to clubs, teams, or schools. Even today, for their participation to be possible, each athlete needs only to be registered in their respective state federation, which must be a member of the Brazilian Volleyball Confederation or, in the case of international competitions, with one of the national federations that is a part of the International Volleyball Federation (FIVB) – such as the Brazilian Volleyball Confederation – (CBV). With this in mind, we believe that it is important to understand the impacts that this process of structuring beach volleyball in Brazil has had on establishing degrees of autonomy and dependence for this modality as a sportive practice in the country, building from an understanding of the operational dynamics of certain practice locations and the conditions under which the practice is integrated in these regions. With this, we seek to investigate how the different forms of practice correlate to the different actors of the field in which this sport is inserted. This study aimed to map the volleyball practice points in the main locations of the modality's development in Brazil and to identify the conditions under which the sport is practiced in these regions. In this sense, the intention is to offer information that contributes to advancing the knowledge pertaining to sports management in beach volleyball, stimulating reflections on the subject and, consequently, the presentation of proposals for the modality's evolution based on the knowledge shared in this chapter.

Contextualizing the Field – Beach Volleyball: from Invention to Spectacularization

The first information on its beginnings around the world appeared in 1915 on the beaches of Hawaii (USA) with matches played by six-player teams (Garcia et al., 2021). Couvillon (2002) mentions in his book "Sands of Time: The History of Beach Volleyball" that the first recorded event of this sport was also in 1915, on the sands of Waikiki Beach, Hawaii, at the Outrigger Canoe Club, a club founded to popularize the sports of that region.

In Brazil, beach volleyball is a tradition dating back to the 1940s and it is possible to find records of this in the written press of the time, more specifically in the country's first ever sports newspaper (Tavares et al., 2021), of amateur tournaments held in 1946 in Rio de Janeiro, a city considered by the Rio de Janeiro Municipal Tourism Company (RIOTUR) to be the birthplace of beach volleyball in Brazil. At the time, the tournaments in Rio de Janeiro were disputed by teams with six players which alternated their composition. Sometimes the teams contained only men and sometimes the teams were mixed. At the time, beach volleyball had no specific official rules, but instead the rules came from social groups of players and were mixed with the rules for indoor volleyball. In 1947, the first official tournament disputed by pairs was held on State Beach, in California, United States of America (Garcia et al., 2021). According to Couvillon (2002), this system was idealized by the American player Pablo Johnson in the 1930s.

In the following years, other championships were held in the United States, causing a beach volleyball "fever" in the country and culminating with the organization of the first American beach volleyball circuit including the cities of Santa Barbara, State Beach, Corona Del Mar, Laguna Beach, and Santa Monica with the participation of hundreds of players (França et al., 2022). In Brazil, the first pairs tournaments began in the 1970s. The Brazilians probably adopted this system (pairs) thanks to influence from United States. In the second half of the 1980s, after the Brazilian men's indoor volleyball team won a silver medal in the 1984 Los Angeles Olympic Games and after beach volleyball began to gain popularity in Brazil, there was a movement to hold tournaments of this modality in Brazil with the aim to provide, through sport, visibility to commercial brands familiar to the public. According to Kasznar and Graça Filho (2002), the characteristics of beach volleyball made this popularization easier, as it is a sport that can be played in the sand on any beach (Tavares et al., 2020). The authors point out that thanks to this characteristic, countless courts could easily be created for use by millions of amateur and professional athletes, as well as by weekend players (Cruz et al., 2020).

In 1986, the first international beach volleyball event was organized in Brazil thanks to a partnership between the Koch Tavares sports marketing company and Sousa Cruz, the country's biggest cigarette producer at the time. Big international volleyball names were brought together at Copacabana Beach in Rio de Janeiro for this exhibition event, which was called Hollywood Volley. In the same year, the same event would be held in Santos and in São Paulo. The participants were mostly from the United States and from Brazil, which were the two countries in which beach volleyball was more developed and popular. After Hollywood Volley's success, FIVB decided to make this modality official and, in 1987, Ipanema Beach hosted the first international beach volleyball tournament accredited by the federation, for men only. The tournament was a huge media and public success and once again brought together thousands of people at the arena (Junior et al., 2021). Later, in 1989, the FIVB implemented the Men's World Tour called the World Champion Series, with events held in Brazil, Japan and Italy after 1992.

Duarte (2007), for example, shows in his work Bank of Brazil's Sports Marketing – A Case Study a history of Banco do Brasil's sports marketing and highlights the institution's sponsorship of beach volleyball as one of the stars within this strategy, analyzing the marketing strategies employed in Brazilian beach volleyball as well as the influence these strategies had on the sport's development in the country.

According to Kasznar and Graça Filho (2006), in the end of the 1980s and the beginning of the 1990s, it was already possible at the time to see that the sport had everything it needed to be a success, both as a sport and as a business (Teixeira et al., 2022). In 1991, the CBV signed a sponsorship contract with the Banco do Brasil financial institution and began to count on this entity's financial support to develop projects in indoor and beach volleyball all over the country, as shown in the institution's webpage (Oliveira et al., 2021).The agreement signed between CBV and Banco do Brasil was part of the bank's marketing strategy to rejuvenate its image. With this association with sport, the bank wanted to attract more clients, preferably young ones, thus overcoming a period of institutional instability they were undergoing at the time. In this context, volleyball was chosen because the entity in charge developed important work in the base categories, as well as because the sport was well-accepted by the young public and had a promising future in terms of medals (Junior, 2021).

For the first time, the CBV's organizational structure gained a beach volleyball department with a work team assigned to deal exclusively with matters related to the sport. Furthermore, a national adult circuit was created with the name "Circuito Banco do Brasil Vôlei de Praia" (Banco do Brasil Beach Volleyball Circuit). From this point, CBV took care of beach volleyball management in Brazil and established the strategic planning for developing the sport in the country. Afonso and Júnior (2012) point out that "From the moment the sport had the possibility of moving large sums of money, institutions/entities quickly appeared with the goal of controlling a specific monopoly". In 1997, CBV began to adopt a business model based on the American concept of Strategic Business Unit (SBU). The entity created five units: Nacional Competitions Unit – NCU (UCN in Portuguese), Teams Unit – TU (USE in Portuguese), Beach Volleyball Unit – BVU (UVP in Portuguese), Events Unit – EU (UE in Portuguese), and the Viva-Vôlei Unit – VVU (UVV in Portuguese) and professionalized the sport's management (Sesinando et al., 2022). This action would mark the beginning of a stage in which Brazilian sports entities were encouraged to become professional based on the CBV's successful case. The strategy used by CBV was based on the understanding of volleyball as a business which generates clear benefits for its stakeholders. Alongside other factors, beach volleyball became an official and Olympic sport.

In 1993, after watching the Rio de Janeiro stage of the world beach volleyball circuit, the president of the International Olympic Committee (IOC), Juan Antonio Samaranch, made beach volleyball an Olympic sport. In 1996, beach volleyball made its debut in the Atlanta Olympic Games. Brazil went down in the history of international beach volleyball by winning the first gold medals for the women's modality with the pair formed by Jackie Silva and Sandra Pires (Garcia et al., 2017). From that moment onward, Brazilian beach volleyball underwent major growth internationally in terms of results and began to occupy a place of honor in the world sports scenario (Tavares et al., 2021). Brazil won 13 medals in the seven editions of the Olympic Games since beach volleyball was included in the program (França et al., 2022). Throughout the regulation process for beach volleyball and its following absorption as an Olympic sport, the creation of official rules was encouraged with the intent to define its practice as a competitive sport and allow athletes to participate in official competitions without having any ties to clubs, teams, or learning institutions (Silva et al., 2020).

In 2019, the CBV calendar contained 24 annual national beach volleyball competitions in the under-17, under-19, under-21, adult, and master. In the same year, 888 athletes appeared as active in the CBV's registration system, 488 men and 400 women. At the same time, the country had an economically active population of approximately 24,570,000 in the metropolitan regions of Recife (PE), Salvador (BA), Belo Horizonte (MG), Rio de Janeiro (RJ), São Paulo (SP), and Porto Alegre (RS) (Tavares et al., 2019). Considering this, some aspects of beach volleyball as a sport are yet to be mentioned:

1 It was an extremely popular sport in the Rio 2016 Olympic Games and was one of the sports with the highest demand for tickets (Gandra, 2016).
2 It is a part of the COB's strategic sports group regarding medals earned in the Olympics (França et al., 2022).
3 Since 1991, the same financial institution (Banco do Brasil) has been the main supporter of most of the beach volleyball projects organized by COB in Brazil (Yamamoto et al., 2021).
4 After the Rio 2016 Olympic Games, there was a reduction of 30% in the value of the annual sponsorship payments from Banco do Brasil to CBV (Brito, 2016).
5 After the reduction mentioned in the previous point, the number of annual beach volleyball competitions held by CBV was reduced from 64 (number from the previous contract) to 24 annual events (number from the contract that was active in 2018, according to CBV). These events possibly represent the absolute majority of beach volleyball projects currently held in the country.
6 The competition formats that have been adopted from the first international tournament to 2018 encouraged the creation of official rules that allow athletes to compete in official competitions without having ties with clubs, teams, or learning institutions (Garcia et al., 2021).
7 Beach volleyball's trajectory is primarily based on the marketing actions implemented by the entities responsible for managing the sport and those of other stakeholders such as event promotors and sponsors.

Method

We conducted field research with the use of websites, open questionnaires, and also the available literature with the objective of investigating the conditions under which beach volleyball is inserted in four Brazilian metropolitan regions

(Fortaleza/CE, João Pessoa/PB, Rio de Janeiro/RJ, and Vitória/ES). A field diary was used to analyze the data. The aforementioned regions were determined through a phone call with the CBV on 11 February 2019 at 11:35 AM in which the confederation named them as the most influential regions in the national beach volleyball scenario in terms of the number of athletes registered with the CBV, the number of events organized by the CBV in each region during this study's cut-off period, and the amount of internationally acclaimed athletes who train in centers located in these regions.

The technique adopted in this study consisted of contacting the entity representatives listed in Table 18.1 as well as consulting the entity websites listed in Tables 18.2 to 18.5. The representatives were contacted through phone calls, e-mail exchanges, and audio messages shared through the WhatsApp messaging application. All information regarding the entities, representatives consulted, dates of contact and tools used are contained in the tables mentioned above, i.e. Tables 18.2–18.5. We sought to select regions with at least one municipality that stood out nationally regarding beach volleyball practice. The study also covered the other municipalities in each region, but the determining factor for each region's selection was the presence of the indicated municipalities. In light of this, we present the criteria used to justify the selection of each location:

1 Fortaleza (CE): According to data collected on the CBV website, the city is, alongside Rio de Janeiro and João Pessoa, one of the most traditional locations for the practice and development of beach volleyball in Brazil. Volta da Jurema beach has one of the best-known training centers in the country, while Iracema beach has been hosting official competitions since the Brazilian adult circuit was created in 1991.
2 João Pessoa (PB): Based on data collected the city is one of the most traditional in the practice and development of beach volleyball in Brazil. Cabo Branco beach has hosted official competitions since the creation of the Brazilian circuit in 1991 and many athletes who train in this city are an important part of the modality's official rankings. The athletes Ricardo (Olympic medalist in Sydney 2000, Athens 2004, and Beijing 2008) and Emanuel (Olympic medalist in Athens 2004, Beijing 2008, and London 2012) used to train at this location.
3 Rio de Janeiro (RJ): The birthplace of beach volleyball in Brazil (Afonso & Junior, 2012). The city hosted the modality's main events in the country. According to data from the CBV the city has the highest number of athletes registered in the modality's entity (Tavares et al., 2021).
4 Vitória (ES): According to data collected, various athletes who train in this city are an important part of the modality's official rankings (Castro et al., 2022).

After defining the analyzed regions, we conducted a cartographic process in order to determine the points where beach volleyball is practiced in these locations and the modality's operational dynamics in each one. According to Romagnoli (2009), cartography is a method, as it does not begin with a pre-established model, instead questioning the object of study based on its own substantiation, affirming

Table 18.1 Entities Participating in the Study

Entity	Participant's job	Contact dates	Communication tools	Observations
CEARÁ VOLLEYBALL FEDERATION	PRESIDENT	06 February 2019 and 13 February 2019	Phone call and WhatsApp	We contacted the representative on 6 February 2019 and informed them of the points we wished to investigate. On 13 February 2019, the representative contacted us, sending the requested information via audio messages recorded on WhatsApp.
PARAÍBA VOLLEYBALL FEDERATION	PRESIDENT	13 February 2019 and 23 August 2019	Phone call, WhatsApp and email	We contacted the representative on 13 February 2019 and informed them of the points we wished to investigate. On 23 August 2019, the representative contacted us by email with the requested information.
BRAZILIAN VOLLEYBALL CONFEDERATION	BEACH VOLLEYBALL DIRECTOR	13 February 2019	Phone call	We contacted the representative on 13 February 2019 and received a phone call on the same day with the requested information.
ESPÍRITO SANTO VOLLEYBALL FEDERATION	TECHNICAL DIRECTOR	11 February 2019 and 13 February 2019	Phone call and WhatsApp	We contacted the representative on 11 February 2019 and informed them of the points we wished to investigate. On 13 February 2019, the representative contacted us, sending the requested information via audio messages recorded on WhatsApp.

Table 18.2 Rio De Janeiro/RJ Metropolitan Region – Websites Used in Search

Region	Entity	Electronic address used in search	Search date
RIO DE JANEIRO-RJ METROPOLITAN REGION	RIO DE JANEIRO MUNICIPAL GOVERNMENT	http://www.rio.rj.gov.br/	8 March 2019
	DUQUE DE CAXIAS MUNICIPAL GOVERNMENT	https://duquedecaxias.rj.gov.br	8 March 2019
	SÃO GONÇALO MUNICIPAL GOVERNMENT	https://www.saogoncalo.rj.gov.br/	8 March 2019
	NOVA IGUAÇU MUNICIPAL GOVERNMENT	http://www.novaiguacu.rj.gov.br/	8 March 2019
	NITERÓI MUNICIPAL GOVERNMENT	http://www.niteroi.rj.gov.br/	8 March 2019
	BELFORD ROXO MUNICIPAL GOVERNMENT	https://prefeituradebelfordroxo.rj.gov.br/	8 March 2019
	SÃO JOÃO DE MERITI MUNICIPAL GOVERNMENT	http://www.meriti.rj.gov.br/semtracite1/	8 March 2019
	PETRÓPOLIS MUNICIPAL GOVERNMENT		8 March 2019
	MAGÉ MUNICIPAL GOVERNMENT	http://mage.rj.gov.br/	8 March 2019
	ITABORAÍ MUNICIPAL GOVERNMENT		8 March 2019
	MESQUITA MUNICIPAL GOVERNMENT	http://www.mesquita.rj.gov.br/pmm/	8 March 2019
	NILÓPOLIS MUNICIPAL GOVERNMENT		8 April 2019
	MARICÁ MUNICIPAL GOVERNMENT	https://www.marica.rj.gov.br/	8 April 2019
	QUEIMADOS MUNICIPAL GOVERNMENT		8 April 2019
	ITAGUAÍ MUNICIPAL GOVERNMENT	https://itaguai.rj.gov.br/	8 April 2019
	JAPERI MUNICIPAL GOVERNMENT	http://www.japeri.rj.gov.br/	8 April 2019
	SEROPÉDICA MUNICIPAL GOVERNMENT	https://www.seropedica.rj.gov.br/	8 April 2019
	RIO BONITO MUNICIPAL GOVERNMENT		8 April 2019
	GUAPIMIRIM MUNICIPAL GOVERNMENT		8 April 2019
	CACHOEIRAS DE MACACU MUNICIPAL GOVERNMENT		8 April 2019
	PARACAMBI MUNICIPAL GOVERNMENT	http://paracambi.rj.gov.br/	8 April 2019
	TANGUÁ MUNICIPAL GOVERNMENT	https://tangua.rj.gov.br/home/	8 April 2019

Table 18.3 João Pessoa/PB Metropolitan Region – Websites Used in Search

Region	Entity	Electronic address used in search	Search date
JOÃO PESSOA – PB METROPOLITAN REGION	JOÃO PESSOA MUNICIPAL GOVERNMENT	www.joaopessoa.pb.gov.br/secretarias/setur/joaopessoa/	13 February 2019
	JOÃO PESSOA AABB		23 August 2019
	PARAHYBA OLYMPIC VILLAGE		23 August 2019
	APECEF/PB		23 August 2019
	JOÃO PESSOA UNIVERSITY CENTER-UNIPÊ	https://unipe.edu.br/2018/11/05/atletas-do-unipe-competem-no-jubs-2018-no-parana/	23 August 2019
	SANTA RITA MUNICIPAL GOVERNMENT	https://www.santarita.pb.gov.br/	13 February 2019
	BAYEUX MUNICIPAL GOVERNMENT	https://www.bayeux.pb.gov.br/	14 February 2019
	CABEDELO MUNICIPAL GOVERNMENT	http://cabedelo.pb.gov.br/	14 February 2019
	PEDRAS DE FOGO MUNICIPAL GOVERNMENT	http://www.pedrasdefogo.pb.gov.br/	14 February 2019
	CONDE MUNICIPAL GOVERNMENT	https://conde.pb.gov.br/	14 February 2019
	RIO TINTO MUNICIPAL GOVERNMENT	http://www.riotinto.pb.gov.br/	14 February 2019
	CAAMPORÃ MUNICIPAL GOVERNMENT		14 February 2019
	ALHANDRA MUNICIPAL GOVERNMENT		14 February 2019
	PITIMBU MUNICIPAL GOVERNMENT	https://www.pitimbu.pb.gov.br/	14 February 2019
	CRUZ DO ESPÍRITO SANTO MUNICIPAL GOVERNMENT	https://cruzdoespiritosanto.pb.gov.br/	14 February 2019
	LUCENA MUNICIPAL GOVERNMENT		14 February 2019

Table 18.4 Vitória/ES Metropolitan Region – Websites Used in Search

Region	Entity	Electronic address used in search	Search date
VITÓRIA-ES METROPOLITAN REGION	SERRA MUNICIPAL GOVERNMENT	http://www.serra.es.gov.br/	18 February 2019
	AEST CLUB	https://clubeaest.com.br/	18 February 2019
	VILA VELHA MUNICIPAL GOVERNMENT	http://www.vilavelha.es.gov.br/	18 February 2019
	CARIACICA MUNICIPAL GOVERNMENT		18 February 2019
	VITÓRIA MUNICIPAL GOVERNMENT	http://vitoria.es.gov.br/	18 February 2019
	ÁLVARO CABRAL SWIMMING AND REGATTA CLUB	https://clubealvarescabral.com.br/	18 February 2019
	CENTRO DE TREINAMENTO DA SESPORT - VITÓRIA	https://sesport.es.gov.br/	18 February 2019
	GUARAPARI MUNICIPAL GOVERNMENT	https://www.guarapari.es.gov.br/	18 February 2019
	VIANA MUNICIPAL GOVERNMENT	http://www.viana.es.gov.br/	18 February 2019
	FUNDÃO MUNICIPAL GOVERNMENT	http://www.fundao.es.gov.br/	18 February 2019

Table 18.5 Fortaleza/CE Metropolitan Region – Websites Used in Search

Region	Entity	Electronic address used in search	Search date
FORTALEZA-CE METROPOLITAN REGION	FORTALEZA MUNICIPAL GOVERNMENT		15 February 2019
	AYO GYM	https://ayofitnessclub.com.br/	15 February 2019
	BNB CLUB		15 February 2019
	AQUIRAZ MUNICIPAL GOVERNMENT	https://www.aquiraz.ce.gov.br	15 February 2019
	CASCAVEL MUNICIPAL GOVERNMENT	https://www.cascavel.ce.gov.br	15 February 2019
	CAUCAIA MUNICIPAL GOVERNMENT	https://www.caucaia.ce.gov.br/	15 February 2019
	CHOROZINHO MUNICIPAL GOVERNMENT	http://chorozinho.ce.gov.br/	16 February 2019
	EUSÉBIO MUNICIPAL GOVERNMENT	http://eusebio.ce.gov.br/	16 February 2019
	GUAIÚBA MUNICIPAL GOVERNMENT	http://www.guaiuba.ce.gov.br/	16 February 2019
	HORIZONTE MUNICIPAL GOVERNMENT		16 February 2019
	ITAITINGA MUNICIPAL GOVERNMENT	https://www.itaitinga.ce.gov.br/	16 February 2019
	MARACANAÚ MUNICIPAL GOVERNMENT	http://www.maracanau.ce.gov.br/	16 February 2019
	MARANGUAPE MUNICIPAL GOVERNMENT	http://www.maranguape.ce.gov.br/	16 February 2019
	PACAJUS MUNICIPAL GOVERNMENT	https://www.pacajus.ce.gov.br/	16 February 2019
	PACATUBA MUNICIPAL GOVERNMENT	https://pacatuba.ce.gov.br/	16 February 2019
	PINDORETAMA MUNICIPAL GOVERNMENT	http://pindoretama.ce.gov.br/	16 February 2019
	SÃO GONÇALO DO AMARANTE MUNICIPAL GOVERNMENT	http://saogoncalodoamarante.ce.gov.br/portal/	16 February 2019
	SÃO LUIS DO CURU MUNICIPAL GOVERNMENT	https://www.saoluisdocuru.ce.gov.br/	17 February 2019
	PARAIPABA MUNICIPAL GOVERNMENT	https://www.paraipaba.ce.gov.br/	17 February 2019
	PARACURU MUNICIPAL GOVERNMENT	https://www.paracuru.ce.gov.br/	17 February 2019
	TRAIRI MUNICIPAL GOVERNMENT	http://www.trairi.ce.gov.br/	17 February 2019

a difference in an attempt to re-encounter knowledge faced with complexity. Cartography, as the bearer of a certain concept of world and of subjectivity, shown below, brings about a new standard of problematization, contributing to the articulation of a set of knowledge, including other types besides scientific knowledge, favoring the revision of hegemonic and dichotomic conceptions. In this proposal, the researcher's role is central, as the production of knowledge occurs through perceptions, sensations, and affections which happen during encounters with their field, which is neither neutral nor empty of interference, nor even centered in the meanings attributed by them (Romagnoli, 2009, pp. 169–170).

Mairesse (2003) states that different forces are present in the encounter between a researcher and their object, changing both from what they were and, also according to the author, cartography would occur as a mechanism in this process. Furthermore, investigations were conducted through the application of open questionnaires for representatives from the CBV and from each state volleyball federation linked to the agency, who are responsible for managing volleyball in the regions in which the selected cities are located (Table 18.1) and in the available literature on the subject, as well as through internet searches in websites (Tables 18.2 to 18.5). The mapping consisted of the following:

1 Discovering on which beaches the beach volleyball modality is regularly practiced in the selected regions and in which way the operational dynamics develop in the identified locations.
2 Investigating which existing clubs (sports and social), learning institutions, and teams have beach volleyball in their scope of activities in the selected regions.
3 Researching which entities and teams promote beach volleyball regularly in the selected regions, without the financial support of Banco do Brasil and without the participation of the CBV.
4 Verifying how the activities mapped in the previous item are financed.

Results and Discussion

The field research was conducted between 22 October 2018 and 23 August 2019 with the intent to investigate the previously described matters, aiming to construct a cartography of the beach volleyball practice dynamics in the locations determined in this study. According to Passos et al. (2015):

> Cartography as a research-intervention method presupposes a guidance of the researcher's work that does not occur in a prescriptive manner, with previously made rules, nor with previously established objectives. However, the action is not without direction as cartography reverses the traditional sense of method without relinquishing the research trajectory guidance.

(p. 17)

The authors in question (p.17) emphasize that "the cartographic guideline is constructed by clues that guide the research trajectory, always considering the effects of the research process on the research object, the researcher and the results". In this direction, the field research was used to understand the autonomy of the established regions, in accordance with the question that guides this study.

According to Thiry-Cherques (2006), what occurs within a field represents a symbolic expression that is refracted by its own internal logic. Through field research, we sought to investigate in which manner the field's internal dynamics develop in each studied region and how certain aspects are organized, bringing up other data pertaining to the social dynamics of specific regions. Derived from the report by D'Oliveira (2019), in Tables 18.1 to 18.5, we list the sources that were used in data collection and other details that will be mentioned throughout the subsequent analyses. Since the author of the present article resides in the city of Rio de Janeiro, the information on this region was collected in person through searches and queries, as shown in Table 18.2.

Fortaleza Metropolitan Region

The second most populous region of the North-Northeast, the sixth largest metropolitan region of Brazil, and the 129th largest urban area in the world, the Fortaleza Metropolitan Region is comprised of 19 municipalities. It is located in the State of Ceará and has a total of 4,074,730 inhabitants. The larger Fortaleza area ended 2014 with a GDP of 22 billion BRL (Brazilian real). This number established the Fortaleza Metropolitan Region as the third richest in the North-Northeast, behind the Salvador and Recife areas and the 11th richest in the country.

According to the data collected from the Ceará Volleyball Federation (FCV) and the CBV, beach volleyball practice in the region can be observed at four beaches: Iracema, Futuro, Meireles, and Cumbuco. Aside from these locations, this sport is also practiced at the BNB Club beach location, at the AYO Gym, and at the training center located within the residence of one of the members of the team of instructors which manages the training of the athletes who use the location. At the moment this study was conducted, there are no reports of beach volleyball courts located in the area's learning institutions and there are no reports of activities linked to this modality held by these institutions outside the structural limits of their premises.

From the collected material, it is possible to consider that beach volleyball practice in the investigated region is concentrated in the municipality of Fortaleza and it is evident that the activities geared toward participation in competitions (high performance) mostly happen in the location known as Volta da Jurema, on Meireles Beach. As informed by the FCV, the location is the modality's main practice point in the region, concentrating some of the main training centers and initiation schools in Fortaleza, as well as most of the region's informal practitioners. In this location, it became evident that the activities geared toward athlete preparation are motivated by the existence of competitions held by the CBV and by the FCV, and the activities geared toward beginners (initiation schools) also appear to suffer this influence. We further understand that the informal practice found at Volta da Jurema may be stimulated by the other activities that are simultaneously held at that location (high performance and beach volleyball initiation), though that does not mean there is a direct relationship between the observed informal practice and the verified competitive practices.

Another location that is geared toward the development of activities specifically for high performance athletes is the Juliana and Larissa Training Center, which was constructed at instructor Oliveira's residence and is located in the Restinga neighborhood. This training center possesses the best structure in the region for beach volleyball, containing a sand court with Olympic dimensions, a swimming pool, meeting room, media room, physical therapy and preventative weight training room, and also dressing rooms and a press room. The activities developed in this location are directly motivated by the existence of competitions held by the CBV and the FCV, since the training is exclusively geared toward high performance. As for the practice at the BNB Club's beach location, we observed that the activities related to beach volleyball within the establishment's premises have the main objective of serving the club's members. Despite this, we found that there are also activities related to the interclub competition held by the CBC (Brazilian Club Committee) in a joint effort with the FCV and the CBV. These activities are related to the preparation of athletes for participating in said competition and using the club's premises to hold stages of the Brazilian Interclub Competition (Collet et al., 2021).

We found that Futuro Beach concentrates the largest number of beach volleyball courts in a same area within the analyzed region. The practice is not consistent or regular in any of the courts, with all of them holding spontaneous activities involving society and tourists, supported only by the local merchants who manage the traditional beach kiosks and have a commercial interest in the participants' presence at the location. Also, according to our research, the courts are located on the sand and the aforementioned support is restricted to offering consumer products such as food and drinks, provided by the merchants in exchange for payment. The equipment must be provided by the participants themselves and there does not seem to be any link between the beach volleyball practice observed at Futuro Beach and the activities held by the FCV or the CBV. Regarding the practice at Ayo Gym, we observed that the beach volleyball activities held at the establishment have the specific objective of serving the gym's members, with no ties to the activities developed by the FCV or the CBV. The courts at Cumbuco Beach are informally attended by the local population and it was not possible to observe any correlation with the activities developed by the FCV or the CBV. The same is true of the activities held at Trinta e Um de Março Square, in the Praia do Futuro neighborhood.

João Pessoa Metropolitan Region

The second researched location was the João Pessoa Metropolitan Region. Located in the State of Paraíba, the region possesses approximately 138 km of beaches and is formed by the municipalities of João Pessoa, Santa Rita, Bayeux, Cabedelo, Pedras de Fogo, Conde, Rio Tinto, Caaporã, Alhandra, Pitimbú, Cruz do Espírito Santo, and Lucena. It contains 51 beaches with clear, warm waters and the most popular ones are the urban beaches Cabo Branco, Tambaú, and Bessa (João Pessoa, 2018). According to the information collected from the Paraíba Volleyball Federation (FPV) and the CBV's Beach Volleyball Unit as well as records from the websites of the public agencies that manage this region (Table 18.3), beach volleyball practices in João Pessoa can be found at different beaches, public locations, clubs, and associations.

Based on the collected material, it is possible to consider that beach volleyball practice in the analyzed region is concentrated at the 26 courts scattered along the Cabo Branco and Tambaú beaches, both of which are located in the municipality of João Pessoa (capital). As verified through the FPV, these locations can be considered the main modality practice points in the region, hosting the main training centers and initiation schools, as well as a large portion of the informal participants. In these locations, it became evident that the activities geared toward base category and high-performance athletes are motivated by the existence of competitions held by the CBV and the Paraíba Volleyball Federation, and the activities geared toward beginners (initiation schools) are also influenced by this situation. We also understand that the informal practice observed at the previously mentioned locations may be stimulated by the competition-related activities that are simultaneously held at those locations, though that does not mean there is a direct relationship between the observed informal practice and the verified competitive practices.

Another location to be mentioned is the João Pessoa University Center (UNIPÊ). This is due to it being one of the only learning institutions located in the analyzed metropolitan regions to have a beach volleyball court within its premises and activities linked to the modality's practice in its scope. The institution sponsors base category and high-performance athletes, also preparing student-athletes to compete in university competitions for this sport The existing beach volleyball court is used by the students during classes and institutionally supervised recreational activities. We emphasize that it is possible to consider that the activities supported by this entity that are geared toward base category and high-performance competitions are directly related to the competitions organized by the CBV and the FPV. However, it is possible to conclude that the activities related to student participation in university competitions and the practice involving other students enrolled at the institution have no ties to the projects developed by the previously mentioned sportive management agencies. With the exception of the Parahyba Olympic Village, a sportive complex constructed by the State's Youth, Sports and Leisure Office (SEJEL), which offers beach volleyball initiation lessons to the local community (Madruga, 2015), the other points identified in this search are characterized by the development of activities based on the informal, spontaneous practice by the local population, with no direct participation of sportive entities or public agencies in the provision and maintenance of the necessary structure.

As reported by the FPV, the operational dynamics of the registered courts on the beaches consist of a practice that is inconsistent regarding the participants' frequency of use. The same occurs with the courts in the public squares, with the difference that in these locations, the public agencies are responsible for maintaining the courts in adequate shape for sportive practice. Similarly, in courts located in the João Pessoa AABB and at the Caixa Economica Federal da Paraíba Staff Association (APCEF), the proprietary institutions are the ones responsible for preserving and maintaining the spaces and, in these last two cases, the institutions themselves are responsible for providing the equipment for their members to practice the modality. It is important to emphasize that there is no evidence of a relationship between the practice in said locations and the projects organized by the CBV and the FPV.

To finish the region's cartography, we note that the FPV supports certain training centers located at Cabo Branco Beach and Tambaú Beach by providing technical materials and equipment, while the support given to other beach volleyball development projects in the region is limited to the entity's approval of certain competitions that are held by independent associations which they recognize.

Vitória Metropolitan Region (Grande Vitória)

The third search was conducted in the Grande Vitória Metropolitan Region, which is comprised of the Cariacica, Fundão, Guarapari, Serra, Viana, Vila Velha, and Vitória municipalities. These seven municipalities hold almost half of Espírito Santo's total population (46%) and 57% of the state's urban population. Through the search, it was possible to observe the existence of beach volleyball practice at six beaches, two public squares, two clubs, and one training center belonging to the Municipal Office of Sports and Leisure. According to the data collected from the Espírito Santo Volleyball Federation (FESV) and the CBV, as well as records from the websites of public agencies that manage this region, in the year 2019, there were no records of beach volleyball courts located within the learning institutions in the Grande Vitória Metropolitan Region and there were no records of activities linked to this modality being developed by these institutions outside of the structural limits of their facilities. Below, we have the demonstrative tables with the data that was collected.

From the collected material, it is possible to see that the region's beach volleyball practice is concentrated at the 38 courts scattered on the beaches that are a part of the coastlines for the municipalities of Vitória and Vila Velha. It is clear that the activities geared toward participation in base category and professional competitions are mostly held at Camburi Beach, Costa Beach, and at the Municipal Sports and Leisure Office Training Center in Vitória. As verified with the FESV, these locations can be considered the main points for the modality's practice in the region, hosting some of the main training centers and initiation schools in the Grande Vitória area, as well as most of the region's informal practitioners. In these locations, it is clear that the activities geared toward athlete preparation are motivated by the existence of the competitions held by the CBV and the FESV. It is also possible to consider that the activities geared toward beginners (initiation schools) are also influenced by this situation. We can also infer that the informal practices observed in the aforementioned locations may be stimulated by the other competition-related activities that are developed simultaneously in these places, which does not mean that we believe there is necessarily a link between the observed informal practices and the verified competitive practices.

Another analyzed location that is aligned with the development of activities specifically geared toward athlete preparation for base category competitions is the Tubarão Steelworkers Sportive Association (AEST), located in the Serra municipality. This training center has the basic structure that is needed for beach volleyball training and for hosting base category competitions, such as stages of the Brazilian Interclub Championship held by the CBC in a joint effort with the FESV and the CBV. The activities held in this location are directly motivated by the existence of competitions held by the CBC, the CBV, and the FESV, since the structure is used exclusively for athlete preparation and training activities. In the same municipality, there are also two locations in which there is only spontaneous practice by the local population. Those are the Jacaraípe and Nova Almeida beaches. In both locations, the equipment must be provided by the participants themselves and there is no obvious link between the beach volleyball practices observed at these beaches and the activities conducted by the FESV or by the CBV.

Concluding the region's cartography, we observed the existence of beach volleyball practice in two public squares located in Vitória. They are the Namorados Square, which is located at Canto Beach and the Recreio dos Olhos Square, located in a neighborhood with the same name. Both locations have similar operational dynamics, as they host two types of beach volleyball practices, which are the schools (geared toward sportive initiation) and the informal practice developed spontaneously by the local population. In both squares, the initiation schools that function during the week have the objective of conducting social work and are made possible by structural support from the municipal government, which provides the equipment and the instructors.

Rio de Janeiro Metropolitan Region (Grande Rio)

The fourth search was conducted in the five municipalities of the Rio de Janeiro Metropolitan Region that present the largest population contingents according to the Brazilian Institute of Geography and Statistics. They are: Rio de Janeiro (6,688,927), São Gonçalo (1,077,687), Duque de Caxias (914,383), Nova Iguaçu (818,875), and Niterói (511,786). Initially, the data collection was going to occur in the 21 municipalities that comprise the Rio de Janeiro Metropolitan Region, but due to the number of beach volleyball practice locations found in the aforementioned municipalities, we made the decision to consider only the numbers found in Rio de Janeiro, São Gonçalo, Duque de Caxias, Nova Iguaçu, and Niterói, as we consider them sufficient for the debate proposed in this study; that is, the aspect that is relevant to the debate proposed by the present study is not exactly related to the number of locations or of participants, but has more to do with the manner in which the groups that are a part of the analyzed fields organize themselves and establish their operational dynamics.

The first municipality that was analyzed was Rio de Janeiro. With 72.3 km of beaches (Praias, 2018), it is the region with the largest number of beach volleyball courts and the highest rate of modality practice among all locations observed in this study. At its 25 beaches (Praias, 2018), it was possible to observe the existence of beach volleyball practice at 194 courts distributed among the Urca, Flamengo, Leme, Copacabana, Ipanema, Leblon, and Barra da Tijuca beaches. It was also possible to observe beach volleyball practice at eight institutions such as clubs and associations. We also found activities linked to this sport in certain public spaces. The research also verified the existence of beach volleyball practice at one public learning institution.

We observed that the region in question possesses characteristics that are quantitatively different when compared to the other three regions that were analyzed in this study, despite the fact that all four regions demonstrate similar operational dynamics pertaining to their autonomy. Thus, although this does not make a difference in the central discussion concerning the areas' relative degrees of autonomy and the manner in which they are organized, this characteristic may be considered an advantage over the other three analyzed areas, as it is possible to consider the existence of a numerical superiority influenced by the association between the cultural capital and the economic capital of certain areas within this region, resulting in a larger number of active practice locations.

Conclusion

From the analyses and discussions that emerged from the collected material, we observed that beach volleyball practice is concentrated in locations with specific structural and geographic characteristics and is basically organized by participants who live near these locations, leaving out groups that are located more distantly from the practice points. We discovered that the informal practice of beach volleyball is relatively independent in the analyzed regions and the participants in these locations are organized autonomously in relation to the entities that manage the modality regionally and nationally, as well as in relation to the sport's sponsors. However, we understand that this analysis must be conducted with a broad focus. In this sense, we believe that the autonomy of informal beach volleyball practice would merely represent this activity's survival in certain regions. Nonetheless, we understand that this statement should not be understood as a signal that this representativity would be enough for beach volleyball to maintain itself as a sport in general, such as in competitive terms. Considering this, the possibilities of implementing any type of strategy geared toward the democratization of beach volleyball would be even more reduced.

It is also not possible to affirm that this spontaneous practice on the part of society would not be reduced in case Brazil's international representativity in this modality in world championships and in the Olympic Games underwent a reduction, which happened recently in the Tokyo 2020 Olympic competition where, for the first time, no Brazilian teams reached the tournament's semifinals. Regarding this aspect, we believe it is necessary to conduct a study in which the object is a debate on the true impacts of sportive results, such as those cited above, on said modality's practice in society as a whole and in the sub-field of spontaneous practice. Another aspect we consider to be important in this conclusion refers to the fact that we observed that during the beach volleyball regulation process in Brazil, priority was given to the creation of official regulations that would allow base category and high-performance athletes to participate in official competitions without needing official ties with clubs, teams, or learning institutions. We believe this strategy may have helped to isolate these groups from the modality's structuring and development process throughout the country, and, consequently, may have contributed to the sport's low inclusion rate in the activity scopes of clubs (social and sportive), teams, and learning institutions in the cities of Fortaleza, João Pessoa, Rio de Janeiro, and Vitória.

Another important point we would like to mention refers to the fact that the rules of the game that are adopted by informal practitioners in the analyzed regions are adaptations of the official rules, as is the case with the different court sizes and fundamental movement execution techniques that are not permitted in official competitions. We believe that these aspects demonstrate how the previously mentioned groups are independently organized and how certain areas would probably not be obviously affected in case the hypothetical situation of the modality losing the CBV's support were to become a reality. Nevertheless, we believe that some conclusions can be established from the data that was directly collected through the searches. However, other points we can emphasize are the result of reflections on aspects that did not appear within the information that was directly provided by the respondents or the data present in bibliographical sources.

Among the conclusions stemming from explicit ideas, it is possible to highlight the need to include actors such as learning institutions and clubs in the beach volleyball development process. This path appeared rather clearly within the debates conducted in this study. As for the conclusions reached through inference, we underscore the absence of a strategy aiming to democratize beach volleyball. This point was not mentioned by any of the interviewees and it was not discussed in the literary sources consulted for this study. Despite this, we understand that our inability to find records of debates on this specific point demonstrates that this aspect was not the object of reflection on the part of the actors who protagonized and conducted the transition periods undergone by the modality and that, by implementing their plans of action, they directed beach volleyball to the pathways it has been following since the first transition mentioned in this study.

References

Afonso, G. F., & Júnior, W. M. (2012). Como Pensar o voleibol de Praia sociologicamente. *Revista Motriz, 18*(1), 72–83.

Brito, D. (2016, December 28). *Banco do Brasil corta R$16 milhões da CBV em novo acordo de patrocínio*. UOL. Retrieved from https://blogdobrito.blogosfera.uol.com.br/2016/12/28/banco-do-brasil-corta-r-16-milhoes-da-cbv-em-novo-acordo-de-patrocinio/

Castro, H. O., Aguiar, S. S., Figueiredo, L. S., Laporta, L., Costa, G. C. T., Afonso, J., Gomes, S. A., & Oliveira, V. (2022). Prevalence of the relative age effect in the elite Brazilian volleyball: an analysis based on gender, the playing position, and performance indicators. *Journal of Human Kinetics, 84*(1), 148–157.

Collet, C., Folle, A., Ibáñez, S. J., & Nascimento, J. V. (2021). Practice context on sport development of elite Brazilian volleyball athletes. *Journal of Physical Education, 32*(1), e-3268.

Couvillon, A. (2002). *Sands of time: the history of beach volleyball, volume # 1: 1895-1969*. Information Guides.

D'Oliveira, F. C. M. (2019). *Determinantes histórico-financeiros e de gestão no desenvolvimento do vôlei de Praia: uma cartografia dos limites e possibilidades*. [Masters Thesis, Universidade do Estado do Rio de Janeiro] Biblioteca Digital de Teses e Dissertações UERJ. Retrieved from https://www.bdtd.uerj.br:8443/handle/1/8257

Duarte, L. (2007). *Marketing esportivo do banco do Brasil: Um estudo de caso*. UniCEUB.

França, F. C. Q., Pereira, A. M. A., Leitão, J. C. G., Costa, R. L., & Silva, M. I. (2022). Fatores determinantes para a excelência no volei de praia: o caso de uma dupla de elite. *Motrivivência, 34*(65), 1–18.

Gandra, A. (2016). Comitê libera Venda de 100 mil ingressos da Rio 2016 a partir de amanhã. Empresa Brasil de Comunicação. Retrieved from http://agenciabrasil.ebc.com.br/rio-2016/noticia/2016-07/comite-libera-venda-de-100-mil-ingressos-da-Rio-2016-a-partir-de-amanha

Garcia, R. M., Nascimento, D. R., & Pereira, E. G. B. (2017). The migratory process and the volleyball ranking: First approaches. *American Journal of Sports Science, 5*(4), 21–26.

Garcia, R. M., Meireles, C. H. A., & Pereira, E. G. B. (2021). Evolução e adaptação histórica do voleibol. *Lecturas: Educación Física y Deportes, 26*(281), 183–203.

João Pessoa. (2018). *Programas e Projetos*. Governo de João Pessoa. Retrieved from https://www.joaopessoa.pb.gov.br/programas-e-projetos/

Junior, N. K. M. (2021). Breve história do voleibol brasileiro e a contribuição da educação física para esse desporto – Anos 90. *Revista Edu-Física, 13*(28), 30–47.

Kasznar, I. K., & Graça Filho, A. S. (2002). *O esporte como indústria: Solução para a criação de riqueza e emprego*. Ediouro.

Kasznar, I. K., & Graça Filho, A. S. (2006). *Estratégia empresarial: Modelo de gestão vitorioso e inovador da confederação brasileira de voleibol*. M. Books.

Madruga, E. (2015, March 29). Vila Olímpica Parahyba: excelência na natação e falhas no atletismo. Globo Esporte. Retrieved from http://globoesporte.globo.com/pb/noticia/2015/03/vila-olimpica-parahyba-excelencia-na-natacao-e-falhas-no-atletismo.html

Mairesse, D. (2003). Cartografia: Do método à arte de fazer pesquisa. In T. M. G. Fonseca, & P. G. Kirst (Eds.), *Cartografias e devires: A construção do presente* (pp. 259–271). UFRGS.

Oliveira, M. H., Nascimento, A. S., & Toledo, E. (2021). Diferentes perspectivas sobre o patrocínio esportivo no volei feminino brasileiro: um estudo de caso do Osasco Voleibol Clube. *Revista Intercontinental de Gestão Desportiva, 11*(4), e110025.

Passos, E., Kastrup, V., & Escóssia, L. (2015). *Pistas do método da cartografia: Pesquisa-intervenção e produção de subjetividade*. Editora Sulina.

Pizzolato, E. A. (2004). *Profissionalização de organizações esportivas: estudo de caso do voleibol brasileiro*. Dissertação de Mestrado em Administração. Pontifícia Universidade Católica, Rio de Janeiro.

Praias. (2018). *Praias do Rio de Janeiro*. Praias.com.br. Retrieved from http://www.praias.com.br/estado-rio-de-janeiro/praias-do-rio-de-janeiro.html.

Romagnoli, R. C. (2009). Cartografia e a relação pesquisa e vida. *Revista Psicologia & Sociedade, 21*(2), 166–173.

Será encerrada hoje a distribuição de formulários de inscrição. (1946). *Jornal dos Sports*.

Sesinando, A. D., Segui-Urbaneja, J., & Teixeira, M. C. (2022). Professional development, skills, and competences in sports: a survey in the field of sport management among public managers. *Journal of Physical Education and Sport, 22*(11), 2800–2809.

Silva, L. S., Sucupira, G. B., Junior, J. C., Rodrigues, L. G., & Junior, A. A. (2020). Analise do calendário competitivo brasileiro e mundial de volei de praia (1989-2019). *Revista Intercontinental de Gestao Desporto, 10*(2), e10015.

Tavares, M., Vaz, L., & Matos, M. C. (2020). Sports and public Space: volleyball practice in Copacabana and Carcavelos/Cascais beaches. *Journal of Engineering and Architeture, 14,* 92–99.

Tavares, M. L. R. S., Garcia, R. M., Nascimento, D. R., Ribeiro, C. H. V., & Pereira, E. G. B. (2019). O sistema de ranqueamento do voleibol brasileiros e seus desdobramentos. *Movimento, 25,* e25054.

Tavares, M. R., Vaz, L. F., & Matos, M. C. (2021). Copacabana e o vôlei: uma história de lazer e esportes de praia. *Oculum Ensaios, 18,* 1–16.

Teixeira, M. C., Rijo, V. A., & Sesinando, A. D. (2022). Sports management research: analysis of scientific development in Portugal (2008-2017). *Journal of Physical Education, 33*(1), e-3353.

Thiry-Cherques, H. R. (2006). Pierre Bourdieu: A teoria na prática. Rio de Janeiro: *RAP, 40*(1), 27–55.

Yamamoto, P. Y., Quevedo-Silva, F., & Mazzei, L. C. (2021). Sponsorship in beach volleyball: effects of event quality, spectator satisfaction and brand experience on brand equity. *Revista Brasileira de Educação Física e Esporte, 35*(2), 207–227.

Index

Note: *Italicized* and **bold** page numbers refer to figures and tables.

2030 Agenda 2–3, 82
Abbott World Marathon Majors 226
Academic development of sport
    management 4–5
AEST *see* Tubarão Steelworkers Sportive
    Association (AEST)
Afonso, G. F. 277
Alava, M. 254
Alemany-Hormaeche, M. 228
ALGEDE *see* Latin American Association
    of Sport Management (ALGEDE)
Allan, G. 197
Allen, J. 190
Amendola, G. 229
American College of Sport Medicine 123
Ammar, A. 37
Argentina: academic development of sport
    management 5; *Asociación*
    de Clubes de Básquetbol 176
Ávila, D. 18, 21
Aznar, M. 116

Babiak, K. 78
Bandsports 178
Bangkok Charter for Health Promotion 87
Bank of America Chicago Marathon
    227, 233
Barajas, A. 196
Bartunek, J. M. 30
Bastos, F. 5
Batista, C. 55
beach volleyball management, in Brazil
    274–292; Fortaleza Metropolitan
    Region 286–287; invention
    275–278; João Pessoa Metropolitan
    Region 287–289; method

278–285, **280**–**284**; Rio de Janeiro
    Metropolitan Region (Grande Rio)
    290–291; spectacularization
    275–278; Vitória Metropolitan
    Region (Grande Vitória) 289–290
Bernal, A. 116
BMW Berlin Marathon 233
BNB Club 286, 287
Boceta, M. 116
Boira-Maiques, J. V. 229
Bouziri, H. 35
BowTie Labs 19
BoxMagic 6, 18–23, *22*
BrainTree 20
Brazil: 1984 Los Angeles Olympic Games
    276; 2006 National Basketball
    Championship 171; 2011 World
    Military Games 43; 2013 FIFA
    Confederation Cup 43; 2014 FIFA
    World Cup 43, 168, 178, 180, 208;
    2016 Rio Olympic and Paralympic
    Games 43, 50–51, 168, 178,
    180–181; academic development
    of sport management 4, 5;
    Banco do Brasil 277; Basketball
    Development League (*Liga de*
    Desenvolvimento de Basquete –
    LDB) 176; beach volleyball
    management in 274–292; *Bolsa*
    Atleta 48–50; *Bolsa Atleta Podium*
    48; Brazilian Aquatic Sports
    Confederation (*Confederação*
    Brasileira de Desportos Aquáticos –
    CBDA) 180; Brazilian Basketball
    Clubs Association (*Associação de*
    Clubes de Basquete do Brasil –

ACBB) 171; Brazilian Basketball Confederation (*Confederação Brasileira de Basketball* – CBB) 169–175, 180; Brazilian Club Committee (CBC) 43, 287, 290; Brazilian Football Confederation (CBF) 182; Brazilian Institute of Geography and Statistics (IBGE) 54; Brazilian Olympic Committee (*Comitê Olímpico Brasileiro* – COB) 43, 48, 51, 52, 168, 170, 180, 275; Brazilian Paralympic Committee (CPB) 43; Brazilian School Games (BSG) 48, 51–52; Brazilian Volleyball Confederation (CBV) 10, 275, 277–279, 285–288, 290; Constitution 43; Decree-Law 3199 of 1941 43; Espírito Santo Volleyball Federation (FESV) 289, 290; Esporte Clube Pinheiros 175; *Gestão do Esporte nos Estados e Municípios* (GEEM) 49; *Gestão e Governança em Entidades Nacionais de Administração do Esporte* (GGEnae) 49; Golden League (*Liga Ouro*) 176, 178; Good Law of 2005 45; *Governance Booklet on Sport Entities* 52; Governance of National Sport Entities 49; Innovation Act of 2004 45; innovation and public policies in 45–46; innovation and sport policy in 42–55, 49; Innovation Virtuous Cycle 181, *182*; Management of Sport within the State and Municipalities program (GEEM) 53–54; managerial perspectives of sports management 179–182; Men's National Basketball Championship 171, 173–175; Ministry of Citizenship 168; Ministry of Education 55; National Basketball League (*Liga Nacional de Basquete* – LNB) 8–9, 170–179, 181–182; National Institute of Educational Studies and Research Anísio Teixeira (INEP) 55; National Olympic Committee (NOC) 52; National Sport System for Brazil 49; National Training Network (RNT) 48, 50–51; NBA (National Basketball Association) 172, 173, 175–177; NBA All-Star Game 175; NBB (*Novo Basquete Brasil* – New Brazilian Basketball) 171, 174–176, 182; NBB All-Star Game 175–176; New Basketball Brazil (*Novo Basquete Brasil* – NBB) 172, 179; NFL (National Football League) 173; *Nossa Liga de Basquete* – NLB (Our Basketball League) 171, 172; Olympic Development League (*Liga de Desenvolvimento Olímpico* – LDO) 176; Oscar League 171; Paraíba Volleyball Federation (FPV) 288, 289; Premier League 173; Rio de Janeiro 2007 Pan American Games 43; Sport Confederation 43; Sport Federation 43; Sport Intelligence eco-system 47; Sport Intelligence Project (*Projeto Inteligência Esportiva*) 44, 55; Sport Intelligence Research Institute (*Instituto de Pesquisa Inteligência Esportiva*, IPIE) 6, 44–49, 46, 53–55; Sport Law 9615 of 1998 52; State's Youth, Sports and Leisure Office (SEJEL) 288; Super 8 Cup 178; *Supercopa* (Supercup) 171, 172; *Taça Brasil de Basquete* (Brazil Basketball Cup) 170–171; *Taça Interligas de Desenvolvimento* 176; *Torneio Interligas de Basquetebol* 176; *TV Globo* 177, 178; Working Group of the National Sport System, Ministry of Sport 53

Brubaker, M. D. 160
Bull, C. 261

Calatrava, S. 234
"Calatrava Model, The" 239, 240
Campos-Izquierdo, A. 79
Cannon, T. F. 196, 197
Carmichael, F. 248
Carnevale, J. B. 30
Carrasco, A. 231
Carvalho, P. 261
Ceará Volleyball Federation (FCV) 286, 287
Center for Research and Studies of Sport (Centro de Investigación y Estudios del Deporte, CIED) 7, 82–83
Chappelet, J.-L. 206–207
Chebet, E. 9

Chen, N. 197
Chen, P. 26, 37
Chile: academic development of sport management 5; BoxMagic 6, 18–23, *22*; Chilean Olympic Committee 17; Chilean Paralympic Committee 17; demographics of 15; digitalization in sports industry 15–23; economic sphere 16; fitness industry 18; innovations in sport management 6; Institution of Federated Sports 17; Instituto Nacional de Deportes (IND) 16, 17; Instituto Nacional de Estadísticas 15; Ministerio del Deporte (MINDEP) 16, 18; municipal sports 16–17; National Registry of Organizations 17; Organic Constitutional Law of Municipalities 16; political-administrative sphere 15–16; public spending on sports 16, *17*; Servicio de Impuestos Internos (SII) 20
CIED *see* Center for Research and Studies of Sport (Centro de Investigación y Estudios del Deporte, CIED)
Coleman, R. 227
Colombia: academic development of sport management 5
Community of Portuguese Speaking Countries (CPLP) 187
consumer behavior, products and services innovations impact on 123–134
consumers' expectations 126–127
consumption behaviour 266–268, **266, 267**
corporate social responsibility (CSR) 37
Corporate Well-being Programme (MSM) 25–38, *27*; framework for adapting 36; method 30–31, *31*; results 31–35; telework associated risks **28**
Correal, J. 144
Council of Europe 187, 232
Couvillon, A. 275, 276
Coye, R. W. 127
CPLP *see* Community of Portuguese Speaking Countries (CPLP)
crisis management during COVID-19 58–67, **62**; managerial perspectives of 66–67
Crompton, J. L. 189
CrossFit 19, 21, 130

CSR *see* corporate social responsibility (CSR)
Cuba: academic development of sport management 4
customer lifetime value 128

Danish Institute for Sport Studies IDAN 54
Darwin, C.: Theory of Evolution 246
Desbordes, M. 195
Dionisio, P. 260
disability 149–150; rights 151
Dixon, A. W. 196, 197
d'Oliveira, F.M. 286
Dorado, A. 140
Duarte, L.: Bank of Brazil's Sports Marketing – A Case Study 277

Ecuador: 2014 Adventure Race World Championship 10, 248; 2016 Galapagos CAMTRI Sprint Triathlon American Cup 10, 248; academic development of sport management 5; Center for Research and Studies of Sport (Centro de Investigación y Estudios del Deporte, CIED) 75–76; Center for Research and Studies of Sport (Centro de Investigación y Estudios del Deporte-CIED) 7; conferences, trends and prospects of 80–81; as destination for international events 246–256; Direction for Research and Cooperation in Physical Culture (Dirección de Investigación y Cooperación en Cultura Física) 74; Direct TV Cup 75; Ecuador National Institute of Statistics and Census (Instituto Nacional de Estadística y Censos Ecuador) 74; Ecuador Olympic Committee 74; Galapagos Islands 246; General Regulation of the Sport Law, Physical Education and Recreation (Reglamento General a la Ley del Deporte, Educación Física y Recreación) 74; Huairasinchi Adventure Race 10, 248; innovations in sport management training service 7, 10, 73–83; Ironman 70.3 Ecuador 10, 248, 254; Law of Sport, Physical

Education and Recreation (Ley del Deporte, Educación Física y Recreación) 74; manifestos from statements of the speakers 82; Ministry of Education 74; Ministry of Sport 74, 248; National Sport Structure 74; Oceanman Manta 2021 10, 248–255; Physical Education Teacher Education (PETE) 76; Sports Capital of Ecuador 253; sport structures in 247–249

educational quality in physical education during Covid-19 pandemic 138–145; management of 139–140; quality appraisal, in educative/sportive services 140; SERVQUAL Model see SERVQUAL Model

Egas, D. 253
Elasri, A. 116
Elias, N. 197
Emir Öksüz, E. 160
employee's health management 25–38
environmental analysis 268–269
ESPN 178
Eurobarometer 123, 187
Europe Active 123
European Institute of Sport Development and Leisure Studies 54
European Sport Management Association 5
EVENTQUAL model 210, **210**

Faulkner, B. 63
FCPF see Futebol Clube of Paços de Ferreira (FCPF)
FCV see Ceará Volleyball Federation (FCV)
Federal University of Paraná (UFPR) 44, 46; Sport Intelligence Research Institute 6
FIBA (International Basketball Federation) 170, 171, 173, 175
Fickenscher, L. 227
FIFA (International Federation of Association Football) 180
First Ibero-American Summit of Heads of State and Government (1991) 2
FitMetrix 19
Fitness Hut 131
FIVB (International Volleyball Federation) 275, 276

Ford, J. 196, 197
Foster, G. 231, 233
Foundation Trinidad Alfonso 233
Fox Sports 178
Franke, F. 37
Funk, C. D. 197
Futebol Clube of Paços de Ferreira (FCPF) 191, 198

Gabert, T. E. 195
Gallardo, L. 140
García-Fernández, J. 134
García-Vallejo, A. 228
German Sport University 54
GFNY see Gran Fondo New York (GFNY)
Gholipour, H. F. 237
Gisbert, V. 239
Globe News Wire 19
GloFox 19
GO Fit 131–133
Graça Filho, A. S. 276, 277
Gran Fondo New York (GFNY) 254
Gratton, C. 195, 227
Grix, J. 248
Groönroos, C. 141, 143

Hall, J. 226, 227
Hall, T. 229
Harvey, D. 229
Hatak, I. 30
Heise, T. L. 37
Hepp, K. 18, 20
Higham, J. E. 261
Hinch, T. D. 261
HRM see human resources management (HRM)
Huang, H. 227
Hubbard, P. 229
Human Development Index Development 16
Human resources management (HRM) 26
Hyysalo, S. 77

Ibero-American Forum of Sport Management (IFSM, Foro Iberoamericano de Gerencia Deportiva) 7, 78
Ibero-American sport management 1–11; academic development 4–5; governance 3–4; innovations 5–10
IBOPE Repucom 169

Index

IFSM *see* Ibero-American Forum of Sport Management (IFSM, *Foro Iberoamericano de Gerencia Deportiva*)

Iglesias-Sánchez, P. P. 37

Importance-Performance Analysis (IPA) 9; discrepancy and satisfaction or dissatisfaction, relationship between **212**; field of knowledge **213**; of International Horse Show Jumping 212–217, *214–216*, **214**, **216**, **217**; matrix 210–211, *211*, *212*, *216*; sports scope **213**; success factors in sporting events through 204–218

Ingesport 131

innovations, in sport management 5–10

innovative management model 167–182

International Health 123, 125

International Horse Show Jumping 204–218

International Olympic Committee (IOC) 52, 74, 180

International Research Network in Sport Tourism (IRNIST) 262

International Symbol of Accessibility (ISA) 160

IOC *see* International Olympic Committee (IOC)

IPA *see* Importance-Performance Analysis (IPA)

Irigoyen, S. 131

IRNIST *see* International Research Network in Sport Tourism (IRNIST)

ISA *see* International Symbol of Accessibility (ISA)

James, J. C. 210

Júnior, W. M. 277

Kahn, K. 76

Kasznar, I. K. 276, 277

Kelley, K. 195

Kent, K. 29, 37

key performance indicators (KPIs) 32, 34

Koch Tavares 276

Kotler, P. 90

KPIs *see* key performance indicators (KPIs)

Kumar, V. 128

Lance! 181

Latin America: academic development of sport management 4–5; innovations in sport management 5

Latin American Association of Sport Management (ALGEDE) 5, 82

Lee, S. 189

Lera-López, F. 196

Levenburg, N. M. 211

Liu, Y. D. 115

Lourenço, R. 261

Madeira, B. 260

Magal, S. R. 211

Mahou San Miguel (MSM): "A tu Salud" (At your Health) programme 30; Corporate Well-being Programme 25–38, *27*; Cuidarme en Casa 31

Mairesse, D. 285

Mariana Tek 19

Martilla, J. A. 210

Martin, J. 226, 227

Marujo, M. N. 261

McCormack, M. 256

Medina-Rodríguez, R. 115, 116

Meeting of Ministers of Foreign Affairs 2

Melo, S. 261

Mexico: academic development of sport management 4; General Law of Physical Culture and Sports 107; innovations in sport management 7, 8; Mexican Olympic Committee 107; Municipal Sports Committees 107; National Commission of Physical Culture and Sports (CONADE) 107; National Institute of Statistics and Geography (Instituto Nacional de Estadística y Geografía) 107, 108; National System of Physical Culture and Sports (SINADE) 107; Official Journal of the Federation 107; Paralympic Committee 107; satisfaction with public sport organization services 106–118, *112*, **112–115**, *117*; SERVQUAL Model 8; Sonora State Sports Commission (CODESON) 109; Sonora State Sports Institute 110; State Sports Institutes 107

Miller, R. 227

Mindbody 18–19

Misra, M. 37
Morales-Sánchez, V. 140, 143, 144
MSM *see* Mahou San Miguel (MSM)
Müller, M. 240
multiplatform distribution content
167–182

NATO *see* North Atlantic Treaty
Organization (NATO)
Nebrija University: Program of Physical
Activity and Sport in the Work
Environment 7, 86–101; University
Sports Service 88
new money 189, 196
New York Road Runners 227
non-resident spectators, innovative
promotions to attract 186–199,
193, 194, *198*
North Atlantic Treaty Organization
(NATO) 187
Núñez-Sánchez, J. M. 25, 29, 30
Nuviala, R. 116
Nuzman, C. A. 52, 180

Oceanman Manta 2021, Ecuador:
background of 249–254; franchise
250–251, **250**; functional structure
of 256; managerial perspectives
of 255–256; traditional and social
media outlets 254–255
OECD *see* Organization for Economic
Cooperation and Development
(OECD)
Ohio University 77
Organization for Economic Cooperation
and Development
(OECD) 187
Outrigger Canoe Club 275

Palacios, S. 249–253
Pan, D. W. 195
Parasuraman, A., 127, 141, 143
Parent, M. M. 206–207
Parra-Camacho, D. 228
Passos, E. 285
Paule-Koba, A. L. 226
Pedrosa Carrera, M. J. 228
Pellicer, M. 231
Perez, J. 248
Pérez, J. 74
Pike13 19
Pill, S. 76

Pires, S. 277
Pizzolato, E. A. 275
Play the Game 52
Portugal: academic development of sport
management 4, 5; Fitness Hut
131; fitness industry 123–134,
131, 133; GO Fit 131–133; Half
Marathon of the Discoveries in
Lisbon 261–262; innovation in
fitness industry 124–126, **125**;
innovations in sport management
7–8, 10; Liga NOS 189, 191, 192,
198, 199; managerial perspectives
on fitness industry 133–134;
Ministry of Education 187;
National Health Survey (NHS)
123–124; National Programme for
the Promotion of Physical Activity
(PNPAF) 124; non-resident
spectators, innovative promotions
to attract 186–199; Portuguese
Institute for Sport and Youth, I. P.
(IPDJ) 187; "Quality Road Race"
261; sport events, as catalyst for
economic, sociocultural, tourism
and environmental sustainability
258–271, **263–267**
*Proceedings of the Encounter of Students-
Latin American Forum of Sport
Management* 78
*Proceedings of the Ibero-American Forum of
Sport Management 2020* 78
Program of Physical Activity and Sport in
the Work Environment, Nebrija
University 7, 86–101; analysis of
88–100, 90; claim's proposal 91;
development of **96**; dissemination
of **95**; Evaluation and Satisfaction
Questionnaire 94, 103–105; hourly
compensation **99**; lines of action
96; practical implications 100–101,
101; promotion and recruitment
campaign for **93**; registration and
monitoring of **98**; satisfaction
measurement **99**; slogan proposal
91; SWOT analysis 88, 88; user
profiles **92**
Prytherch, D. 229

quality appraisal, in educative/sportive
services 140
Quilende, M. 260

Index   301

Racquet and Sportsclub Association
123, 125
Ramchandani, G. 227
Ratten, V. 78, 174, 177–179
return on investment (ROI) 26
Reyes-Robles, M. 110
Rial, J. 140
Ribó, J. 230
Rio de Janeiro Municipal Tourism
Company (RIOTUR) 276
RIOTUR *see* Rio de Janeiro Municipal
Tourism Company (RIOTUR)
Rius-Ulldemolins, J. 239
Roche, M. 226, 229
Rogers, E. 76
ROI *see* return on investment (ROI)
Roig, J. 233
Romagnoli, R. C. 279
Roschel, H. 28
Ruíz-Alejos, C. 116
Running for all European Athletics 261
Running USA 227

Salanova, M. 37
Salgado-Aranda, R. 28
Samaranch, J. A. 277
Santos, L. 195
Santos, S. C. 62
SBU *see* Strategic Business Unit (SBU)
Scheerder, J. 231
Schmidt, O. 171
SDC *see* Sociedad Deportiva Correcaminos
(SDC)
SDGs *see* Sustainable Development Goals
(SDGs)
SERVPERF model 209, **210**
SERVQUAL Model 8, 145, 209,
210; application in sportive
organizations 143–144; dimensions
of **209**; origins and structure of
141, 143; in physical education
141, **142**
Silva, J. 277
Singh, K. 37
SIRC *see* Sport Information Resource
Center (SIRC)
Sivrikaya, K. 77
Smith, A. C. 172, 225
Sociedad Deportiva Correcaminos (SDC)
9, 232
Sou do Esporte ('I am from Sport') 52
Sousa Cruz, 276

Spain: 2010 *Sport Strategic Plan of
Valencia* 225; 2016 Palma
de Mallorca Marathon 228;
academic development of
sport management 4, 5; crisis
management during COVID-19
58–67, **62**; equestrianism 205;
Gross Domestic Product (GDP) 58,
60; High Spanish Sports Council
(Consejo Superior de Deportes,
CSD) 205–206; industry of sport
events 206–209, **207**; innovations
in sport management 8;
Instituto Valenciano de
Investigaciones Económicas (IVIE)
225; International Horse Show
Jumping 204–218; Longines Global
Champions Tour 206; Madrid
Horse Week 206; Ministry of
Health 88; Mutua Madrid Tennis
Open 206; National Census of
Sports Facilities 59; REMUS
(Madrid Network of Healthy
Universities) 87–88; Royal Spanish
Equestrian Federation 205; *Sociedad
Deportiva Correcaminos* (SDC)
224; Spanish Network of Healthy
Universities (REUS) 87; spectators'
experience, understanding
208–209; sport events evaluation
209–212; sport events industry and
city marathons 225–228; Valencia
Marathon (Marathon Popular de
Valencia) 9, 224–240, 240–245
Sparling, P. B. 37
spectators' experience, understanding
208–209
sport centres, innovation in 148–161, *152*,
152–155, *153*, *155*, *156*, **157**,
158, **159**; academic education
of managers 156; activities **157**;
business model **154**; customer
census *153*; employees *155*;
facilities **155**, *158*; inclusion
policies of managers and directors
159; size *152*
"*Sport for All*" movement 230, 232
Sport Information Resource Center
(SIRC) 54
Sport Intelligence Research Institute,
Brazil 6
sport literacy 76

sport management curriculum standards 150
sport marketing 190
SPORTSERV model 210, **210**
sport tourism 188, 226
Sprinklr 180
starchitects 229, 230
Stewart, B. 172
Strategic Business Unit (SBU) 277
Stripe 20
Sustainable Development Goals (SDGs) 2, 81, 82
SWOT analysis 88, 88, 255

TCS New York City Marathon 226, 227, 231, 232
TEAMQUAL model 210, **210**
Thiry-Cherques, H. R. 286
Thomson, A. 226
Tjønndal, A. 76, 125, 172–174
Triib 19
Trougakos, J. P. 37
Tubarão Steelworkers Sportive Association (AEST) 290

UFPR *see* Federal University of Paraná (UFPR)
UNDP *see* United Nations Development Program (UNDP)
UNESCO Statistic Institute 74
United Kingdom Sport 237
United Nations Development Program (UNDP) 16
Universidad Europea Sports Management Research Group 206
University of Bayreuth 77

Valencia: 5K Circuit Jardin del Turia 240; 2020 Platinum Label Road Race 234; as *European Capital of Sport* 233; Formula One Grand Prix 230; Great Recession (2008–2015) 230; MVTA EDP 224, 225, 228, 231, 233, 234, 237, 239, 240; Open Tennis 500 tournament 230, 231; political and socioeconomic context of 228–231; Sport Department (*Fundación Deportiva Municipal Valencia*) 230, 232; *Strategic Sport Plan of Valencia* 230, 232, 233; Valencia City Council 229, 230, 233, 239
Valencia Marathon (Marathon Popular de Valencia) 9, 224–240, 240–245; participants' feedback for improvement 234–238, **235, 236, 238**; strategy in action 231–234
Venezuela: academic development of sport management 4
Verdu, P. 255
Virgin London Marathon 227
Virgin Money London Marathon (now TCS London Marathon) 233

Washington, K. 227
Wearable Fitness Technology (WFT) 124, 131, 132
WebPay 20, 21
Weed, M. 261
WFT *see* wearable fitness technology (WFT)
WHO *see* World Health Organisation (WHO)
Wicker, P. 197, 227, 228
Winand, M. 173
Wodify 19, 20
World Bank Group 167–168
World Health Organisation (WHO) 26, 87, 123, 124
World Open Water Swimming Association (WOWSA) 249
WOWSA *see* World Open Water Swimming Association (WOWSA)
Wright, T. A. 28
WSC Sports 179, 181

Yin, R. K. 251

ZeeZor 19
ZenPlanner 19
Zhang, J. J. 195